# Accounting for AQA: A-level year 2

the complete resource for the AQA examinations

David Cox

osborne
BOOKS

Published by Osborne Books Limited
Tel 01905 748071
Email books@osbornebooks.co.uk
Website www.osbornebooks.co.uk

Cover design by Windrush Group (www.windrushgroup.co.uk)

Printed by CPI Group (UK) Limited, Croydon, CR0 4YY.

British Library Cataloguing in Publication Data
A catalogue record for this book is available from the British Library

ISBN 978 1911198 253

# Contents

# Introduction

**Accounting for AQA: A-level year 2** has been written to provide a study resource for students of the Assessment and Qualifications Alliance's A-level year 2 in Accounting. It develops the accounting techniques – financial and management – covered in our year 1 book **Accounting for AQA: AS and A-level year 1**.

The book is divided into two sections:

- **Financial Accounting**, which develops the accounting techniques acquired in A-level year 1 and studies the financial statements of partnerships and limited companies.

- **Management Accounting**, which develops the knowledge and understanding of management accounting, including budgeting, standard costing and capital investment appraisal.

**Accounting for AQA: A-level year 2** has been designed to be user-friendly and contains:

- clear explanations and numerous worked examples
- chapter summaries to help with revision
- a wide range of questions, appropriate for the AQA examinations
- answers to selected questions, set out in the fully worked layout that should be used

# Resources for tutors – Tutor Zone

For the questions where answers are not given in this book, separate **tutor support material** provides the answers, together with a range of photocopiable layouts.

These resources are available to tutors who adopt this textbook for their students. For more information, visit www.osbornebooks.co.uk.

Thanks are due to Sage (UK) Ltd for permission to use screen images in the chapter on computer accounting.

# Use of Accounting Terminology

The AQA examinations in Accounting make full use of international terminology as set out in International Financial Reporting Standards (IFRSs). The following shows the international terminology, together with the terminology used previously.

| International Terminology | Terminology used previously |
|---|---|
| **Financial statements** | |
| Appropriation account (partnership) | Profit and loss appropriation account |
| Cash and cash equivalents (limited companies) | Cash in hand, cash at bank/bank overdraft |
| Financial statements | Final accounts and balance sheets |
| Income statement | Trading and profit and loss account |
| Inventory | Stock |
| Irrecoverable debt | Bad debt |
| Loss for year | Net loss |
| Non-current assets | Fixed assets |
| Non-current liabilities | Long-term liabilities |
| Other payables | Expenses due; income received in advance |
| Other receivables | Expenses prepaid; income due |
| Profit for year | Net profit |
| Revenue (within an income statement) | Sales |
| Statement of financial position | Balance sheet |
| Trade payables | Trade creditors (creditors) |
| Trade receivables | Trade debtors (debtors) |
| **Accounting ratios** | |
| Expenses in relation to revenue % | Expenses in relation to sales % |
| Profit to revenue % | Net profit to sales % |
| Rate of inventory turnover | Rate of stock turnover |
| Trade payable days | Creditor payment period |
| Trade receivable days | Debtor collection period |

**A note about year dates**

Please note that year dates used throughout this book, for the sake of simplicity, are expressed as 20-1, 20-2, 20-3 etc, unlike in a real business where the actual date is shown (ie 2011, 2012, 2013 etc). Occasionally in this book 20-9 is followed by 20-0, ie when the decade changes.

# Electronic Resources for students

**Online Multiple Choice Tests for each chapter**

At the beginning of the questions at the end of most chapters you will see a screen that indicates that an additional 'True or False' multiple choice test is available online to test understanding of the chapter. These tests can be accessed in the Products and Resources section of www.osbornebooks.co.uk

**Online Resource Documents**

Also available in the Products and Resources section of www.osbornebooks.co.uk are downloadable pdf files which will help with the practice questions in this book. These include:

- limited company income statement, statement of changes in equity and statement of financial position
- statement of cash flows
- cash budget

# Financial Accounting

This section of the book develops further the financial accounting techniques you have acquired in year 1 studies. The areas it covers include:

- incomplete records – the techniques used to draw up financial statements when some of the required accounting data is missing

- partnerships – the format of partnership financial statements and the implications of changes in partnerships

- limited company financial statements – the formats used and their relevance to user groups

- statements of cash flow

- the use of international accounting standards

- the legal and regulatory framework of accounting

- the application of ethical principles to accounting

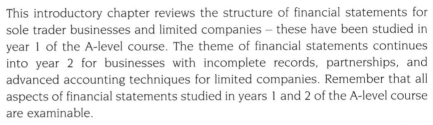

# 1 FINANCIAL STATEMENTS AND INTRODUCTION TO ETHICS

This introductory chapter reviews the structure of financial statements for sole trader businesses and limited companies – these have been studied in year 1 of the A-level course. The theme of financial statements continues into year 2 for businesses with incomplete records, partnerships, and advanced accounting techniques for limited companies. Remember that all aspects of financial statements studied in years 1 and 2 of the A-level course are examinable.

The chapter also gives an introduction to ethics and sets out the ethical principles that must be applied in accounting. Ethics is an important aspect of accounting and is one that we will be studying in more detail in later chapters.

The chapter concludes with an explanation of the differences between financial accounting and management accounting.

## FINANCIAL STATEMENTS

As you will remember from your studies in year 1, the trial balance usually forms the starting point for the preparation of financial statements. These comprise:

- income statement (also referred to as a statement of profit or loss)
- statement of financial position

Such financial statements can be produced more often than once a year in order to give information to the owner/owners on how the business is progressing. However, it is customary to produce annual accounts for the benefit of HM Revenue & Customs, lenders such as a bank, and other stakeholders. In this way the income statement covers an accounting period of a financial year (which can end at any date – it doesn't have to be the calendar year), and the statement of financial position shows the state of the business at the end of the accounting period.

## INCOME STATEMENT

| **income** | **minus** | **expenses** | **equals** | **profit/loss** |
|---|---|---|---|---|
| *revenue from sales* | | *costs of running the business* | | *which adds to/subtracts from capital/equity* |

The income statement (examples shown on pages 9 and 13) shows the income a business has received over a given period for goods sold or services provided (together with any small amounts of other income, eg rent received). It also sets out the expenses incurred – the cost of the product, and the expenses (eg wages, administration expenses, rent, and so on). The difference between income and expenses is the profit for the year of the business. If expenses are greater than income, then a loss has been made. The profit (or loss) belongs to the owner/owners of the business. For a business that trades in goods, a figure for gross profit shows the profit made before expenses are deducted, and a profit for the year after expenses are deducted.

The format of an income statement is as follows:

|  | Revenue (Sales) |
|---|---|
| *less* | Cost of sales* (cost of purchases of goods, adjustment for change in inventory) |
| *equals* | **Gross profit** |
| *less* | Expenses (wages, administration expenses, rent paid, etc) |
| *equals* | **Profit for the year** |

*often referred to as 'cost of goods sold'

## STATEMENT OF FINANCIAL POSITION

| **assets** | **minus** | **liabilities** | **equals** | **capital/equity** |
|---|---|---|---|---|
| *what a business owns* | | *what a business owes* | | *how the business has been financed* |

The statement of financial position (examples shown on pages 11 and 15) uses the accounting equation to give a 'snapshot' of the business at a particular date – the end of the financial year. A typical business statement of financial position will show:

**assets**   What the business owns:

- non-current assets comprise the long-term items owned by a business:
  - intangible non-current assets which do not have material substance, eg goodwill (the amount paid for the reputation and connections of a business that has been taken over)

- tangible non-current assets which have material substance, eg property, vehicles, machinery, office equipment (shown at their carrying amount, ie cost price or revaluation less depreciation to date)

- current assets comprise short-term assets which change regularly, eg inventory held for resale, trade receivables, bank and cash balances (cash and cash equivalents)

**liabilities**     What the business owes:

- current liabilities, where payment is due within twelve months of the date of the statement of financial position, eg trade payables, bank overdraft

- non-current liabilities, where payment is due in more than one year from the date of the statement of financial position, eg loans, mortgages, long-term bank loans

**net assets**     The total of non-current and current assets, less current and non-current liabilities. The net assets are financed by the owner/owners of the business, in the form of capital/equity. Net assets therefore equals the total of the 'financed by' section – the statement of financial position 'balances'.

**capital/equity**     Where the resources (eg money) to finance the business have come from – the investment of the owner/owners and business profits. The financial statements of limited companies use the term 'equity' in place of capital.

# FINANCIAL STATEMENTS: POINTS TO NOTE

## assets and the order of liquidity

In the statement of financial position it is customary to list the assets – non-current assets and current assets – in an 'increasing order of liquidity'. In accounting, liquidity means nearness to cash, so the most permanent assets – ie those that are furthest away from cash – are listed first. Thus property, which would take time to turn into cash, heads the list, with other non-current assets – such as shop fittings, machinery and vehicles – following. For current assets, the usual order is to start with inventory, then trade receivables, bank (if not overdrawn), and cash. In this way, the assets are listed from the most permanent (usually property) to the most liquid (cash itself).

The reason for this order is historical – nineteenth-century business owners wanted to impress upon readers of their financial statements the solid assets that they owned. The top line of the balance sheet (as the statement of financial position was known then) was the first to be read and that showed the value of their property. The following lines listed their other assets. This traditional approach lives on into twenty-first century financial statements.

## adjustments to financial statements

Whilst the starting point for the preparation of financial statements is the bookkeeper's two-column trial balance, if we used only the trial balance figures (which record the financial transactions that have taken place) the resultant financial statements would show an inaccurate picture of the state of the business. Adjustments are made with the aim of improving the accuracy of the financial statements in showing the profit, and the assets and liabilities of the business.

The main adjustments to financial statements are for:

- closing inventory
- accruals and prepayments of expenses and income
- depreciation of non-current assets
- irrecoverable debts written off
- allowance for doubtful debts

These adjustments, including inventory valuation, have been studied in year 1 of the A-level course.

# FINANCIAL STATEMENTS: LAYOUT

The following pages show the layout of financial statements for:

- a sole trader business (pages 8-11)
- a limited company (pages 12-15)

These layouts will be familiar to you from your studies in year 1 and form the basis of the financial accounting covered in year 2. We will be amending them slightly as we go on to study incomplete records accounting, partnership accounting and aspects of the financial statements of limited companies.

## a note on the layout of the statement of financial position

In the layouts that follow, the statement of financial position shows the assets used by the business and how they have been financed:

|  |  |
|---|---|
|  | Non-current assets |
| *plus* | Net current assets |
| *less* | Non-current liabilities |
| *equals* | Net assets |
| *equals* | Capital/Equity |

This columnar presentation statement of financial position agrees the figure for net assets, with capital/equity.

However, you may see alternative columnar layouts for the statement of financial position, for example:

| | |
|---|---|
| | Non-current assets |
| *plus* | Current assets |
| *equals* | Total assets |

which balances against

| | |
|---|---|
| | Capital/Equity |
| *plus* | Non-current liabilities |
| *plus* | Current liabilities |
| *equals* | Capital/Equity and liabilities |

Here the same information is used, it is just that the sections for non-current liabilities and current liabilities are brought down and added to capital/equity. This presentation agrees the figure for total assets with the figure for capital/equity plus liabilities.

**a note about showing deductions**

In financial statements, where amounts are to be deducted, they can be indicated either as 'less' or they can be bracketed. For example, 'less closing inventory £10,500' (as shown in the sample financial statements later in this chapter) or 'closing inventory (£10,500)'.

**sample layouts**

The sample layouts for a sole trader business and a limited company are on pages 8-15.

# ETHICAL PRINCIPLES

Ethics is an important aspect of accounting that applies to all accounting staff – bookkeepers when recording financial transactions and accountants when preparing financial statements. Accounting requires a high level of ethics so that the users of accounts can be assured that they have been prepared to the highest professional standards. Accordingly, accounting staff follow the five ethical principles of:

- integrity
- objectivity
- professional competence and due care
- confidentiality
- professional behaviour

The meaning and application of these ethical principles is now explained.

**Integrity** means being straightforward and honest in all professional and business relationships. When recording transactions, accounting staff should identify whether transactions are genuine and valid for inclusion in the records of the business. For example, a bookkeeper who records an inflated or bogus expenses claim submitted by a member of staff would not be following the principle of integrity.

**Objectivity** means not allowing bias, conflict of interest or the undue influence of others to override professional or business judgements. In addition accounting staff must appreciate the importance of:

- transparency, being confident of showing to others decisions made
- fairness, being certain that decisions made will be considered fair by those affected by them

**Professional competence and due care** means maintaining professional knowledge and skill at the level required to provide a competent professional service to an employer or client. For example, a bookkeeper who has not studied taxation and has never completed a tax return but, nevertheless, advertises a tax advice service, would not be following the principle of professional competence and due care.

**Confidentiality** means that information acquired as a result of professional or business relationships should not be disclosed to third parties, except where permission is given or there is a legal or professional duty to disclose. For example, an accountant who tells a friend about the losses made by a client would not be following the principle of confidentiality.

**Professional behaviour** means complying with relevant laws and regulations and avoiding bringing the accountancy profession into disrepute. This includes dealing with the pressures, whether actual or perceived, of familiarity and authority. Familiarity means that accounting staff must not, because of a close or personal relationship, become too sympathetic to the interests of others. Authority means not being deterred from acting professionally despite pressure from managers, supervisors and business owners.

Note that the application of ethical principles relates to all aspects of accounting. In Chapter 9 the impact of ethical considerations is considered in further detail.

**SOLE TRADER**

The **income statement** includes a figure for gross profit for businesses that trade in goods. The income statement finishes with profit for the year for the accounting period, ie profit after expenses.

The amounts for **revenue (sales)** and **purchases** include only items in which the business trades – eg a clothes shop buying clothes from the manufacturer and selling to the public. Note that any items bought for use in the business, such as a new till for the shop, are not included with purchases but are *capital expenditure* shown as assets on the statement of financial position.

**Cost of sales** represents the cost to the business of the goods which have been sold in this financial year. Cost of sales is:

|  | opening inventory | (inventory bought previously) |
|---|---|---|
| *plus* | purchases | (purchased during the year) |
| *minus* | closing inventory | (inventory left unsold at the end of the year) |
| *equals* | cost of sales | (cost of what has actually been sold) |

**Gross profit** is calculated as:

*revenue – cost of sales = gross profit*

**Expenses**, or overheads, are the running costs of the business – known as *revenue expenditure.* The categories of expenses or overheads used vary according to the needs of each business.

**Profit for the year** is calculated as:

*gross profit – expenses = profit for the year*

If expenses are more than gross profit, the business has made a loss.

The profit for the year is the amount the business earned for the owner/owners, and is subject to taxation. The owner/owners can take some or all of the profit in the form of drawings. Part of the profit might well be left in the business in order to help build up the business for the future.

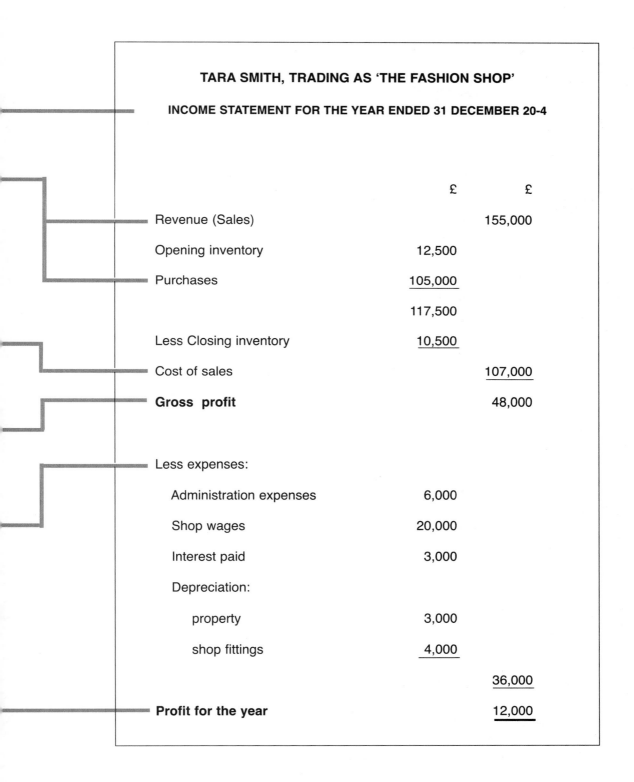

**TARA SMITH, TRADING AS 'THE FASHION SHOP'**

**INCOME STATEMENT FOR THE YEAR ENDED 31 DECEMBER 20-4**

|  | £ | £ |
|---|---|---|
| Revenue (Sales) | | 155,000 |
| Opening inventory | 12,500 | |
| Purchases | 105,000 | |
|  | 117,500 | |
| Less Closing inventory | 10,500 | |
| Cost of sales | | 107,000 |
| **Gross profit** | | 48,000 |
|  | | |
| Less expenses: | | |
| Administration expenses | 6,000 | |
| Shop wages | 20,000 | |
| Interest paid | 3,000 | |
| Depreciation: | | |
| property | 3,000 | |
| shop fittings | 4,000 | |
|  | | 36,000 |
| **Profit for the year** | | 12,000 |

**SOLE TRADER**

**Non-current assets** comprise the long-term items owned by a business, eg property, vehicles, machinery, office equipment, shop fittings (shown at their carrying amount, ie cost/valuation less depreciation to date).

**Current assets** comprise short-term assets which change regularly, eg inventory held for resale, trade receivables, bank balances and cash. These items will alter as the business trades, eg inventory will be sold, or more will be bought; trade receivables will make payment to the business, or sales on credit will be made; the cash and bank balances will alter with the flow of money in and out of the bank account.

**Current liabilities** are where payment is due within twelve months of the date of the statement of financial position, eg trade payables, and bank overdraft (which is usually repayable on demand, unlike a bank loan which is negotiated for a particular time period).

**Net current assets** is the excess of current assets over current liabilities, ie current assets − current liabilities = net current assets. Without adequate net current assets, a business will find it difficult to continue to operate. Net current assets is also often referred to as *working capital*.

**Non-current liabilities** are where payment is due in more than one year from the date of the statement of financial position; they are often loans, mortgages or long-term bank loans.

**Net assets** is the total of non-current and current assets, less current and non-current liabilities. The net assets are financed by the owner/owners of the business, in the form of capital. Net assets therefore equals the total of the 'financed by' section − ie the statement of financial position 'balances'.

**Capital** is the investment of the owner/owners, and is a liability of a business, ie it is what the business owes the owner/owners. Opening capital + capital injection added during the year (if any) + profit for the year − drawings = closing capital (the investment of the owner/owners at the end of the year).

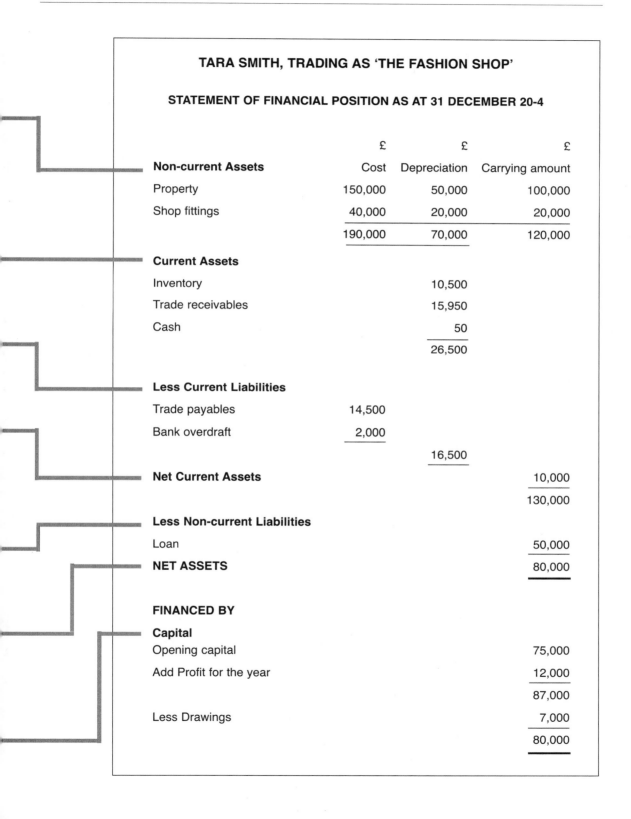

**TARA SMITH, TRADING AS 'THE FASHION SHOP'**

**STATEMENT OF FINANCIAL POSITION AS AT 31 DECEMBER 20-4**

| | £ | £ | £ |
|---|---|---|---|
| **Non-current Assets** | Cost | Depreciation | Carrying amount |
| Property | 150,000 | 50,000 | 100,000 |
| Shop fittings | 40,000 | 20,000 | 20,000 |
| | 190,000 | 70,000 | 120,000 |
| **Current Assets** | | | |
| Inventory | | 10,500 | |
| Trade receivables | | 15,950 | |
| Cash | | 50 | |
| | | 26,500 | |
| **Less Current Liabilities** | | | |
| Trade payables | 14,500 | | |
| Bank overdraft | 2,000 | | |
| | | 16,500 | |
| **Net Current Assets** | | | 10,000 |
| | | | 130,000 |
| **Less Non-current Liabilities** | | | |
| Loan | | | 50,000 |
| **NET ASSETS** | | | 80,000 |
| | | | |
| **FINANCED BY** | | | |
| **Capital** | | | |
| Opening capital | | | 75,000 |
| Add Profit for the year | | | 12,000 |
| | | | 87,000 |
| Less Drawings | | | 7,000 |
| | | | 80,000 |

**LIMITED COMPANY**

**Revenue** is sales less sales returns, ie the turnover of the company.

**Other income** could include rental income, cash discount, profit on sale of assets, etc.

The **expenses** of a limited company are usually split between the expenses of distribution, sales and marketing, and administration, although different headings can be used, eg wages, depreciation of assets, etc.

The company has recorded a **profit for the year from operations** (operating profit) of £49,000, before deduction of finance costs (such as debenture interest, bank and loan interest) and tax.

**Tax**, the corporation tax that a company has to pay, based on its profits, is shown. We shall not be studying the calculations for corporation tax in this book. It is, however, important to see how the tax is recorded in the financial statements.

The company has recorded a **profit for the year after tax**, of £28,000. This amount is taken to the statement of changes in equity.

The **statement of changes in equity** demonstrates how profit for the year is added to the brought forward balance of retained earnings (a revenue reserve), while dividends paid during the year are deducted. The resultant balance of retained earnings at the end of the year is shown in the statement of financial position in the equity section.

Also included in the statement of changes in equity could be other items such as an issue of shares and the unrealised profits from, for example, an upwards revaluation of property (see pages 121 and 123).

**ORION LIMITED**

**INCOME STATEMENT FOR THE YEAR ENDED 31 DECEMBER 20-6**

|  | £ | £ |
|---|---|---|
| Revenue |  | 725,000 |
| Opening inventory | 45,000 |  |
| Purchases | 381,000 |  |
|  | 426,000 |  |
| Less Closing inventory | 50,000 |  |
| Cost of sales |  | 376,000 |
| **Gross profit** |  | 349,000 |
| Other income |  | 10,000 |
|  |  | 359,000 |
| Less expenses: |  |  |
| Distribution expenses | 85,000 |  |
| Sales and marketing expenses | 100,000 |  |
| Administration expenses | 125,000 |  |
|  |  | 310,000 |
| **Profit/(loss) for the year from operations** |  | 49,000 |
| Less Finance costs |  | 6,000 |
| **Profit/(loss) for the year before tax** |  | 43,000 |
| Less Tax |  | 15,000 |
| **Profit/(loss) for the year after tax** |  | 28,000 |

**STATEMENT OF CHANGES IN EQUITY FOR THE YEAR ENDED 31 DECEMBER 20-6**

|  | Share capital £ | Share premium £ | Retained earnings £ | Total £ |
|---|---|---|---|---|
| Balances at start | 400,000 | 30,000 | 41,000 | 471,000 |
| Profit for the year |  |  | 28,000 | 28,000 |
| Dividends paid |  |  | (20,000) | (20,000) |
| Balances at end | 400,000 | 30,000 | 49,000 | 479,000 |

**LIMITED COMPANY**

The **non-current assets** section of a limited company statement of financial position usually distinguishes between:

**intangible non-current assets**, which do not have material substance but belong to the company and have value, eg goodwill (the amount paid for the reputation and connections of a business that has been taken over), patents and trademarks; the intangible non-current assets are amortised (depreciated).

**property, plant and equipment**, which are tangible (ie have material substance) non-current assets and are depreciated over their useful lives.

As well as the usual **current liabilities**, for limited companies, this section also contains the amount of tax to be paid within the next twelve months.

**Non-current liabilities** are those liabilities that are due to be repaid more than twelve months from the date of the statement of financial position, eg loans and debentures.

**Equity** is assets minus liabilities, representing the stake of ordinary shareholders in the company.

**Issued share capital** shows the shares that have been issued. In this statement of financial position, the ordinary shares are described as being fully paid, meaning that the company has received the full amount of the nominal value of each share from the shareholders. Sometimes shares will be partly paid, eg ordinary shares of £1, but 75p paid. This means that the company can make a call on the shareholders to pay the extra 25p to make the shares fully paid.

**Capital reserves** (see page 121) are created as a result of a non-trading profit, such as share premium and revaluation – these surpluses cannot be distributed as dividends.

**Revenue reserves** (see page 123) are retained earnings from the statement of changes in equity and are available to be distributed as dividends.

**Total equity** is the stake of the ordinary shareholders in the company. It comprises issued ordinary share capital, plus capital and revenue reserves.

## ORION LIMITED

### STATEMENT OF FINANCIAL POSITION AS AT 31 DECEMBER 20-6

| | £ Cost | £ Amortisation/ Depreciation | £ Carrying amount |
|---|---|---|---|
| **Non-current Assets** | | | |
| *Intangible* | | | |
| Goodwill | 50,000 | 20,000 | 30,000 |
| *Property, plant and equipment* | | | |
| Freehold land and buildings | 280,000 | 40,000 | 240,000 |
| Machinery | 230,000 | 100,000 | 130,000 |
| Fixtures and fittings | 100,000 | 25,000 | 75,000 |
| | 660,000 | 185,000 | 475,000 |
| | | | |
| **Current Assets** | | | |
| Inventory | | 50,000 | |
| Trade and other receivables | | 38,000 | |
| Cash and cash equivalents | | 21,000 | |
| | | 109,000 | |
| | | | |
| **Less Current Liabilities** | | | |
| Trade and other payables | 30,000 | | |
| Tax liabilities | 15,000 | | |
| | | 45,000 | |
| **Net Current Assets** | | | 64,000 |
| | | | 539,000 |
| | | | |
| **Less Non-current Liabilities** | | | |
| 7% debentures (repayable in 20-9) | | | 60,000 |
| **NET ASSETS** | | | 479,000 |
| | | | |
| **EQUITY** | | | |
| | | | |
| **Issued Share Capital** | | | |
| 400,000 ordinary shares of £1 each fully paid | | | 400,000 |
| | | | |
| **Capital Reserve** | | | |
| Share premium | | | 30,000 |
| | | | |
| **Revenue Reserve** | | | |
| Retained earnings | | | 49,000 |
| **TOTAL EQUITY** | | | 479,000 |

**Note:** the statement of financial position can be presented using a number of columns, as required.

# FINANCIAL ACCOUNTING AND MANAGEMENT ACCOUNTING

These two types of accounting, although they produce different reports and statements, obtain their data from the same set of transactions carried out by a business over a given period. This is illustrated in the diagram below.

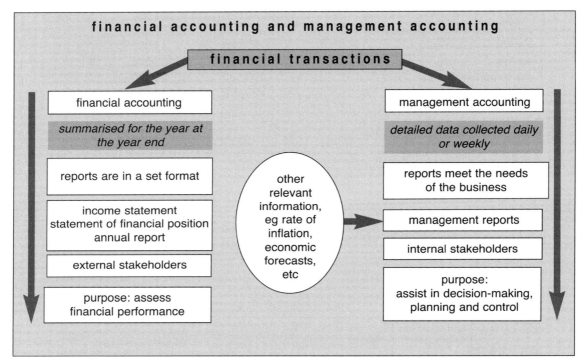

Financial accounting uses the financial data relating to transactions carried out over a period of time. The information is processed through the accounting records and transferred to the financial statements – the income statement, the statement of financial position and the company's annual report. The statements are often required to be produced by law, eg the Companies Act 2006, and are available to stakeholders such as shareholders, suppliers, lenders, government.

Management accounting uses the same data to produce reports containing financial information on the recent past and projections for the future. The reports are available to internal stakeholders, such as management, employees, and owners (but not to shareholders generally), and may also be made available to third parties (such as lenders). There is no legal requirement to produce this information and the content of the report and the principles used can be suited to the activities of the business and the requirements of its managers. The information is prepared as frequently as it is required, and speed is often vital as the information may go out-of-date very quickly. It is important that the information is prepared accurately and in line with the **ethical principle of integrity** – accounting staff are straightforward and honest in all professional and business relationships.

## CHAPTER SUMMARY

● Financial statements comprise:
  - income statement
  - statement of financial position

● Gross profit is revenue minus cost of sales.

● Profit for the year is gross profit minus expenses.

● The statement of financial position records:
  - assets (non-current and current)
  - liabilities (current and non-current)
  - capital/equity

● Ethical principles for accounting staff are:
  - integrity
  - objectivity
  - professional competence and due care
  - confidentiality
  - professional behaviour

● Financial accounting focuses on accounting records and the preparation of financial statements, mainly for external stakeholders.

● Management accounting prepares reports for internal stakeholders to assist in decision-making, planning and control of the business.

In the next chapter we move on to the preparation of financial statements from incomplete records – where the financial records of the business have not followed double-entry principles.

# QUESTIONS

visit
**www.osbornebooks.co.uk**
to take an online test

An asterisk (*) after the question number means that the answer is given at the end of this book.

**1.1\*** The following trial balance has been extracted by Nick Johnson on 31 December 20-3:

|  | Dr £ | Cr £ |
|---|---|---|
| Opening inventory | 25,000 | |
| Purchases | 210,000 | |
| Revenue (Sales) | | 310,000 |
| Administration expenses | 12,000 | |
| Wages | 41,000 | |
| Interest paid | 9,000 | |
| Property at cost | 200,000 | |
| Depreciation of property | | 40,000 |
| Machinery at cost | 40,000 | |
| Depreciation of machinery | | 24,000 |
| Sales ledger control (trade receivables) | 31,000 | |
| Bank | 900 | |
| Cash | 100 | |
| Capital | | 100,000 |
| Drawings | 10,000 | |
| Loan | | 80,000 |
| Purchases ledger control (trade payables) | | 25,000 |
| | 579,000 | 579,000 |

Notes:
- Inventory at 31 December 20-3 cost £21,000.
- Depreciate property by £4,000 for the year and machinery by £6,000.

**REQUIRED:**

You are to prepare the financial statements of Nick Johnson for the year ended 31 December 20-3.

**1.2** Crantock Limited prepares its financial statements to 31 March each year. At 31 March 20-2 its trial balance was as follows:

|  | Dr | Cr |
| --- | --- | --- |
|  | £000 | £000 |
| Administration expenses | 240 |  |
| Issued share capital – ordinary shares |  | 700 |
| Trade and other receivables | 525 |  |
| Cash and cash equivalents | 75 |  |
| Share premium |  | 200 |
| Distribution expenses | 500 |  |
| Plant and equipment at cost | 1,600 |  |
| Depreciation of plant and equipment |  | 500 |
| Retained earnings at 1 April 20-1 |  | 350 |
| Purchases | 1,200 |  |
| Inventory at 1 April 20-1 | 160 |  |
| Trade and other payables |  | 395 |
| Revenue |  | 2,295 |
| Dividends paid | 140 |  |
|  | 4,440 | 4,440 |

Notes:

- Inventory at 31 March 20-2 cost £180,000.
- The tax charge based on the profits for the year is £65,000.
- Depreciation on plant and equipment has already been provided for in the list of balances above and allocated to distribution expenses and administration expenses accordingly.

**REQUIRED:**

You are to prepare the financial statements of Crantock Limited for the year ended 31 March 20-2.

**1.3\*** You are the bookkeeper at JC Trading. A sales executive passes to you an expenses claim for car miles to visit a client. You know that the executive travelled in another colleague's car when they both visited the client.

Indicate the **two** ethical principles for accounting staff that are at issue.

| A | Integrity | |
|---|---|---|
| B | Objectivity | |
| C | Professional competence and due care | |
| D | Confidentiality | |
| E | Professional behaviour | |

**1.4** Indicate the ethical principle at issue for accounting staff for each of the following.

| A | No compromise of professional judgement | |
|---|---|---|
| B | Transactions are genuine and valid for inclusion in the records of the business | |
| C | Compliance with relevant laws and regulations | |
| D | Non-disclosure of information to third parties | |
| E | Knowledge and skill is maintained at the level required to provide a competent professional service | |

Choose from the following list:
- Integrity
- Objectivity
- Professional competence and due care
- Confidentiality
- Professional behaviour

**1.5\*** Describe the main differences between financial accounting and management accounting.

# 2 INCOMPLETE RECORDS

In our studies for AQA Accounting we have concentrated on the double-entry system and, from this, we have extracted a trial balance and prepared the income statement and the statement of financial position. However, many smaller businesses do not use the double-entry system, and no trial balance is available. Such businesses keep some records – but these are the single-entry system of incomplete records – and, at the end of the year, it is the task of the accountant to construct the financial statements from these.

This chapter looks at:

- the information available when constructing financial statements from incomplete records
- how information that is required can be calculated, including the use of a statement of affairs
- preparing financial statements from the single-entry system of incomplete records
- the use of gross profit mark-up and margin in incomplete records accounting
- the calculation of cash shortfalls – cash missing as a result of poor cash handling procedures, or as a result of theft
- the calculation of goods taken by the owner of a business for own use
- benefits and limitations of incomplete records
- commenting on financial statements prepared from incomplete records

## WHAT HAPPENS WHEN THERE'S NO DOUBLE-ENTRY?

Many small businesses do not use a double-entry system but, instead, rely on a single-entry cash book to record receipts and payments. At the same time they collect together – often in a box file – their paid invoices, credit notes, copies of invoices issued, bank statements and other bank documentation, notes and jottings, and bits and pieces. At the end of the financial year, it is the task of the accountant to use this 'box file' information – or incomplete records – to construct the income statement and statement of financial position. The owner of the business can then see how much profit has been made during the year, and the assets, liabilities and owner's stake in the business at the end of the year.

# ACCOUNTING RECORDS

Incomplete records is the term used where the bookkeeping system does not use double-entry principles and no trial balance is available. Some records are kept using the single-entry system – eg cash book – and the accountant will construct financial statements by:

- using the information available
- seeing what information may not be available, and how 'missing' figures can be calculated

## information available to the accountant

The basic financial record kept by most businesses is a cash book, often operated as a single-entry system. In practice, even if a cash book has not been kept, it is usually possible to reconstruct it from banking records, although this task can prove to be time-consuming. Other financial information will be available so that, in all, the accountant has the following to work from:

- cash book – the basic record for any single entry system
- banking details – statements, paying-in books, cheque counterfoils, etc
- invoices – both received (for purchases) and sent (for sales) during the year
- expenses – during the year
- records of assets and liabilities – non-current and current assets, non-current and current liabilities, both at the beginning and end of the year
- records of non-current assets – bought or sold during the year

Information which may not be available, and will need to be calculated includes:

- capital at the beginning of the financial year
- purchases and sales for the year
- cash book summary to calculate cash and bank balances
- profit for the year

## acting with integrity

It is important that accounting staff preparing financial statements must always act with integrity. This means that they must be straightforward and honest in all professional and business relationships.

## the tools of accounting

In the two Worked Examples which follow we construct the accounts that are required by taking the financial information that is available and using the following accounting techniques:

- an opening trial balance, or a statement of assets and liabilities
- the construction of a cash account and/or a bank account
- control accounts (also known as totals accounts) – sales ledger control account and purchases ledger control account

In addition, the following may be of use:

- the accounting equation (assets – liabilities = capital)
- gross profit mark-up and margin
- inventory turnover
- profit in relation to revenue
- the format of the income statement and the statement of financial position

The two Worked Examples make use of these accounting techniques, although it should be emphasised that no two incomplete records situations are the same; however practice will help to develop your skills in this aspect of accounting.

## WORKED EXAMPLE: JAYNE PERRY – STATIONERY SUPPLIES

### situation

The following information has been taken from the incomplete records of Jayne Perry, who runs a small stationery supplies business.

**LIST OF ASSETS AND LIABILITIES**

|  | 1 Jan 20-4 | 31 Dec 20-4 |
|---|---|---|
|  | £ | £ |
| Shop fittings | 8,000 | 8,000 |
| Inventory | 25,600 | 29,800 |
| Trade receivables | 29,200 | 20,400 |
| Bank balance | 5,000 | not known |
| Trade payables | 20,800 | 16,000 |
| Expenses owing | 200 | 300 |

**BANK SUMMARY FOR 20-4**

|  | £ |
|---|---|
| Receipts from trade receivables | 127,800 |
| Payments to trade payables | 82,600 |
| Drawings | 12,500 |
| Expenses | 30,600 |

### solution

In the text which follows we shall see how Jayne Perry's accountant will construct the financial statements for 20-4 from incomplete records. The information to be calculated is:

- opening capital, at the beginning of the financial year
- cash book summary for the year
- purchases and sales for the year
- profit for the year
- year end statement of financial position

# OPENING CAPITAL

## the statement of affairs

Opening capital is needed in Jayne Perry's case because a year end statement of financial position is to be prepared. In other situations with incomplete records, opening capital may be stated, being the difference between assets and liabilities. To calculate the capital at the beginning of the financial year, we use the formula *assets – liabilities = capital*.

This is presented in a *statement of affairs* as follows:

| JAYNE PERRY STATEMENT OF AFFAIRS AS AT 1 JANUARY 20-4 | £ | £ |
|---|---|---|
| **Assets** | | |
| Shop fittings | | 8,000 |
| Inventory | | 25,600 |
| Trade receivables | | 29,200 |
| Bank balance | | 5,000 |
| | | 67,800 |
| **Less Liabilities** | | |
| Trade payables | 20,800 | |
| Expenses owing | 200 | |
| | | 21,000 |
| **Capital at 1 January 20-4** | | 46,800 |

*Notes*:

- Here, the bank balance is an asset, ie money in the bank; if it was marked as an overdraft, it would be included amongst the liabilities.

- Look out for the opening bank balance or overdraft being stated elsewhere in the information; for example, a bank summary may be given which starts with the bank figure at the beginning of the year – this figure must be included in the statement of affairs, which is used to calculate opening capital.

## changes in capital over time

A statement of affairs can be used to calculate capital at the start of the year, as above. It can also be used to calculate capital at the end of the year (or at any other time). The change in capital over time shows the amount of profit or loss of the business after the owner has taken out any drawings.

For example, in the statement of affairs above, Jayne Perry's capital at 1 January 20-4 is calculated at £46,800. If her capital at 31 December 20-4 is calculated from a statement of affairs to be £49,000, then we can say that her retained profit for the year is:

|                                          | £      |
|------------------------------------------|--------|
| capital at start of year                 | 46,800 |
| capital at end of year                   | 49,000 |
| retained profit for year after drawings  | 2,200  |

If we then know that Jayne Perry's drawings for the year were £12,500, we can say that the profit for the year of her business was £2,200 + £12,500 = £14,700. Later on we will see from Jayne Perry's income statement (page 29) that £14,700 is her profit for the year.

Remember that changes in capital over time can indicate either a profit or a loss – a fall in the value of capital would show that the business has made a loss. Don't forget to allow for drawings taken by the owner to get to the profit or loss figure for the year.

# CASH BOOK SUMMARY

A cash book summary enables us to find out the cash and bank balances at the year-end. (Sometimes this is not necessary, as a cash book may have been prepared already by the owner of the business.) In practice, the entries on the firm's bank statement can be used to produce a summary of receipts and payments for the year. In the case of Jayne Perry's business, the bank account columns of the cash book are:

| Dr | | | **Bank Account** | | Cr |
|----|----|----|----|----|----|
| **20-4** | | £ | **20-4** | | £ |
| 1 Jan | Balance b/d | 5,000 | | Payments to trade payables | 82,600 |
| | Receipts from trade receivables | 127,800 | | Drawings | 12,500 |
| | | | | Expenses | 30,600 |
| | | | 31 Dec | Balance c/d | 7,100 |
| | | 132,800 | | *missing figure* | 132,800 |
| **20-5** | | | **20-5** | | |
| 1 Jan | Balance b/d | 7,100 | | | |

The bank balance of £7,100 on 31 December 20-4 is calculated by filling in the missing figure.

*Notes*:

- When preparing a bank account summary, be on the look out for an opening bank balance that is *overdrawn*; this is entered on the credit side.
- At the end of the bank account summary, a credit balance brought down is an overdraft.
- In some incomplete records questions a cash account summary will also be needed, if there are separate cash and bank balances (an example of cash account is shown on page 41).

# PURCHASES AND SALES

In calculating purchases and sales, we need to take note of the trade payables and trade receivables at both the beginning and the end of the year. The important point to note is that payments to trade payables are not the same as purchases for the year (because of the change in the level of trade payables). Likewise, receipts from trade receivables are not the same as sales (because of the change in trade receivables). Only in a business which trades solely on cash terms and has no trade receivables and trade payables would the receipts and payments be the figures for sales and purchases.

## calculating purchases and sales

The method of calculating the purchases and sales figures is:

- **purchases for year** = payments to trade payables in the year, *less* trade payables at the beginning of the year, *plus* trade payables at the end of the year
- **sales for year** = receipts from trade receivables in the year, *less* trade receivables at the beginning of the year, *plus* trade receivables at the end of the year

When calculating purchases and sales, also take note of any cash discounts received and allowed, and – for sales – irrecoverable debts written off.

The figures from Jayne Perry's business are:

purchases = £82,600 – £20,800 + £16,000 = £77,800

sales = £127,800 – £29,200 + £20,400 = £119,000

## use of control accounts

The use of control accounts (or total accounts) is recommended for calculating purchases and sales in incomplete records questions. We can use the information for purchases given in the Worked Example as follows:

| Dr | | £ | **Purchases Ledger Control Account** | | Cr | £ |
|---|---|---|---|---|---|---|
| 20-4 | | | 20-4 | | | |
| | Payments to trade payables | 82,600 | 1 Jan | Balance b/d | | 20,800 |
| 31 Dec | Balance c/d | 16,000 | | Purchases *(missing figure)* | | ? |
| | | 98,600 | | | | 98,600 |
| 20-5 | | | 20-5 | | | |
| | | | 1 Jan | Balance b/d | | 16,000 |

The missing figure of purchases for the year is:

£98,600 – £20,800 = £77,800

In a similar way, the sales figure can be calculated:

| Dr | | **Sales Ledger Control Account** | | Cr |
|---|---|---|---|---|
| 20-4 | £ | 20-4 | | £ |
| 1 Jan Balance b/d | 29,200 | Receipts from trade receivables | | 127,800 |
| Sales (*missing figure*) | ? | 31 Dec Balance c/d | | 20,400 |
| | 148,200 | | | 148,200 |
| 20-5 | | 20-5 | | |
| 1 Jan Balance b/d | 20,400 | | | |

The missing figure of sales for the year is £148,200 – £29,200 = £119,000

The control account method – which may be called for in examination questions – does bring a discipline to calculating the two important figures of purchases and sales. Do not forget that the control accounts give the figures for *credit* purchases and sales: *cash* purchases and sales need to be added, where applicable, to obtain total purchases and sales for the year.

## purchases and sales – summary

Whichever method of calculating purchases or sales is used – calculation, or a control account – four pieces of information are usually required:

- opening balance
- closing balance
- payments or receipts for the year
- purchases or sales for the year

Provided that any three are known, the fourth can be calculated – the figure for purchases and sales was the missing figure in the examples above. However if, for example, we know the opening and closing trade receivables totals, together with sales for the year, then it is a simple matter to calculate the missing figure for receipts from trade receivables.

Remember that, if they are applicable, cash discounts allowed and received, sales and purchases returns and – for sales – irrecoverable debts written off, should also be incorporated into the control accounts.

# PREPARATION OF THE FINANCIAL STATEMENTS

## income statement

Having calculated the figures for purchases and sales, we can now prepare the income statement. The section as far as gross profit is:

**JAYNE PERRY**

**INCOME STATEMENT FOR THE YEAR ENDED 31 DECEMBER 20-4**

|  | £ | £ |
|---|---|---|
| Revenue (Sales) | | 119,000 |
| Opening inventory | 25,600 | |
| Purchases | 77,800 | |
| | 103,400 | |
| Less Closing inventory | 29,800 | |
| Cost of sales | | 73,600 |
| **Gross profit** | | 45,400 |

The expenses section of the income statement follows but, before we are able to complete this, we need to know the figure for expenses for the year. The relevant information from the Worked Example is:

- bank payments for expenses during year, £30,600
- expenses owing at 1 January 20-4, £200
- expenses owing at 31 December 20-4, £300

Like the calculation of purchases and sales, we cannot simply use the bank payments figure for expenses; we must take note of cash payments, together with accruals and prepayments. The calculation is:

> **expenses for year** = bank and cash payments in the year, *less* accruals/plus prepayments at beginning of the year, *plus* accruals/less prepayments at end of the year

Thus the figure for Jayne Perry's business expenses is:

> £30,600 − £200 + £300 = £30,700.

Alternatively, expenses can be calculated by means of a control account:

| Dr | | **Expenses Control Account** | | | Cr |
|---|---|---|---|---|---|
| **20-4** | | £ | **20-4** | | £ |
| | Cash/bank | 30,600 | 1 Jan | Balance b/d | 200 |
| 31 Dec | Balance c/d | 300 | 31 Dec | Income statement (missing figure) | ? |
| | | 30,900 | | | 30,900 |
| **20-5** | | | **20-5** | | |
| | | | 1 Jan | Balance b/d | 300 |

The missing figure of expenses for the year is £30,900 − £200 = £30,700

Jayne Perry's income statement concludes as follows:

|  | £ |
|---|---|
| **Gross profit** | 45,400 |
| Less: | |
| Expenses | 30,700 |
| **Profit for the year** | 14,700 |

## statement of financial position

The statement of financial position can now be prepared using the assets and liabilities from the Worked Example.

**JAYNE PERRY**
**STATEMENT OF FINANCIAL POSITION AS AT 31 DECEMBER 20-4**

|  | £ | £ | £ |
|---|---|---|---|
| **Non-current Assets** | | | |
| Shop fittings | | | 8,000 |
| **Current Assets** | | | |
| Inventory | | 29,800 | |
| Trade receivables | | 20,400 | |
| Bank | | 7,100 | |
| | | 57,300 | |
| **Less Current Liabilities** | | | |
| Trade payables | 16,000 | | |
| Accruals | 300 | | |
| | | 16,300 | |
| **Net Current Assets** | | | 41,000 |
| **NET ASSETS** | | | 49,000 |
| | | | |
| **FINANCED BY** | | | |
| **Capital** | | | |
| Opening capital | | | 46,800 |
| Add Profit for the year | | | 14,700 |
| | | | 61,500 |
| Less Drawings | | | 12,500 |
| | | | 49,000 |

## WORKED EXAMPLE: ELECTROPARTS

We will now look at a more comprehensive example of incomplete records accounting. This incorporates points on depreciation and the sale of a non-current asset and concludes with the production of financial statements. You may like to work through the Worked Example before comparing your solution with the one shown.

### situation

John Anstey owns a small business, Electroparts, which supplies spare parts for a wide range of electrical goods – cookers, fridges, freezers, dishwashers, etc. Most of his customers are self-employed repairers who buy parts for specific jobs from his trade counter – John allows them credit terms; some sales are made to members of the public carrying out 'do-it-yourself' repairs – these customers pay in cash at the time of sale. All purchases from suppliers are made on credit.

John does not keep a full set of accounting records; however, the following statement of affairs and bank account sumary has been produced for the year ended 31 December 20-4:

---

**ELECTROPARTS**

**STATEMENT OF AFFAIRS AS AT 1 JANUARY 20-4**

|  |  | £ | £ |
|---|---|---:|---:|
| **ASSETS** | Property at cost | 100,000 | |
| | Less depreciation | 10,000 | |
| | | | 90,000 |
| | Fixtures and fittings at cost | 15,000 | |
| | Less depreciation | 7,500 | |
| | | | 7,500 |
| | | | 97,500 |
| | Inventory | 24,400 | |
| | Trade receivables | 21,650 | |
| | Prepayment: general expenses | 140 | |
| | Cash | 250 | |
| | | | 46,440 |
| | TOTAL ASSETS | | 143,940 |
| **LIABILITIES** | Trade payables | 15,950 | |
| | Bank overdraft | 12,850 | |
| | TOTAL LIABILITIES | | 28,800 |
| **CAPITAL** | | | 115,140 |

### SUMMARY OF BANK ACCOUNT (YEAR ENDED 31 DECEMBER 20-4)

| | £ | | £ |
|---|---|---|---|
| Cash sales | 45,280 | Balance b/d | 12,850 |
| Receipts from trade receivables | 177,410 | Payments to trade payables | 149,620 |
| Sale proceeds of fixtures | | General expenses | 17,340 |
| and fittings | 1,950 | Wages | 18,280 |
| | | Drawings | 25,390 |
| | | Balance c/d | 1,160 |
| | 224,640 | | 224,640 |
| Balance b/d | 1,160 | | |

**other information for the year ended 31 December 20-4**

–  On 31 December 20-4, inventory was valued at £28,400

–  Depreciation is calculated at the rate of 2% on the cost of property and 10% on the cost of fixtures and fittings held at the end of the financial year. No depreciation is calculated in the year of sale/disposal

–  Fixtures and fittings purchased on 1 January 20-2 for £2,500 were sold on 30 September 20-4, the purchaser paying by cheque

–  The proceeds from cash sales are placed in the till and paid into the bank account at the end of the day, apart from a cash float which is retained in the till; the amount of the cash float was £250 until October, when it was increased to £500

–  On 31 December 20-4, trade payables were £18,210, trade receivables were £23,840 and £210 was owing for general expenses

–  During the year, irrecoverable debts of £870 have been written off

John Anstey asks you to:

1  Calculate the amount of credit sales during the year, using a control account

2  Calculate the total sales during the year, using a control account

3  Calculate the amount of purchases during the year, using a control account

4  Calculate the profit or loss on the sale of fixtures and fittings

5  Calculate the figure for general expenses to be shown in the income statement for the year ended 31 December 20-4, using a control account

6  Prepare the income statement for the year ended 31 December 20-4

7  Prepare the statement of financial position at 31 December 20-4

## solution

**1** Dr                        **Sales Ledger Control Account**                     Cr

| 20-4 | | £ | 20-4 | | £ |
|---|---|---|---|---|---|
| 1 Jan | Balance b/d | 21,650 | | Receipts from trade receivables | 177,410 |
| | Credit sales | | | Irrecoverable debts written off | 870 |
| | (missing figure) | 180,470 | 31 Dec | Balance c/d | 23,840 |
| | | 202,120 | | | 202,120 |
| 20-5 | | | 20-5 | | |
| 1 Jan | Balance b/d | 23,840 | | | |

**2** Dr                                **Sales Account**                           Cr

| 20-4 | | £ | 20-4 | | £ |
|---|---|---|---|---|---|
| 31 Dec | Income statement | | | Credit sales (see above) | 180,470 |
| | (sales for year) | 226,000 | | Cash sales (from bank) | 45,280 |
| | | | | Increase in cash float | 250 |
| | | 226,000 | | | 226,000 |

**3** Dr                       **Purchases Ledger Control Account**                   Cr

| 20-4 | | £ | 20-4 | | £ |
|---|---|---|---|---|---|
| | Payments to trade payables | 149,620 | 1 Jan | Balance b/d | 15,950 |
| 31 Dec | Balance c/d | 18,210 | | Purchases | |
| | | | | (missing figure) | 151,880 |
| | | 167,830 | | | 167,830 |
| 20-5 | | | 20-5 | | |
| | | | 1 Jan | Balance b/d | 18,210 |

**4**     **Profit or loss on disposal of fixtures and fittings**

| | |
|---|---|
| Depreciation per year | £250 |
| Number of years' depreciation | 2     (20-2, 20-3; no depreciation in year of sale) |
| Depreciation | £500 |

| Dr | | **Disposals Account** | | Cr |
|---|---|---|---|---|
| **20-4** | | £ | **20-4** | £ |
| 30 Sep | Fixtures and fittings | 2,500 | 30 Sep   Depreciation | 500 |
| | | | 30 Sep   Bank (sale proceeds) | 1,950 |
| | | | 31 Dec   Income statement | |
| | | | (loss on sale) | 50 |
| | | 2,500 | | 2,500 |

**5**

| Dr | | **General Expenses Control Account** | | | Cr |
|---|---|---|---|---|---|
| **20-4** | | £ | **20-4** | | £ |
| 1 Jan | Balance b/d | 140 | 31 Dec | Income statement | |
| | Bank | 17,340 | | *(missing figure)* | 17,690 |
| 31 Dec | Balance c/d | 210 | | | |
| | | 17,690 | | | 17,690 |
| **20-5** | | | **20-5** | | |
| | | | 1 Jan | Balance b/d | 210 |

**6**

### JOHN ANSTEY, TRADING AS 'ELECTROPARTS'
### INCOME STATEMENT FOR THE YEAR ENDED 31 DECEMBER 20-4

|  | £ | £ |
|---|---|---|
| Revenue (Sales) |  | 226,000 |
| Opening inventory | 24,400 |  |
| Purchases | 151,880 |  |
|  | 176,280 |  |
| Less Closing inventory | 28,400 |  |
| Cost of sales |  | 147,880 |
| **Gross profit** |  | 78,120 |
|  |  |  |
| Less expenses: |  |  |
| General expenses | 17,690 |  |
| Loss on sale of fixtures and fittings | 50 |  |
| Depreciation: property | 2,000 |  |
| fixtures and fittings | *1,250 |  |
| Irrecoverable debts | 870 |  |
| Wages | 18,280 |  |
|  |  | 40,140 |
| **Profit for the year** |  | 37,980 |

| *Note |  |
|---|---|
| Fixtures and fittings at cost on 1 January 20-4 | £15,000 |
| Less cost price of fixtures and fittings sold 30 September 20-4 | £2,500 |
| Fixtures and fittings at cost on 31 December 20-4 | £12,500 |
| Depreciation at 10% | £1,250 |

**7**

### JOHN ANSTEY, TRADING AS 'ELECTROPARTS'
### STATEMENT OF FINANCIAL POSITION AS AT 31 DECEMBER 20-4

| | £ | £ | £ |
|---|---|---|---|
| **Non-current Assets** | Cost | Depreciation | Carrying amount |
| Property | 100,000 | 12,000 | 88,000 |
| Fixtures and fittings | 12,500 | *8,250 | 4,250 |
| | 112,500 | 20,250 | 92,250 |
| | | | |
| **Current Assets** | | | |
| Inventory | | 28,400 | |
| Trade receivables | | 23,840 | |
| Bank | | 1,160 | |
| Cash | | 500 | |
| | | 53,900 | |
| | | | |
| **Less Current Liabilities** | | | |
| Trade payables | 18,210 | | |
| Accrual of expenses | 210 | | |
| | | 18,420 | |
| **Net Current Assets** | | | 35,480 |
| **NET ASSETS** | | | 127,730 |
| | | | |
| **FINANCED BY** | | | |
| **Capital** | | | |
| Opening capital (from assets and liabilities at 1 January 20-4) | | | 115,140 |
| Add Profit for the year | | | 37,980 |
| | | | 153,120 |
| Less Drawings | | | 25,390 |
| | | | 127,730 |

| *Note | |
|---|---|
| Depreciation of fixtures and fittings at 1 January 20-4 | 7,500 |
| Less depreciation on asset sold | 500 |
| | 7,000 |
| Depreciation for year (see income statement) | 1,250 |
| Depreciation of fixtures and fittings at 31 December 20-4 | 8,250 |

# USING ACCOUNTING RATIOS FOR INCOMPLETE RECORDS

It is often necessary to use accounting ratios and percentages in the preparation of financial statements from incomplete records. The topic of ratios and percentages has already been covered in your year 1 studies.

## margins and mark-ups

Two useful percentages for incomplete records accounting are:

* gross profit mark-up
* gross profit margin

It is quite common for a business to establish its selling price by reference to either a mark-up or a margin. The difference between the two is that:

* mark-up is a profit percentage added to the cost of sales
* margin is a percentage profit based on revenue

For example, a product is bought by a retailer at a cost of £100; the retailer sells it for £125, ie

$$\text{cost of sales} + \text{gross profit} = \text{revenue}$$
$$£100 \quad + \quad £25 \quad = \quad £125$$

The **mark-up** is:

$$\frac{\text{gross profit}}{\text{cost of sales}} \times \frac{100}{1} = \frac{£25}{£100} \times \frac{100}{1} = \mathbf{25\%}$$

The **margin** is:

$$\frac{\text{gross profit}}{\text{revenue}} \times \frac{100}{1} = \frac{£25}{£125} \times \frac{100}{1} = \mathbf{20\%}$$

In incomplete records accounting, mark-up or the margin percentages can be used to calculate figures for sales and purchases, as shown by the following examples.

## WORKED EXAMPLE: USING MARGINS AND MARK-UPS

### example 1 - calculation of sales

* Cost of sales is £150,000
* Mark-up is 40%
* What is the sales revenue amount?

Gross profit $= £150,000 \times \dfrac{40}{100} = £60,000$

**Sales** = cost of sales + gross profit, ie £150,000 + £60,000 = **£210,000**

**example 2 – calculation of purchases**

- Sales revenue is £450,000
- Margin is 20%
- Opening inventory is £40,000; closing inventory is £50,000
- What is the purchases amount?

Gross profit $= £450,000 \times \dfrac{20}{100} =$ £90,000

Cost of sales = sales – gross profit, ie £450,000 – £90,000 = £360,000

The purchases calculation is:

| | |
|---|---|
| Opening inventory | £40,000 |
| + Purchases (missing figure) | ? |
| – Closing inventory | £50,000 |
| = Cost of sales | £360,000 |
| **Purchases =** | **£370,000** |

## inventory turnover

Inventory turnover in days measures the number of days' inventory held on average. It is expressed as:

$$\frac{\text{Average inventory}}{\text{Cost of sales}} \times 365 \text{ days} = \text{Inventory turnover (days)}$$

Inventory turnover can also be expressed as times per year:

$$\frac{\text{Cost of sales}}{\text{Average inventory}} = \text{Inventory turnover (times per year)}$$

For incomplete records accounting, provided we know any two figures (eg average inventory and inventory turnover) we are able to calculate the third figure (eg cost of sales), as shown by the following examples.

We can also use inventory turnover as a check when we have reconstructed an income statement from missing figures, ie for the same business inventory turnover from year-to-year should be a similar number of days or times per year. A significant difference – particularly when compared with others in the same line of business – would need investigation as to the reasons for the change.

## WORKED EXAMPLE: USING INVENTORY TURNOVER

### example 1 – calculation of cost of sales

- Average inventory is £12,000
- Inventory turnover is 30 days
- What is the cost of sales amount?

$$\frac{£12,000}{\text{cost of sales}} = 30 \text{ days inventory turnover}$$

$$= \frac{£12,000}{30} \times 365 \qquad = \textbf{£146,000 cost of sales}$$

### example 2 – calculation of average inventory

- Cost of sales is £150,000
- Inventory turnover is 12 times per year
- What is the average inventory?

$$\frac{£150,000}{\text{average inventory}} = 12 \text{ times inventory turnover}$$

$$= \frac{£150,000}{12 \text{ times}} \qquad = \textbf{£12,500 average inventory}$$

## profit in relation to revenue

This ratio measures the percentage of profit before tax in relation to revenue, expressed as:

$$\frac{\text{Profit before tax}}{\text{Revenue}} \times \frac{100}{1} = \text{Profit in relation to revenue percentage}$$

We can use this ratio when preparing financial statements from incomplete records to compare the same business from year-to-year – which should be similar – and also to compare with others in the same line of business.

For incomplete records accounting, once we know the revenue figure for the year, by using the previous year's percentage or the industry average, we can make an estimate of profit before tax.

## WORKED EXAMPLE: USING PROFIT IN RELATION TO REVENUE

### example 1 – calculation of profit before tax

- Revenue is £250,000
- Profit in relation to revenue is 20 per cent
- What is profit before tax?

$$\frac{\text{profit before tax}}{£250,000} = 20 \text{ per cent}$$

$$= £250,000 \times 20 \text{ per cent} = \textbf{£50,000 profit before tax}$$

### example 2 – calculation of sales revenue

- Profit in relation to revenue is 25 per cent
- Profit before tax is £40,000
- What is sales revenue?

$$\frac{£40,000}{\text{revenue}} = 25 \text{ per cent (ie 0.25/1)}$$

$$= \frac{£40,000}{0.25} = \textbf{£160,000 revenue}$$

Note: Both of these calculations can be used for checking that figures used within the incomplete records meet the test of 'reasonableness' when compared with the same business for previous years and with others in the same line of business.

## REASONABLENESS OF FIGURES

When preparing financial statements from calculated figures, it is appropriate to 'step back' and, before using the figure, to ask 'does this seem reasonable?' For example, where profit in relation to revenue is 50% this year compared with 10% last year, it would make sense to question and to double-check the calculation.

There is a need to be aware that, when using a calculated figure, it may differ from an actual balance. Wherever possible, when preparing incomplete records, an actual balance is preferable to a calculated figure.

As with all calculated figures, accounting staff should exercise an element of professional judgement as to the reasonableness of given figures in a particular context.

# CHECKING THE CASH

It is always good business practice for a business that receives a lot of cash – such as a shop – to ensure that all cash is accounted for. The techniques used in incomplete records accounting can help to identify cash shortfalls which may occur as a result of poor cash-handling procedures (eg by not banking cash regularly) or, more seriously, as a result of theft. The value of cash shortfalls can be calculated either by preparing a cash book summary and/or using margins and mark-ups to work out how much cash should have been received. The Worked Example which follows shows the calculations of cash shortfalls in two common situations.

## WORKED EXAMPLE: CHECKING THE CASH

### example 1 – cash book summary

There was a theft of cash from a business on 30 January. From the following information, calculate how much cash was stolen.

|  | £ |
|---|---|
| Cash balance at 1 January | 1,056 |
| Cash balance at 31 January | 955 |
| Cash sales for January | 12,112 |
| Cash paid into bank in January | 9,648 |
| Expenses paid from cash in January | 2,235 |

A cash account summary is prepared for January:

| Dr | | | Cash Account | | Cr |
|---|---|---|---|---|---|
| | | £ | | | £ |
| 1 Jan | Balance b/d | 1,056 | | Bank | 9,648 |
| | Cash sales | 12,112 | | Expenses | 2,235 |
| | | | 31 Jan | Balance c/d | 955 |
| | | | 31 Jan | Amount of cash stolen | |
| | | | | (missing figure) | 330 |
| | | 13,168 | | | 13,168 |
| 1 Feb | Balance b/d | 955 | | | |

By preparing a cash accounting summary and filling in the missing figure, the amount of cash stolen on 30 January is found to be **£330**.

## example 2 – margins and mark-ups

The owner of a shop thinks that there may be a shortfall of cash for the month of April. From the following information, calculate the shortfall.

* A mark-up of 50% is used for all goods.
* All takings are banked at the end of each day.
* The following figures are available:

|                                   |    £   |
|-----------------------------------|-------:|
| Inventory at 1 April              | 1,550  |
| Inventory at 30 April             | 1,790  |
| Purchases for April               | 4,560  |
| Trade receivables at 1 April      | 2,075  |
| Trade receivables at 30 April     | 2,695  |
| Cash paid into bank in April      | 5,270  |

**Step 1**  Calculating cost of sales, gross profit and sales

|                               |   £   |
|-------------------------------|------:|
| Opening inventory             | 1,550 |
| Purchases                     | 4,560 |
|                               | 6,110 |
| Less Closing inventory        | 1,790 |
| Cost of sales                 | 4,320 |
| Gross profit at mark-up of 50% | 2,160 |
| Sales                         | 6,480 |

*Note:* the mark-up is applied to cost of sales rather than purchases.

**Step 2**  Using a sales ledger control account

| Dr     |              | **Sales Ledger Control Account** |        |        |              | Cr    |
|--------|--------------|-------:|--------|--------|--------------|------:|
|        |              |    £   |        |        |              |   £   |
| 1 Apr  | Balance b/d  | 2,075  |        |        | Bank *(missing figure)* | 5,860 |
|        | Sales        | 6,480  |        | 30 Apr | Balance c/d  | 2,695 |
|        |              | 8,555  |        |        |              | 8,555 |
|        |              |        |        |        |              |       |
| 1 May  | Balance b/d  | 2,695  |        |        |              |       |

**Step 3** Calculating the cash shortfall

| | £ |
|---|---|
| Cash expected to be banked (from control account) | 5,860 |
| Cash actually banked | 5,270 |
| Cash shortfall | **590** |

## measures to prevent cash shortfalls

- maintaining accurate records of cash transactions
  - keeping a detailed cash book
  - keeping a copy of all cash receipts issued
  - use of a numbering system for all receipts and invoices
  - preparation of a bank reconciliation statement each time a bank statement is received
  - using margin and/or mark-up to compare expected sales with actual sales figures
- office procedures
  - recording cash transactions as they occur, eg by using tills that issue receipts
  - collecting cash from tills regularly, and placing the cash in a safe in the office
  - banking cash regularly, so that there is a low level of cash on the premises at any time
  - paying bills by cheque or bank transfer rather than in cash, so avoiding the need to carry cash when paying trade payables
  - dividing duties within the business, ensuring that no one person is responsible for all cash handling
  - carrying out cash checks at regular intervals, eg to ensure that cash in the tills balances against receipts
  - improving security, eg use of a safe in the office for cash to be banked, keeping the office door locked when the office is empty, use of security cameras
  - checking references for new employees
  - setting authorisation limits for employees who pay bills, to ensure that large amounts cannot be paid out by newer employees

# GOODS FOR OWN USE

The value of goods taken by the owner of a business for his or her own use may need to be calculated as part of incomplete records accounting.

The value of inventory taken by the owner is calculated by preparing an accounting summary which often makes use of margins and mark-ups. The calculation is best carried out in three steps:

1. Opening inventory
   + Purchases
   = Cost of inventory available for sale

2. Sales
   − Gross profit (using normal gross profit margin)
   = Cost of sales

3. Cost of inventory available for sale (from 1, above)
   − Cost of sales (2, above)
   = Estimated closing inventory
   − Value of inventory remaining
   = Value of inventory taken by the owner for own use

## WORKED EXAMPLE: CLOTHING SUPPLIES − GOODS FOR OWN USE

**situation**

Peter Kamara runs Clothing Supplies, a small clothing wholesalers. During the year he has taken clothes for his own use but has kept no records. He asks you to calculate, from the accounting details, the value of the goods he has taken. The following information is available:

- sales for the year, £500,000
- opening inventory at the beginning of the year, £15,000
- purchases for the year, £310,000
- closing inventory at the end of the year, £24,000
- the gross profit margin achieved on all sales is 40 per cent

**solution**

| CALCULATION OF GOODS FOR OWN USE FOR THE YEAR | | |
|---|---|---|
| | £ | £ |
| Opening inventory | | 15,000 |
| Purchases | | 310,000 |
| **Cost of inventory available for sale** | | 325,000 |
| Sales | 500,000 | |
| Less Normal gross profit margin (40%) | 200,000 | |
| **Cost of sales** | | 300,000 |
| Estimated closing inventory | | 25,000 |
| Less Actual closing inventory | | 24,000 |
| **Value of goods taken for own use** | | 1,000 |

**Tutorial note:** The same format of calculation can be used where there is a shortfall of inventory − caused by events such as a fire, a flood or a theft.

# BENEFITS AND LIMITATIONS OF INCOMPLETE RECORDS

Whilst the use of a double-entry system is the preferred way to keep business accounting records, there are many smaller businesses that use a single-entry system of incomplete records. The availability of accounting software (see Chapter 3) may encourage some businesses to switch to double-entry accounts, but there will still be a role for the accountant in the preparation of financial statements and especially to deal with the tax authorities. It is also true that many people, and often those setting up in business for the first time, have a limited knowledge of keeping accounting records – hence the approach of incomplete records used in this chapter.

The main benefits of the single-entry system of incomplete records include:

- knowledge of double-entry is not required – a person with no knowledge of the principles of double-entry can keep the books of the business

- less expensive on a day-to-day basis – the single-entry system costs less than double-entry (but an accountant's costs to prepare financial statements will be higher)

- time-saving – a quick and easy method which, at its most basic, only requires a cash book

- convenient – the single-entry method can be adapted to suit the needs of the business with no double-entry principles to be followed

- suitable for small businesses – the owner of the business can keep the records as can an employee who works on other aspects of the business

- a cash-based income statement can be prepared – but the assistance of an accountant will be needed to complete the financial statements

The limitations and drawbacks of the single-entry system of incomplete records include:

- higher cost at the year end – because it is time-consuming, an accountant usually charges more to prepare financial statements from incomplete records than from records kept using double-entry

- lack of up-to-date management information – details are not readily available of such things as trade receivables (how much are we owed?), bank (what is the bank balance?), sales (what have we sold this month?), expenses (how much have we spent on fuel for the vehicles this month?), etc

- statements of account sent to trade receivables may not be completely accurate – this will also make chasing payments from trade receivables difficult

- dangers of shortfall or theft of cash and inventory – may be difficult to verify if the accounting records are not up-to-date

- there may be a lack of accuracy – a number of amounts, such as sales and purchases, are calculated by means of a missing figure; there may be other items that should be included in the calculations

- additional costs may be incurred – eg the costs of obtaining duplicate bank statements and paid cheques from the bank

- reliability of figures may be questioned – eg by lenders and the tax authorities' lack of an independent verification (double-check) of figures – the assumption with incomplete records is that if something has been calculated, then it must be correct

- items may be missed from the financial statements – eg an asset or a liability may be overlooked

- no trial balance – with single entry a trial balance cannot be prepared, so the accuracy of the bookkeeping cannot be checked

- difficulty in preparing financial statements – the assistance of an accountant will be needed

## COMMENTING ON YEAR END FINANCIAL STATEMENTS

From time-to-time examination questions will ask you, after you have prepared financial statements from incomplete records, to make comments on the figures, or give advice to the owner of the business or other interested party. Questions asked can include a commentary on the profitability, liquidity, efficiency, and capital structure of the business. To answer these, you will need to make use of accounting ratios learned previously in AQA Accounting: AS and A-level year 1, eg profit margins, return on capital employed, current asset and liquid capital ratios, etc.

Be ready to make comparisons from one year to the next in order to indicate a trend – eg falling profitability, increasing expenses – and to suggest ways in which adverse trends can be corrected – eg by increasing sales/sales prices, keeping a tight rein on expenses. Also, be prepared to make comparisons between two businesses – eg to compare the business whose financial statements you have prepared with those of a similar business, or with an industry average.

The owner of the business may seek advice such as, 'should I expand the business?'; if so, 'how should I finance the expansion?'; or, 'should I consider selling the business and retiring?' Make sure that the advice you give is backed up with financial figures – eg if the owner is thinking of selling up and retiring, see how much profit the business is currently making and compare this with the interest that could be earned from investing the sale proceeds in a savings account. For a business which is seeking to expand, you will need to suggest appropriate sources of finance – eg a bank overdraft or loan.

As always, with any 'commentary' question, ensure you finish with a conclusion that summarises your findings.

# STEP-BY-STEP GUIDE TO PREPARING FINANCIAL STATEMENTS FROM INCOMPLETE RECORDS

Note that, depending on the information given in a question, not all of these steps will be required.

**1. calculate opening capital**

use a statement of affairs to list:

assets

less liabilities

equals capital at start

(remember to include the bank balance or overdraft – it could be found in another part of the question)

*Using opening capital and closing capital, profit for the year can be calculated as:*

*closing capital*
*less opening capital*
*plus drawings*
*equals profit for the year*

**2. calculate closing cash and/or bank balance**

use a cash account or a bank account to record:

| Cash Account or Bank Account ||
|---|---|
| Balance b/d* | Payments |
| Receipts _____ | Balance c/d _____ |
| ‗‗‗‗‗ | ‗‗‗‗‗ |

\* bank overdraft at the start will be a credit balance b/d

**3. calculate credit purchases for the year**

use a purchases ledger control account to record:

*Include cash discounts received where applicable*

| Purchases Ledger Control Account ||
|---|---|
| Payments to trade payables | Balance b/d |
| Balance c/d _____ | Purchases for the year _____ |
| ‗‗‗‗‗ | ‗‗‗‗‗ |

**4. calculate credit sales for the year**

use a sales ledger control account to record:

| Sales Ledger Control Account | |
|---|---|
| Balance b/d | Receipts from trade receivables |
| Sales for the year | Balance c/d |

*Include cash discounts allowed and irrecoverable debts where applicable*

**5. calculate total sales for the year**

credit sales + cash sales (if any)

= total sales for the year

**6. calculate expenses for the year**

| Expenses Control Account | |
|---|---|
| Prepayments b/d | Accruals b/d |
| Cash/bank payments | Expense for year (to income statement) |
| Accruals c/d | Prepayments c/d |

*Use an expenses control account where there are accruals and/or prepayments*

**7. calculate profit or loss on disposal of non-current assets**

| Disposals Account | |
|---|---|
| NCAs at cost | Depreciation |
| Profit on disposal (to income statement) | Bank (sale proceeds) |
| | Loss on disposal (to Income statement) |

**8. prepare the income statement**

|            | revenue             |
|------------|---------------------|
| less       | cost of sales       |
| equals     | gross profit        |
| less       | expenses            |
| equals     | profit for the year |

**9. prepare the statement of financial position**

|            | non-current assets  |
|------------|---------------------|
| plus       | net current assets  |
| equals     | net assets          |
|            |                     |
| financed by| opening capital     |
| plus       | profit for the year |
| less       | drawings            |
| equals     | closing capital     |

Note: These steps provide a logical approach to preparing financial statements from incomplete records. However, they may need to be adapted to meet the requirements of an individual question.

# CHAPTER SUMMARY

● Incomplete records is the term used where the bookkeeping system does not use double-entry principles.

● In order to prepare financial statements, the accountant may well have to calculate:
  • capital at the beginning of the financial year, using a statement of affairs
  • purchases and sales for the year
  • cash account and bank account summary
  • profit for the year

● It is important that accounting staff preparing financial statements act with integrity.

● The change in capital over time shows the profit or loss of the business after the owner has taken out any drawings.

● On the basis of these calculations, the accountant can then construct the financial statements without recourse to a trial balance.

● Ratios and percentages that can be used in incomplete records accounting are:
  • gross profit mark-up, which is the profit percentage added to the cost of sales
  • gross profit margin, which is the profit percentage based on revenue
  • inventory turnover
  • profit in relation to revenue

● The value of cash shortfalls and goods for own use may be calculated using margins and mark-ups.

● The main benefits and limitations of incomplete records include:
  • benefits: knowledge of double-entry not required; less expensive on a day-to-day basis; time saving; convenient
  • limitations: higher cost at the year end; lack of up-to-date management information; dangers of shortfall or theft of cash or inventory; lack of accuracy; no trial balance

● Commenting on year end financial statements prepared from incomplete records will often include consideration of the profitability, liquidity, efficiency and capital structure of the business.

● Use the step-by-step guide on pages 47-49 to help with the preparation of financial statements from incomplete records.

The next chapter looks at the way in which computers are used to handle accounting records and to overcome some of the drawbacks of incomplete records accounting.

# QUESTIONS

visit
**www.osbornebooks.co.uk**
to take an online test

An asterisk (*) after the question number means that the answer is given at the end of this book.

**2.1\***  A retailer has never kept accounting records, but wishes to know the value of the business. Which **one** of the following would provide the retailer with the value of the business?

| A | Bank reconciliation statement | |
|---|-------------------------------|---|
| B | Trial balance | |
| C | Statement of affairs | |
| D | Income statement | |

**2.2\***  The following information was provided by a sole trader for the year ended 31 December 20-8.

| | £ |
|---|---|
| Capital 1 January 20-8 | 55,000 |
| Capital 31 December 20-8 | 51,000 |
| Drawings | 15,000 |

What was the business's profit or loss for the year ended 31 December 20-8?

| A | Loss £19,000 | |
|---|--------------|---|
| B | Loss £11,000 | |
| C | Profit £19,000 | |
| D | Profit £11,000 | |

**2.3**  The following information was provided by a sole trader for the year ended 30 June 20-3.

| | £ |
|---|---|
| Capital 1 July 20-2 | 47,000 |
| Capital 30 June 20-3 | 38,000 |
| Drawings | 5,000 |

What was the business's profit or loss for the year ended 30 June 20-3?

| A | Loss £4,000 | |
|---|-------------|---|
| B | Loss £14,000 | |
| C | Profit £4,000 | |
| D | Profit £14,000 | |

**2.4\***  A sole trader has not maintained proper books of account. The following information is available relating to trade receivables for the year ended 31 December 20-4.

|                                        | £       |
| -------------------------------------- | ------- |
| Receipts from trade receivables        | 164,000 |
| Irrecoverable debts                    | 2,000   |
| Trade receivables, 1 January 20-4      | 18,000  |
| Trade receivables, 31 December 20-4    | 22,000  |

What is the value of credit sales for the year ended 31 December 20-4?

| A | £158,000 |  |
| - | -------- | -- |
| B | £162,000 |  |
| C | £168,000 |  |
| D | £170,000 |  |

**2.5**  A sole trader has not maintained proper books of account. The following information is available relating to trade payables for the year ended 31 March 20-6.

|                                    | £       |
| ---------------------------------- | ------- |
| Payments to trade payables         | 195,000 |
| Purchases returns                  | 6,000   |
| Trade payables, 1 April 20-5       | 10,000  |
| Trade payables, 31 March 20-6      | 14,000  |

What is the value of credit purchases for the year ended 31 March 20-6?

| A | £193,000 |  |
| - | -------- | -- |
| B | £197,000 |  |
| C | £205,000 |  |
| D | £225,000 |  |

**2.6\***  The following information is available relating to rent paid for the year ended 30 June 20-5.

|  | £ |
|---|---|
| Debit balance brought down, 1 July 20-4 | 750 |
| Payments during year ended 30 June 20-5 | 8,350 |
| Credit balance carried down at 30 June 20-5 | 550 |

How much should be shown as an expense in the income statement for the year ended 30 June 20-5?

| A | £7,050 | |
|---|---|---|
| B | £8,150 | |
| C | £8,550 | |
| D | £9,650 | |

**2.7**  The following information is available relating to rent received for the year ended 31 December 20-8.

|  | £ |
|---|---|
| Credit balance brought down, 1 January 20-8 | 600 |
| Receipts during year ended 31 December 20-8 | 4,800 |
| Credit balance carried down at 31 December20-8 | 350 |

How much should be shown as income in the income statement for the year ended 31 December 20-8?

| A | £3,850 | |
|---|---|---|
| B | £4,550 | |
| C | £5,050 | |
| D | £5,750 | |

**2.8\***
- Cost of sales for the year is £200,000.
- Mark-up is 30%.

  What are sales for the year?

**2.9**
- Sales for the year are £100,000.
- Gross profit margin is 25%.
- Opening inventory is £10,000; closing inventory is £12,000.

  What are purchases for the year?

**2.10\***
- Cost of sales is £320,000.
- Inventory turnover is 16 times per year.

What is the average inventory for the year?

**2.11**
- Profit in relation to revenue is 20 per cent.
- Profit before tax is £25,000.

What is revenue for the year?

**2.12\*** Jayne Harvey runs a stationery supplies shop. During the year she has taken stationery for her own use, but has kept no records. She asks you to calculate from the accounting records the value of the goods she has taken. The following information is available for the year ended 30 June 20-8:

- sales for the year, £180,000
- opening inventory at the beginning of the year, £21,500
- purchases for the year, £132,000
- closing inventory at the end of the year, £26,000
- the gross profit margin achieved on all sales is 30 per cent

**You are to** calculate the value of goods Jayne has taken for her own use during the year ended 30 June 20-8.

**2.13** Talib Zabbar owns a shop selling clothes. During the year he has taken clothes for his own use but has kept no records. He asks you to calculate from the accounting records the value of the goods he has taken.

The following information is available for the year ended 30 September 20-7:

- sales for the year, £160,000
- opening inventory at the beginning of the year, £30,500
- purchases for the year, £89,500
- closing inventory at the end of the year, £23,500
- the gross profit margin achieved on all sales is 40 per cent

**You are to** calculate the value of goods Talib has taken for his own use during the year ended 30 September 20-7.

**2.14\*** Jane Price owns a fashion shop called 'Trendsetters'. She has been in business for one year and, although she does not keep a full set of accounting records, the following information has been produced for the first year of trading, which ended on 31 December 20-4:

**Summary of the business bank account for the year ended 31 December 20-4:**

|  | £ |
|---|---|
| Capital introduced | 60,000 |
| Receipts from trade receivables | 153,500 |
| Payments to trade payables | 95,000 |
| Advertising | 4,830 |
| Shop wages | 15,000 |
| Shop rent | 8,750 |
| General expenses | 5,000 |
| Shop fittings | 50,000 |
| Drawings | 15,020 |

**Summary of assets and liabilities at 31 December 20-4:**

|  | £ |
|---|---|
| Shop fittings at cost | 50,000 |
| Inventory | 73,900 |
| Trade receivables | 2,500 |
| Trade payables | 65,000 |

**Other information:**

- Jane wishes to depreciate the shop fittings at 20% per year using the straight-line method
- At 31 December 20-4, shop rent is prepaid by £250, and shop wages of £550 are owing

**You are to:**

**(a)** Calculate the amount of sales during the year.

**(b)** Calculate the amount of purchases during the year.

**(c)** Calculate the figures for:
- shop rent
- shop wages

to be shown in the income statement for the year ended 31 December 20-4

**(d)** Prepare Jane Price's income statement for the year ended 31 December 20-4.

**(e)** Prepare Jane Price's statement of financial position at 31 December 20-4.

**2.15** Colin Smith owns a business which sells specialist central heating parts to trade customers. He has been in business for a number of years. Although he does not keep a full set of accounting records, the following information is available in respect of the year ended 30 June 20-5:

**Summary of assets and liabilities:**

|  | 1 July 20-4 | 30 June 20-5 |
|---|---|---|
|  | £ | £ |
| **Assets** |  |  |
| Inventory | 25,000 | 27,500 |
| Fixtures and fittings (cost £50,000) | 40,000 | 35,000 |
| Trade receivables | 36,000 | 35,000 |
| Bank | 1,500 | 1,210 |
|  |  |  |
| **Liabilities** |  |  |
| Trade payables | 32,500 | 30,000 |
| Accrual of expenses | 500 | 700 |

**Summary of the business bank account for the year ended 30 June 20-5:**

|  | £ |
|---|---|
| Expenses | 30,000 |
| Drawings | 28,790 |
| Receipts from trade receivables | 121,000 |
| Payments to trade payables | 62,500 |

**Other information:**

• Fixtures and fittings are being depreciated at 10% per year using the straight-line method

• Irrecoverable debts of £550 have been written off during the year

**You are to:**

**(a)** Calculate the amount of sales during the year ended 30 June 20-5.

**(b)** Calculate the amount of purchases during the year ended 30 June 20-5.

**(c)** Calculate the figure for expenses to be shown in the income statement for the year ended 30 June 20-5.

**(d)** Prepare Colin Smith's income statement for the year ended 30 June 20-5.

**(e)** Prepare Colin Smith's statement of financial position at 30 June 20-5.

**2.16**  Samantha owns a kitchenware shop called 'Sam's Trading'. She does not keep proper books of account and asks for your help in preparing her financial statements for the year ended 31 December 20-6.

The following information is available for the year ended 31 December 20-6.

| 20-6 | 1 January £ | 31 December £ |
|---|---|---|
| Shop fittings at carrying amount | 18,240 | 14,360 |
| Inventory | 32,170 | 35,470 |
| Trade payables | 14,560 | 16,830 |
| Other payables: rent of shop premises | – | 1,230 |
| Other receivables: rent of shop premises | 860 | – |

An analysis of the bank statements for Samantha's business for 20-6 is summarised as follows:

| 20-6 | Debit £ | Credit £ | Balance £ | |
|---|---|---|---|---|
| Balance at 1 January | | | 1,270 | Cr |
| Cash takings banked | | 247,840 | 249,110 | Cr |
| Payments to trade payables | 180,890 | | 68,220 | Cr |
| Rent of shop premises | 20,840 | | 47,380 | Cr |
| General expenses | 25,170 | | 22,210 | Cr |
| Drawings | 18,410 | | 3,800 | Cr |
| Sale of shop fittings | | 610 | 4,410 | Cr |
| Balance at 31 December | | | 4,410 | Cr |

Samantha provides you with the following additional information:

- All purchases are made on credit; all sales are cash sales.

- Samantha's policy is to have a mark-up on all goods sold of 40%.

- At 31 December 20-6 there are unpresented cheques sent to trade payables of £1,590 and amounts for cash takings paid into the bank but not yet credited of £1,220.

- The shop fittings sold during the year had a carrying amount of £1,250 at 1 January 20-6; no new shop fittings have been purchased during the year.

- During 20-6, Samantha has taken goods for her own use but does not know the amount.

**You are to:**

**(a)**  Calculate the purchases for 20-6.

**(b)**  Calculate the rent of shop premises for 20-6.

**(c)**  Calculate the depreciation of shop fittings for 20-6.

**(d)**  Calculate the profit or loss on sale of shop fittings.

**(e)**  Prepare the business's income statement for the year ended 31 December 20-6 showing clearly the value of goods taken for her own use by Samantha.

**(f)**  Prepare the business's statement of financial position as at 31 December 20-6.

# 3  COMPUTER ACCOUNTING

In the previous chapter we have seen how some businesses keep incomplete records, usually on a single-entry system. Other businesses may use a paper-based double-entry system. However, many small and medium-sized businesses buy 'off-the-shelf' accounting programs from suppliers such as Sage, while larger businesses often have custom-designed programs.

Computer accounting programs carry out functions such as invoicing, dealing with payments, paying wages and providing regular accounting reports such as the income statement and the statement of financial position.

The introduction of a computer accounting system can provide major advantages such as speed and accuracy of operation. There are also certain disadvantages, such as cost and training needs which the management of a business must appreciate before taking the decision to convert from a manual to a computerised accounting system.

Businesses also make considerable use of computer spreadsheets, particularly for budgets. They can also be used for speeding up the processes in manual accounting systems, setting up a trial balance, for example.

> **Tutorial note:** within this chapter there is reference to Value Added Tax (VAT) – an aspect of accounting that computer accounting programs handle with ease. You should note, however, that the AQA Accounting Specifications do not require a knowledge of how to account for VAT.

## FEATURES OF COMPUTER ACCOUNTING

### facilities

A typical computer accounting program will offer a number of facilities:

- on-screen input and printout of sales invoices
- automatic updating of customer accounts in the sales ledger
- recording of suppliers' invoices
- automatic updating of supplier accounts in the purchases ledger
- recording of bank receipts
- making payments to suppliers and for expenses
- automatic updating of the general (nominal) ledger
- automatic adjustment of inventory records

## management reports

A computer accounting program can provide instant reports for management, for example:

- aged trade receivables' summary – a summary of customer accounts, showing overdue amounts
- trial balance, income statement and statement of financial position
- inventory valuation
- VAT return

## computer accounting – ledger system

The 'Ledger' – which basically means 'the books of the business' is a term used to describe the way the accounts of the business are grouped into different sections:

- **sales ledger**, containing the accounts of trade receivables (customers)
- **purchases ledger**, containing the accounts of trade payables (suppliers)
- **cash books**, containing the cash account and the bank account
- **general ledger** (also called nominal ledger) containing the remaining accounts, eg expenses (including purchases), income (including sales), assets, loans, inventory, VAT

The screens of a ledger computer accounting system are designed to be user-friendly. Look at the menu of the opening screen of a computer accounting system shown below and then read the explanatory notes.

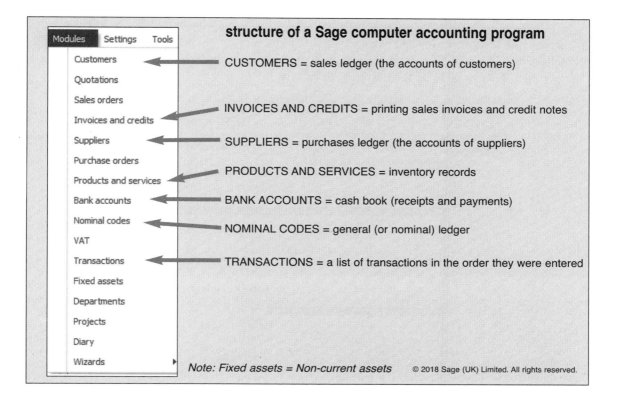

**structure of a Sage computer accounting program**

Modules | Settings | Tools

- Customers — CUSTOMERS = sales ledger (the accounts of customers)
- Quotations
- Sales orders
- Invoices and credits — INVOICES AND CREDITS = printing sales invoices and credit notes
- Suppliers — SUPPLIERS = purchases ledger (the accounts of suppliers)
- Purchase orders
- Products and services — PRODUCTS AND SERVICES = inventory records
- Bank accounts — BANK ACCOUNTS = cash book (receipts and payments)
- Nominal codes — NOMINAL CODES = general (or nominal) ledger
- VAT
- Transactions — TRANSACTIONS = a list of transactions in the order they were entered
- Fixed assets
- Departments
- Projects
- Diary
- Wizards

*Note: Fixed assets = Non-current assets*

## using a computer accounting system

Computer input screens are designed to be easy to use. Their main advantage is that each transaction needs only to be input as a single entry, unlike in a manual double-entry system where two (or three) entries are required. In the example below, payment is made for copy paper costing £45.50 plus Value Added Tax. The input line includes the nominal account number of bank account (1200), the date of payment, the cheque number (234234), and the nominal account code for stationery expenses (7500). The net amount of £45.50 is entered and the computer automatically calculates the VAT. The appropriate amounts are then transferred by the computer to bank account, stationery expenses account and VAT account.

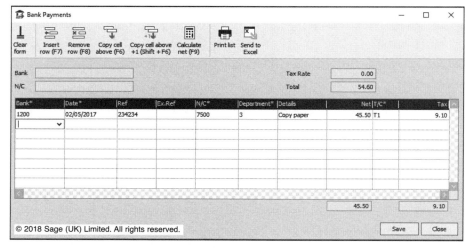

The screen below shows an invoice input screen. In this example 20 Enigma 35s are being invoiced to R Patel & Co in Salisbury. The computer will in due course print the invoice, which will contain the name of the seller as well as all the customer details held in the accounting program's database.

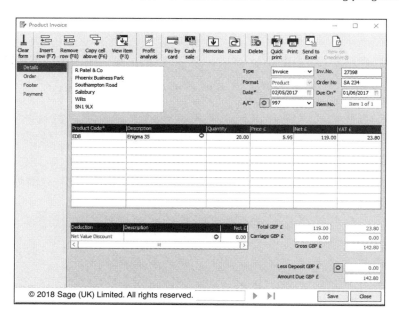

## computerised ledgers – an integrated system

A computerised ledger system is **fully integrated**. This means that when a business transaction is input on the computer it is recorded in a number of different accounting records as a single entry. For example, when the sales invoice on the previous page is entered on the screen and the ledgers are 'updated' an integrated program will:

- record the amount of the invoice in the customer account of R Patel & Co in the sales ledger
- record the amount of the invoice in the sales account and VAT account (if appropriate) in the general ledger
- reduce the quantity of goods held (in this case Enigmas) in the inventory records

At the centre of an integrated program is the nominal ledger which deals with all the accounts except customers' accounts and suppliers' accounts. It is affected one way or another by most transactions.

The diagram below shows how the purchases ledger, sales ledger and bank link with the nominal (general) ledger. You can see how an account in the nominal ledger is affected by each of these three transactions. This is the double-entry bookkeeping system at work. The advantage of the computer system is that in each case only a single entry transaction has to be made.

Note that Value Added Tax account is omitted from this diagram for the sake of simplicity of illustration. VAT account will be maintained in the nominal (general) ledger and will be updated by all three of the transactions shown.

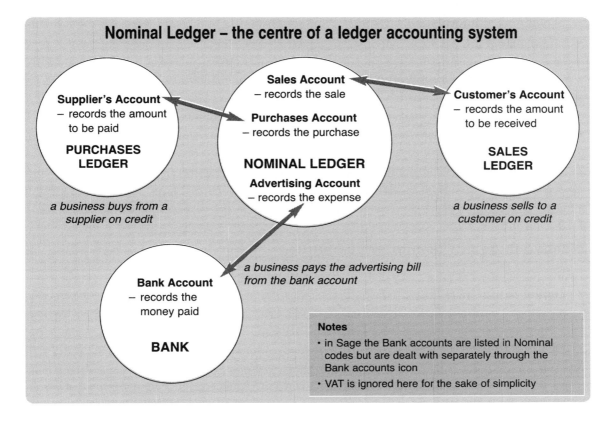

### Nominal Ledger – the centre of a ledger accounting system

**Supplier's Account**
– records the amount to be paid

**PURCHASES LEDGER**

*a business buys from a supplier on credit*

**Sales Account**
– records the sale

**Purchases Account**
– records the purchase

**NOMINAL LEDGER**

**Advertising Account**
– records the expense

**Customer's Account**
– records the amount to be received

**SALES LEDGER**

*a business sells to a customer on credit*

**Bank Account**
– records the money paid

**BANK**

*a business pays the advertising bill from the bank account*

**Notes**
- in Sage the Bank accounts are listed in Nominal codes but are dealt with separately through the Bank accounts icon
- VAT is ignored here for the sake of simplicity

# ADVANTAGES AND DISADVANTAGES OF COMPUTER ACCOUNTING

In this chapter so far we have stressed the advantages of the introduction of computers to carry out accounting functions in a business. There are, however, some disadvantages as well, and any business introducing computer accounting will need to weigh up carefully the 'pros and cons'.

These advantages and disadvantages follow, together with a Worked Example based on the effect on employees of the introduction of a new computer accounting system.

## advantages of computer accounting

The main advantages of using a computer accounting program include:

- **speed** – data entry on the computer with its formatted screens and built-in databases of customer and supplier details and inventory records can be carried out far more quickly than any manual processing

- **automatic document production** – fast and accurate invoice and credit note printing, statement runs, payroll processing

- **accuracy** – there is less room for error as only a single entry is needed for each transaction rather than the two (or three) required in a manual double-entry system

- **up-to-date information** – the accounting records are automatically updated and so account balances (eg customer accounts) will always be up-to-date

- **availability of information** – the data can be made available to different users at the same time

- **management information** – reports can be produced which will help management monitor and control the business, for example the aged trade receivables' analysis which shows which customer accounts are overdue for payment, trial balance, income statement and statement of financial position

- **VAT return** – the automatic production of figures for the VAT return

- **legibility** – the on-screen and printed data should always be legible and so will avoid errors caused by poor figures

- **efficiency** – better use is made of resources and time; cash flow should improve through better debt collection from trade receivables

- **staff motivation** – the system will require staff to be trained to use new skills, which can make them feel more valued

## disadvantages of computer accounting

The main disadvantages of using computer accounting programs include:

- **capital cost of installation** – the hardware and software will need to be budgeted for, not only as 'one-off' expenditure but also as recurrent costs because computers will need replacing and software updating

- **cost of training** – the staff will need to be trained in the use of the hardware and software

- **staff opposition** – motivation may suffer as some staff may not like computers, also there may be staff redundancies (as fewer people may be needed in the accounts department), all of which create bad feeling

- **disruption** – loss of work time and changes in the working environment when the computerised system is first introduced
- **system failure** – the danger of the system crashing and the subsequent loss of work when no back-ups have been made
- **back-up requirements** – the need to keep regular and secure back-ups in case of system failure
- **breaches of security** – the danger of people hacking into the system from outside, the danger of viruses, the incidence of staff fraud
- **health dangers** – the problems of bad backs, eyestrain and muscular complaints such as RSI (Repetitive Strain Injury)
- **errors** – there is still the danger of errors of omission (data entry not made at all), errors of original entry (the wrong figure is entered), errors of principle (the entry is in the wrong type of account) and mispost (entry is in the wrong person's account)

## WORKED EXAMPLE

### situation

Stitch-in-time Limited is an old-fashioned company which manufactures sewing machines. The Finance Director, Charles Cotton, is considering the introduction of a computer accounting system which will completely replace the existing manual double-entry system.

He is worried because he knows that the proposition will not go down very well with employees who have been with the company for a long time.

He asks you to prepare notes in which you are to set out:

(a) the benefits to staff of the new scheme

(b) the likely causes of staff dissatisfaction with the new scheme

### solution

(a) **potential benefits to staff**
- the staff will be able to update their skills
- they will receive training
- they may get an increase in pay
- the training will increase their career prospects
- they will be motivated
- they will get job satisfaction

(b) **causes of staff dissatisfaction**
- staff prefer doing the job in a way which is familiar to them
- they do not like computers

- they may see their jobs threatened as they worry that redundancies will occur
- they do not look forward to the disruption at the time of the changeover
- they worry about the possible bad effects to their health, having heard about RSI (Repetitive Strain Injury) and radiation and eye damage from computer screens
- they will be demotivated as they consider the new system 'mechanical' – they will have to sit in front of a computer for hours at a time and not be able to communicate so well with their colleagues as they have in the past

# COMPUTER SPREADSHEETS

A spreadsheet is a grid of boxes – 'cells' – set up on the computer, organised in rows and columns into which are entered text and numbers. It enables calculations to be made with the figures. The computer program will work out the calculations automatically once an appropriate formula is entered in the cell where the result of the calculations is required.

The major advantage of a spreadsheet is that if any of the figures are changed the computer will automatically recalculate the total, saving much time and effort.

Spreadsheets are used for a variety of functions in business:

- producing invoices – working out costs of products sold, calculating and adding on VAT and producing a sales total
- working out budgets (see Chapter 10) – such as cash, sales, purchases, production and labour
- working out sales figures for different products or areas

A commonly used spreadsheet program is Microsoft Excel.

Spreadsheets may be used in a wide variety of accounting functions. The first of the two examples illustrated on the next page is very simple: it shows the two columns of a **trial balance**. The spreadsheet has been set up with columns for account names, debit balances, credit balances and totals for the columns. When the figures have been entered, they will automatically produce totals which should balance.

The second example (on the next page) of a computer spreadsheet used in the accounting process is a form of cash budget, often known as a **cash flow forecast**. This is a projection of the cash receipts and payments of a business over a period of months. Each month the spreadsheet calculates the total receipts (row 11) and payments (row 23) and uses them to calculate the cash flow (row 24). This figure is then used to calculate the projected bank balance of the business (row 26). This figure is useful as it will show if the business needs to borrow from the bank.

The advantage of the spreadsheet in this example is that if the business wishes to change any of the receipt or payment amounts – eg if the sales receipts increase – then the cash flow figures will automatically be recalculated, potentially saving hours of work.

| | A | B | C | D | E | F | G |
|---|---|---|---|---|---|---|---|
| 1 | | Dr | Cr | | | | |
| 2 | | | | | | | |
| 3 | | | | | | | |
| 4 | Plant and machinery | 35000 | | | | | |
| 5 | Office equipment | 15000 | | | | | |
| 6 | Furniture and fixtures | 25000 | | | | | |
| 7 | Sales ledger control | 45500 | | | | | |
| 8 | Bank current account | 12450 | | | | | |
| 9 | Purchases ledger control | | 32510 | | | | |
| 10 | Sales tax control account | | 17920 | | | | |
| 11 | Purchase tax control account | 26600 | | | | | |
| 12 | Loans | | 35000 | | | | |
| 13 | Ordinary Shares | | 75000 | | | | |
| 14 | Hardware sales | | 85000 | | | | |
| 15 | Software sales | | 15000 | | | | |
| 16 | Computer consultancy | | 2400 | | | | |
| 17 | Materials purchased | 69100 | | | | | |
| 18 | Advertising | 12400 | | | | | |
| 19 | Gross wages | 16230 | | | | | |
| 20 | Rent | 4500 | | | | | |
| 21 | General rates | 450 | | | | | |
| 22 | Electricity | 150 | | | | | |
| 23 | Telephone | 275 | | | | | |
| 24 | Stationery | 175 | | | | | |
| 25 | | | | | | | |
| 26 | | | | | | | |
| 27 | Total | 262830 | 262830 | | | | |

| | A | B | C | D | E | F | G |
|---|---|---|---|---|---|---|---|
| 1 | **CORIANNE LIMITED** | | | | | | |
| 2 | **Cash flow forecast for the six months ending** 30 June 20-X | | | | | | |
| 3 | | JANUARY | FEBRUARY | MARCH | APRIL | MAY | JUNE |
| 4 | | £ | £ | £ | £ | £ | £ |
| 5 | *Receipts* | | | | | | |
| 6 | | | | | | | |
| 7 | | | | | | | |
| 8 | Sales Receipts | 3,000 | 3,000 | 4,000 | 4,000 | 4,000 | 4,000 |
| 9 | | | | | | | |
| 10 | Capital | 10,000 | | | | | |
| 11 | TOTAL RECEIPTS | 13,000 | 3,000 | 4,000 | 4,000 | 4,000 | 4,000 |
| 12 | *Payments* | | | | | | |
| 13 | Purchases | 5,000 | 1,750 | 1,750 | | 1,750 | 1,750 |
| 14 | Non-current Assets | 4,500 | 5,250 | | | | |
| 15 | Rent/Rates | 575 | 575 | 575 | 575 | 575 | 575 |
| 16 | Insurance | 50 | 50 | 50 | 50 | 50 | 50 |
| 17 | Electricity | 25 | 25 | 25 | 25 | 25 | 25 |
| 18 | Telephone | 150 | 15 | 15 | 15 | 15 | 15 |
| 19 | Stationery | 10 | 10 | 10 | 10 | 10 | 10 |
| 20 | Postage | 15 | 15 | 15 | 15 | 15 | 15 |
| 21 | Bank charges | 100 | | 75 | | | 75 |
| 22 | Advertising | 150 | 30 | 30 | 30 | 30 | 30 |
| 23 | TOTAL PAYMENTS | 10,575 | 7,720 | 2,545 | 720 | 2,470 | 2,545 |
| 24 | CASHFLOW FOR MONTH | 2,425 | - 4,720 | 1,455 | 3,280 | 1,530 | 1,455 |
| 25 | Bank Balance *brought forward* | - | 2,425 | - 2,295 | - 840 | 2,440 | 3,970 |
| 26 | Bank Balance *carried forward* | 2,425 | - 2,295 | - 840 | 2,440 | 3,970 | 5,425 |

# CHAPTER SUMMARY

● Computer accounting systems save businesses time and money by automating many accounting processes, including the production of reports for management.

● Most computer accounting programs are based on the ledger system and integrate a number of different functions – a single entry transaction will change accounting data in a number of different parts of the system.

● The different functions can include: sales ledger, purchases ledger, nominal (general) ledger, cash and bank payments, inventory control, invoicing, and reports.

● A business must consider carefully the advantages and disadvantages of computer accounting before installing a computerised system. The main advantages are speed, accuracy, availability of up-to-date information; the main disadvantages are cost, security implications and possible opposition from employees.

● Computer spreadsheets are often also used to carry out individual functions in an accounting system, for example the creation of budgets.

In the next chapter we turn our attention to the accounting and financial statements of partnerships.

# QUESTIONS

An asterisk (*) after the question number means that an answer is given at the end of this book.

**3.1*** Explain **two** advantages to a business of using a computer accounting system to record financial transactions.

**3.2*** Describe **two** advantages of using a computer spreadsheet for a document such as a cash flow forecast (cash budget).

**3.3*** Explain how **three** different areas of the accounting system might benefit from the introduction of computer accounting.

**3.4*** A business is planning to introduce a computer accounting system and holds an employee meeting to explain the implications of the change. One employee says 'I have heard that there are all sorts of risks to the computer data which could cause us to lose the lot'. Describe **two** of the main risks to the security of computer data.

**3.5**

Gerry Mann is the finance director of Colourways Limited, a design company. He wants to introduce a computer accounting system into the business, but is encountering opposition from Helen Baxill, who works in the finance department.

Describe:

**(a)** The objections relating to staff working conditions and welfare that Helen is likely to raise to try and block or delay the introduction of a computer system.

**(b)** The advantages to staff of a computer system that Gerry could use to persuade Helen to accept its introduction.

# 4 PARTNERSHIP FINANCIAL STATEMENTS

Partnerships, which were considered briefly as a type of business organisation in Accounting for AQA: AS and A-level year 1, can be found in the form of:

- sole traders who have joined together with others in order to raise finance and expand the business
- family businesses, such as builders, car repairers, gardeners
- professional firms such as solicitors, accountants, doctors, dentists

In this chapter we examine:

- the definition of a partnership
- the accounting requirements of the Partnership Act 1890
- the accounting requirements which may be incorporated into a partnership agreement
- the use of capital accounts and current accounts
- the appropriation of profits
- the layout of the capital section of the statement of financial position
- the preparation of a partnership statement of financial position from a trial balance

## WHAT DOES A PARTNERSHIP INVOLVE?

The Partnership Act of 1890 defines a partnership as:

**the relation which subsists between persons carrying on a business in common with a view of profit**

Normally, partnerships consist of between two and twenty partners. Exceptions to this include large professional firms, eg solicitors and accountants, who sometimes set up what are known as 'limited liability partnerships' (LLPs). Partnerships are often larger businesses than sole traders because, as there is more than one owner, there is likely to be more capital. A partnership may be formed to set up a new business or it may be the logical growth of a sole trader taking in partners to increase the capital.

## advantages and disadvantages

Partnerships are cheap and easy to set up; their advantages are:

- there is the possibility of increased capital
- individual partners may be able to specialise in particular areas of the business
- with more people running the business, there is more cover for illness and holidays

The disadvantages are:

- as there is more than one owner, decisions may take longer because other partners may need to be consulted
- there may be disagreements amongst the partners
- each partner is liable in law for the dealings and business debts of the *whole* firm – unless it is a 'limited liability partnership' (LLP) set up under the Limited Liability Partnerships Act 2000
- the retirement or death of one partner may adversely affect the running of the business

## accounting requirements of a partnership

The accounting requirements of a partnership are:

- either to follow the rules set out in the Partnership Act 1890
- or – and more likely – for the partners to agree amongst themselves, by means of a partnership agreement (see page 71), to follow different accounting rules

Unless the partners agree otherwise, the Partnership Act 1890 states the following accounting rules:

- profits and losses are to be shared equally between the partners
- no partner is entitled to a salary
- partners are not entitled to receive interest on their capital
- interest is not to be charged on partners' drawings
- when a partner contributes more capital than agreed, he or she is entitled to receive interest at five per cent per annum on the excess

As noted above, the partners may well decide to follow different accounting rules – these will be set out in a partnership agreement (see page 71).

# FINANCIAL STATEMENTS OF A PARTNERSHIP

A partnership prepares the same type of financial statements as a sole trader business:

- income statement
- statement of financial position

The main difference is that, immediately after the income statement, follows the **partnership appropriation account**. This shows how the profit from the income statement is shared amongst the partners.

## sharing profits

Ela, Fay and Gen are partners sharing profits and losses equally; for 20-4 their income statement shows a profit for the year of £60,000. Their partnership appropriation account appears as:

**ELA, FAY AND GEN**
**PARTNERSHIP APPROPRIATION ACCOUNT**
**FOR THE YEAR ENDED 31 DECEMBER 20-4**

|  | £ |
|---|---|
| Profit for the year | 60,000 |
| Share of profits: |  |
| Ela | 20,000 |
| Fay | 20,000 |
| Gen | 20,000 |
|  | 60,000 |

The above is a simple appropriation of profits. A more complex partnership appropriation account (see Worked Example on page 75) deals with other accounting points which may be included in the partnership agreement.

## separate capital accounts

Each partner has a separate capital account, which operates in the same way as for a sole trader. Thus the partner's capital accounts show:

- capital introduced
- share of profits/losses
- drawings

Continuing the example of Ela, Fay and Gen (above), if each partner started the year with capital of £100,000 and drawings were £10,000 for Ela and £15,000 for Fay and Gen, the capital section of their statement of financial position at 31 December 20-4 appears as:

**ELA, FAY AND GEN**
**STATEMENT OF FINANCIAL POSITION (EXTRACT) AS AT 31 DECEMBER 20-4**

| | £ | £ | £ | £ |
|---|---|---|---|---|
| **FINANCED BY** | | | | |
| **Capital Accounts** | | | | |
| | Ela | Fay | Gen | |
| Opening capital | 100,000 | 100,000 | 100,000 | |
| Add Profit for the year | 20,000 | 20,000 | 20,000 | |
| | 120,000 | 120,000 | 120,000 | |
| Less Drawings | 10,000 | 15,000 | 15,000 | |
| Closing capital | 110,000 | 105,000 | 105,000 | 320,000 |

*Note:* £320,000 is the total of all partners' capital accounts at the date of the statement of financial position.

The above is a simple illustration of the use of capital accounts – in practice most partnerships use both a capital account and a current account (see page 73) to record partners' contributions to the business.

# PARTNERSHIP AGREEMENT

The accounting rules from the Partnership Act are often varied with the agreement of all partners by means of a partnership agreement. A partnership agreement will usually cover the following:

- division of profits and losses between partners
- partners' salaries/commission
- whether interest is to be allowed on capital, and at what rate
- whether interest is to be charged on partners' drawings, and at what rate

The money amounts involved for each of these points (where allowed by the partnership agreement) are shown in the partnership appropriation account (see Worked Example on page 75).

## division of profits and losses between partners

The Partnership Act states that, in the absence of an agreement to the contrary, profits and losses are to be shared equally. A partner's share of the profits is normally taken out of the business in the form of drawings. Clearly, if one partner has contributed much more capital than the other partner(s), it would be unfair to apply this clause from the Act. Consequently, many partnerships agree to share profits and losses on a different basis – often in the same proportions as they have contributed capital. Note that, in examination questions, you will normally be told the agreed division of profits; however, if there is no mention of this, you should assume that the partners receive an equal share.

## partners' salaries/commission

Although the Act says that no partner is entitled to a salary, it is quite usual in the partnership agreement for one or more partners to be paid a salary. The reason for doing this is that often in a partnership, one of the partners spends more time working in the partnership than the other(s). The agreement to pay a salary is in recognition of the work done. Note that partners' salaries are not shown as an expense in the income statement; instead they appear in the partnership appropriation account (see the example on page 75).

Many professional partnerships, such as solicitors and accountants, have junior partners who receive a partnership salary because they work full-time in the business, but have not yet contributed any capital. In a partnership, there may not be a requirement to contribute capital, unless the partnership agreement states otherwise; however, most partners will eventually do so.

As an alternative to a salary, a partner might be paid a commission on sales. As with a salary, this is not shown as an expense in the income statement, but appears in the partnership appropriation account.

## interest allowed on capital

Many partnerships include a clause in their partnership agreement which allows interest to be paid on capital; the rate of interest will be stated also. This clause is used to compensate partners for the loss of use of their capital, which is not available to invest elsewhere. Often, interest is allowed on capital in partnerships where profits and losses are shared equally – it is one way of rewarding partners for different capital balances. As noted earlier, the Partnership Act does not permit interest to be paid on capital, so reference to it must be made in the partnership agreement.

When calculating interest on capital, it may be necessary to allow for part years. For example:

| | |
|---|---|
| 1 January 20-4 capital balance | £20,000 |
| 1 July 20-4 additional capital contributed | £4,000 |
| the rate of interest allowed on capital | 10% per annum |
| the partnership's financial year end | 31 December 20-4 |

Interest allowed on capital is calculated as:

| | |
|---|---|
| 1 January – 30 June  £20,000 x 10% x 6 months | £1,000 |
| 1 July – 31 December  £24,000 x 10% x 6 months | £1,200 |
| Interest allowed on capital for year | £2,200 |

## interest charged on partners' drawings

In order to discourage partners from drawing out too much money from the business early in the financial year, the partnership agreement may stipulate that interest is to be charged on partners' drawings, and at what rate. This acts as a penalty against early withdrawal when the business may be short of cash. For example:

| | |
|---|---|
| a partner's drawings during the year | £24,000 |
| withdrawal at the end of each quarter (31 March, 30 June, 30 September, 31 December) | £6,000 |
| the rate of interest charged on partners' drawings | 10% per annum |
| the partnership's financial year end | 31 December |

Interest charged on this partner's drawings is calculated as:

| | |
|---|---|
| 31 March: £6,000 x 10% x 9 months | £450 |
| 30 June: £6,000 x 10% x 6 months | £300 |
| 30 September: £6,000 x 10% x 3 months | £150 |
| Interest charged on the partner's drawings for year | £900 |

No interest is charged on the withdrawal on 31 December, because it is at the end of the financial year. The amount of interest charged on drawings for the year is shown in the partnership appropriation account, where it increases the profit to be shared amongst the partners.

## interest paid on loans

If a partner makes a loan to the partnership, the rate of interest to be paid needs to be agreed, otherwise the rate specified in the Partnership Act 1890 applies – five per cent per annum.

Interest on loans is charged as an expense in the income statement, and is not shown in the partnership appropriation account and the loan amount is shown as a liability – either short- or long-term – in the statement of financial position.

Note that, where a partner lends money to the partnership, the loan account is kept entirely separate from that partner's capital account and current account and is shown as a liability – either short- or long-term – in the statement of financial position.

# CAPITAL ACCOUNTS AND CURRENT ACCOUNTS

As noted previously, each partner has a separate capital account to record his or her permanent contribution to the business. Often, this will suffice for partnerships where the agreement is simply to split profits and losses equally. With more complex partnership agreements, each partner usually has both a capital account and a current account. The capital account is normally **fixed**, and only alters if a permanent increase or decrease in capital contributed by the partner takes place. The current account is **fluctuating** and it is to this account that:

- share of profit is credited
- share of loss is debited
- salary/commission is credited
- interest allowed on partners' capital is credited
- drawings and goods for own use are debited
- interest charged on partners' drawings is debited

Thus, the current account is a working account, while capital account remains fixed, except for capital introduced or withdrawn, or when changes are made to the partnership (see Chapter 5). With this arrangement the fixed capital account makes interest on capital – where permitted by the partnership agreement – easy to calculate, while at the same time shows whether or not partners are maintaining their permanent capital in the business. The fluctuating current account shows whether or not partners have withdrawn more profit from the business than they are earning. However, it should be pointed out that separate capital and current accounts require more work and are, therefore, more time-consuming for the bookkeeper than using the partners' capital accounts for all transactions. As to which is used will depend on the size and complexity of the partnership business.

A partner's current account has the following layout:

| Dr | **Partner Aye: Current Account** | Cr |
|---|---|---|
| | £ | £ |
| Share of loss | Balance b/d | |
| Drawings/goods for own use | Share of profit | |
| Interest charged on drawings* | Salary/commission* | |
| Balance c/d | Interest on capital* | |

* if these items are allowed by the partnership agreement

Note that the normal balance on a partner's current account is credit. However, when a partner has drawn out more than his or her share of the profits, then the balance will be debit – as shown by Ali's current account in the Worked Example which follows.

As noted earlier, any loan account in the name of a partner – used to account for money loaned by the partner to the partnership – is kept entirely separate from that partner's capital account and current account. Such a loan does not receive a share of the profits and is only entitled to receive interest at the rate stated in the partnership agreement, otherwise the rate specified in the Partnership Act 1890 applies – five per cent per annum. Such interest is charged in the income statement as an expense before any appropriation of profit is made.

## WORKED EXAMPLE: APPROPRIATION OF PARTNERSHIP PROFITS

As we have seen earlier in this chapter, the partnership appropriation account follows the income statement and shows how profit for the year is divided amongst the partners. This Worked Example shows a partnership salary (which is not shown in the income statement) and interest allowed on partners' capital.

### situation

Ali and Bob are in partnership sharing profits and losses 60 per cent and 40 per cent respectively. Profit for the year ended 31 March 20-4 is £42,000.

At 1 April 20-3 (the start of the year), the partners have the following balances:

|  | Capital account | Current account |
|---|---|---|
|  | £ | £ |
| Ali | 40,000 | 2,000 Cr |
| Bob | 30,000 | 400 Cr |

- There have been no changes to the capital accounts during the year; interest is allowed on partners' capitals at the rate of eight per cent per year.
- Bob is entitled to a salary of £16,000 per year.
- On 30 September 20-3 (half-way through the financial year), partners' drawings were made: Ali £18,000, Bob £24,000; there were no other drawings. Interest is charged on partners' drawings at the rate of ten per cent per year.

### solution

The appropriation of profits will be made as follows:

| ALI AND BOB, IN PARTNERSHIP | | |
|---|---|---|
| **PARTNERSHIP APPROPRIATION ACCOUNT FOR THE YEAR ENDED 31 MARCH 20-4** | | |
|  | £ | £ |
| **Profit for the year** |  | 42,000 |
| Add interest charged on partners' drawings: |  |  |
| Ali (£18,000 x six months x 10%) | 900 |  |
| Bob (£24,000 x six months x 10%) | 1,200 |  |
|  |  | 2,100 |
|  |  | 44,100 |
| **Less appropriation of profit:** |  |  |
| Salary: Bob |  | 16,000 |
| Interest allowed on partners' capitals: |  |  |
| Ali       £40,000 x 8% | 3,200 |  |
| Bob       £30,000 x 8% | 2,400 |  |
|  |  | 5,600 |
|  |  | 22,500 |
| **Share of remaining (residual) profit:** |  |  |
| Ali (60%) | 13,500 |  |
| Bob (40%) | 9,000 |  |
|  |  | 22,500 |

Note that all of the available profit – after allowing for any salary, and interest allowed on capital and charged on drawings – is shared amongst the partners, in the ratio in which they share profits and losses.

The partners' current accounts for the year are shown below. Here the layout for the partners' current accounts uses a normal 'T' account but in a side-by-side format with a column for each partner on both the debit and credit sides. As an alternative, separate current accounts can be produced for each partner.

| Dr | | | | | Partners' Current Accounts | | | | Cr |
|---|---|---|---|---|---|---|---|---|---|
| | | Ali | Bob | | | | | Ali | Bob |
| 20-3/4 | | £ | £ | 20-3/4 | | | | £ | £ |
| 31 Mar | Drawings | 18,000 | 24,000 | 1 Apr | Balances b/d | | | 2,000 | 400 |
| 31 Mar | Interest on drawings | 900 | 1,200 | | Salary | | | – | 16,000 |
| 31 Mar | Balance c/d | – | 2,600 | 31 Mar | Interest on capital | | | 3,200 | 2,400 |
| | | | | 31 Mar | Share of profit | | | 13,500 | 9,000 |
| | | | | 31 Mar | Balance c/d | | | 200 | – |
| | | 18,900 | 27,800 | | | | | 18,900 | 27,800 |
| 20-4/5 | | | | 2004/5 | | | | | |
| 1 Apr | Balance b/d | 200 | – | 1 Apr | Balance b/d | | | – | 2,600 |

From the current accounts we can see that Ali has drawn more out than the balance of the account; accordingly, at the end of the year, Ali has a debit balance of £200 on current account. By contrast, Bob has a credit balance of £2,600 on current account.

# STATEMENT OF FINANCIAL POSITION

The statement of financial position of a partnership must show the year end balances on each partner's capital and current account. However, the transactions that have taken place on each account can be shown in summary form – in the same way that, in a sole trader's statement of financial position, profit for the year is added and drawings for the year are deducted.

The other sections of the statement of financial position – non-current assets, current assets, current and non-current liabilities – are presented in the same way as for a sole trader.

The following is an example statement of financial position layout for the 'financed by' section (the other sections are not shown). It details the capital and current accounts of the partnership of Ali and Bob (see Worked Example above).

**ALI AND BOB, IN PARTNERSHIP**
**STATEMENT OF FINANCIAL POSITION (EXTRACT) AS AT 31 MARCH 20-4**

| | £ | £ |
|---|---|---|
| **FINANCED BY** | | |
| **Capital Accounts** | | |
| Ali | 40,000 | |
| Bob | 30,000 | |
| | | 70,000 |
| **Current Accounts** | | |
| Ali | (200) | |
| Bob | 2,600 | |
| | | 2,400 |
| | | 72,400 |

# PARTNERSHIP FINANCIAL STATEMENTS FROM THE TRIAL BALANCE

The financial statements of a partnership are prepared in exactly the same way as for sole traders. The only differences to note are that partners' capital and current accounts are shown in the statement of financial position. Transactions affecting the partners' current accounts – such as share of profits, partners' salaries, drawings, etc – can be shown either in the form of a double-entry 'T' account (see previous page for an example), or directly on the face of the statement of financial position (see the following Worked Example). Whichever way this is done, it is the closing balances of the current accounts that are added in to the 'financed by' section of the statement of financial position.

## WORKED EXAMPLE: PARTNERSHIP FINANCIAL STATEMENTS

### situation

The trial balance for the partnership of Ramjit Singh and Veta Bix, trading as 'Rave Music', at 31 December 20-5 is shown on the next page.

**RAMJIT SINGH AND VETA BIX IN PARTNERSHIP, TRADING AS 'RAVE MUSIC'**
**TRIAL BALANCE AS AT 31 DECEMBER 20-5**

|  | | Dr £ | Cr £ |
|---|---|---|---|
| Inventory at 1 January 20-5 | | 20,000 | |
| Revenue | | | 250,000 |
| Purchases | | 120,000 | |
| Property at cost | | 200,000 | |
| Depreciation: freehold property | | | 9,000 |
| Fixtures and fittings at cost | | 20,000 | |
| Depreciation: fixtures and fittings | | | 8,000 |
| Wages and salaries | | 35,000 | |
| Shop expenses | | 20,000 | |
| Trade receivables | | 3,000 | |
| Trade payables | | | 7,000 |
| Bank overdraft | | | 6,000 |
| Long-term loan from Ramjit Singh | | | 80,000 |
| Capital accounts: | Ramjit Singh | | 50,000 |
| | Veta Bix | | 45,000 |
| Current accounts: | Ramjit Singh | | 4,000 |
| | Veta Bix | | 1,000 |
| Drawings: | Ramjit Singh | 24,000 | |
| | Veta Bix | 18,000 | |
| | | 460,000 | 460,000 |

Notes at 31 December 20-5:
- inventory was valued at £30,000
- wages and salaries owing £1,700
- shop expenses prepaid £800
- depreciate the property by £3,000, and the fixtures and fittings by 10 per cent (straight-line method)
- interest of £4,000 on the loan from Ranjit Singh is owing
- goods taken for own use, Ramjit £500, Veta £400
- Veta is to receive a partnership salary of £10,000
- interest is to be allowed on partners' capital accounts at 10 per cent per year
- remaining profits and losses are to be shared equally
- there is no interest charged on partners' drawings

**solution**
The financial statements of the partnership of Ramjit Singh and Veta Bix, trading as 'Rave Music', are shown on the next page.

**RAMJIT SINGH AND VETA BIX IN PARTNERSHIP, TRADING AS 'RAVE MUSIC'**
**INCOME STATEMENT FOR THE YEAR ENDED 31 DECEMBER 20-5**

|  | £ | £ | £ |
|---|---|---|---|
| **Revenue** | | | 250,000 |
| Opening inventory | | 20,000 | |
| Purchases | 120,000 | | |
| Less Goods for own use | 900 | | |
| | | 119,100 | |
| | | 139,100 | |
| Less Closing inventory | | 30,000 | |
| Cost of sales | | | 109,100 |
| **Gross profit** | | | 140,900 |
| Less expenses: | | | |
| Wages and salaries | | 36,700 | |
| Shop expenses | | 19,200 | |
| Depreciation: | | | |
| property | | 3,000 | |
| fixtures and fittings | | 2,000 | |
| Loan interest | | 4,000 | |
| | | | 64,900 |
| **Profit for the year** | | | 76,000 |
| | | | |
| **Less appropriation of profit:** | | | |
| Salary:  Veta Bix | | | 10,000 |
| Interest allowed on partners' capitals: | | | |
| Ramjit Singh | £50,000 x 10% | 5,000 | |
| Veta Bix | £45,000 x 10% | 4,500 | |
| | | | 9,500 |
| | | | 56,500 |
| | | | |
| **Share of remaining (residual) profit:** | | | |
| Ramjit Singh (50%) | | | 28,250 |
| Veta Bix (50%) | | | 28,250 |
| | | | 56,500 |

**RAMJIT SINGH AND VETA BIX IN PARTNERSHIP, TRADING AS 'RAVE MUSIC'**
**STATEMENT OF FINANCIAL POSITION AS AT 31 DECEMBER 20-5**

| | £ | £ | £ |
|---|---|---|---|
| **Non-current Assets** | Cost | Depreciation | Carrying amount |
| Freehold property | 200,000 | 12,000 | 188,000 |
| Fixtures and fittings | 20,000 | 10,000 | 10,000 |
| | 220,000 | 22,000 | 198,000 |
| | | | |
| **Current Assets** | | | |
| Inventory | | 30,000 | |
| Trade receivables | | 3,000 | |
| Other receivable | | 800 | |
| | | 33,800 | |
| **Less Current Liabilities** | | | |
| Trade payables | 7,000 | | |
| Other payables (wages & salaries, loan interest) | 5,700 | | |
| Bank overdraft | 6,000 | | |
| | | 18,700 | |
| **Net Current Assets** | | | 15,100 |
| | | | 213,100 |
| **Less Non-current Liabilities** | | | |
| Loan from Ramjit Singh | | | 80,000 |
| **NET ASSETS** | | | 133,100 |
| | | | |
| **FINANCED BY** | | | |
| **Capital Accounts** | | | |
| Ramjit Singh | | 50,000 | |
| Veta Bix | | 45,000 | |
| | | | 95,000 |

| **Current Accounts** | R Singh | V Bix | |
|---|---|---|---|
| Opening balance | 4,000 | 1,000 | |
| Add: Salary | – | 10,000 | |
| Interest on capital | 5,000 | 4,500 | |
| Share of profit | 28,250 | 28,250 | |
| | 37,250 | 43,750 | |
| Less: Drawings | 24,000 | 18,000 | |
| Goods for own use* | 500 | 400 | |
| Closing balance | 12,750 | 25,350 | |
| | | | 38,100 |
| | | | 133,100 |

* goods for own use can be included with the amount for drawings – shown here separately
  so that the accounting treatment can be seen clearly.

## COMMENTING ON PARTNERSHIP FINANCIAL STATEMENTS

In examination questions you will be asked to prepare different accounting aspects of partnerships, eg partners' capital and current accounts, appropriation accounts, and partnership financial statements. Examination questions may also ask you to discuss or comment on a variety of aspects of partnerships. Topics could include:

- the terms of the Partnership Act 1890, including reference to sharing profits and losses
- the merits of having a partnership agreement
- the circumstances under which partners use capital accounts only
- the arguments for and against the use of capital and current accounts (to include the meaning of debit or credit balances on current accounts)
- the distinction between a partner's loan account and capital account, and the accounting treatment of each, including interest allowed

Some questions may also link to other parts of the AQA Accounting course – for example, a partnership may not keep double-entry accounts, instead using incomplete records; you might then be asked to prepare partnership financial statements from such incomplete records.

## CHAPTER SUMMARY

- A partnership is formed when two or more (usually up to a maximum of twenty) people set up in business.

- The Partnership Act 1890 states certain accounting rules, principally that profits and losses must be shared equally.

- Many partnerships over-ride the accounting rules of the Act by having a partnership agreement which covers the following main points:
  - division of profits and losses between partners
  - partners' salaries/commission
  - whether interest is to be allowed on capital, and at what rate
  - whether interest is to be charged on partners' drawings, and at what rate
  - the rate of interest to be paid on loans made by partners to the partnership

- A common way to account for partners' capital is to maintain a fixed capital account for each partner. This is complemented by a fluctuating current account which is used as a working account for share of profits, drawings, etc.

● The financial statements of partnerships are similar to those of sole traders, but incorporate:

- an appropriation account, as a continuation of the income statement, to show the share of profits and losses

- accounts for each partner – usually separate capital and current accounts – shown in the statement of financial position

In the next chapter we continue the theme of partnerships and look at changes in partnerships, such as the admission of a new partner, and the retirement of a partner.

# QUESTIONS

visit
www.osbornebooks.co.uk
to take an online test

An asterisk (*) after the question number means that the answer is given at the end of this book.

**4.1\*** Which **one** of the following contravenes the provisions of the Partnership Act 1890?

| A | No partner is entitled to a salary | |
|---|---|---|
| B | Profits and losses are to be shared in proportion to capital | |
| C | Partners are not entitled to receive interest on their capital | |
| D | Interest is not to be charged on partners' drawings | |

**4.2\*** A partnership may choose to over-ride some or all of the accounting rules in the Partnership Act 1890 by the partners entering into a separate:

| A | Appropriation account | |
|---|---|---|
| B | Accounting policy | |
| C | Partnership agreement | |
| D | Loan agreement | |

**4.3\*** Which **one** of the following correctly states items that should be shown in a partnership appropriation account?

| A | Interest on partners' capital accounts; share of residual losses; partnership salaries | |
|---|---|---|
| B | Interest on a partner's loan; share of residual profits; interest on partners' drawings | |
| C | Share of residual losses; interest on partners' drawings; interest on a partner's loan | |
| D | Drawings, share of residual profits; partnership salaries | |

**4.4**

Profits of a two-person partnership are £32,800 before the following are taken into account:

- Interest allowed on partners' capital accounts, £1,800
- Salary of one partner, £10,000
- Interest on partners' drawings, £600

If the remaining profits are shared equally, how much will each partner receive?

| A | £10,800 | |
|---|---------|---|
| B | £12,000 | |
| C | £16,400 | ✓ |
| D | £22,000 | |

**4.5**

Fay is a partner in a recently formed business. The bookkeeper has made errors in completing her partnership current account.

Her current account is shown below:

| Dr | | **Fay: Current Account** | | Cr |
|----|---|---|---|---|
| | £ | | £ | |
| Share of profit | 2,500 | Interest charged on drawings | 250 | |
| Drawings | 4,500 | Salary | 8,750 | |
| Balance c/d | 2,000 | | | |
| | 9,000 | | 9,000 | |
| | | Balance b/d | 2,000 | |

What is the correct closing balance brought down on Fay's current account?

| A | £1,500 debit | |
|---|---|---|
| B | £6,500 debit | |
| C | £1,500 credit | |
| D | £6,500 credit | ✓ |

**4.6**

The current account of a partner, Tara Shah, has a balance at the beginning of the financial year of £550 debit. During the year, the following transactions pass through her current account:

- interest allowed on capital, £900

- partnership salary, £10,000

- drawings, £14,000

- share of profits, £4,230

What is the balance of Tara Shah's current account at the end of the financial year?

| A | £1,220 debit | |
|---|---|---|
| B | £6,750 debit | |
| C | £580 credit | |
| D | £1,680 credit | |

**4.7***

Lysa and Mark are in partnership and own a shop, 'Trends', which sells fashionable teenage clothes. The following figures are extracted from their accounts for the year ended 31 December 20-4:

| | £ | |
|---|---|---|
| Capital accounts at 1 January 20-4: | | |
| Lysa | 50,000 | Cr |
| Mark | 40,000 | Cr |
| Current accounts at 1 January 20-4: | | |
| Lysa | 420 | Cr |
| Mark | 1,780 | Cr |
| Drawings for the year: | | |
| Lysa | 13,000 | |
| Mark | 12,250 | |
| Interest on capital for the year: | | |
| Lysa | 2,500 | |
| Mark | 2,000 | |
| Share of profits for the year: | | |
| Lysa | 9,300 | |
| Mark | 9,300 | |

Notes:
- neither partner is entitled to receive a salary
- there is no interest charged on partners' drawings

**You are to** show the partners' capital and current accounts for the year ended 31 December 20-4.

**4.8**

Mike and Bernie are in partnership as 'M & B Builders'. The follo
from their accounts for the year ended 31 December 20-4:

| | | |
|---|---:|---|
| Capital accounts at 1 January 20-4: | £ | |
| Mike | 30,000 | Cr |
| Bernie | 20,000 | Cr |
| | | |
| Current accounts at 1 January 20-4: | | |
| Mike | 1,560 | Cr |
| Bernie | 420 | Dr |
| | | |
| Drawings for the year: | | |
| Mike | 21,750 | |
| Bernie | 17,350 | |
| | | |
| Partnership salary: | | |
| Bernie | 7,500 | |
| | | |
| Interest on capital for the year: | | |
| Mike | 1,500 | |
| Bernie | 1,000 | |
| | | |
| Share of profits for the year: | | |
| Mike | 20,200 | |
| Bernie | 10,100 | |

Note: there is no interest charged on partners' drawings.

**You are to** show the partners' capital and current accounts for the year ended 31 December
20-4.

**4.9\***

Sigrid and Tomascz are in partnership as 'S & T Plumbers'. Their partnership agreement
states:

- profits and losses are to be shared in the ratio 60:40
- interest is to be allowed on partners' capital accounts at the rate of 10% per year
- interest is to be charged on drawings
- Tomascz is to receive a partnership salary of £12,000 per year

Profit for the year ended 30 June 20-2 is £50,500. The following data is also available:

| | Sigrid | | Tomascz | |
|---|---:|---|---:|---|
| | £ | | £ | |
| Capital accounts at 1 July 20-1 | 40,000 | | 30,000 | |
| Current accounts at 1 July 20-1 | 1,200 | Cr | 2,500 | Dr |
| Drawings for the year | 26,000 | | 21,500 | |
| Salary | – | | 12,000 | |
| Interest on drawings | 1,280 | | 920 | |

**You are to:**

(a)    Prepare the partnership appropriation account for the year ended 30 June 20-2.

(b)    Show the partners' capital and current accounts for the year ended 30 June 20-2.

**4.10***    John James and Steven Hill are in partnership and own a wine shop called 'Grapes'. The following trial balance has been taken from their accounts for the year ended 31 December 20-4, after the calculation of gross profit:

|  | Dr £ | Cr £ |
|---|---|---|
| Capital accounts: | | |
| James | | 38,000 |
| Hill | | 32,000 |
| Current accounts: | | |
| James | 3,000 | |
| Hill | | 1,000 |
| Drawings: | | |
| James | 10,000 | |
| Hill | 22,000 | |
| Gross profit | | 89,000 |
| Rent and rates | 7,500 | |
| Advertising | 12,000 | |
| Heat and light | 3,500 | |
| Wages and salaries | 18,000 | |
| Sundry expenses | 4,000 | |
| Shop fittings at cost | 20,000 | |
| *Closing inventory | 35,000 | |
| Bank | 29,000 | |
| Trade receivables | 6,000 | |
| Trade payables | | 10,000 |
| | 170,000 | 170,000 |

*    Only the closing inventory is included in the trial balance because gross profit for the year has already been calculated.

Notes at 31 December 20-4:
- depreciation is to be charged on the shop fittings at 10 per cent per year
- Steven Hill is to receive a partnership salary of £15,000 per year
- interest is to be allowed on partners' capital accounts at 10 per cent per year
- remaining profits and losses are to be shared equally
- there is no interest charged on partners' drawings

**You are to:**

**(a)** Show the partners' capital and current accounts for the year ended 31 December 20-4.

**(b)** Prepare the partnership financial statements for the year ended 31 December 20-4.

**(c)** On receiving the accounts, John James asks a question about the partners' current accounts. He wants to know why the balances brought down at the start of the year for the two partners are on opposite sides.

Write a note to John James explaining:

- what the balance on a partner's current account represents
- what a debit balance on a partner's current account means
- what a credit balance on a partner's current account means

**4.11\*** Clark and Pearce are in partnership selling business computer systems. The following trial balance has been taken from their accounts for the year ended 30 June 20-4, after the calculation of gross profit:

|  | | Dr £ | Cr £ |
|---|---|---:|---:|
| Gross profit | | | 105,000 |
| Salaries | | 30,400 | |
| Electricity | | 2,420 | |
| Telephone | | 3,110 | |
| Rent and rates | | 10,000 | |
| Discount allowed | | 140 | |
| Office expenses | | 10,610 | |
| *Closing inventory | | 41,570 | |
| Trade receivables and trade payables | | 20,000 | 12,190 |
| Irrecoverable debts written off | | 1,200 | |
| Provision for doubtful debts | | | 780 |
| Office equipment at cost | | 52,000 | |
| Depreciation on office equipment | | | 20,800 |
| Clark: | Capital account | | 60,000 |
| | Current account | | 430 |
| | Drawings | 20,600 | |
| Pearce: | Capital account | | 30,000 |
| | Current account | | 300 |
| | Drawings | 15,700 | |
| Bank | | 21,750 | |
| | | 229,500 | 229,500 |

\* Only the closing inventory is included in the trial balance because gross profit has been calculated already.

Notes at 30 June 20-4:

- depreciate the office equipment at 20 per cent per year, using the straight-line method
- Pearce is to receive a partnership salary of £12,000
- remaining profits and losses are shared as follows: Clark two-thirds, Pearce one-third
- there is no interest allowed on partners' capital accounts or charged on partners' drawings

**You are to:**

**(a)** Show the partners' capital and current accounts for the year.

**(b)** Prepare the partnership financial statements for the year ended 30 June 20-4.

**4.12** Sara and Simon Penny are in partnership running a catering service called 'Class Caterers'. The following trial balance has been taken from their accounts for the year ended 31 March 20-5:

|  |  | Dr | Cr |
|---|---|---|---|
|  |  | £ | £ |
| Capital accounts: | Sara |  | 10,000 |
|  | Simon |  | 6,000 |
| Current accounts: | Sara |  | 560 |
|  | Simon |  | 1,050 |
| Drawings: | Sara | 12,700 |  |
|  | Simon | 7,400 |  |
| Purchases |  | 11,300 |  |
| Revenue (Sales) |  |  | 44,080 |
| Opening inventory |  | 2,850 |  |
| Wages |  | 8,020 |  |
| Rent and rates |  | 4,090 |  |
| Sundry expenses |  | 1,390 |  |
| Equipment |  | 8,000 |  |
| Trade receivables |  | 4,500 |  |
| Trade payables |  |  | 7,200 |
| Bank |  | 8,640 |  |
|  |  | 68,890 | 68,890 |

Notes at 30 June 20-5:
* inventory was valued at £3,460
* sundry expenses owing, £110
* depreciation is to be charged on the equipment at 10 per cent per year
* Sara is to receive a partnership salary of £8,000
* interest is to be allowed on partners' capital accounts at 10 per cent per year
* remaining profits and losses are to be shared equally
* there is no interest charged on partners' drawings

**You are to:**

**(a)** Show the partners' capital and current accounts for the year.

**(b)** Prepare the partnership financial statements for the year ended 31 March 20-5.

**4.13** Anne Adams and Jenny Beeson are partners in an electrical supplies shop called 'A & B Electrics'. They do not have a partnership agreement. The following trial balance has been taken from their accounts for the year ended 30 June 20-5:

|  |  | Dr | Cr |
|---|---|---:|---:|
|  |  | £ | £ |
| Capital accounts: | A Adams |  | 30,000 |
|  | J Beeson |  | 20,000 |
| Current accounts: | A Adams |  | 780 |
|  | J Beeson |  | 920 |
| Drawings: | A Adams | 14,000 |  |
|  | J Beeson | 12,000 |  |
| Opening inventory |  | 26,550 |  |
| Purchases and Revenue (Sales) |  | 175,290 | 250,140 |
| Returns |  | 1,360 | 850 |
| Rent and rates |  | 8,420 |  |
| Wages |  | 28,700 |  |
| Vehicle expenses |  | 2,470 |  |
| General expenses |  | 6,210 |  |
| Vehicle at cost |  | 12,000 |  |
| Fixtures and fittings at cost |  | 4,000 |  |
| Depreciation:  vehicle |  |  | 3,000 |
| fixtures and fittings |  |  | 800 |
| Trade receivables and trade payables |  | 6,850 | 14,770 |
| Bank |  | 22,009 |  |
| Cash |  | 1,376 |  |
| Irrecoverable debts written off |  | 175 |  |
| Provision for doubtful debts |  |  | 150 |
|  |  | 321,410 | 321,410 |

Notes at 30 June 20-5:

- inventory is valued at £27,750

- rates paid in advance £250

- wages owing £320

- provision for doubtful debts to be equal to 2 per cent trade receivables

- depreciation on fixtures and fittings to be provided at 10 per cent per year, using the straight-line method

- depreciation on vehicles to be provided at 25 per cent per year, using the reducing balance method

**You are to:**

**(a)**   Show the partners' capital and current accounts for the year.

**(b)**   Prepare the partnership financial statements for the year ended 30 June 20-5.

# 5 CHANGES IN PARTNERSHIPS

In this chapter we continue our study of partnerships by looking at the principles involved and the accounting entries for:

- admission of a new partner
- retirement of a partner
- revaluation of assets
- partnership changes when there are split years

Before we look at each of these, we need to consider the goodwill of the partnership business.

## GOODWILL

The statement of financial position of a partnership, like that of many businesses, rarely indicates the true 'going concern' value of the business: usually the recorded figures underestimate the worth of a business. There are two main reasons for this:

- **Prudence** – where there is any doubt about the value of assets, they are usually stated at a conservative (lower) figure, but caution should be exercised.
- **Goodwill** – a going concern business will often have a value of goodwill, because of various factors, such as the trade that has been built up, the reputation of the business, the location of the business, the skill of the workforce, and the success at developing new products.

### definition of goodwill

Goodwill is an intangible non-current asset without physical form. It is defined formally in accounting terms as:

*the difference between the value of a business as a whole, and the net value of its separate assets and liabilities.*

For example, an existing business is bought for £500,000, with the separate assets and liabilities being worth £450,000 net; goodwill is, therefore, £50,000.

Thus goodwill has a value as an intangible non-current asset to the owner or owners of a going concern business, whether or not it is recorded on the statement of financial position. As you will see in the sections which follow, a valuation has to be placed on goodwill when changes take place in a partnership.

## valuation of goodwill

The valuation of goodwill is always subject to negotiation between the people concerned if, for instance, a partnership business is to be sold. It is, most commonly, based on the profits of the business – eg the average profit per year over the last, say, three years and multiplied by an agreed figure, perhaps six times.

We will now see how goodwill is created when changes are made to partnerships, such as the admission of a new partner or retirement of an existing partner. For these changes, a value for goodwill is agreed and this amount is temporarily debited to goodwill account, and credited to the partners' capital accounts in their profit-sharing ratio. After the change in the partnership, it is usual practice for the goodwill to be written off – the partners' capital accounts are debited and goodwill account is credited. Thus a 'nil' balance remains on goodwill account and, therefore, it is not recorded on the partnership statement of financial position. This follows the prudence concept, and is the method commonly followed when changes are made to partnerships.

# ADMISSION OF A NEW PARTNER

A new partner – who can only be admitted with the consent of all existing partners – is normally charged a premium for goodwill. This is because the new partner will start to share in the profits of the business immediately and will benefit from the goodwill established by the existing partners. If the business was to be sold shortly after the admission of a new partner, a price will again be agreed for goodwill and this will be shared amongst all the partners (including the new partner).

To make allowance for this benefit it is necessary to make bookkeeping adjustments in the partners' capital accounts. The most common way of doing this is to use a goodwill account which is opened by the old partners with the agreed valuation of goodwill and, immediately after the admission of the new partner, is closed by transfer to the partners' capital accounts, including that of the new partner.

The procedures on admission of a new partner are:
- **agree a valuation for goodwill**
- **old partners: goodwill created**
  - debit goodwill account with the amount of goodwill
  - credit partners' capital accounts (in their old profit-sharing ratio) with the amount of goodwill

- **old partners + new partner: goodwill written off**
    - debit partners' capital accounts (in their new profit-sharing ratio) with the amount of goodwill
    - credit goodwill account with the amount of goodwill

The effect of this is to charge the new partner with a premium for goodwill.

## WORKED EXAMPLE: ADMISSION OF A NEW PARTNER

### situation

Al and Ben are in partnership sharing profits and losses equally. Their statement of financial position as at 31 December 20-4 is as follows:

| AL AND BEN | |
|---|---|
| **STATEMENT OF FINANCIAL POSITION AS AT 31 DECEMBER 20-4** | |
| | £ |
| Net assets | 80,000 |
| Capital accounts: | |
| Al | 45,000 |
| Ben | 35,000 |
| | 80,000 |

On 1 January 20-5 the partners agree to admit Col into the partnership, with a new profit-sharing ratio of Al (2), Ben (2) and Col (1). Goodwill has been agreed at a valuation of £25,000. Col will bring £20,000 of cash into the business as his capital, part of which represents a premium for goodwill.

### solution

The accounting procedures on the admission of Col into the partnership are as follows:

- goodwill has been valued at £25,000
- old partners: goodwill created
    - debit goodwill account     £25,000
    - credit capital accounts (in their old profit-sharing ratio)
        - Al          £12,500
        - Ben        £12,500
- old partners + new partner: goodwill written off
    - debit capital accounts (in their new profit-sharing ratio)
        - Al          £10,000
        - Ben        £10,000
        - Col        £5,000
    - credit goodwill account     £25,000

The capital accounts of the partners, after the above transactions have been recorded, appear as:

| Dr | Al £ | Ben £ | Col £ | **Partners' Capital Accounts** | Al £ | Ben £ | Col £ | Cr |
|---|---|---|---|---|---|---|---|---|
| Goodwill written off | 10,000 | 10,000 | 5,000 | Balances b/d | 45,000 | 35,000 | – | |
| Balances c/d | 47,500 | 37,500 | 15,000 | Goodwill created | 12,500 | 12,500 | – | |
| | | | | Bank | – | – | 20,000 | |
| | 57,500 | 47,500 | 20,000 | | 57,500 | 47,500 | 20,000 | |
| | | | | Balances b/d | 47,500 | 37,500 | 15,000 | |

The statement of financial position, following the admission of Col, appears as:

**AL, BEN AND COL**
**STATEMENT OF FINANCIAL POSITION AS AT 1 JANUARY 20-5**

| | | £ |
|---|---|---|
| Net assets (£80,000 + £20,000) | | 100,000 |
| Capital accounts: | | |
| Al | (£45,000 + £12,500 - £10,000) | 47,500 |
| Ben | (£35,000 + £12,500 - £10,000) | 37,500 |
| Col | (£20,000 - £5,000) | 15,000 |
| | | 100,000 |

In this way, the new partner has paid the existing partners a premium of £5,000 for a one-fifth share of the profits of a business with a goodwill value of £25,000.

Although a goodwill account has been used, it has been fully utilised with adjusting entries made in the capital accounts of the partners, as follows:

| Dr | | £ | **Goodwill Account** | | Cr £ |
|---|---|---|---|---|---|
| Capital accounts: | | | Capital accounts: | | |
| Al | goodwill created | 12,500 | Al | goodwill written off | 10,000 |
| Ben | | 12,500 | Ben | | 10,000 |
| | | | Col | | 5,000 |
| | | 25,000 | | | 25,000 |

# RETIREMENT OF A PARTNER

When a partner retires it is necessary to calculate how much is due to the partner in respect of capital and profits. The partnership agreement normally details the procedures to be followed when a partner retires. The most common procedure requires goodwill to be valued and this operates in a similar way to the admission of a new partner, as follows:

- **agree a valuation for goodwill**
- **old partners: goodwill created**
  - debit goodwill account with the amount of goodwill
  - credit partners' capital accounts (in their old profit-sharing ratio) with the amount of goodwill
- **remaining partners: goodwill written off**
  - debit partners' capital accounts (in their new profit-sharing ratio) with the amount of goodwill
  - credit goodwill account with the amount of goodwill

The effect of this is to credit the retiring partner with the amount of the goodwill built up whilst he or she was a partner. This amount, plus the retiring partner's capital and current account balances can then be paid out of the partnership bank account. (If there is insufficient money for this, it is quite usual for a retiring partner to leave some of the capital in the business as a loan, which is repaid over a period of time.)

As well as agreeing an amount for goodwill, the retirement of a partner often includes a revaluation of assets – see page 98. Such changes – either upwards or downwards – in the value of assets are recorded in the accounts by using a revaluation account.

## WORKED EXAMPLE: RETIREMENT OF A PARTNER

### situation

Jane, Kay and Lil are in partnership sharing profit and losses in the ratio of 2:2:1 respectively. Partner Jane decides to retire on 31 December 20-4 when the partnership statement of financial position is as follows:

| JANE, KAY AND LIL STATEMENT OF FINANCIAL POSITION AS AT 31 DECEMBER 20-4 | |
|---|---:|
| | £ |
| Net assets | 100,000 |
| Capital accounts: | |
| Jane | 35,000 |
| Kay | 45,000 |
| Lil | 20,000 |
| | 100,000 |

Goodwill is agreed at a valuation of £30,000. Kay and Lil are to continue in partnership and will share profits and losses in the ratio of 2:1 respectively. Jane agrees to leave £20,000 of the amount due to her as a loan to the new partnership.

## solution

The accounting procedures on the retirement of Jane from the partnership are as follows:

- goodwill has been valued at £30,000
- old partners: goodwill created
  - debit goodwill account    £30,000
  - credit capital accounts (in their old profit-sharing ratio of 2:2:1)

|  |  |
|---|---|
| Jane | £12,000 |
| Kay | £12,000 |
| Lil | £6,000 |

- remaining partners: goodwill written off
  - debit capital accounts (in their new profit-sharing ratio of 2:1)

|  |  |
|---|---|
| Kay | £20,000 |
| Lil | £10,000 |

  - credit goodwill account   £30,000

The capital accounts of the partners, after the above transactions have been recorded, appear as:

| Dr | | | | Partners' Capital Accounts | | | Cr |
|---|---|---|---|---|---|---|---|
| | Jane<br>£ | Kay<br>£ | Lil<br>£ | | Jane<br>£ | Kay<br>£ | Lil<br>£ |
| Goodwill written off | – | 20,000 | 10,000 | Balances b/d | 35,000 | 45,000 | 20,000 |
| Loan account | 20,000 | | | Goodwill created | 12,000 | 12,000 | 6,000 |
| Bank | 27,000 | | | | | | |
| Balances c/d | – | 37,000 | 16,000 | | | | |
| | 47,000 | 57,000 | 26,000 | | 47,000 | 57,000 | 26,000 |
| | | | | Balances b/d | – | 37,000 | 16,000 |

Note: After recording goodwill, the balance of Jane's capital account is £47,000 (ie £35,000 + £12,000, being her share of the goodwill). Of this, £20,000 will be retained in the business as a loan, and £27,000 will be paid to her from the partnership bank account.

The statement of financial position, after the retirement of Jane, appears as follows (see next page):

**KAY AND LIL**
**STATEMENT OF FINANCIAL POSITION AS AT 1 JANUARY 20-5**

| | | £ |
|---|---|---|
| Net assets (£100,000 – £27,000 paid to Jane) | | 73,000 |
| Less Loan account of Jane | | 20,000 |
| | | 53,000 |
| | | |
| Capital accounts: | | |
| Kay | (£45,000 + £12,000 – £20,000) | 37,000 |
| Lil | (£20,000 + £6,000 – £10,000) | 16,000 |
| | | 53,000 |

The effect of this is that the remaining partners have bought out Jane's £12,000 share of the goodwill of the business, ie it has cost Kay £8,000, and Lil £4,000. If the business was to be sold later, Kay and Lil would share the goodwill obtained from the sale in their new profit-sharing ratio.

## REVALUATION OF ASSETS

So far in this chapter we have looked at the adjustments made for goodwill when changes are made to partnerships. Goodwill, however, reflects only one aspect of a partner's interest in the business. For example, some of the assets may have appreciated in value, but adjustments may not have been made in the accounts; other assets may have fallen in value, while provisions for depreciation and/or doubtful debts may have been too much or too little. With a change in the partnership, a revaluation account may be needed to correct any discrepancies in values. The accounting procedure is:

*   **increase in the value of an asset**
    *   debit asset account with the amount of the increase
    *   credit revaluation account with the amount of the increase
*   **reduction in the value of an asset**
    *   debit revaluation account with the amount of the reduction
    *   credit asset account with the amount of the reduction
*   **increase in provision for depreciation/doubtful debts**
    *   debit revaluation account with the amount of the increase
    *   credit provision account with the amount of the increase

- **reduction in provision for depreciation/doubtful debts**
  - debit provision account with the amount of the reduction
  - credit revaluation account the amount of the reduction

After these adjustments have been recorded in the books of account, the balance of the revaluation account is divided among the partners in their profit-sharing ratios.

## WORKED EXAMPLE: REVALUATION OF ASSETS

### situation

Matt, Nia and Olly are in partnership sharing profits and losses equally. On 31 December 20-1 their statement of financial position is as follows:

| | | |
|---|---:|---:|
| **MATT, NIA AND OLLY** | | |
| **STATEMENT OF FINANCIAL POSITION AS AT 31 DECEMBER 20-1** | | |
| | £ | £ |
| **Non-current Assets** | | |
| Property (carrying amount) | | 100,000 |
| Machinery (carrying amount) | | 40,000 |
| | | 140,000 |
| **Current Assets** | | |
| Inventory | 30,000 | |
| Trade receivables | 20,000 | |
| Bank | 5,000 | |
| | 55,000 | |
| **Less Current Liabilities** | | |
| Trade payables | 25,000 | |
| **Net Current Assets** | | 30,000 |
| **NET ASSETS** | | 170,000 |
| | | |
| **FINANCED BY** | | |
| **Capital accounts** | | |
| Matt | | 60,000 |
| Nia | | 60,000 |
| Olly | | 50,000 |
| | | 170,000 |

Olly decides to retire at 31 December 20-1; Matt and Nia are to continue the partnership and will share profits and losses equally. The following valuations are agreed:

| | |
|---|---|
| Goodwill | £30,000 |
| Property | £150,000 |
| Machinery | £30,000 |
| Inventory | £21,000 |

A provision for doubtful debts equal to five per cent of trade receivables is to be made.

Olly agrees that the monies owing on retirement are to be retained in the business as a long-term loan.

Show revaluation account, goodwill account and the adjusted statement of financial position at 1 January 20-2.

### solution

| Dr | | Revaluation Account | | Cr |
|---|---|---|---|---|
| | £ | | | £ |
| Machinery | 10,000 | Property | | 50,000 |
| Inventory | 9,000 | | | |
| Provision for doubtful debts | 1,000 | | | |
| Capital accounts: | | | | |
| Matt (one-third) | 10,000 | | | |
| Nia (one-third) | 10,000 | | | |
| Olly (one-third) | 10,000 | | | |
| | 50,000 | | | 50,000 |

| Dr | | | Goodwill Account | | | Cr |
|---|---|---|---|---|---|---|
| | | £ | | | | £ |
| Capital accounts: | | | Capital accounts: | | | |
| Matt (one-third) | goodwill | 10,000 | Matt (one-half) | goodwill | | 15,000 |
| Nia (one-third) | created | 10,000 | Nia (one-half) | written off | | 15,000 |
| Olly (one-third) | | 10,000 | | | | |
| | | 30,000 | | | | 30,000 |

Note: goodwill created is credited to the partners' capital accounts, and goodwill written off is debited – in this way goodwill will not be shown on the statement of financial position.

**MATT AND NIA**
**STATEMENT OF FINANCIAL POSITION AS AT 1 JANUARY 20-2**

| | £ | £ |
|---|---|---|
| **Non-current Assets** | | |
| Property (revaluation) | | 150,000 |
| Machinery (revaluation) | | 30,000 |
| | | 180,000 |
| **Current Assets** | | |
| Inventory | 21,000 | |
| Trade receivables | 20,000 | |
| Less provision for doubtful debts | 1,000 | |
| | 19,000 | |
| Bank | 5,000 | |
| | 45,000 | |
| **Less Current Liabilities** | | |
| Trade payables | 25,000 | |
| **Net Current Assets** | | 20,000 |
| | | 200,000 |
| | | |
| **Less Non-current Liabilities** | | |
| Loan account of Olly (£50,000 + £10,000 + £10,000) | | 70,000 |
| **NET ASSETS** | | 130,000 |
| | | |
| **FINANCED BY** | | |
| **Capital accounts** | | |
| Matt (£60,000 + £10,000 + £10,000 – £15,000) | | 65,000 |
| Nia (£60,000 + £10,000 + £10,000 – £15,000) | | 65,000 |
| | | 130,000 |

# PARTNERSHIP CHANGES: SPLIT YEARS

The changes in partnerships that we have looked at so far in this chapter may occur during the course of an accounting year, rather than at the end of it.

For example, part-way through the year:

- the partners might decide to admit a new partner
- a partner might retire

To avoid having to prepare financial statements at the date of the change, it is usual to continue the accounts until the normal year end. Then, when profit for the year has been calculated, it is necessary to apportion the profit between the two parts of the financial year, ie to split the year into the period before the change, and the period after the change. This is often done by assuming that the profit for the year has been earned at an equal rate throughout the year.

The apportionment is done by dividing the partnership appropriation account between the two time periods.

## WORKED EXAMPLE: PARTNERSHIP SPLIT YEARS

### situation

Raj and Sam are in partnership; their partnership agreement states:

* interest is allowed on partners' capital accounts at the rate of ten per cent per annum
* Sam receives a partnership salary of £18,000 per annum
* the balance of partnership profits and losses are shared between Raj and Sam in the ratio 2:1 respectively

At the beginning of the financial year, on 1 January 20-4, the balances of the partners' capital accounts were:

Raj     £70,000

Sam     £50,000

During the year ended 31 December 20-4, the profit of the partnership was £50,500 before appropriations. The profit had accrued evenly throughout the year.

On 1 October 20-4, Raj and Sam admitted Tom as a partner. Tom introduced £40,000 of cash into the business as his capital.

The partnership agreement was amended on 1 October 20-4 as follows:

* interest is allowed on partners' capital accounts at the rate of ten per cent per annum
* Sam and Tom are each to receive a partnership salary of £12,000 per annum
* the balance of partnership profits and losses is to be shared between Raj, Sam and Tom in the ratio of 2:2:1 respectively

*Note:* no accounting entries for goodwill are to be recorded.

### solution

The partnership appropriation account for the year is shown on the next page.

**RAJ, SAM AND TOM**
**PARTNERSHIP APPROPRIATION ACCOUNT**
**FOR THE YEAR ENDED 31 DECEMBER 20-4**

|  | | 9 months to 30 September £ | 3 months to 31 December £ | Total for year £ |
|---|---|---|---|---|
| **Profit for the year** | | 37,875 | 12,625 | 50,500 |
| **Less appropriation of profit** | | | | |
| Salaries: | | | | |
| Sam | £18,000 pa x 9 months | 13,500 | – | |
| | £12,000 pa x 3 months | | 3,000 | 16,500 |
| Tom | £12,000 pa x 3 months | | 3,000 | 3,000 |
| Interest on partners' capitals: | | | | |
| Raj | £70,000 @ 10% pa x 9 months | 5,250 | – | |
| | £70,000 @ 10% pa x 3 months | – | 1,750 | 7,000 |
| Sam | £50,000 @ 10% pa x 9 months | 3,750 | – | |
| | £50,000 @ 10% pa x 3 months | – | 1,250 | 5,000 |
| Tom | £40,000 @ 10% pa x 3 months | – | 1,000 | 1,000 |
| | | *15,375 | **2,625 | 18,000 |

| | 9 months to 30 September | 3 months to 31 December | Total for year |
|---|---|---|---|
| **Share of remaining (residual) profit** | | | |
| Raj | (2/3) 10,250 | (2/5) 1,050 | 11,300 |
| Sam | (1/3) 5,125 | (2/5) 1,050 | 6,175 |
| Tom | – | (1/5) 525 | 525 |
| **Total profit distributed** | 15,375 | 2,625 | 18,000 |

\*   Raj and Sam shared profits 2:1 respectively
\*\* Raj, Sam and Tom shared profits 2:2:1 respectively

# CHAPTER SUMMARY

● Goodwill is an intangible non-current asset.

● With partnerships, goodwill is usually valued for transactions involving changes in the structure of the business to cover:

- admission of a new partner
- retirement of a partner

A goodwill account is created just before the change, and then written off immediately after the change, ie it does not appear on the partnership statement of financial position.

● A revaluation account is used whenever assets are revalued prior to making changes to the partnership.

● When partnership changes take place part-way through the financial year, it is necessary to apportion the profit between the two parts of the financial year, usually by assuming that the profit has been earned at a uniform rate throughout the year.

In the next chapter we turn our attention to the financial statements of limited companies. These must be prepared in accordance with the Companies Act 2006 and with international accounting standards.

# QUESTIONS

visit
www.osbornebooks.co.uk
to take an online test

An asterisk (*) after the question number means that the answer is given at the end of this book.

5.1

(a) Explain the concept of goodwill in partnership accounting.

(b) Using figures of your choice, demonstrate the accounting procedures that must be undertaken in order to admit a new partner to the business where goodwill is valued and then eliminated from the books of account.

**5.2\***

Where changes in partnerships take place, a goodwill account is opened, usually temporarily. After the change has taken place, this goodwill account is usually written off. This follows the accounting concept of:

| A | Prudence | ✓ |
|---|---|---|
| B | Accruals | |
| C | Going concern | |
| D | Consistency | |

**5.3\***

Andrew and Barry are in partnership sharing profits equally. Colin is admitted to the partnership and the profit sharing ratios now become Andrew (2), Barry (2) and Colin (1). Goodwill at the time of Colin joining is valued at £50,000. What will be the goodwill adjustments to Andrew's capital account?

| A | Debit £25,000,  Credit £25,000 | |
|---|---|---|
| B | Debit £20,000,  Credit £25,000 | |
| C | Debit £20,000,  Credit £20,000 | |
| D | Debit £25,000,  Credit £20,000 | |

**5.4**

You have the following information about a partnership:

The partners are Kay and Lee.

- Mel was admitted to the partnership on 1 April 20-1 when she introduced £30,000 to the bank account.

- Profit share, effective until 31 March 20-1:
  - Kay    50%
  - Lee    50%

- Profit share, effective from 1 April 20-1:
  - Kay    40%
  - Lee    40%
  - Mel    20%

- Goodwill was valued at £24,000 on 31 March 20-1.

- Goodwill is to be introduced into the partners' capital accounts on 31 March and then eliminated on 1 April.

**You are to:**

**(a)** Prepare the capital account for Mel, the new partner, showing clearly the balance carried down as at 1 April 20-1. (Dates are not required.)

**Capital Account – Mel**

|  | £ |  | £ |
|---|---|---|---|
|  |  | Balance b/d | 0 |
|  |  |  |  |
|  |  |  |  |
|  |  |  |  |

**(b)** Complete the following sentence by circling the appropriate phrase in each case:

Goodwill can be defined as the difference between **(the value of the business/the balance at bank)**, and the **(accumulated depreciation/net value)** of the separate **(trade receivables and trade payables/assets and liabilities)**.

**5.5\*** Jim and Maisie are in partnership sharing profits and losses in the ratio 3:2 respectively. At 31 December 20-4 the balances of their capital accounts are £60,000 and £40,000 respectively. Current accounts are not used by the partnership.

On 1 January 20-5, Matt is admitted into the partnership, with a new profit-sharing ratio of Jim (3), Maisie (2) and Matt (1). Goodwill has been agreed at a valuation of £48,000. Matt will bring £28,000 of cash into the business as his capital and premium for goodwill. Goodwill is to be eliminated from the accounts.

For the year ended 31 December 20-5, the partnership profits amount to £60,000, and the partners' drawings were:

|  | £ |
|---|---|
| Jim | 12,000 |
| Maisie | 12,000 |
| Matt | 8,000 |

**You are to** show the partners' capital accounts for the period from 31 December 20-4 to 1 January 20-6.

**5.6\***   Andy, Beth and Cath are in partnership sharing profits and losses in the ratio 3:2:1 respectively. Andy has decided to retire and the partners have agreed the following.

- Tangible assets are to be revalued creating a surplus of £24,000
- Goodwill is to be valued at £30,000. It has been agreed that a goodwill account is not to be maintained in the books of account.
- The amount due to Oliver on his retirement is to be paid in full from the business bank account.
- Beth and Cath are to continue in partnership sharing profits and losses equally.
- In the new partnership Beth and Cath's capital account balances are to be equal to £17,500 each; this is to be achieved by paying in or withdrawing cash using the partnership bank account.

The balances on the partners' capital accounts immediately prior to implementing this agreement were: Andy £30,000, Beth £15,000, Cath £10,000.

**You are to** complete the partnership capital accounts after the above transactions have taken place.

Dr                            **Partners' Capital Accounts**                            Cr

|  | Andy | Beth | Cath |  | Andy | Beth | Cath |
|---|---|---|---|---|---|---|---|
|  | £ | £ | £ |  | £ | £ | £ |
|  |  |  |  |  |  |  |  |
|  |  |  |  |  |  |  |  |
|  |  |  |  |  |  |  |  |
|  |  |  |  |  |  |  |  |
|  |  |  |  |  |  |  |  |
|  |  |  |  |  |  |  |  |
|  |  |  |  |  |  |  |  |

**5.7** Reena, Sam and Tamara are in partnership sharing profits in the ratio 4:2:2 respectively. Sam is to retire on 31 August 20-4 and is to be paid the amount due to him by cheque.

The statement of financial position drawn up immediately before Sam's retirement was as follows:

|  | £ |
|---|---|
| Non-current Assets | 50,000 |
| Current Assets | 10,000 |
| Bank | 25,000 |
|  | 85,000 |
| Trade payables | (10,000) |
|  | 75,000 |
| Capital Accounts: |  |
| Reena | 33,000 |
| Sam | 12,000 |
| Tamara | 30,000 |
|  | 75,000 |

Goodwill is to be valued at £16,000 and non-current assets are to be revalued at £74,000. No goodwill is to remain in the accounts after Sam's retirement.

In the new partnership Reena and Tamara are to share profits equally.

Note that current accounts are not used by the partnership.

**You are to:**

(a) Prepare the revaluation account, goodwill account and partners' capital accounts to show the amount to be paid to Sam upon retirement.

(b) Show the statement of financial position immediately after Sam's retirement from the partnership.

**5.8\***  Henry and Jenny are in partnership sharing profits and losses in a 3:2 ratio. Their statement of financial position at 31 December 20-8 is as follows:

| STATEMENT OF FINANCIAL POSITION AS AT 31 DECEMBER 20-8 | | |
|---|---|---|
| **Non-current Assets** | £ | £ |
| Property (carrying amount) | | 150,000 |
| Vehicles (carrying amount) | | 30,000 |
| | | 180,000 |
| **Current Assets** | | |
| Inventory | 20,000 | |
| Trade receivables | 25,000 | |
| Bank | 3,000 | |
| | 48,000 | |
| **Less Current Liabilities** | | |
| Trade payables | 28,000 | |
| **Net Current Assets** | | 20,000 |
| **NET ASSETS** | | 200,000 |
| | | |
| **FINANCED BY** | | |
| **Capital accounts** | | |
| Henry | | 100,000 |
| Jenny | | 90,000 |
| | | 190,000 |
| **Current accounts** | | |
| Henry | 8,500 | |
| Jenny | 1,500 | |
| | | 10,000 |
| | | 200,000 |

On 1 January 20-9 the partners decide to admit Kylie into the partnership. On this date:

- goodwill was valued at £40,000
- the property was valued at £180,000
- the inventory valuation includes £3,000 of inventory which is obsolete and should be written off
- an amount of £2,000, owed by a trade receivable, is considered to be irrecoverable, and the balance was written off

The new partnership agreement states that Henry, Jenny and Kylie are to share profits and losses in a 2:2:1 ratio.

Kylie will pay £50,000 into the business bank account as her capital, part of which represents a premium for goodwill.

**You are to prepare the following**:

- the revaluation account for Henry and Jenny in partnership
- the goodwill account for the partnership
- partners' capital accounts
- the statement of financial position at 1 January 20-9 for Henry, Jenny and Kylie in partnership

**5.9**

You have the following information about a partnership business:

- The financial year ends on 31 March.

- The partners at the beginning of the year were Amy, Ben and Col.

- Amy retired on 30 September 20-2.

- Partners' annual salaries:

  - Amy £24,000

  - Ben £21,000

  - Col nil

- Partners' interest on capital:

  - Amy £1,000 per full year

  - Ben £1,500 per full year

  - Col £500 per full year

- Profit share, effective until 30 September 20-2:

  - Amy 50%

  - Ben 25%

  - Col 25%

- Profit share, effective from 1 October 20-2:

  - Ben 60%

  - Col 40%

Profit for the year ended 31 March 20-3 was £72,000. You can assume that profits accrued evenly during the year.

**You are to** prepare the partnership appropriation account (on the next page) for the year ended 31 March 20-3.

**AMY, BEN AND COL**

**PARTNERSHIP APPROPRIATION ACCOUNT FOR THE YEAR ENDED 31 MARCH 20-3**

| | 1 Apr 20-2 – 30 Sep 20-2 6/12 £ | 1 Oct 20-2 – 31 Mar 20-3 6/12. £ | Total for year £ |
|---|---|---|---|
| Profit for the year | 36,000 | 36,000 | 72,000 |
| Less appropriation of profit | | | |
| Salaries: | | | |
| Amy | | | |
| Ben | | | |
| Col | | | |
| Interest on partners' capitals: | | | |
| Amy | | | |
| Ben | | | |
| Col | | | |
| | | | |

| | | | |
|---|---|---|---|
| **Share of remaining (residual) profit** | | | |
| Amy | | | |
| Ben | | | |
| Col | | | |
| **Total profit distributed** | | | |

# 6 ACCOUNTING FOR LIMITED COMPANIES

In this chapter we look at:

- the main elements of limited company financial statements and their purpose
- the format of published accounts
- interpretation of the auditors' report
- the accounting policies followed by a particular company
- how published accounts are used by a variety of stakeholders

The chapter makes much reference to the published accounts of limited companies. To help with your studies you should obtain a set of published accounts from a public limited company that is of interest to you.

## INTRODUCTION TO LIMITED COMPANY FINANCIAL STATEMENTS

Preparation of the financial statements of limited companies is a natural progression from the financial statements of sole traders and partnerships. The layouts of financial statements are similar; however, some of the terminology is different and is fully explained in the chapter.

The major development to note is that we will be applying international accounting standards which, together with the Companies Act 2006, form the framework within which company financial statements must be prepared. For the chapters which follow we will be referring to international accounting standards which apply to financial accounting. In particular, in this chapter, we use IAS 1, *Presentation of Financial Statements*, to study the form and content of limited company financial statements.

## THE LEGAL AND REGULATORY FRAMEWORK OF ACCOUNTING

The legal and regulatory framework forms the 'rules' of accounting. When preparing financial statements – especially those of limited companies – accountants seek to follow the same set of rules so that broad comparisons can be made between the financial results of different companies. At the same time the framework gives guidance on aspects of accounting such as the definition of assets and liabilities, the distinction between capital and revenue expenditure, depreciation methods for non-current assets, the valuation of inventory, and so on.

The legal and regulatory framework of accounting comprises:

- accounting standards
- company law
- Conceptual Framework for Financial Reporting

This legal and regulatory framework is discussed in detail in Chapter 9.

# PUBLISHED ACCOUNTS

All limited companies have shareholders. Each shareholder is a stakeholder in the company and, although they do not take part in the day-to-day running of the company (unless they are also directors), they are entitled to know the financial results of the company.

Every limited company, whether public or private, is required by law to produce financial statements each year, which are also available for anyone to inspect if they so wish. We need to distinguish between the **statutory accounts** and the **annual report and accounts**. The **statutory accounts** are those which are required to be produced under company law, and a copy of these is filed with the Registrar of Companies. Note that public limited companies must file their accounts within six months of the end of their accounting period (nine months for private limited companies).

The **annual report and accounts** is available to every shareholder and contains the main elements of published accounts:

- income statement (also known as a 'statement of profit or loss')
- statement of financial position
- statement of cash flows (see Chapter 7)
- statement of changes in equity
- notes to the financial statements, including a statement of the company's accounting policies
- directors' report
- auditors' report

The annual report and accounts – often referred to as the corporate report – of large well-known companies are often presented in the form of a glossy booklet, well illustrated with photographs and diagrammatic presentations. Companies often include the annual report and accounts on their websites, where they are readily accessible.

## stakeholders of published accounts

A number of groups – internal and external – are the stakeholders who are interested in reading and interpreting the annual report and accounts of a company, particularly the accounts of large public limited companies. These stakeholders and their interests include:

**Internal stakeholders**, who have a stake in the ownership of the company or are employed by the company. They include:

- shareholders – the profits of the company and dividends paid
- management – to see if the company is expanding and offering management opportunities for the future
- employees – to ensure continued employment and the ability to fund pay increases

**External stakeholders**, who have business dealings with the company or are interested in the company at a national or local level. They include:

- customers – to ensure that goods and services provided by the company will still be available in the future
- suppliers – the ability of the company to pay for goods and services supplied
- lenders – to see security available for loans and the ability to repay loans as they fall due
- the Government and government agencies – to obtain business statistics and to ensure that taxes are paid
- the local community – the contribution of the company to the economy

It is important for the company to be aware of these differing groups. The annual report and accounts is a means of communicating with them and to address their interests on an annual basis. Large companies often produce interim accounts halfway through the accounting year and frequently give much additional information – beyond the legal and accounting framework – about their activities. Company websites are a good source of information for stakeholders.

In Chapter 8 we will see how stakeholders analyse and interpret the accounting information from published accounts.

## RESPONSIBILITIES OF DIRECTORS

The directors of a limited company are elected by the shareholders to manage the company on their behalf. The directors are put in a position of trust by the shareholders to be responsible for the stewardship of the company's accounting information.

Directors have a general duty under the Companies Act 2006 to:

- act within their powers (normally derived from the company's constitution, eg the Articles of Association)
- promote the success of the company
- exercise independent judgement
- exercise reasonable care, skill and diligence
- avoid conflicts of interest
- not accept benefits from third parties
- disclose an interest in any proposed transactions involving the company

The directors are responsible for ensuring that the provisions of the Companies Act 2006 which relate to accounting records and financial statements are followed.

# IAS 1 – PRESENTATION OF FINANCIAL STATEMENTS

The objective of this international accounting standard is to set out how financial statements should be presented to ensure comparability with previous accounting periods and with other companies. The standard states that the purpose of financial statements is to *'provide information about the financial position, financial performance and cash flows of an entity that is useful to a wide range of users in making economic decisions'*.

Note the following from the definition:

- *financial position* – is reported through the statement of financial position
- *financial performance* – is reported through the income statement
- *cash flows* – are reported through the statement of cash flows (see Chapter 7)
- *entity* – an organisation, such as a limited company
- *wide range of users* – financial statements are used by a number of stakeholders
- *economic decisions* – information from financial statements is used to help in making decisions about investment in the company

## components of financial statements

IAS 1 states that a complete set of financial statements comprises:

- income statement
- statement of financial position
- statement of changes in equity
- statement of cash flows
- accounting policies and explanatory notes

## accounting concepts

IAS 1, and other accounting standards, require that companies comply with a number of accounting concepts as follows:

- *going concern* – financial statements are prepared on the basis that the company will continue to operate in the foreseeable future
- *accruals* – financial statements are prepared on the basis that income and expenses occurring in the same accounting period are matched
- *consistency* – presentation and classification of information shown in financial statements from one period to the next should remain the same
- *materiality* – some items of expenditure are so low in value that to record them separately would be inappropriate; this allows aggregation of similar items rather than showing them separately in the financial statements, eg in the classification of assets as non-current or current

There are a number of further accounting concepts which continue to be used when preparing financial statements; these continue to provide the 'bedrock' of accounting:

- *prudence* – financial statements should take a conservative approach where there is any doubt in the reporting of profits or the valuation of assets

- *business entity* – financial statements should not include the personal expenses or income, or record personal assets and liabilities, for any of the people involved in owning or running the company

- *money measurement* – only transactions which can be measured in money terms can be included in financial records or financial statements

- *realisation* – all financial transactions are recorded when legal title passes between buyer and seller, which may not be at the same time as payment is made

- *duality* – every accounting transaction has a dual aspect, one aspect considers the assets of the company, the other considers any claims against the assets

## other considerations

As well as complying with accounting concepts, IAS 1 gives two other considerations that must be taken into account when preparing company financial statements:

- *offsetting* – generally it is not permitted to set-off assets and liabilities, and income and expenses against each other in order to show a net figure, eg cash at bank is not to be netted off against a bank overdraft

- *comparative information* – it is a requirement to show the figures from previous time periods in the financial statements in order to help users of the statements

## structure and content – general principles

IAS 1 sets out the detailed disclosures to be shown on the face of the income statement, statement of financial position, and statement of changes in equity. We shall be covering these later in this chapter.

There are some general principles that IAS 1 requires.

- the financial statements are clearly shown separately from other information which may be provided for stakeholders
- the name of the company is shown
- the period covered by the financial statements is shown, eg for the year ended 31 December 20-9
- the currency of the financial statements is indicated, eg £ Sterling
- the level of rounding for money amounts is stated, eg thousands, millions

Generally, financial statements are to be prepared at least annually. However, if the reporting period changes, the financial statements will be prepared for longer or shorter than a year. In these circumstances the company must disclose the reason for the change and give a warning that figures may not be comparable with those of previous periods.

# INCOME STATEMENT

> **Tutorial note:**
>
> An example of an income statement which complies with IAS 1 is shown on page 119, together with a statement of changes in equity.

The published income statement does not have to detail every single overhead or expense incurred by the company – to do so would be to disclose important management information to competitors. Instead, the main items are summarised; however, IAS 1 requires that certain items must be detailed on the face of the income statement, including:

* revenue
* finance costs
* tax expense

Note that further detail may be needed to give information relevant to an understanding of financial performance.

The income statement concludes by showing the profit or loss for the year after tax.

Expenses must be analysed either by nature (raw materials, employee costs, depreciation, etc) or by function (cost of sales, distribution expenses, sales and marketing expenses, administration expenses, etc) – depending on which provides the more reliable and relevant information. The analysis by nature is often appropriate for manufacturing companies, while the analysis by function is commonly used by trading companies. The example income statement on page 119 shows an analysis by function.

Much of the detail shown in the income statement is summarised. For example:

* distribution expenses include warehouse costs, post and packing, delivery drivers' wages, running costs of delivery vehicles, depreciation of delivery vehicles, etc
* sales and marketing expenses include advertising costs, the salaries of sales people, the running costs of sales people's cars, the cost of sales promotions, etc
* administration expenses include office costs, rent and rates, heating and lighting, depreciation of office equipment, etc.

# DEALING WITH DIVIDENDS IN THE FINANCIAL STATEMENTS

Dividends are distributions to the shareholders, who own the company, as a return on their investment. Many companies pay dividends twice a year – an *interim dividend*, which is usually paid just over halfway through the financial year, and a *final dividend* which is paid early in the next financial year. The interim dividend is based on the profits reported by the company during the first half of the year, while the final dividend is based on the profits reported for the full year. The final dividend is proposed by the directors but has to be approved by shareholders at a meeting of the company. Thus the financial calendar for a company with a financial year end of 31 December 20-8 might take the following form:

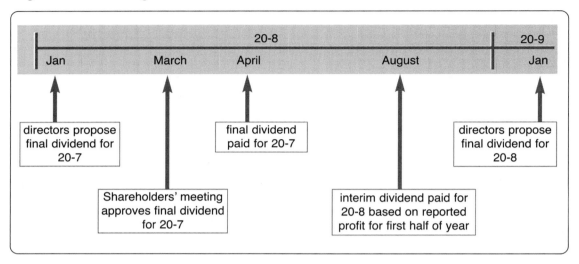

Only the dividends paid during the year can be recorded in the financial statements (a requirement of international accounting standard number 10, *Events after the Reporting Period*. In the above example, the dividends paid in April 20-8 (final dividend for the previous year) and August 20-8 (interim dividend for the current year) are recorded in the financial statements for the year ended 31 December 20-8. The proposed final dividend for the year ended 31 December 20-8 is disclosed as a note, stating that it is subject to approval by the shareholders at a company meeting. All dividends for the year which have been paid are shown in the statement of changes in equity.

## STATEMENT OF CHANGES IN EQUITY

IAS 1 requires that a statement of changes in equity is one of the year end financial statements. As its name implies, it shows the changes that have taken place to the shareholders' stake in the company – not only the *realised* profit or loss from the income statement, but also *unrealised* profits (such as the gain on the upwards revaluation of property) which are taken directly to reserves.

Note that IAS 1 requires information to be given, either on the face of the statement of changes in equity, or in the notes to the financial statements, on:

• details of transactions with shareholders, showing dividends paid to shareholders

• opening and closing balances of retained earnings and changes during the period

• opening and closing balances of each reserve and changes during the period

An example statement of changes in equity of XYZ PLC (with sample figures, including dividends paid) is shown on the next page.

**XYZ PLC**

**INCOME STATEMENT FOR THE YEAR ENDED 31 DECEMBER 20-9**

|  | £000 |
|---|---|
| Revenue | 30,000 |
| Less Cost of sales | 16,000 |
| **Gross profit** | 14,000 |
| Less expenses: | |
| Distribution expenses | 5,000 |
| Administration expenses | 4,000 |
| **Profit/(loss) for the year from operations** | 5,000 |
| Less Finance costs | 1,000 |
| **Profit/(loss) for the year before tax** | 4,000 |
| Less Tax | 1,500 |
| **Profit/(loss) for the year after tax** | 2,500 |

**STATEMENT OF CHANGES IN EQUITY FOR THE YEAR ENDED 31 DECEMBER 20-9**

|  | Share capital | Share premium | Revaluation reserve | Retained earnings | Total |
|---|---|---|---|---|---|
|  | £000 | £000 | £000 | £000 | £000 |
| **Balance at 1 January 20-9** | 3,000 | 200 | – | 2,400 | 5,600 |
| **Profit for the year** | – | – | – | 2,500 | 2,500 |
| Revaluation surplus | – | – | 500 | – | 500 |
| Dividends paid | – | – | – | (600) | (600) |
| Issue of share capital | 1,000 | 200 | – | – | 1,200 |
| **Balance at 31 December 20-9** | 4,000 | 400 | 500 | 4,300 | 9,200 |

**Notes:**

- All material items of income and expense are to be disclosed separately, either on the face of the income statement or in the notes.
- In this example expenses are analysed by function – cost of sales, distribution costs, administration expenses, etc.
- A revaluation surplus – an example of which is seen here in the statement of changes in equity – is explained on page 121.

## STATEMENT OF FINANCIAL POSITION

> An example of a statement of financial position which complies with IAS 1 is shown on page 122.
>
> IAS 1 does not set out a required format for statements of financial position: assets can be presented first, then equity and liabilities; or, in a version common in the UK, non-current assets can be followed by net current assets (current assets minus current liabilities), then non-current liabilities, all balanced against equity. This latter layout is shown in the example statement of financial position (with specimen figures).

IAS 1 specifies the items to be shown on the face of the statement of financial position as a minimum. The Standard does not, however, state the order in which the items are to be presented.

The items to be shown on the face of the statement of financial position include:

* property, plant and equipment
* investment property
* intangible assets
* inventory
* trade and other receivables
* cash and cash equivalents
* trade and other payables
* tax liabilities
* issued capital and reserves

In statements of financial position, IAS 1 requires most companies to separate out current and non-current assets and liabilities:

*Current assets* are

* cash or cash equivalent
* those to be realised, sold or used within the normal operating cycle
* assets held for trading and expected to be realised within twelve months

Examples of current assets are trade receivables, inventory, and cash and cash equivalents.

All other assets are non-current.

*Current liabilities* are:

* those expected to be settled within the normal operating cycle
* liabilities held for trading and expected to be settled within twelve months
* where the company does not have the right to defer payment beyond twelve months

Examples of current liabilities are trade payables, tax liabilities and bank overdraft.

All other liabilities are non-current.

Further detail can be given about statement of financial position items – either on the face of the statement or in the notes. Examples include:

- property, plant and equipment may be shown by different classes – such as property, machinery, motor vehicles, office equipment, etc

- receivables may be split into amounts due from trade customers, prepayments, etc

- inventory can be sub-classified into raw materials, work-in-progress, finished goods, etc

- share capital and reserves can be shown by the various classes of shares and reserves

In particular, IAS 1 requires the following disclosures about share capital (either on the face of the statement of financial position or in the notes):

- the number of shares authorised (if applicable)

- the number of shares issued and fully paid, and issued but not fully paid

- the par (or nominal) value per share, or that the shares have no value

# RESERVES

A limited company rarely distributes all its profits to its shareholders. Instead, it will often keep part of the profits earned each year in the form of reserves. There are two types of reserves:

- capital reserves, which are created as a result of a non-trading profit
- revenue reserves, which include retained earnings from the income statement

## capital reserves

Examples of capital reserves (which cannot be used to fund dividend payments, ie they are non-distributable) include:

- **Revaluation reserve.** This occurs when a non-current asset, most probably property, is revalued (in an upwards direction). The amount of the revaluation surplus is recorded in the statement of changes in equity and shown as a revaluation reserve on the statement of financial position where it increases the value of the shareholders' investment in the company. Note, however, that this is purely a 'book' adjustment – no cash has changed hands.

  In the example on the page 123 a company revalues its property upwards by £250,000 from £500,000 to £750,000.

*continued on page 123*

**XYZ PLC**
**STATEMENT OF FINANCIAL POSITION AS AT 31 DECEMBER 20-9**

|  | £000 | £000 | £000 |
|---|---|---|---|
| **Non-current Assets** | | | |
| Intangible – Goodwill | | | 50 |
| Property, plant and equipment | | | 9,750 |
| | | | 9,800 |
| **Current Assets** | | | |
| Inventory | | 1,190 | |
| Trade and other receivables | | 1,600 | |
| Cash and cash equivalents | | 10 | |
| | | 2,800 | |
| **Less Current Liabilities** | | | |
| Trade and other payables | 900 | | |
| Tax liabilities | 850 | | |
| Bank overdraft | 50 | | |
| | | 1,800 | |
| **Net Current Assets** | | | 1,000 |
| | | | 10,800 |
| **Less Non-current Liabilities** | | | |
| Loan | | | 1,600 |
| **NET ASSETS** | | | 9,200 |
| | | | |
| **EQUITY** | | | |
| Share capital (£1 ordinary shares, fully paid) | | | 4,000 |
| Share premium | | | 400 |
| Revaluation reserve | | | 500 |
| Retained earnings | | | 4,300 |
| **TOTAL EQUITY** | | | 9,200 |

**Note:** The share capital shown in the equity section, above, is the **issued** share capital. Some companies may also have **authorised** share capital – this may be shown (but not added into the equity total) as a note on the face of the statement of financial position, or as a separate note to the accounts.

---

**STATEMENT OF FINANCIAL POSITION (EXTRACTS)**

| | £ |
|---|---|
| **Before revaluation** | |
| Non-current asset: property at cost | 500,000 |
| Share capital: ordinary shares of £1 each | 500,000 |
| **After revaluation** | |
| Non-current asset: property at revaluation | 750,000 |
| Share capital: ordinary shares of £1 each | 500,000 |
| Capital reserve: revaluation reserve | 250,000 |
| | 750,000 |

---

- **Share premium.** An established company may issue additional shares to the public at a higher amount than the nominal value. For example, an established company could seek finance for further expansion by issuing additional ordinary shares. Although the shares may have been issued originally at a price of £1 each, now that the company is established, the shares might be issued at £1.50 each. Of this amount, £1 is recorded in the share capital section, and the extra 50p is the share premium.

## revenue reserves

Revenue reserves are profits generated from trading activities; they have been retained in the company to help build the company for the future. Revenue reserves include the balance of retained earnings from the statement of changes in equity. Also, there may be named revenue reserve accounts, such as *general reserve*, or a revenue reserve for a specific purpose, such as *reserve for the replacement of plant and equipment*. Transfers to or from these named revenue reserve accounts are made in the statement of changes in equity. Revenue reserves are distributable, ie they can be used to fund dividend payments.

## reserves: profits not cash

It should be noted that reserves – both capital and revenue – are not cash funds to be used whenever the company needs money, but are in fact represented by assets shown on the statement of financial position. The reserves record the fact that the assets belong to the shareholders via their ownership of the company.

# SCHEDULE OF NON-CURRENT ASSETS

In the AQA Accounting A-level examination, you may be required to prepare a schedule of non-current assets. The two Worked Examples which follow are similar to the type of questions you may be asked to answer in the examination.

## WORKED EXAMPLE 1: SCHEDULE OF NON-CURRENT ASSETS

### situation

The directors of Durning plc provide the following statement of financial position extracts:

|  | 31 December 20-8 | 31 December 20-9 |
|---|---|---|
| **Non-current Assets** | £000 | £000 |
| *Property, plant and equipment* | 5,091 | 4,579 |

Additional information:

- In the year to 31 December 20-9, property, plant and equipment, which had originally cost £1,352,000, was sold. The depreciation charge on these non-current assets up to 31 December 20-9 was £480,000. The loss on disposal was £122,000.

- In the year to 31 December 20-9, new property, plant and equipment was purchased at a cost of £845,000.

The directors of Durning plc ask you to prepare the detailed note for the financial statements for the year to 31 December 20-9 which shows the movements in property, plant and equipment.

### solution

For the purposes of the note for the statement of financial position you should ignore any profit or loss on sale – this will have been shown in the income statement. The note can be set out either vertically or horizontally – both versions are shown below.

| **Non-current Assets** | £000 |
|---|---|
| *Property, plant and equipment* | |
| Carrying amount at start of year | 5,091 |
| Additions at cost | 845 |
| Less Disposals during year (£1,352 – £480) | 872 |
| Less Depreciation for year | *485 |
| Carrying amount at end of year | 4,579 |
| *note that depreciation for the year is calculated as a 'missing figure' | |

|  | Carrying amt at start | Additions at cost | Disposals during year | Depreciation for year | Carrying amt at end |
|---|---|---|---|---|---|
| **Non-current Assets** | £000 | £000 | £000 | £000 | £000 |
| *Property, plant and equipment* | 5,091 | 845 | (872) | (485) | 4,579 |

## WORKED EXAMPLE 2: SCHEDULE OF NON-CURRENT ASSETS

### situation

The directors of Goodwin plc provide the following statement of financial position extracts at 30 June 20-3:

|  | Cost £ | Depreciation £ | Carrying amount £ |
|---|---|---|---|
| *Property, plant and equipment* | | | |
| Land and buildings | 200,000 | 55,000 | 145,000 |
| Plant and machinery | 75,000 | 35,800 | 39,200 |
| Fixtures and fittings | 50,000 | 12,400 | 37,600 |
|  | 325,000 | 103,200 | 221,800 |

During the year ended 30 June 20-4, the following transactions took place:

*   Land and buildings were revalued at £260,000 on 1 July 20-3
*   Plant and machinery was purchased at a cost of £25,000
*   Fixtures and fittings purchased on 1 July 20-1 for £10,000 were sold during the year for £6,000
*   Fixtures and fittings were purchased at a cost of £15,000

Goodwin plc's depreciation policy is as follows:

*   Land and buildings are depreciated using the straight-line method at 2% per annum
*   Plant and machinery is depreciated using the reducing balance method at 25% per annum
*   Fixtures and fittings are depreciated at 15% per annum on cost
*   All non-current assets are depreciated for a whole year in the year of purchase but are not depreciated during the year of disposal

The directors of Goodwin plc ask you to prepare a schedule of non-current assets at 30 June 20-4 (a total column is not required).

**solution**

**SCHEDULE OF NON-CURRENT ASSETS AT 30 JUNE 20-4**
**PROPERTY, PLANT AND EQUIPMENT**

|  | Land and buildings £ | Plant and machinery £ | Fixtures and fittings £ |
|---|---|---|---|
| *Cost* |  |  |  |
| As at 1 July 20-3 | 200,000 | 75,000 | 50,000 |
| Additions at cost |  | 25,000 | 15,000 |
| Less Disposals |  |  | 10,000 |
| Revaluation | 60,000 |  |  |
| As at 30 June 20-4 | 260,000 | 100,000 | 55,000 |
| *Depreciation* |  |  |  |
| As at 1 July 20-3 | 55,000 | 35,800 | 12,400 |
| Charge for the year | 5,200 | 16,050 | 8,250 |
| Less Eliminated on disposal |  |  | 3,000 |
| Less Eliminated on revaluation | (55,000) |  |  |
| As at 30 June 20-4 | 5,200 | 51,850 | 17,650 |
| Carrying amount at 30 June 20-4 | 254,800 | 48,150 | 37,350 |

**workings**
- Land and buildings depreciation charge:

  260,000 x 2% = 5,200
- Plant and machinery depreciation charge:

  (75,000 – 35,800 = 39,200 + 25,000) x 25% = 16,050
- Fixtures and fittings depreciation charge:

  (50,000 – 10,000 + 15,000) x 15% = 8,250
- Fixtures and fittings eliminated depreciation:

  (10,000 x 15%) x 2 years = 3,000

# DIRECTORS' REPORT

The directors' report, which forms part of the published accounts, contains details of the following:
- the principal activities of the company
- a review of the activities of the company over the past year
- likely developments that will affect the company in the future, including research and development activity
- directors' names and their shareholdings in the company

- proposed dividends
- any significant differences between the book value and market value of property
- political and charitable contributions
- actions taken on employee involvement and consultation
- the company's policies on:
  - employment of disabled people
  - health and safety at work of employees
  - payment of suppliers

## STATEMENT OF CASH FLOWS

International accounting standard number 7, *Statement of Cash Flows*, requires that limited companies must include, as part of their accounts, a statement of cash flows, which we will look at in detail in Chapter 7. Such a statement shows an overall view of money flowing in and out during an accounting period. It links profit with changes in assets and liabilities and the effect on the cash of the company.

## AUDITORS' REPORT

The directors are responsible for preparing the company's published accounts. The accounts must then – for larger companies – be audited by external auditors appointed by the shareholders to check them. The auditors' report, which is printed in the published accounts, is the culmination of their work. The three main sections of the auditors' report are:

- **respective responsibilities of directors and auditors** – the auditors' report states that directors are responsible for preparing the financial statements, while the auditors are responsible for forming an opinion on the accounts
- **basis of audit opinion** – the way in which the audit was conducted, other assessments, and the way in which the audit was planned and performed
- **opinion** – the auditors' view of the company's financial statements

The opinion is 'unqualified' if the auditors are of the opinion that:

- the financial statements have been prepared properly
- they give a true and fair view of the company's affairs in accordance with company law and accounting standards
- the information given in the directors' report is consistent with the financial statements

Note that the auditors' report may be 'qualified' if the auditors feel that certain parts of the financial statements have not been dealt with correctly and that this is important enough to be brought to the attention of the Registrar of Companies and other stakeholders of the financial statements, such as investors or suppliers.

Note that most smaller private companies are exempt from audit requirements.

## ACCOUNTING POLICIES

Accounting policies are the specific accounting methods selected by the directors and followed by the company, such as the method of depreciation. IAS 1 requires companies to include details of the accounting policies used. In selecting and applying accounting policies:

- where an accounting policy is given in an international accounting standard then that policy must apply
- where there is no standard then managers of a company must use their judgement to provide information that is relevant and reliable

Once adopted by a company, accounting policies are to be applied consistently for similar transactions – unless an accounting standard allows differing policies to be applied to categories of items. Changes of accounting policies can only occur:

- if the change is required by an accounting standard; or
- if the change results in the financial statements providing reliable and more relevant information

When there are changes in accounting policies, they are to be applied retrospectively. Any changes require the figure for equity and other figures from the income statement and statement of financial position to be altered for previous financial statements.

Accounting policies are important to the stakeholders of published accounts as they enable them to:

- understand the accounts
- rely on the accounts as being free from bias
- make comparison with different companies
- make reliable decisions based on the information given

## NOTES TO THE FINANCIAL STATEMENTS

IAS 1 requires notes to the financial statements. These notes provide detailed information regarding:

- the basis of preparation used in the financial statements and the specific accounting policies used
- information required by international accounting standards that is not already included in the financial statements
- any additional information that is relevant to the understanding of the financial statements

## PUBLISHED ACCOUNTS AND INTERNAL USE ACCOUNTS

It is the regulatory framework of accounting – which includes the Companies Act 2006 and international accounting standards – that sets out the requirements for published accounts. The regulatory framework details the financial statements that are to be produced, together with their content. The objective is to ensure that 'standard' sets of published accounts are produced – for example, income statements are in the same format, statement of financial positions use the same headings, notes to the accounts give the same level of information. All this enables the published accounts of two or more companies – even if they are from different sorts of business – to be compared. At the same time, published accounts are audited by external auditors who give their opinion on the company's accounts.

By contrast, internal use company accounts are not subject to regulation and do not need to be audited. As their name suggests, they are for the internal use of the company's directors and managers. This means that they can be presented in a form that suits the stakeholders – both in the format of the financial statements and also the level of detail provided. Often internal use accounts provide additional figures for sales and costs which are useful within the company, but would disclose too much information to rivals if it were included in the published accounts.

Whilst published accounts must be produced each year, internal use accounts can be prepared as often as the company wishes.

## benefits of published accounts

- published accounts are produced annually and are available to shareholders and other stakeholders
- public companies file their statutory accounts with the Registrar of Companies within six months of the financial year end – they are then available for inspection by interested stakeholders
- the accounts of most larger companies are audited by external auditors and an audit report is included in the published accounts
- the accounting framework ensures that published accounts follow the same legal and accounting standards, making them comparable from year-to-year for the same company and enabling comparison with other companies

## limitations of published accounts

- published accounts are produced annually – the fortunes of a company could change quite considerably within such a time period
- public companies must file their statutory accounts with the Registrar of Companies within six months of the financial year end – this means that, by the time the information is available, the accounts are out-of-date
- the regulatory framework for accounting details the requirements for published accounts – invariably companies will not disclose additional information
- published accounts report on what has gone on in the past and give little indication of what will happen in the future – eg changing markets or the state of the economy which could impact on the performance of the business in the future
- published accounts cannot record aspects of the company which will affect future performance – eg quality of management, motivation of the workforce, product life cycles, environmental input, ethical considerations

# Issue of Shares, Bonus Issues and Rights Issues

An **issue of shares** usually takes place once a limited company has been set up. The initial share issue provides the company with its equity capital.

Shares are issued either at par value (ie the nominal value) – such as 5p, 25p, 50p, £1 – or at more than par value, which is an issue at a premium. Share premium often comes about when an established and successful company issues additional shares – the new shareholders are paying extra to buy a stake in a profitable business.

## issue of shares at par

The bookkeeping entries to record an issue of ordinary shares at par are:

- Dr bank account (with the amount of the issue)
- Cr ordinary shares account

For example, Avon Ltd has recently been set up and issues 10,000 £1 ordinary shares. The issue is recorded as:

| Dr | **Bank Account** | | Cr |
|---|---|---|---|
| | £ | | £ |
| Ordinary shares | 10,000 | | |

| Dr | **Ordinary Shares Account** | | Cr |
|---|---|---|---|
| | £ | | £ |
| Bank | 10,000 | | |

If this share issue is the first transaction of the company, the statement of financial position after the issue is:

|  | £ |
|---|---|
| Current assets – bank | 10,000 |
| Ordinary shares of £1 each, fully paid | 10,000 |

## issue of shares at a premium

The share premium is the difference between the issue price of the shares and the nominal value. The amount of the premium is credited to share premium account.

For example, Teme Ltd issues 5,000 £1 ordinary shares at £1.50 per share. The issue is recorded as:

| Dr | **Bank Account** | | Cr |
|---|---|---|---|
| | £ | | £ |
| Ordinary shares | 5,000 | | |
| Share premium | 2,500 | | |

| Dr | **Ordinary Shares Account** | | Cr |
|---|---|---|---|
| | £ | | £ |
| | Bank | 5,000 | |

| Dr | **Share Premium Account** | | Cr |
|---|---|---|---|
| | £ | | £ |
| | Bank | | 2,500 |

If this share issue is the first transaction of the company (although issues at a premium are more often made by established and profitable companies), the statement of financial position after the issue is:

|  | £ |
|---|---|
| Current assets – bank | 7,500 |
| Ordinary shares of £1 each, fully paid | 5,000 |
| Share premium | 2,500 |
|  | 7,500 |

Limited companies – and particularly public limited companies – quite often increase their issued share capital by means of either **bonus issues** or **rights issues** of shares. Whilst both of these have the effect of increasing the number of shares in issue, they have quite different effects on the equity of the company's statement of financial position.

Note that, with bonus issues and rights issues, the calculations are made on the basis of the issued share capital. Some examination questions may show an amount for authorised share capital at a higher amount than the amount for issued share capital – only use the issued share capital in your calculations.

## bonus issues

A bonus issue is made when a company issues free shares to existing ordinary shareholders; it does this by using reserves that have built up and capitalising them (ie they are turned into permanent share capital). The bonus issue is distributed on the basis of existing shareholdings – for example, one bonus share for every two shares already held.

With a bonus issue no cash flows in or out of the company. The shareholders are no better off: with more shares in issue the stock market price per share will fall in proportion to the bonus issue, ie the company's net assets are now spread among a greater number of shares.

Bonus issues are made in order to acknowledge the fact that reserves belong to shareholders. Often a build-up of reserves occurs because a company hasn't the cash to pay dividends, so a bonus issue is a way of passing the reserves to ordinary shareholders.

Note that capital or revenue reserves can be used for bonus issues. If there is a choice, then capital reserves are used first – this is because it is one of the few uses of a capital reserve, which cannot be used to fund the payment of dividends.

## rights issues

A rights issue is used by a company seeking to raise further finance through the issue of shares. Instead of going to the considerable expense of offering additional shares to the public, it is cheaper to offer shares to existing shareholders at a favourable price (a little below the current market value). As with a bonus issue the extra shares are offered in proportion to the shareholders' existing holding. The shareholder may take up the rights by subscribing for the shares offered; alternatively the rights can often be sold on the stock market.

### WORKED EXAMPLE: BONUS ISSUES AND RIGHTS ISSUES

#### situation

The following are the summary statements of financial position of Severn plc and Wye plc:

|  | Severn | Wye |
|---|---|---|
|  | £ | £ |
| Non-current assets | 300,000 | 300,000 |
| Current assets (including bank) | 100,000 | 100,000 |
|  | 400,000 | 400,000 |
|  |  |  |
| Ordinary shares of £1 each, fully paid | 200,000 | 200,000 |
| Revenue reserve: retained earnings | 200,000 | 200,000 |
|  | 400,000 | 400,000 |

Severn is planning a one-for-two bonus issue.

Wye is seeking finance for a major expansion programme through a one-for-two rights issue at a price of £1.80 per share.

#### solution

After the issues, the statements of financial position are:

|  | Severn | Wye |
|---|---|---|
|  | £ | £ |
| Non-current assets | 300,000 | 300,000 |
| Current assets (including bank) | 100,000 | 280,000 |
|  | 400,000 | 580,000 |
|  |  |  |
| Ordinary shares of £1 each, fully paid | 300,000 | 300,000 |
| Capital reserve: share premium | – | 80,000 |
| Revenue reserve: retained earnings | 100,000 | 200,000 |
|  | 400,000 | 580,000 |

The changes are:

**Severn** Reserves are reduced by £100,000, whilst share capital is increased by the same amount; the ordinary share capital is now more in balance with non-current assets; no cash has been received.

**Wye** The bank balance has increased by £180,000, being 100,000 shares (assuming that all shareholders took up their rights) at £1.80; share capital has increased by £100,000, whilst 80p per share is the share premium, ie £80,000 in total. The company now has the money to finance its expansion programme. There are also significant reserves which could be used for a bonus issue in the future.

The statements of changes in equity for each company are:

**Severn plc: Statement of changes in equity**

|  | Share capital £ | Share premium £ | Retained earnings £ | Total £ |
|---|---|---|---|---|
| At start | 200,000 | – | 200,000 | 400,000 |
| Issue of bonus shares | 100,000 | – | (100,000) | – |
| After share issue | 300,000 | – | 100,000 | 400,000 |

**Wye plc: Statement of changes in equity**

|  | Share capital £ | Share premium £ | Retained earnings £ | Total £ |
|---|---|---|---|---|
| At start | 200,000 | – | 200,000 | 400,000 |
| Issue of shares at a premium | 100,000 | 80,000 | – | 180,000 |
| After share issue | 300,000 | 80,000 | 200,000 | 580,000 |

**Tutorial note:**

Take care when calculating the number of new shares issued under bonus and rights issues. Check the nominal value of each share – which will be stated in the question. Many ordinary shares have a nominal value of £1, but other values could be 5p, 10p, 25p, 50p or indeed for any amount.

For example, a one-for-four bonus issue where a company currently has £100,000 of ordinary shares at 50p each (ie 200,000 shares) means that 50,000 new shares will be issued at a value of £25,000.

## differences between a bonus issue and a rights issue

| bonus issue | rights issue |
|---|---|
| • additional shares given free to existing ordinary shareholders | • additional shares offered for sale to existing shareholders in proportion to their holdings |
| • the capitalisation of reserves into share capital | • offer price is below the current market value |
| • distributed in proportion to existing shareholdings | • shareholders can either buy the additional shares or can sell the rights on the stock market |
| • no payment made for shares | • company receives payment from shares sold |
| • stock market price of shares falls in proportion to bonus issue | • stock market price of shares may fall slightly (because offer price is below current market price) |

# CHAPTER SUMMARY

● The regulatory framework of accounting includes:
  – accounting standards
  – company law

● The annual report and accounts is available to every shareholder of a limited company. It includes the financial statements and the directors' report and auditors' report.

● Stakeholders in published accounts include:
  – internal: shareholders, management, employees
  – external: customers, suppliers, lenders, the Government and government agencies, the local community

● The directors are responsible for ensuring that the company keeps accounting records and that financial statements are prepared.

● IAS 1, *Presentation of Financial Statements*, sets out how financial statements should be prepared to ensure comparability. It states that a complete set of financial statements comprises:
  • income statement
  • statement of financial position
  • statement of changes in equity

- statement of cash flows
- accounting policies and explanatory notes

- IAS 1 requires compliance with a number of accounting concepts and other considerations:
  - going concern
  - accruals
  - consistency
  - materiality
  - offsetting
  - comparative information

- For larger companies, external auditors report to the shareholders and give their opinion on the company's financial statements as to whether they give a true and fair view of the financial position of the company.

- The directors establish the accounting policies, which are the specific accounting methods to be followed by the company.

- An issue of shares could be at par value (nominal value) or at a premium.

- A bonus issue is the capitalisation of reserves – either capital or revenue – in the form of free shares issued to existing ordinary shareholders in proportion to their holdings; no cash flows into the company.

- A rights issue is the raising of cash by offering shares to existing shareholders, in proportion to their existing holding.

The next chapter focuses on the statement of cash flows – this uses information from the income statement and statement of financial position to show the effect on the cash of the business.

# QUESTIONS

visit
**www.osbornebooks.co.uk**
to take an online test

An asterisk (*) after the question number means that the answer is given at the end of this book.

**6.1** Explain what is contained within the annual report and accounts of a public limited company.

**6.2*** Outline the benefits to a company's shareholders of the statement of changes in equity.

**6.3** Indicate which of the following are internal stakeholders and which are external stakeholders.

| | Internal stakeholders | External stakeholders |
|---|---|---|
| Customers | | |
| Shareholders | | |
| Local community | | |
| Employees | | |

**6.4*** List **four** items that have to be included in a directors' report.

**6.5** The directors of Presingold plc, a recently-formed trading company, seek your guidance on the following issues:

**(a)** What items do we have to show on the face of the income statement?

**(b)** How should we analyse our expenses for the income statement?

**6.6*** **(a)** Define the following terms used in published accounts, giving an example for each:

(1) current assets

(2) current liabilities

**(b)** Published accounts also include a directors' report and an auditors' report.

(1) Identify **three** areas you would expect the directors' report to cover.

(2) What is the difference between the duties of directors and auditors with regard to published accounts?

**6.7** The following is an extract from the statement of financial position of Chiverton plc as at 30 September 20-9:

|  | £000 | £000 |
|---|---|---|
| **EQUITY** | | |
| **Issued Share Capital** | | |
| Ordinary shares of £1 each fully paid | | 500 |
| **Capital Reserves** | | |
| Share premium | 100 | |
| Revaluation reserve | 200 | |
| | | 300 |
| **Revenue Reserve** | | |
| Retained earnings | | 175 |
| **TOTAL EQUITY** | | 975 |

**REQUIRED:**

**(a)** Explain the meaning of the following:

- share premium
- revaluation reserve

**(b)** One of the directors of Chiverton plc asks if £100,000 of the retained earnings can be used to build a new warehouse for the company. How would you reply?

**(c)** What is the difference between 'equity' and 'non-current liabilities'.

**6.8\*** The directors of Perran plc provide the following statement of financial position extracts:

|  | 31 December 20-1 | 31 December 20-2 |
|---|---|---|
|  | £000 | £000 |
| **Non-current assets** | | |
| Property, plant and equipment | 3,832 | 3,584 |

**Additional information**

- In the year to 31 December 20-2, property, plant and equipment, which had originally cost £1,076,000 was sold. The depreciation charge on these non-current assets up to 31 December 20-2 was £695,000. The loss on disposal was £54,000.

- In the year to 31 December 20-2, new property, plant and equipment was purchased at a cost of £722,000.

**REQUIRED:**

Prepare the detailed note for the published accounts for the year to 31 December 20-2 which shows the movements in property, plant and equipment during the year.

**6.9** The directors of Zelah plc provide the following statement of financial position extracts:

|  | 30 June 20-4 | 30 June 20-5 |
|---|---|---|
|  | £000 | £000 |
| Non-current assets |  |  |
| Property, plant and equipment | 8,074 | 7,647 |

**Additional information**

- In the year to 30 June 20-5, property, plant and equipment, which had originally cost £2,168,000 was sold. The depreciation charge on these non-current assets up to 30 June 20-5 was £970,000. The profit on disposal was £85,000.

- In the year to 30 June 20-5, new property, plant and equipment was purchased at a cost of £1,175,000.

**REQUIRED:**

Prepare the detailed note for the published accounts of Zelah plc for the year to 30 June 20-5 which shows the movements in property, plant and equipment during the year.

**6.10\*** Nelson Plc prepares its financial statements to 31 March each year. At 31 March 20-2 its trial balance was as follows:

|  | Debit | Credit |
|---|---|---|
|  | £000 | £000 |
| Administration expenses | 285 | |
| Ordinary shares of £1 each, fully paid | | 500 |
| Trade and other receivables | 570 | |
| Cash and cash equivalents | 35 | |
| Share premium | | 140 |
| Distribution expenses | 420 | |
| Property cost | 400 | |
| Plant and equipment – cost | 550 | |
| Depreciation on plant and machinery at 1 April 20-1 | | 320 |
| Retained earnings at 1 April 20-1 | | 245 |
| Purchases | 960 | |
| Inventory at 1 April 20-1 | 140 | |
| Trade and other payables | | 260 |
| Revenue | | 1,935 |
| Dividends paid | 40 | |
| | 3,400 | 3,400 |

**Further information:**

- Inventory at 31 March 20-2 cost £180,000.

- The tax charge based on the profits for the year is £15,000.

- The property is to be revalued at £500,000.

- Depreciation of plant and equipment is to be provided for the year at 20% on a straight-line basis, and is to be apportioned 40% to administration expenses and 60% to distribution costs.

**REQUIRED:**

As far as the information permits, prepare the company's published income statement and statement of changes in equity for the year ended 31 March 20-2 and the statement of financial position as at that date.

6.11

The following list of balances was extracted from the books of Mithian Plc on 31 December 20-2:

|  | £ |
|---|---:|
| Revenue | 2,640,300 |
| Administration expenses | 220,180 |
| Distribution expenses | 216,320 |
| Interest paid on loan stock | 20,000 |
| Dividends paid | 20,000 |
| Share premium | 40,000 |
| Purchases | 2,089,600 |
| Inventory at 1 January 20-2 | 318,500 |
| Cash and cash equivalents | 20,640 |
| Trade and other receivables | 415,800 |
| Irrecoverable debts | 8,900 |
| Trade and other payables | 428,250 |
| 10% Loan stock | 200,000 |
| Office equipment | 110,060 |
| Depreciation on office equipment | 48,200 |
| Vehicles | 235,000 |
| Depreciation on vehicles | 55,000 |
| Ordinary shares of £1 each, fully paid | 200,000 |
| Retained earnings at 1 January 20-2 | 63,250 |

**Notes:**

- Inventory at 31 December 20-2 cost £340,600.

- Provide for tax of £30,000 which is payable on 1 October 20-3.

- Depreciation has already been provided for in the list of balances above and allocated to distribution expenses and administration expenses accordingly.

**REQUIRED:**

As far as the information permits, prepare the company's published income statement and statement of changes in equity for the year ended 31 December 20-2 and the statement of financial position as at that date.

**6.12\*** The directors of Pryce Ltd have to repay a loan in July 20-4. They propose to make a rights issue on 1 May 20-4 on the basis of one new share for every four shares in issue at a premium of 20p per share.

The issued share capital of Pryce Ltd at 30 April 20-4 was:

|                          | £       |
|--------------------------|---------|
| Ordinary share of 50p each | 500,000 |

How much cash will be received from the rights issue assuming that it is fully subscribed?

| A | £100,000 | |
|---|----------|---|
| B | £125,000 | |
| C | £175,000 | |
| D | £212,500 | |

**6.13** The equity section of the statement of financial position of a company is shown below.

|                                      | £       |
|--------------------------------------|---------|
| Ordinary shares of 50p each, fully paid | 100,000 |
| Retained earnings                    | 50,000  |
| TOTAL EQUITY                         | 150,000 |

The company's directors have decided to make a two-for-five bonus issue of ordinary shares.

How many shares will make up the bonus issue?

| A | 40,000 shares  | |
|---|----------------|---|
| B | 60,000 shares  | |
| C | 80,000 shares  | |
| D | 120,000 shares | |

**6.14\***  The equity section of the statement of financial position of Durning plc at 30 June 20-4 is shown below:

| Equity | £ |
|---|---|
| Share capital (ordinary shares) | 600,000 |
| Share premium | 90,000 |
| Retained earnings | 330,000 |
| TOTAL EQUITY | 1,020,000 |

The ordinary shares have a nominal value of 25p each and are fully paid.

On 1 January 20-5, a rights issue of shares was completed. The shares were issued on the basis of one new share for every four existing shares at the issue price of 40p per share. The issue was fully subscribed.

During the year ended 30 June 20-5, dividends paid totalled £220,000.

The profit for the year ended 30 June 20-5 was £365,000.

Prepare the statement of changes in equity of Durning plc for the year ended 30 June 20-5. Use the table provided.

**DURNING PLC**

**STATEMENT OF CHANGES IN EQUITY FOR THE YEAR ENDED 30 JUNE 20-5**

| | Share capital £ | Share premium £ | Retained earnings £ | Total £ |
|---|---|---|---|---|
| At 1 July 20-4 | 600,000 | 90,000 | 330,000 | 1,020,000 |
| Issue of shares | | | | |
| Profit for the year | | | | |
| Dividends paid | | | | |
| **At 30 June 20-5** | | | | |

**6.15**   The equity section of the statement of financial position of Polbreen Ltd at 1 January 20-2 is shown below:

| Equity | £ |
|---|---|
| Ordinary shares of 50p each, fully paid | 220,000 |
| Retained earnings | 118,000 |
| TOTAL EQUITY | 338,000 |

On 1 November 20-2, a rights issue of shares was completed. The shares were issued on the basis of one new share for every two shares held at a price of 80p per share. The issue was fully subscribed.

During the year ended 31 December 20-2, dividends paid totalled £45,000.

The profit for the year ended 31 December 20-2 was £79,000.

Prepare the statement of changes in equity of Polbreen Ltd for the year ended 31 December 20-2. Use the table provided.

**POLBREEN LTD**

**STATEMENT OF CHANGES IN EQUITY FOR THE YEAR ENDED 31 DECEMBER 20-2**

| | Share capital £ | Share premium £ | Retained earnings £ | Total £ |
|---|---|---|---|---|
| At 1 January 20-2 | 220,000 | – | 118,000 | 338,000 |
| Issue of shares | | | | |
| Profit for the year | | | | |
| Dividends paid | | | | |
| **At 31 December 20-2** | | | | |

6.16

The equity section of the statement of financial position of Perran Ltd at 31 March 20-6 is shown below:

| Equity | £ |
|---|---|
| Ordinary shares of 25p each fully paid | 800,000 |
| Share premium | 225,000 |
| Revaluation reserve | 185,000 |
| Retained earnings | 215,000 |
| TOTAL EQUITY | 1,425,000 |

On 1 April 20-6, the directors made a bonus issue of ordinary shares on the basis of two new shares for every five existing shares held. The directors intend to retain the reserves in their most distributable form.

**REQUIRED:**

**(a)**  Calculate the number of bonus shares issued.

**(b)**  Prepare the equity section of the statement of financial position of Perran Ltd immediately after the bonus issue.

# 7 STATEMENT OF CASH FLOWS

In this chapter we study the statement of cash flows, which links profit from the income statement with changes in assets and liabilities in the statement of financial position, and the effect on the cash of the company over a period of time. We will cover:

● an appreciation of the need for a statement of cash flows

● the format of a statement of cash flows

● the cash flows for the sections of the statement

● how the cash flows relate to the areas of business activity

● the interpretation of a statement of cash flows

This chapter focuses on the preparation of statements of cash flow for limited companies, although they can be used by sole traders and partnership businesses.

## WHAT ARE CASH FLOWS?

Cash flows are receipts and payments of money flowing in and out of a business during an accounting period.

With most transactions it is easy to identify the cash flow and we will soon see how they fit into the statement of cash flows. For example:

- cash purchase of goods, paid for by bank transfer – here there is a cash outflow (note that the term 'cash purchase' means that the buyer is paying for the goods immediately)

- purchase of a new non-current asset, paying by bank transfer – clearly this is another cash outflow (as we will see later, we need to note that this is for the purchase of non-current assets)

- raising a loan by issuing debentures – this is a cash inflow for a loan raised

- paying dividends – a cash outflow, paid to the shareholders

It is important to note that some transactions do not have an effect on cash, for example:

- selling goods on credit – this is a 'non-cash' transaction, with the money being received at a later date (but note that the profit on the sale will be taken immediately)

- allowing for depreciation of non-current assets – this is a non-cash transaction (because the fall in value of non-current assets does not directly affect the cash of a business, eg a car depreciating over time, does not cause a cash outflow)

# FUNCTION OF THE STATEMENT OF CASH FLOWS

The income statement shows profitability, and the statement of financial position shows asset strength. While these two financial statements give us a great deal of information on the progress of a company during an accounting period, profit does not equal cash, and strength in assets does not necessarily mean a large bank balance.

The **statement of cash flows** links profit with changes in assets and liabilities, and the effect on the cash of the company over a period of time.

A *statement of cash flows uses information from the accounting records (particularly the income statement and statement of financial position) to show an overall view of money flowing in and out of a company during an accounting period.*

Such a statement explains to the shareholders why, after a year of good profits for example, there is a reduced balance at the bank or a larger bank overdraft at the year end than there was at the beginning of the year. The statement of cash flows concentrates on the liquidity of the business: it is often a lack of cash (a lack of liquidity) that causes businesses to fail.

Such is the importance of cash flows that companies preparing and presenting accounts in accordance with international accounting standards are required to include a statement of cash flows as an integral part of their financial statements.

The format used in this chapter for the statement of cash flows is that which is set out in IAS 7, *Statement of Cash Flows.*

# FORMAT OF THE STATEMENT OF CASH FLOWS

Statements of cash flow are divided into three sections:

- Operating activities – the main revenue-producing activities of the business, together with the payment of interest and tax
- Investing activities – the purchase and sale of non-current assets, and other investments, together with interest and dividends received
- Financing activities – receipts from the issue of new shares, payments to repay shares, changes in non-current loans, payment of dividends

The cash flows for the year affecting each of these areas of business activity are shown in the statement.

At the bottom of the statement of cash flows is shown the net increase in cash and cash equivalents for the period, together with the cash and cash equivalents, both at the beginning and at the end of the period.

Note the following terms:

- *cash*, which comprises cash on hand and on-demand deposits
- *cash equivalents*, which are short-term, highly liquid investments that can easily be converted into cash (an example of a cash equivalent is money held in a term account, provided that the money can be withdrawn within three months from the date of deposit)

Bank overdrafts which are payable on demand are included as a part of cash and cash equivalents.

The diagram on the next page shows the main cash flows (inflows and outflows of cash and cash equivalents) under each heading, and indicates the content of the statement of cash flows. The first section – operating activities – needs a word of further explanation, particularly as it is the main source of cash flow for most companies.

## operating activities

The cash flow from operating activities is calculated by using figures from the income statement and statement of financial position as follows:

|  |  |
|---|---|
| | profit from operations (before deduction of finance costs) |
| *add* | depreciation expense for the year |
| *add* | loss on sale of non-current assets, or *deduct* profit on sale of non-current assets) – see page 154 |
| *less* | dividends received (which is shown in investing activities) |
| *add* | decrease in inventory or *deduct* increase in inventory |
| *add* | decrease in trade and other receivables, or *deduct* increase in trade and other receivables |
| *add* | increase in trade and other payables, or *deduct* decrease in trade and other payables |
| *equals* | **cash from operating activities** |
| *less* | interest paid |
| *less* | tax paid (eg corporation tax) |
| *equals* | **net cash from operating activities** |

Notes:

- Depreciation is added to profit because depreciation is a non-cash expense, that is, no money is paid out by the company in respect of depreciation expensed to the income statement.
- Cash flows relating to the purchase and sale of non-current assets are shown in the investing activities section.
- Dividends received are deducted here and will then be added in to the investing activities section.

# LAYOUT OF A STATEMENT OF CASH FLOWS

A statement of cash flows uses a common layout which can be amended to suit the particular needs of the company for which it is being prepared. The example layout shown on the next page (with specimen figures included) is commonly used – note that brackets are used to indicate negative amounts.

---

**STATEMENT OF CASH FLOWS**

**Operating activities**

- Profit from operations
- Add depreciation expense for the year
- Add loss or deduct profit on sale of non-current assets (see page 154)
- Less dividends received (shown in investing activities)
- Increase or decrease in inventory, trade and other receivables and trade and other payables
- Less interest paid
- Less tax paid (eg corporation tax)

**Investing activities**

- Inflows: proceeds from sale of non-current assets
- Outflows: purchase cost of non-current assets
- Interest received
- Dividends received

**Financing activities**

- Inflows: receipts from increase in share capital and loans
- Outflows: repayment of share capital and loans
- Dividends paid

---

*(handwritten annotations: 3600 / at cost / disp / NBV - 3600 800 / Prof(loss) 2800 / Prof 2800 / x Reps / taxation 32,860 / Prov yr 105,000)*

**ABC LIMITED**
**STATEMENT OF CASH FLOWS FOR THE YEAR ENDED 31 DECEMBER 20-6**

|  | £ | £ |
|---|---:|---:|
| Profit from operations | 75,000 | |
| Depreciation | 10,000 | |
| Profit/loss on sale of Property, plant and equipment (PPE) | – | |
| Decrease in inventory | 2,000 | |
| Increase in trade receivables | (5,000) | |
| Increase in trade payables | 7,000 | |
| **Cash from operating activities** | 89,000 | |
| Interest paid (note: amount paid during year) | (5,000) | |
| Tax paid (note: amount paid during year) | (6,000) | |
| *Net cash from operating activities* | | 78,000 |
| **Investing activities** | | |
| Purchase of non-current assets | (125,000) | |
| Proceeds from sale of non-current assets | 15,000 | |
| Interest received | 10,000 | |
| Dividends received | – | |
| *Net cash used in investing activities* | | (100,000) |
| **Financing activities** | | |
| Proceeds of share issue | 275,000 | |
| New bank loans | – | |
| Bank loans repaid | (140,000) | |
| Dividends paid (note: amount paid during year) | (22,000) | |
| *Net cash from financing activities* | | 113,000 |
| **Net increase in cash and cash equivalents** | | 91,000 |
| **Cash and cash equivalents at start of year** | | 105,000 |
| **Cash and cash equivalents at end of year** | | 196,000 |

### notes on the statement of cash flows

- The separate amounts shown for each section can, if preferred, be detailed in a note to the statement of cash flows.
- Money amounts shown in brackets indicate a deduction or, where the figure is a sub-total, a negative figure.
- The changes in the working capital items of inventory, trade and other receivables, and trade and other payables have an effect on cash balances. For example, a purchase of inventory decreases cash, while a decrease in trade receivables means the customer has paid, so cash increases.
- IAS 7 allows some flexibility in the way in which companies present their statements of cash flows. In particular, the cash flows from interest and dividends received and paid can be classified as operating or investing or financing activities.
- The statement of cash flows concludes with a figure for the net increase or decrease in cash and cash equivalents for the year. This is calculated from the subtotals of each of the three sections of the statement. Added to this is the amount of cash and cash equivalents at the beginning of the year. Thus the final figure of the statement is that of cash and cash equivalents at the end of the year.

## WORKED EXAMPLE:

## LIMITED COMPANY STATEMENT OF CASH FLOWS

### question

The statements of financial position of Newtown Trading Company Limited for 20-5 and 20-6 are shown on the next page.

Prepare a statement of cash flows for the year ended 31 December 20-6 and comment on the main points highlighted by the statement.

*Additional information*

During the year ended 31 December 20-6:

- Property was revalued.
- Additional plant and equipment was purchased.
- There were no other disposals or purchases of non-current assets.
- Taxation paid totalled £1,000.
- Dividends paid totalled £2,000.
- The income statement for the year ended 31 December 20-6 included:
  - depreciation charges, £2,700
  - finance costs, £400
  - taxation of £1,500

> **Tutorial note:** When preparing a statement of cash flows from financial statements, take a moment or two to establish which is the earlier year and which is the later year. In this worked example they are set out from left to right, ie 20-5 followed by 20-6. In some questions, the later year is shown first, ie 20-6 followed by 20-5.

### NEWTOWN TRADING COMPANY LIMITED
### STATEMENT OF FINANCIAL POSITION AS AT 31 DECEMBER

| | 20-5 | | | 20-6 | | |
|---|---|---|---|---|---|---|
| | £ | £ | £ | £ | £ | £ |
| | Cost | Dep'n | Carrying amount | Cost or reval'n | Dep'n | Carrying amount |
| **Non-current Assets** | | | | | | |
| Property | 75,000 | – | 75,000 | 125,000 | – | 125,000 |
| Plant and equipment | 22,200 | 6,200 | 16,000 | 39,000 | 8,900 | 30,100 |
| | 97,200 | 6,200 | 91,000 | 164,000 | 8,900 | 155,100 |
| | | | | | | |
| **Current Assets** | | | | | | |
| Inventory | | 7,000 | | | 11,000 | |
| Trade receivables | | 5,000 | | | 3,700 | |
| Bank | | 1,000 | | | 500 | |
| | | 13,000 | | | 15,200 | |
| | | | | | | |
| **Less Current Liabilities** | | | | | | |
| Trade payables | 5,500 | | | 6,800 | | |
| Tax liability | 1,000 | | | 1,500 | | |
| | | 6,500 | | | 8,300 | |
| **Net Current Assets** | | | 6,500 | | | 6,900 |
| | | | 97,500 | | | 162,000 |
| **Less Non-current Liabilities** | | | | | | |
| Debentures | | | 5,000 | | | 3,000 |
| **NET ASSETS** | | | 92,500 | | | 159,000 |
| | | | | | | |
| **EQUITY** | | | | | | |
| Share capital | | | 80,000 | | | 90,000 |
| Share premium | | | 1,500 | | | 2,500 |
| Revaluation reserve | | | – | | | 50,000 |
| Retained earnings | | | 11,000 | | | 16,500 |
| **TOTAL EQUITY** | | | 92,500 | | | 159,000 |

Note that this statement of financial position is set out in the form of net assets (non-current assets plus current assets – current and non-current liabilities) = equity. In some AQA examination questions you may be presented with the set out of total assets = total equity and liabilities. Practice questions 7.9 and 7.10 use this layout so that you can familiarise yourself with it before the examination.

**answer**

### NEWTOWN TRADING COMPANY LIMITED
### STATEMENT OF CASH FLOWS FOR THE YEAR ENDED 31 DECEMBER 20-6

|  | £ | £ |
|---|---|---|
| Profit from operations (see working) | 9,400 | |
| Depreciation £8,900 – £6,200 | 2,700 | |
| Increase in inventory | (4,000) | |
| Decrease in trade receivables | 1,300 | |
| Increase in trade payables | 1,300 | |
| **Cash from operating activities** | 10,700 | |
| Interest paid | (400) | |
| Tax paid | (1,000) | |
| *Net cash from operating activities* | | 9,300 |
| **Investing activities** | | |
| Purchase of non-current assets (plant and equipment) | | |
| £39,000 – £22,200 | (16,800) | |
| *Net cash used in investing activities* | | (16,800) |
| **Financing activities** | | |
| Issue of ordinary shares at a premium | | |
| ie £10,000 + £1,000 = | 11,000 | |
| Repayment of debentures | (2,000) | |
| Dividends paid | (2,000) | |
| *Net cash from financing activities* | | 7,000 |
| **Net decrease in cash and cash equivalents** | | (500) |
| **Cash and cash equivalents at start of year** | | 1,000 |
| **Cash and cash equivalents at end of year** | | 500 |

| *Working for profit from operations* | £ | £ |
|---|---|---|
| Increase in retained earnings: | | |
| Retained earnings at 31 December 20-6 | 16,500 | |
| Less Retained earnings at 31 December 20-5 | 11,000 | |
| | | 5,500 |
| Add back: | | |
| Dividends paid | | 2,000 |
| Tax provision | | 1,500 |
| Finance costs | | 400 |
| Profit from operations | | 9,400 |

*Take note of this working as you will need to use it in practice questions and in the examination.*

Note that the revaluation of property does not feature in the statement of cash flows because it is a non-cash transaction – see page 157.

## how useful is the statement of cash flows?

The following points are highlighted by the statement on the previous page:

- cash from operating activities is £10,700 (this is before interest and tax is paid for the year)

- net cash from operating activities is £9,300

- a purchase of plant and equipment of £16,800 (ie £39,000 – £22,200) has been made, financed partly by operating activities, and partly by an issue of shares at a premium

- the bank balance during the year has fallen by £500, ie from £1,000 to £500

In conclusion, the picture shown by the statement of cash flows is that of a business which is generating cash from its operating activities and using the cash to build for the future.

# PROFIT OR LOSS ON SALE OF NON-CURRENT ASSETS

## a difference between book value and sale proceeds

When a company sells non-current assets it is most unlikely that the resultant sale proceeds will equal the carrying amount (cost/revaluation less accumulated depreciation).

## dealing with a profit or loss on sale

The accounting solution is to transfer any small profit or loss on sale – non-cash items – to the income statement. However, such a profit or loss on sale must be handled with care when preparing a statement of cash flows because, in such a statement we have to adjust for non-cash items when calculating the net cash from operating activities; at the same time we must separately identify the amount of the sale proceeds of non-current assets in the investing activities section.

## WORKED EXAMPLE:

## PROFIT OR LOSS ON SALE OF NON-CURRENT ASSETS

### question

H & J Wells Limited is an electrical contractor. For the year ended 30 June 20-6 its income statement is as shown on the next page.

|  | £ | £ |
|---|---|---|
| Gross profit | | 37,500 |
| Less expenses: | | |
| General expenses | 23,000 | |
| Depreciation: plant | 2,000 | |
| equipment | 3,000 | |
| | | 28,000 |
| Profit for the year from operations | | 9,500 |

## profit on sale

During the course of the year the company has sold the following non-current asset; the effects of the sale transaction have not yet been recorded in the income statement:

| | | £ |
|---|---|---|
| Plant: | cost price | 1,000 |
| | *less* depreciation to date | 750 |
| | *equals* carrying amount | 250 |
| | sale proceeds | 350 |

Use a working such as the following to calculate the profit or loss on disposal of a non-current asset (figures from above):

| Working for profit or loss on disposal of a non-current asset | £ |
|---|---|
| Cost of asset sold | 1,000 |
| Less Depreciation on asset sold | 750 |
| | 250 |
| Proceeds of sale | 350 |
| Profit on disposal | 100 |

The income statement incorporates this profit on sale as follows:

|  | £ | £ |
|---|---|---|
| Gross profit | | 37,500 |
| Profit on sale of non-current assets | | 100 |
| | | 37,600 |
| Less expenses: | | |
| General expenses | 23,000 | |
| Depreciation: plant | 2,000 | |
| equipment | 3,000 | |
| | | 28,000 |
| Profit for the year from operations | | 9,600 |

The statement of cash flows, based on the amended income statement, will include the following figures:

---

**STATEMENT OF CASH FLOWS (EXTRACT) OF H & J WELLS LIMITED
FOR THE YEAR ENDED 30 JUNE 20-6**

|  | £ |
|---|---|
| Profit from operations | 9,600 |
| Adjustments for: | |
| Depreciation | 5,000 |
| Profit on sale of non-current assets | (100) |
| (Increase)/decrease in inventory | . . . |
| (Increase)/decrease in trade and other receivables | . . . |
| Increase/(decrease) in trade and other payables | . . . |
| *Net cash from operating activities* | 14,500 |
| | |
| **Investing activities** | |
| Purchase of non-current assets | (. . .) |
| Proceeds from sale of non-current assets | 350 |
| *Net cash from investing activities* | 350 |

Note that the profit on sale of non-current assets is deducted in the operating activities section because it is non-cash income. (Only the sections of the statement of cash flows affected by the sale are shown above.)

---

## loss on sale

If the plant in the Worked Example had been sold for £150, this would have given a 'loss on sale' of £100. This amount would be debited to the income statement, to give an amended profit from operations of £9,400. The effect on the statement of cash flows would be twofold:

1   In the operating activities section, loss on sale of non-current assets of £100 would be added; the net cash from operating activities remains at £14,500 (which proves that both profit and loss on sale of non-current assets are items which do not affect cash)

2   In the investing activities section, proceeds from sale of non-current assets would be £150

## conclusion: profit or a loss on sale of non-current assets

The rule for dealing with a profit or a loss on sale of non-current assets in a statement of cash flows is:

- add the amount of the loss on sale to the profit from operations, or deduct the profit on sale from the profit from operations, when calculating the net cash from operating activities

- show the total sale proceeds, ie the amount of the payment received, as proceeds from sale of non-current assets in the investing activities section

# REVALUATION OF NON-CURRENT ASSETS

From time-to-time some non-current assets are revalued upwards and the amount of the revaluation is recorded in the statement of financial position. The most common asset to be treated in this way is property. The value of the non-current asset is increased and the amount of the revaluation is placed to a revaluation reserve in the equity section of the statement of financial position where it increases the value of the shareholders' investment in the company. As a revaluation is purely a 'book' adjustment, ie no cash has changed hands, it does not feature in a statement of cash flows – see the Worked Example of Newtown Trading Company Limited on pages 151 to 154.

# INTERPRETING THE STATEMENT OF CASH FLOWS

The statement of cash flows is important because it identifies the sources of cash flowing into the company and shows how they have been used. To get an overall view of the company, we need to read the statement in conjunction with the other main financial statements – income statement and statement of financial position – and also in the context of the previous year's statements.

The following points should be borne in mind:

- Like the other financial statements, the statement of cash flows uses the money measurement concept. This means that only items which can be recorded in money terms can be included; also we must be aware of the effect of inflation if comparing one year with the next.

- Look for positive cash flows from the operating activities section. In particular, look at the subtotal 'cash from operating activities' – this shows the cash from the revenue-producing activities of the company.

- Make a comparison between the amount of profit and the amount of cash from operating activities. Identify the reasons for major differences between these figures – look at the changes in inventory, trade and other receivables, and trade and other payables, and put them into context. For example, it would be a warning sign if there were large increases in these items in a company with falling profits, as such a trend would put a strain on the liquidity of the business.

- The investing activities section of the statement shows the amount of investment made during the year (eg the purchase of non-current assets). In general there should be a link between the cost of the investment and an increase in loans and/or share capital – it isn't usual to finance non-current assets from short-term sources, such as a bank overdraft.

- In the financing activities section of the statement, where there has been an increase in loans and/or share capital, look to see how the money has been used. Was it to buy non-current assets or other investments, or to finance inventory and trade receivables, or other purposes?

- Look at the amount of dividends paid – this is an outflow of cash that will directly affect the change in the bank balance. As a quick test, the amount of net cash from operating activities should, in theory, be sufficient to cover dividends paid; if it doesn't, then it is likely that the level of dividends will have to be reduced in future years.

- The statement of cash flows, as a whole, links profit with changes in cash. Both of these are important: without profits the company cannot generate cash (unless it sells non-current assets), and without cash it cannot pay bills as they fall due.

# CHAPTER SUMMARY

- The objective of a statement of cash flows is to show an overall view of money flowing in and out of a company during an accounting period.

- IAS 7 is the international accounting standard that sets out the requirements of statements of cash flows.

- A statement of cash flows is divided into three sections:
  1 operating activities – the main revenue-producing activities of the business, together with the payment of interest and tax
  2 investing activities – the purchase and sale of non-current assets, and other investments, together with interest and dividends received
  3 financing activities – receipts from the issue of new shares, payments to repay shares, changes in non-current loans, payment of dividends

- Limited companies are required to include a statement of cash flows as a part of their financial statements.

In the next chapter we look at the important area of interpreting and understanding what the financial statements tell us about the strengths and weaknesses of a business. To help us in this we shall be calculating ratios, percentages and other performance indicators.

# QUESTIONS

visit
**www.osbornebooks.co.uk**
to take an online test

An asterisk (*) after the question number means that the answer is given at the end of this book.

**7.1\*** Which **one** of the following items, in a statement of cash flows, would be shown in the operating activities section?

| A | Dividends paid | |
|---|---|---|
| B | Loss on sale of non-current assets | |
| C | Repayment of debentures | |
| D | Purchase of non-current assets | |

**7.2** Which **one** of the following items, in a statement of cash flows, would be shown in the investing activities section?

| A | Profit on sale of non-current assets | |
|---|---|---|
| B | Proceeds on sale of non-current assets | |
| C | Loss on sale of non-current assets | |
| D | Depreciation of non-current assets | |

**7.3\*** Raven Limited has a profit from operations of £30,000 for 20-5, and there were the following movements in the year:

| | £ |
|---|---|
| depreciation charge | 10,000 |
| increase in inventory | 5,000 |
| decrease in trade receivables | 4,000 |
| increase in trade payables | 6,000 |

What is the cash from operating activities for the year?

| A | £40,000 | |
|---|---|---|
| B | £45,000 | |
| C | £50,000 | |
| D | £55,000 | |

**7.4** Meadow Limited has a loss from operations of £10,000 for 20-6, and there were the following movements in the year:

|  | £ |
|---|---|
| depreciation charge | 8,000 |
| decrease in inventory | 4,000 |
| increase in trade receivables | 5,000 |
| decrease in trade payables | 3,000 |

What is the cash from operating activities for the year?

| A | (£6,000) | |
|---|---|---|
| B | (£10,000) | |
| C | (£18,000) | |
| D | (£30,000) | |

**7.5\*** Complete the following table to show the effect on cash – inflow, outflow, or no effect – of the transactions.

The first item has been completed as an example.

| Transaction | | Inflow of cash | Outflow of cash | No effect on cash |
|---|---|---|---|---|
| | Cash sales | ✓ | | |
| A | Cash purchases | | | |
| B | Sold goods on credit | | | |
| C | Bought goods on credit | | | |
| D | Bought a non-current asset, paying by cheque | | | |
| E | A trade receivable pays by bank transfer | | | |
| F | Paid expenses in cash | | | |
| G | Paid a trade payable by bank transfer | | | |

**7.6** The following extract is taken from the statement of cash flows of Durning Limited for the year ended 31 December 20-8. It gives the reconciliation of profit before tax to cash from operations.

|  | £ |
|---|---|
| Profit from operations | 71,250 |
| Depreciation | 6,500 |
| Increase in inventory | (7,500) |
| Increase in trade receivables | (6,000) |
| Increase in trade payables | 2,400 |
| Cash from operating activities | 66,650 |

**(a)** Explain the terms:

(1) profit from operations

(2) cash from operating activities

**(b)** Explain why the following adjustments have been made to profit from operations:

(1) depreciation – added

(2) increase in inventory – subtracted

(3) increase in trade receivables – subtracted

(4) increase in trade payables – added

**7.7\*** The bookkeeper of Hall Limited has asked for your assistance in producing a statement of cash flows for the company for the year ended 30 September 20-5.

She has derived the information which is required to be included in the statement of cash flows, but is not sure of the format in which it should be presented. The information is set out below:

|  | £ |
|---|---|
| Profit from operations | 24,000 |
| Depreciation for the year | 318,000 |
| Proceeds from sale of non-current assets | 132,000 |
| Issue of shares for cash | 150,000 |
| Cash received from new non-current loan | 200,000 |
| Purchase of non-current assets for cash | 358,000 |
| Interest paid | 218,000 |
| Tax paid | 75,000 |
| Dividends paid | 280,000 |
| Increase in inventory | 251,000 |
| Increase in trade receivables | 152,000 |
| Increase in trade payables | 165,000 |
| Cash and cash equivalents at 1 October 20-4 | 395,000 |
| Cash and cash equivalents at 30 September 20-5 | 50,000 |

**You are to** prepare a statement of cash flows for Hall Limited for the year ended 30 September 20-5.

**7.8\*** John Smith, managing director of J Smith Limited, has been in business for two years. He is puzzled by the company's financial statements because, although they show a profit for each year, the bank balance has fallen and is now an overdraft. He asks for your assistance to explain what has happened. The statements of financial position of J Smith Limited are as follows:

**STATEMENT OF FINANCIAL POSITION AS AT 31 DECEMBER**

| | 20-1 | | | 20-2 | | |
|---|---|---|---|---|---|---|
| | £ | £ | £ | £ | £ | £ |
| | Cost | Depreciation | Carrying amount | Cost | Depreciation | Carrying amount |
| **Non-current Assets** | | | | | | |
| Property, plant & equip't | 3,000 | 600 | 2,400 | 5,000 | 1,600 | 3,400 |
| **Current Assets** | | | | | | |
| Inventory | | 5,500 | | | 9,000 | |
| Trade receivables | | 1,750 | | | 2,300 | |
| Bank (cash and cash equivalents) | | 850 | | | – | |
| | | 8,100 | | | 11,300 | |
| **Less Current Liabilities** | | | | | | |
| Trade payables | 2,500 | | | 2,750 | | |
| Bank overdraft | – | | | 1,200 | | |
| Tax liability | 1,000 | | | 1,750 | | |
| | | 3,500 | | | 5,700 | |
| **Net Current Assets** | | | 4,600 | | | 5,600 |
| **NET ASSETS** | | | 7,000 | | | 9,000 |
| **EQUITY** | | | | | | |
| Share capital | | | 5,000 | | | 5,000 |
| Retained earnings | | | 2,000 | | | 4,000 |
| **TOTAL EQUITY** | | | 7,000 | | | 9,000 |

**Additional information:**

- Additional property, plant and equipment (PPE) was purchased.
- There were no other revaluations, purchases or disposals of non-current assets.
- Taxation paid totalled £1,000.
- Dividends paid totalled £9,000.

- The income statement for the year ended 31 December 20-2 included:
  - depreciation charges, £1,000
  - finance costs, £250
  - taxation of £1,750

**You are to** prepare a statement of cash flows for the year ended 31 December 20-2.

**7.9**

> **Tutorial note:** This statement of financial position is set out in the form of total assets = total equity and liabilities. This set-out could be used in AQA examination questions.

The statements of financial position of Williams Limited for the last two years are as follows:

### STATEMENT OF FINANCIAL POSITION AS AT 30 SEPTEMBER

| | 20-5 | | | 20-6 | | |
|---|---|---|---|---|---|---|
| | £ | £ | £ | £ | £ | £ |
| | Cost | Depreciation | Carrying amount | Cost | Depreciation | Carrying amount |
| **Non-current Assets** | 60,000 | 12,000 | 48,000 | 70,000 | 23,600 | 46,400 |
| **Current Assets** | | | | | | |
| Inventory | | 9,800 | | | 13,600 | |
| Trade receivables | | 10,800 | | | 15,000 | |
| | | | 20,600 | | | 28,600 |
| **TOTAL ASSETS** | | | 68,600 | | | 75,000 |
| **EQUITY** | | | | | | |
| Share capital | | | 50,000 | | | 50,000 |
| Retained earnings | | | 400 | | | 2,700 |
| **TOTAL EQUITY** | | | 50,400 | | | 52,700 |
| **Non-current Liabilities** | | | | | | |
| Bank loan | | | 10,000 | | | 3,000 |
| **Current Liabilities** | | | | | | |
| Trade payables | | 5,700 | | | 12,800 | |
| Bank overdraft | | 1,000 | | | 4,700 | |
| Tax liability | | 1,500 | | | 1,800 | |
| | | | 8,200 | | | 19,300 |
| **TOTAL EQUITY AND LIABILITIES** | | | 68,600 | | | 75,000 |

**Additional information:**

- Additional non-current assets were purchased.
- There were no other revaluations, purchases or disposals of non-current assets.
- Taxation paid totalled £1,500.
- Dividends paid totalled £8,200.
- The income statement for the year ended 30 September 20-6 included:
  - depreciation charges, £11,600
  - finance costs, £2,200
  - taxation of £1,800

**You are to** prepare a statement of cash flows for the year ended 30 September 20-6.

**7.10\*** The statements of financial position of Sheehan Limited for the last two years are as follows:

### STATEMENT OF FINANCIAL POSITION AS AT 31 OCTOBER

|  | 20-3 | | 20-2 | |
|---|---|---|---|---|
|  | £000 | £000 | £000 | £000 |
| **Non-Current Assets** | | | | |
| At cost | 9,000 | | 8,400 | |
| Depreciation to date | (1,800) | 7,200 | (1,500) | 6,900 |
| **Current Assets** | | | | |
| Inventory | 84 | | 69 | |
| Trade receivables | 255 | | 270 | |
| Cash and cash equivalents | 48 | | 30 | |
|  | | 387 | | 369 |
| **TOTAL ASSETS** | | 7,587 | | 7,269 |
| **EQUITY** | | | | |
| Share capital | | 3,000 | | 2,550 |
| Share premium | | 177 | | – |
| Retained earnings | | 3,411 | | 1,953 |
| **TOTAL EQUITY** | | 6,588 | | 4,503 |
| **Non-current Liabilities** | | | | |
| Loans | | 600 | | 2,400 |
| **Current Liabilities** | | | | |
| Trade payables | 108 | | 81 | |
| Tax liability | 291 | | 285 | |
|  | | 399 | | 366 |
| **TOTAL EQUITY AND LIABILITIES** | | 7,587 | | 7,269 |

**Additional Information:**

- Additional non-current assets were purchased, cost £629,000.

- Non-current assets, which had been depreciated by £18,000, were sold for £8,000.

- There were no other disposals or purchases of non-current assets.

- Taxation paid totalled £744,000.

- Dividends paid totalled £144,000.

- The income statement for the year ended 31 October 20-3 included:
  - depreciation charges, £318,000
  - finance costs, £168,000
  - taxation of £750,000

**You are to** prepare a statement of cash flows for the year ended 31 October 20-3.

# 8 INTERPRETATION OF ACCOUNTING INFORMATION

In this chapter we look at how accounting techniques, measures and ratios are used to analyse and interpret accounting information. We recap on the performance measures of profitability, liquidity, efficiency, and capital structure which were covered in year 1, and then move on to look at the ratios that an investor can use to assess a company's performance. As well as investors, the value of published accounts to other internal and external stakeholders is considered.

The chapter includes a Worked Example of a potential investor reviewing accounting information and the conclusions drawn.

Finally, we must always remember that, while accounting ratios can be used to highlight the strengths and weaknesses from financial statements, they should always be considered as a part of the overall assessment of a company, rather than as a whole.

## AVAILABILITY OF FINANCIAL STATEMENTS

Limited company financial statements are far more readily available to stakeholders than the financial statements of sole traders and partnerships:

- all limited companies must submit financial statements to Companies House where they are available for public inspection
- a copy of the financial statements is available to all shareholders, together with a report on the company's activities during the year
- the income statement and statement of financial position of larger public limited companies are commented on and discussed in the media
- the financial statements of larger public limited companies are freely available to potential investors, lenders and other interested parties

It is recommended that you study the published financial statements of a large public limited company. Most plcs include their accounts on their websites – once on a company's website, search for 'financial statements' or 'investors' or 'investment centre'. Here are the links for Tesco, J Sainsbury and Marks and Spencer:

www.tescoplc.com

www.j-sainsbury.co.uk/investor-centre

http://annualreport.marksandspencer.com

# RECAP ON ACCOUNTING RATIOS

Accounting ratios have been covered fully in Chapter 18 of Accounting for AQA: AS and A-level year 1. The main themes of accounting ratios are:

- profitability – the relationship between profit and sales revenue, assets and capital employed
- liquidity – the financial stability of the business on a short-term basis
- efficiency – the effective and efficient use of assets and liabilities
- capital structure – the financial stability of the business on a long-term basis

The ratios that were studied in year 1 are summarised on pages 168 to 170.

## the difference between cash and profits

The accounting ratios for profitability assess the ability of a business to generate profits. Many stakeholders assessing a business are also interested in cash flows – the ability to generate cash.

There is an important difference between profit and cash – it is possible to have a highly profitable company that is using more cash than it is generating so that its bank balance is falling (or its overdraft is increasing). Liquidity is important as it is often a lack of cash that causes businesses to fail.

To distinguish between cash and profit:

- **cash** is the actual amount of money held in the bank or as cash
- **profit** is a calculated figure which shows the surplus of income over expenditure for a period; it takes note of adjustments for accruals and prepayments and non-cash items such as depreciation and provision for doubtful debts

## effect of transactions on profitability and liquidity

A problem for many businesses is that they may have profitable products and services, but they are always short of cash, ie they have liquidity problems.

To distinguish between profitability and liquidity

- **profitability** is a measure of the surplus of income over expenditure for a period against either revenue or capital employed
- **liquidity** is a measure of the ability of a business to meet the short-term obligations of its current liabilities

It is probably true to say that a profitable business can only survive in the short-term without sufficient money in the bank to pay its way. The payment of amounts to trade payables, for salaries and wages and other expenses will prove difficult and will eventually cause the business to fail.

By contrast, an unprofitable business can survive for a while provided it has sufficient liquidity. However, once it has used its balance of cash and collected money from trade receivables it will be heading towards failure.

Various transactions have an unequal effect on profitability and liquidity as shown by the examples in the following diagram:

| Effect on profitability | | Transaction | Effect on liquidity | |
|:---:|:---:|---|:---:|:---:|
| increase | decrease | | increase | decrease |
| | | • purchase of non-current assets | | ✓ |
| | ✓ | • depreciation of non-current assets | | |
| | | • issue of new shares | ✓ | |
| | | • payment of dividends/drawings | | ✓ |
| | | • raising of a loan | ✓ | |
| | | • repayment of a loan | | ✓ |
| ✓ | | • increase in inventory | | ✓ |
| | ✓ | • decrease in inventory | ✓ | |
| | | • increase in trade receivables | | ✓ |
| | | • decrease in trade receivables | ✓ | |
| | ✓ | • increase in provision for doubtful debts | | |
| ✓ | | • reduction in provision for doubtful debts | | |
| | | • increase in trade payables | ✓ | |
| | | • decrease in trade payables | | ✓ |

## PROFITABILITY RATIOS

$$\text{Gross profit margin} = \frac{\text{Gross profit}}{\text{Revenue}} \times \frac{100}{1}$$

$$\text{Gross profit mark-up} = \frac{\text{Gross profit}}{\text{Cost of sales}} \times \frac{100}{1}$$

$$\text{Expenses in relation to revenue} = \frac{\text{Expenses}}{\text{Revenue}} \times \frac{100}{1}$$

$$\text{Profit in relation to revenue} = \frac{\text{Profit before tax}}{\text{Revenue}} \times \frac{100}{1}$$

Return on capital employed = (sole trader)

$$\frac{\text{Profit before interest}}{\text{Capital employed*}} \times \frac{100}{1}$$

\* capital + non-current liabilities (note: either opening or closing capital could be used)

Return on capital employed = (limited company)

$$\frac{\text{Profit from operations}}{\text{Capital employed*}} \times \frac{100}{1}$$

\* equity + non-current liabilities (note: either opening or closing equity could be used)

## LIQUIDITY RATIOS

Current ratio\* =

$$\frac{\text{Current assets}}{\text{Current liabilities}}$$

\* also known as the working capital ratio

Liquid capital ratio\* =

$$\frac{\text{Current assets} - \text{inventory}}{\text{Current liabilities}}$$

\* also known as the acid test or quick ratio

## EFFICIENCY RATIOS

Rate of inventory turnover = (days)

$$\frac{\text{Average inventory*}}{\text{Cost of sales}} \times 365 \text{ days}$$

Rate of inventory turnover = (times per year)

$$\frac{\text{Cost of sales}}{\text{Average inventory*}}$$

\* usually taken as: (opening inventory + closing inventory) ÷ 2; alternatively, if opening inventory figure is not available, use closing inventory from the statement of financial position in the calculation

Trade receivable days =

$$\frac{\text{Trade receivables}}{\text{Credit sales}} \times 365 \text{ days}$$

**Trade payable days** $=$ $\dfrac{\text{Trade payables}}{\text{Credit purchases}}$ x 365 days

## CAPITAL STRUCTURE RATIO

**Capital gearing** $=$ $\dfrac{\text{Non-current liabilities}}{\text{Issued share capital + Reserves + Non-current liabilities}} \times \dfrac{100}{1}$

# INVESTOR RATIOS

Investor ratios are used by business people and investors who intend to buy either a whole business, or holdings of shares in limited companies. The ratios will help to assess the performance of the company in which they wish to invest.

## dividend yield

$$\dfrac{\text{Dividend per share}}{\text{Market price per share}} \quad x \quad \dfrac{100}{1}$$

Investors in companies which are quoted on the Stock Exchange or similar markets can obtain this information from financial newspapers or the internet. The dividend yield gives the investor the annual percentage return paid on a quoted share. However, dividend yield is an inadequate measure because it ignores the overall profits – or 'earnings' – available for the ordinary shareholders; retained earnings (ie that part of profits not paid as dividends) should help to boost the share price, so giving investors capital growth rather than income.

## earnings per share

$$\dfrac{\text{Earnings (profit after tax)}}{\text{Number of issued ordinary shares}}$$

Earnings per share (or EPS) measures the amount of profit (or loss) – usually expressed in pence – earned by each share, after tax. Comparisons can be made with previous years to provide a basis for assessing the company's performance.

## dividend cover

$$\dfrac{\text{Profit after intetest and tax}}{\text{Ordinary share dividends paid}}$$

This figure shows the margin of safety between the amount of profit a company makes and the amount paid out in dividends. The figure must be greater than 1 if the company is not to use past retained earnings to fund the current dividend. A figure of 5 as dividend cover indicates that profit exceeds dividend by five times – a healthy sign.

## price earnings

$$\frac{\textit{Current market price}}{\textit{Earnings per share}} \quad = \quad \textit{Price earnings}$$

The price earnings ratio (or P/E ratio, as it is often abbreviated) compares the current market price of a share with the earnings (profit after tax) of that share. For example, if a particular share has a market price of £3, and the earnings per share in the current year are 30p, then the P/E ratio is 10. This simply means that a person buying the share for £3 is paying ten times the last reported earnings of that share.

Investors use the price earnings ratio to help them make decisions as to the 'expensiveness' of a share. In general, high P/E ratios (ie a higher number) indicate that the market price has been pushed up in anticipation of an expected improvement in earnings: therefore, the share is now expensive. The reason for a low P/E ratio is usually that investors do not expect much (if any) growth in the company's earnings in the foreseeable future.

## interest cover

$$\frac{\textit{Profit before interest and tax}}{\textit{Interest payable}}$$

The interest cover ratio, which is linked closely to capital gearing, considers the safety margin (or cover) of profit over the finance costs of a business. For example, if the profit before interest and tax of a business was £10,000, and finance costs were £5,000, this would give interest cover of 2, which is a low figure. If the interest was £1,000, this would give interest cover of 10 which is a higher and much more acceptable figure. Thus, the conclusion to draw is that the higher the interest cover, the better (although there is an argument for having some debt and paying interest).

# INVESTOR RATIOS

$$\textbf{Dividend yield} \ = \ \frac{\text{Dividend per share}}{\text{Market price per share}} \ \times \frac{100}{1}$$

$$\textbf{Earnings per share} \ = \ \frac{\text{Earnings (profit after tax)}}{\text{Number of issued ordinary shares}} \ \times \frac{100}{1}$$

Dividend cover = $\dfrac{\text{Profit after interest and tax}}{\text{Ordinary share dividends paid}} \times \dfrac{100}{1}$

Price earnings = $\dfrac{\text{Current market price}}{\text{Earnings per share}}$

Interest cover = $\dfrac{\text{Profit before interest and tax}}{\text{Interest payable}}$

## WORKED EXAMPLE: INVESTOR RATIOS

### situation

Nicola has £20,000 available for medium/long-term investment in the ordinary shares of a company. She is wishing, initially, to maximise her income.

She has identified two companies in the same line of business and has gathered together the following information from their most recent financial statements.

|  | Perran plc | Porth plc |
|---|---|---|
| Current market price (per share) | £2.20 | £0.75 |
| Share price (last 52 weeks) |  |  |
| high | £2.35 | £1.10 |
| low | £2.05 | £0.50 |
| Dividend per share | 8.5p | 5.3p |
| Dividend yield | 3.9% | 14.2% |
| Dividend cover | 2.6 times | 2.1 times |
| Earnings per share | 22p | 11p |
| Price earnings ratio | 10.0 | 6.8 |
| Return on capital employed | 7.2% | 11.1% |
| Capital gearing | 35% | 80% |

An extract from the statement of financial position shows the following:

| Property, plant and equipment | Cost | Depreciation | Carrying amount |
|---|---|---|---|
|  | £m | £m | £m |
| Perran plc | 180 | 60 | 120 |
| Porth plc | 60 | 40 | 20 |

Nicola asks you to help her evaluate both companies from an investor's point of view and to advise her which would be better for her investment.

### solution

> **Tutorial note:** this evaluation is best completed by steps to
> - quantify Nicola's possible investment and her expected income
> - compare ratios for the two companies
> - analysis of the information to help make the investment decision
> - conclusion, being a summary of the findings

### step 1

The number of shares that Nicola could purchase and her expected income:

- Perran plc

  £20,000 investment ÷ £2.20 current market price = 9,091 shares

  At current dividends her income is 9,091 shares x 8.5p per share = £773 (approx) per year
- Porth plc

  £20,000 ÷ £0.75 = 26,667 shares

  Income  26,667 x 5.3p = £1,413 (approx) per year

### step 2

A comparison of the investor ratios for the two companies shows:

- Perran is better than Porth
    - dividend per share
    - dividend cover
    - earnings per share
    - price earnings ratio


- Porth is better than Perran
    - dividend yield

Other data shows that:

- Perran appears to be a larger company than Porth (based on PPE amounts)
- Porth has a higher return on capital employed than Perran
- Perran is lower geared than Porth, whose gearing may be too risky for investors
- Perran's share price appears to be more stable – fluctuating within a narrower range than that of Porth

**step 3**

An analysis will help Nicola with the investment decision.

* Nicola wishes, initially, to maximise her income – Porth will give her a much higher income.

* However, Porth's share price is less stable than that of Perran (note that the difference in the share prices is not an indicator of a better or worse company). This could offer larger capital gains for Nicola if it rises, but with the possibility of losses if it falls.

* Porth's higher return on capital employed could be as a result of the company making more efficient use of its capital employed.

* Porth's higher capital gearing represents a riskier investment – 80% means that non-current liabilities are greater than equity.

* Other factors to consider include:
    – what is Nicola's attitude to investment risk?
    – is the line of business in which both companies operate acceptable to Nicola?
    – is other data, both historical and future, available?

**step 4**

The conclusion is that, if Nicola wishes to maximise her income, she should make her investment in Porth. However, this is a more volatile company – share price, gearing – and her investment will be at greater risk. If she wishes to invest for the longer-term, both for income and capital gain (share price increase), she should consider making her investment in Perran.

# STAKEHOLDERS OF PUBLISHED ACCOUNTS

One of the objects of company financial reporting is to provide information to stakeholders. The information includes the income of the company, its statement of financial position (including changes in financial position), and its statement of cash flows. All this information is used by stakeholders to help make decisions, eg to invest in the company, to lend money to the company, to work for the company.

There is a wide variety of stakeholders – both internal and external – of published accounts as shown by the table on the next page.

**Internal stakeholders** include employees, management, owners/shareholders.

**External stakeholders** include customers, suppliers, government (and government agencies), lenders, local community.

Whilst each user is interested in a number of different aspects, as the diagram on the next page shows, most users will assess the stewardship of the management of the company. By stewardship is meant that the management of a company is accountable for the safe-keeping of the company's resources, and for their proper, efficient and profitable use.

As well as the annual published accounts, companies often provide much more information for stakeholders. For example, J Sainsbury plc provides a full strategic report which explains, amongst other things, the company's business model, its market context, its priorities, its principal risks and uncertainties. Most other large companies will include similar information.

## LIMITED COMPANY PUBLISHED ACCOUNTS: stakeholders

| Who is interested? | What are they interested in? | Why are they interested? |
| --- | --- | --- |
| **INTERNAL STAKEHOLDERS** | | |
| Employees | • Has the company made a profit? <br> • Can the company pay its way? | • To assess whether the company is able to pay wages and salaries <br> • To consider the stability of the company in offering employment opportunities in the future |
| Management | • Is the company making a profit? <br> • Can the company pay its way? <br> • How efficiently is the company using its resources? | • To see if the company is expanding or declining <br> • To see if the company will continue in the foreseeable future <br> • To examine the efficiency of the company and to make comparisons with other, similar, companies |
| Owners/ shareholders | • Is the company making a profit? <br> • Can the company pay its way? <br> • What was the sales revenue figure? | • To assess the stewardship of management <br> • To see how much money can be paid in dividends <br> • To see if the company will continue in the foreseeable future <br> • To see if the company is expanding or declining |
| **EXTERNAL STAKEHOLDERS** | | |
| Customers | • Is the company profitable? <br> • What is the value of the assets? <br> • Can the company pay its way? | • To see if the company will continue to supply its products or services <br> • To assess the ability of the company to meet warranty liabilities, and provision of spare parts |
| Suppliers | • Can the company pay its way? <br> • What is the value of the assets? | • To decide whether to supply goods and services to the company <br> • To assess if the company is able to pay its debts |
| Government | • Has the company made a profit? <br> • What was the sales revenue figure? | • To calculate the tax due <br> • To ensure that the company is registered for VAT and completes VAT returns on time <br> • To provide a basis for government regulation and statistics <br> • To see how grants provided have been spent |
| Lenders | • Has the company made a profit? <br> • What amount is currently loaned? <br> • What is the value of the assets? | • To check if the company will be able to pay finance costs and make loan repayments <br> • To assess how far the lender is financing the company <br> • To assess the value of security available to the lender |
| Local community | • Is the company profitable? <br> • Can the company pay its way? | • To assess local employment prospects <br> • To assess the contribution to the local economy |

# LIMITATIONS OF USING ACCOUNTING RATIOS

Although accounting ratios and measures can usefully highlight strengths and weaknesses, it should always be considered as a part of the overall assessment of a business, rather than as a whole. We have already seen the need to place ratios in context and relate them to a reference point or standard. The limitations of financial ratios should always be borne in mind.

## retrospective nature of ratios

Accounting ratios are usually retrospective, based on previous performance and conditions prevailing in the past. They may not necessarily be valid for making forward projections: for example, a large customer may become insolvent, so threatening the business with an irrecoverable debt, and also reducing revenue in the future.

## differences in accounting policies

When the financial statements of a business are compared, either with previous years' figures, or with figures from a similar business, there is a danger that the comparative statements are not drawn up on the same basis as those currently being worked on. Different accounting policies, in respect of depreciation and inventory valuation for instance, may well result in distortion and invalid comparisons.

## inflation

Inflation may prove a problem, as most financial statements are prepared on an historic cost basis, that is, assets and liabilities are recorded at their original cost. As a result, comparison of figures from one year to the next may be difficult. In countries where inflation is running at high levels any form of comparison becomes practically meaningless.

## reliance on standards

From your studies in year 1, you will know guideline standards for some accounting ratios, for instance 2:1 for the current ratio. There is a danger of relying too heavily on such suggested standards, and ignoring other factors in the statement of financial position. An example of this would be to criticise a business for having a low current ratio when the business sells the majority of its goods for cash and consequently has a very low trade receivables figure: this would in fact be the case with many well-known and successful retail companies.

## other considerations

**Economic**: The general economic climate and the effect this may have on the nature of the business, eg in an economic downturn retailers are usually the first to suffer, whereas manufacturers feel the effects later.

**State of the business**: The director's report for a limited company should be read in conjunction with the financial statements to ascertain an overall view of the state of the business. Of great importance are the products of the company and their stage in the product life cycle, eg is a car manufacturer relying on old models, or is there an up-to-date product range which appeals to buyers?

**Comparing like with like**: Before making comparisons between 'similar' businesses we need to ensure that we are comparing 'like with like'. Differences, such as the acquisition of assets – renting property compared with ownership, leasing vehicles compared with ownership – will affect the profitability of the business and the structure of the statement of financial position; likewise, the long-term financing of a business – the capital gearing – will also have an effect.

# CHAPTER SUMMARY

● Limited company financial statements are readily available to stakeholders.

● Accounting ratios can be used to measure:
  - profitability
  - liquidity
  - efficiency
  - capital structure

● Investor ratios include:
  - dividend yield
  - earnings per share
  - dividend cover
  - price earnings
  - interest cover

● Investor ratios are used to help to assess the performance of companies in which an investment is being considered.

● One of the objectives of financial reporting is to provide information to stakeholders:
  - internal stakeholders include employees, management, owners/shareholders
  - external stakeholders include customers, suppliers, government, lenders, local community

● There are a number of limitations to be borne in mind when drawing conclusions from financial ratios:
  - retrospective nature, based on past performance
  - differences in accounting policies
  - effects of inflation when comparing year-to-year
  - reliance on standards
  - economic and other factors

In the next chapter we see how ethical considerations impact on the behaviour of accounting professionals and organisations.

# QUESTIONS

**visit**
www.osbornebooks.co.uk
**to take an online test**

An asterisk (*) after the question number means that the answer is given at the end of this book.

Questions 8.1 to 8.5 relate to the following information from Zelah plc:

| | |
|---|---|
| Current market price per share | £2.50 |
| Profit for the year before interest and tax | £210,000 |
| Profit for the year after tax | £150,000 |
| Dividend on ordinary shares for the year | £60,000 |
| Number of issued ordinary shares of £1 each | 500,000 |
| Interest payable for the year | £35,000 |

**8.1\*** What is the dividend yield of Zelah plc?

| A | 4.8% | |
|---|---|---|
| B | 12.0% | |
| C | 30.0% | |
| D | 48.0% | |

**8.2\*** What is the earnings per share of Zelah plc?

| A | £0.03 | |
|---|---|---|
| B | £0.30 | |
| C | £0.12 | |
| D | £0.42 | |

**8.3\*** What is the dividend cover of Zelah plc?

| A | 0.3 times | |
|---|---|---|
| B | 0.4 times | |
| C | 2.5 times | |
| D | 3.5 times | |

**8.4**

What is the price earnings of Zelah plc?

| A | 12.0 times | |
|---|---|---|
| B | 2.5 times | |
| C | 4.8 times | |
| D | 8.33 times | |

**8.5**

What is the interest cover of Zelah plc?

| A | 6 times | |
|---|---|---|
| B | 4.3 times | |
| C | 1.71 times | |
| D | 14.3 times | |

**8.6**

The following is taken from the statement of financial position of two plcs:

| | ABC plc | XYZ plc |
|---|---|---|
| Ordinary dividend for year | £750,000 | £1,200,000 |
| Number of issued ordinary shares of £1 each | 5,000,000 | 15,000,000 |
| Current market price per share | £1.50 | £4.00 |
| Profit for the year after tax | £1,500,000 | £5,500,000 |

Note:  both companies are in the same industry.

**(a)**    For each business, calculate:

| | ABC plc | XYZ plc |
|---|---|---|
| Dividend yield | | |
| Earnings per share | | |
| Price earnings | | |
| Dividend cover | | |

**(b)**    State in which company you would invest for (1) capital growth, (2) income.

**8.7**

Select a public limited company of your choice and obtain the latest set of published accounts. (Write to the company asking for a set or look on the company's website.)

Read the report and accounts and, from the financial statements, extract the following information for the current and previous year – if there is a choice of figures, use those from the consolidated (or group) accounts:

**income statement**
- revenue for the year
- profit or loss for the year from operations
- profit or loss for the year after tax

**statement of financial position**
- total of non-current assets
- total of current assets
- total of current liabilities
- total of non-current liabilities
- total equity

**statement of cash flows** (see also Chapter 7)
- cash flow from operating activities
- cash flow from investing activities
- cash flow from financing activities
- net increase or decrease in cash

**auditors' report (current year only)**
- does it state that the financial statements show a 'true and fair view'?
- are there any 'qualifications' to the report?

**accounting policies (current year only)**
- state two accounting policies followed by the plc

**You are to compile a short report** – from the point of view of a private investor – which contains:

- an introduction to the selected plc; its structure, size, products, position in its own industry

- the information extracted from the published accounts

- a portfolio of your observations from the report and accounts, eg
  - is the company expanding/declining/remaining static?
  - have the shareholders received higher/lower dividends?

**8.8\***

A friend of yours, Samantha Smith, owns a shop selling children's clothes. You are helping Samantha to understand her financial statements which have been prepared by her accountant. She says to you: "I cannot understand why my bank overdraft has increased in a year when I have made such good profits."

**REQUIRED**

(a) Explain to Samantha the difference between cash and profits.

(b) Give two examples to explain how a business can make good profits during a year when the bank balance reduces or the bank overdraft increases.

**8.9**

A director of Wyvern plc, a medium-sized manufacturing company, is concerned about the liquidity of the company. The company's accountant has provided the following information.

|  | 31 March 20-5 | 31 March 20-4 | Industry average |
|---|---|---|---|
| Current ratio | 1.60:1 | 1.55:1 | 1.50:1 |
| Liquid capital ratio | 0.70:1 | 0.65:1 | 0.75:1 |

The statement of cash flows for the year ended 31 March 20-5 shows a net increase in cash and cash equivalents of £79,000.

**You are to** assess the liquidity of Wyvern plc and the extent to which you agree with the director's concerns.

**8.10\***

Steve Horan is a shareholder in Blenheim plc and has asked you to assist him in assessing the efficiency and effectiveness of the management of the company. You have calculated the following accounting ratios in respect of Blenheim plc's financial statements for the last two years to assist you in your analysis.

|  | 20-1 | 20-0 |
|---|---|---|
| Gross profit margin | 42.0% | 45.0% |
| Profit in relation to revenue | 9.5% | 7.5% |
| Rate of inventory turnover (days) | 84 days | 66 days |
| Trade receivable days | 55 days | 40 days |
| Trade payable days | 50 days | 42 days |

Prepare a report to Steve that includes:

(a) A comment on the relative performance of the company for the two years based on the accounting ratios calculated and what this tells you about the company.

**REPORT**

To:        Steve Horan
From:      AQA Accounting student
Subject:   Shareholding in Blenheim plc
Date:      Today

*If required, continue on a separate sheet*

**(b)**    Advise, with reasons based on the accounting ratios you have calculated, on whether or not Steve should maintain his investment in the company.

*If required, continue on a separate sheet*

8.11  Louise Forsythe is a shareholder in Kingham plc and has asked you to assist her in assessing the effectiveness of the management of the company in using its resources. You have calculated the following accounting ratios in respect of Kingham plc's financial statements for the last two years to assist you in your analysis.

|  | 20-1 | 20-0 |
| --- | --- | --- |
| Gross profit margin | 39.0% | 42.0% |
| Profit in relation to revenue | 10.0% | 9.5% |
| Return on capital employed | 12.0% | 10.5% |
| Capital gearing | 22.2% | 27.4% |
| Interest cover | 10.6 times | 9.1 times |

Prepare a report to Louise that includes:

**(a)**   A comment on the relative performance of the company for the two years based on the accounting ratios calculated and what this tells you about the company.

**REPORT**

To:          Louise Forsythe
From:       AQA Accounting student
Subject:    Shareholding in Kingham plc
Date:        Today

If required, continue on a separate sheet

**(b)** Advise, with reasons based on the accounting ratios you have calculated, on whether or not Louise should maintain her investment in the company.

**8.12**

Jayne Lavendar, an ordinary shareholder in Gresham plc, is debating whether to keep or to sell her shares in the company. Her main concern is the level of income she is receiving from Gresham plc, but she also wishes to ensure that her shareholding is safe.

She has asked you to analyse the company's most recent financial statements with a view to assisting her in her decision.

You have calculated the following three accounting ratios for Gresham plc, for years 20-1 and 20-0, and an extract of the company's statement of cash flows for 20-1 is also provided below.

**Accounting ratios**

|  | **20-1** | **20-0** |
| --- | --- | --- |
| Gearing | 42% | 34% |
| Current ratio | 1.8 times | 2.1 times |
| Interest cover | 3.2 | 5.6 |

**Gresham plc – Statement of cash flows (extract) for year 20-1**

|  | £000 |
| --- | --- |
| Operating activities | 40 |
| Investing activities | (160) |
| Financing activities | 100 |
| Decrease in cash and cash equivalents | (20) |

**REQUIRED:**

Prepare notes for Jayne that include:

**(a)** Comments on the relative performance of Gresham plc in respect of the two years, giving possible reasons for any differences (the extract of the statement of cash flows may assist you in some aspects of this) based upon the three ratios calculated.

**(b)** Advice to Jayne, with **one** principal reason only to support this, as to whether or not she should keep or sell her shares in the company.

**8.13***

Four groups of stakeholders of published accounts are:

- shareholders
- lenders
- suppliers
- employees

For each group:

**(a)** State two items from the financial statements which would be of particular interest.

**(b)** Give reasons for your choice.

**8.14**

The managing director of Chapelporth plc has issued the following statement:

> "I am pleased to report that the profit from operations for the year to 30 November 20-6 was £68 million. These good results were achieved despite higher expenses. After finance costs of £15 million the profit before tax of £53 million was 12 per cent up on the same period in 20-5. Future investment will be concentrated on those areas offering the highest returns and the greatest growth prospects."

This profit will please the stakeholders of Chapelporth plc but for different reasons.

**REQUIRED:**

Explain why the following stakeholders will be pleased with the increase in the profits of Chapelporth plc.

**(a)** Shareholders.

**(b)** Lenders.

**(c)** Employees.

**8.15***

Birgitta has £50,000 available for medium/long-term investment in the ordinary shares of a company. She is wishing, initially, to maximise her income.
She has identified two companies in the same line of business and has gathered together the following information from their most recent financial statements.

| | Avon plc | Severn plc |
|---|---|---|
| Current market price (per share) | £1.20 | £3.50 |
| Share price (last 52 weeks) | | |
| high | £1.40 | £3.60 |
| low | £0.60 | £3.20 |
| Dividend per share | 10.5p | 7.0p |
| Dividend yield | 8.75% | 2.0% |
| Dividend cover | 1.43 times | 3.0 times |
| Earnings per share | 15p | 21p |
| Price earnings ratio | 8.0 | 16.7 |
| Return on capital employed | 9.3% | 4.4% |
| Capital gearing | 70% | 25% |

An extract from the statement of financial position shows the following:

| Property, plant and equipment | Cost £m | Depreciation £m | Carrying amount £m |
|---|---|---|---|
| Avon plc | 90 | 60 | 30 |
| Severn plc | 350 | 80 | 270 |

Birgitta asks you to help her evaluate both companies from an investor's point of view and to advise her which would be better for her investment.

**REPORT**

To:        Birgitta
From:      AQA Accounting student
Subject:   Evaluation of Avon plc and Severn plc
Date:      Today

# 9 ACCOUNTING REGULATIONS AND ETHICS

This chapter focuses on the legal and regulatory framework of the accounting sector – which encompasses accounting standards and company law. The framework includes the role of the professional accounting bodies who require their members to maintain the high standards expected of them by employers, clients, colleagues and the public.

Most of the professional accounting bodies – eg the Institute of Chartered Accountants, the Association of Accounting Technicians – provide a Code of Professional Ethics which gives guidance to their members on how to act ethically.

In this chapter we look at:

● the legal and regulatory framework of the accounting sector

● the role of professional bodies

● the fundamental principles of ethical behaviour

● how ethics impacts on accounting

● acting ethically in the workplace

● handling unethical behaviour and illegal acts

● resolving ethical conflict

## THE LEGAL AND REGULATORY FRAMEWORK OF THE ACCOUNTING SECTOR

The regulatory framework forms the 'rules' of accounting. When drafting company financial statements, accountants seek to follow the same set of rules – thus enabling broad comparisons to be made between the financial results of different companies.

The legal and regulatory framework of the accounting sector comprises:

• accounting standards

• company law

• Conceptual Framework for Financial Reporting

• organisations involved in the regulatory framework

The historical development of the regulatory framework in the UK dates from the first Companies Act in 1862 through to the main Companies Acts of the last thirty years in 1985, 1989 and 2006. Accounting standards have been developed over the last fifty years to provide a framework for accounting. A development in more recent years has been the adoption by large UK companies of international accounting standards.

The following diagram shows the development of the regulatory framework in the UK since 1970:

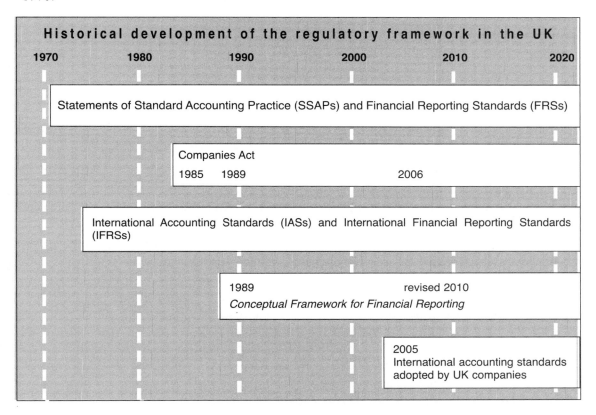

**Historical development of the regulatory framework in the UK**

| 1970 | 1980 | 1990 | 2000 | 2010 | 2020 |
|---|---|---|---|---|---|

Statements of Standard Accounting Practice (SSAPs) and Financial Reporting Standards (FRSs)

Companies Act
1985    1989                    2006

International Accounting Standards (IASs) and International Financial Reporting Standards (IFRSs)

1989                    revised 2010
*Conceptual Framework for Financial Reporting*

2005
International accounting standards adopted by UK companies

## accounting standards

Over the last fifty years, a number of accounting standards have been produced to provide a framework for accounting and to reduce the variety of accounting treatments which companies may use in their financial statements.

The UK's former domestic accounting standards – **Statements of Standard Accounting Practice (SSAPs)** and **Financial Reporting Standards (FRSs)** – have been largely brought together in a single accounting standard, FRS 102. This is entitled *The Financial Reporting Standard Applicable in the UK and Republic of Ireland*, and is issued by the Financial Reporting Council. It is used by smaller limited companies.

International accounting standards – in the form of **International Accounting Standards (IASs)** and **International Financial Reporting Standards (IFRSs)** – have been developed by the International Accounting Standards Board since 1973 with the aim of harmonising international financial reporting. All large companies in the European Union and in the UK prepare their financial statements in accordance with international accounting standards, and the standards are being adopted increasingly on a worldwide basis.

Two international accounting standards that we have studied in recent chapters are IAS 1, *Presentation of Financial Statements* (Chapter 6) and IAS 7, *Statement of Cash Flows* (Chapter 7). A full list of international accounting standards is available at www.ifrs.org (another useful source – which summarises international accounting standards – is www.iasplus.com).

## purposes of accounting standards

The purposes of using accounting standards are:

- to provide a framework for preparing and presenting financial statements – the 'rules' of accounting
- to standardise financial statements so that the same accounting rules apply to all companies
- to reduce the variations of accounting treatments used in financial statements – thus making manipulation of the accounts to show a better position more difficult
- to help to ensure high quality financial accounting for users through the application of the qualitative characteristics of useful financial information
- to enable compliance with the Companies Act and audit requirements that financial statements have been prepared in accordance with accounting standards
- to allow users of financial statements to make comparisons between firms in the knowledge that all the financial statements have been prepared using the same standards

## Company Law

Limited companies are regulated by the Companies Act 2006. In particular, the Act requires that directors of a company state that the financial statements have been prepared in accordance with applicable accounting standards and, if there have been any material departures, they must give details and the reasons for such departures.

## Conceptual Framework for Financial Reporting

Although not an accounting standard, the *Conceptual Framework for Financial Reporting* has been developed by the International Accounting Standards Board to set out the concepts that underlie the preparation and presentation of financial statements for external users.

The *Framework* sets out the objective of financial reporting, identifies the users of financial information, and defines assets, liabilities, equity, profits or losses, income, and expenses.

The purpose of the *Framework* is to:

- assist in the development and review of international accounting standards
- assist in promoting harmonisation of standards by reducing the number of permissible alternative accounting treatments
- help preparers of accounts to deal with issues not yet covered by the standards

- help users of accounts to interpret the information in financial statements which have been prepared in accordance with the standards

## organisations involved in the regulatory framework

In the UK two organisations in particular form part of the regulatory framework of the accounting sector:

- the Financial Reporting Council (FRC)
- the Government Department for Business, Energy and Industrial Strategy (BEIS)

Additionally, the European Union (EU) requires companies operating in the EU to disclose information about their finances and how they operate.

### The Financial Reporting Council

The FRC is the independent statutory regulator for the accounting sector. It promotes transparency and integrity in business. In particular, it sets the UK framework for Corporate Governance and publishes codes and standards for companies, accountants and auditors to adopt. It oversees the accountancy sector and, where appropriate, will monitor and enforce compliance with its codes and standards.

The FRC sees high quality corporate governance and reporting as important in driving forward a successful economy, which gives confidence to investors. It seeks to achieve this through its monitoring of the accounts of public companies, together with assessing the quality of auditing and audit firms.

The FRC takes action and imposes sanctions where appropriate on public companies, accountants and audit firms. It recognises that stakeholders benefit from a well-regulated system of corporate governance and reporting which contributes to a well-run and developing economy. The downside would be a lack of trust by stakeholders in the accounting sector, a fall in company profits, a slide in share prices and a weakening economy.

The FRC is funded by audit firms, accountancy professional bodies, large companies, and others who benefit from FRC regulation.

### The Department for Business, Energy and Industrial Strategy

This Government department is responsible for a wide range of activities to support businesses' productivity and their ability to compete around the world. Its work includes helping businesses to find finance and to write a business plan.

The Department works with a number of other agencies, including Companies House (which deals with starting and running a company, filing company accounts) and the Insolvency Service (which deals with, among other things, companies in administration and company directors who are disqualified from holding office).

The Department's involvement with the regulatory framework of the accounting sector includes:

- business and the environment
- business regulation (including business tax)
- company law reform

**The European Union**

The EU sets out the rules of financial information to be disclosed by companies operating in the European Union. Broadly, large companies must prepare their financial statements in accordance with international accounting standards. The UK's departure from the EU does not change this regulatory framework as all larger UK companies have applied international accounting standards since 2005.

The EU sets out the rules that companies have to follow when preparing financial statements in its 'Accounting Directive'. The aim of this directive is to standardise:

* the presentation and content of financial statements

* the presentation and content of directors' reports

* how companies use measurement bases (eg depreciation) to prepare financial statements

* the audit of financial statements

* the publication of financial statements

* the responsibility of directors for financial reporting

# THE ROLE OF PROFESSIONAL BODIES IN THE ACCOUNTING SECTOR

The professional accounting bodies have a role to play in establishing and enforcing codes of conduct on their members.

The professional bodies are grouped into two:

* the Consultative Committee of Accountancy Bodies (CCAB)

* the Chartered Institute of Management Accountants (CIMA)

The first of these is an 'umbrella' group of professional accounting bodies comprising:

– the Association of Chartered Certified Accountants (ACCA)
– the Chartered Institute of Public Finance and Accountancy (CIPFA)
– the Institute of Chartered Accountants in England and Wales (ICAEW)
– the Chartered Accountants Ireland (CAI)
– the Institute of Chartered Accountants of Scotland (ICAS)

These five organisations have a strong focus on audit, whereas CIMA is involved more with management accounting – hence the separate groupings within the sector.

## ethics and codes of conduct

An ethical code of conduct guides accountants to behaving ethically and sets out the required standards of professional behaviour that accountants should maintain and gives them guidance on how to achieve these standards. Each professional accounting body in the UK has based its own ethical code on that issued by the International Ethics Standards Board for Accountants (IESBA) and this consistent approach to professional ethics means that the public interest will be protected together with the reputation of the professional accounting bodies.

The code of ethics for accountants prescribes a principles-based approach, ie identifying, evaluating and addressing threats to fundamental principles rather than a rules-based approach. Similarly, a principles-based approach should be adopted when applying a code of conduct or practice and these should be used as a guide rather than a set of rules.

The professional accounting bodies in the UK expect their members to comply with the code of ethics and to uphold the high standards that are expected of the accounting profession. Failure by an accountant to comply with applicable regulations and codes of practice may result in the accountant being disciplined. Disciplinary action for misconduct can be taken by the individual accounting bodies and also by the Financial Reporting Council (FRC), which is the independent disciplinary body for accountants, accountancy firms and audit firms in the UK.

Misconduct falls into two main categories:

• bringing the accounting profession into disrepute

• acting in breach of the rules and regulations of the accountant's professional body

Individual accounting bodies in the UK have published disciplinary regulations, which set out the processes and sanctions that the accounting body will carry out if a member is guilty of misconduct. The procedures will involve a disciplinary investigation followed by a decision as to whether the accountant is guilty of misconduct. Depending on the severity of the misconduct penalties range from a fine through to suspension of membership or, at the worst case, being expelled from membership of the body.

# THE FUNDAMENTAL PRINCIPLES OF ETHICAL BEHAVIOUR

In the preparation of financial statements, accountants must ensure that these are accurate and prepared in the public interest and without bias. Behaving ethically is key to achieving this, and consequently accounting professionals are required to comply with a number of fundamental ethical principles that underpin financial reporting.

The fundamental principles are explained on the next page.

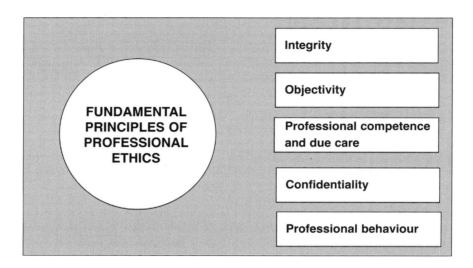

**integrity** – being straightforward and honest in all professional and business relationships.

**objectivity** – not allowing bias, conflict of interest or the undue influence of others to override professional or business judgements.

**professional competence and due care** – an accountant should maintain professional knowledge and skill at the level required to ensure that an employer or client receives a competent professional service. The accountant should act diligently in accordance with current developments in practice, legislation and techniques.

**confidentiality** – information acquired as a result of professional and business relationships should not be disclosed to third parties except when proper and specific authority is given or there is a legal or professional right to disclose. Such confidential information should not to be used for personal advantage or be passed to third parties.

**professional behaviour** – accountants should ensure that their behaviour complies with relevant laws and regulations and avoids bringing the accountancy profession into disrepute.

## THREATS TO THE FUNDAMENTAL ETHICAL PRINCIPLES

The Code of Professional Ethics of accounting bodies provides a framework that their members can apply that will enable them to identify threats to their compliance with the fundamental ethical principles identified above. When faced with an ethical dilemma where his/her fundamental principles are threatened the accountant must consider each individual circumstance and decide how to deal with it. This may be by implementing safeguards that eliminate the threats or reduce them to an acceptable level.

There are a number of potential threats that an accountant may face when preparing financial statements. These threats are summarised in the diagram on the next page.

| potential threats to the fundamental ethical principles |

**self-interest threats**

These may occur where a financial or other interest will inappropriately influence the accountant's judgement or behaviour.

**self-review threats**

These may occur when an accountant has to re-evaluate a judgement or data that he/she has previously made or produced.

**familiarity threats**

These may occur when, because of a close or personal relationship, an accountant becomes too sympathetic to the interests of others.

**intimidation threats**

These may occur when an accountant may be deterred from acting objectively because of real or perceived threats.

**advocacy threats**

These may occur when an accountant promotes a position or opinion (normally of a client) to the point that his/her objectivity may be compromised in the future.

An example of how each of these threats to the fundamental ethical principles can relate to the preparation of financial statements is as follows:

- self-interest threats – an accountant has a financial interest in, or has made a loan to, a company for which he/she prepares the financial statements
- self-review threats – an accountant is involved in the audit of financial statements that have been prepared by him/herself or the firm that he/she works for
- familiarity threats – the accountant has a close family or personal relationship with a director or officer of a company for which he/she prepares the financial statements
- intimidation threats – an accountant is threatened with demotion or dismissal because he/she disagrees with the way in which accounting principles have been applied in the company's financial statements
- advocacy threats – an accountant promotes shares in a company for which he/she is responsible for preparing the financial statements

## safeguards against threats to the fundamental ethical principles

Safeguards are actions or other measures that can be put in place to eliminate threats or to reduce them to acceptable levels. These safeguards fall into two broad categories:

- safeguards created by the accounting profession, legislation or regulation
- safeguards in the work environment

*Safeguards created by the profession, legislation or regulation include:*

- education, training and experience requirements for entry into the accountancy profession
- continuing professional development (CPD) requirements
- corporate governance regulations

- professional standards
- professional or regulatory monitoring and disciplinary procedures
- external review of work completed by the accountant carried out by a legally empowered third party

*Safeguards in the work environment of the accountant in business include*:

- the employer's systems and structures of oversight
- the employer's ethics and conduct programme
- recruitment of high calibre, competent staff
- strong internal controls
- appropriate disciplinary procedures
- leadership, focussing on the importance of ethical behaviour
- policies and procedures to implement and monitor employee performance
- communication of policies and procedures to staff, together with training and education
- policies and procedures that encourage employees to discuss ethical issues with senior colleagues
- consultation with another appropriate professional

*Safeguards in the work environment of the accountant in public practice include*:

- emphasising the importance of complying with the fundamental principles
- the expectation that staff will act in the public interest
- policies and procedures to implement and monitor the quality of work
- policies and procedures to ensure compliance with the fundamental principles
- policies to identify threats to compliance with the fundamental principles, and how to deal with them
- identification of interests or relationships between staff and clients
- different staff used for separate aspects of a client's work
- ensuring that staff who are not involved in a client's work are not able to influence decisions
- communication of policies and procedures to staff, together with training and education
- a senior manager overseeing the quality control system
- encouraging staff to consult with senior colleagues over compliance issues
- appropriate disciplinary mechanisms to provide compliance with policies and procedures

## APPLYING THE SAFEGUARDS TO RESOLVE ETHICAL CONFLICT

When an accountant is faced with an ethical conflict in the application of the fundamental ethical principles, he/she will need to find a method for resolving this conflict. This may involve a formal conflict resolution process if there is one. If not the accountant may wish to resolve the issue informally. In either case the accountant should consider each of the following points:

- the relevant facts relating to the ethical conflict
- the ethical issues involved
- the fundamental principles relating to the ethical conflict
- established internal procedures and how they might be applied to the conflict
- alternative courses of action available to the accountant

With these points in mind, the accountant then needs to determine the course of action to follow and to apply relevant safeguards and thereby resolve the ethical conflict.

We will now take each of the fundamental ethical principles and identify what action an accountant should take to prevent or minimise ethical conflict.

## integrity

An accountant must not be associated with reports, returns, communications, or other information that:

- contain false or misleading statements
- contain statements or information furnished recklessly
- omits or obscures information so as to be misleading

If an accountant realises that he/she has been associated with this type of information, the accountant should disassociate from the information.

## objectivity

An accountant must avoid situations and relationships that bias or unduly influence professional judgement. He/she must not carry out professional services if a relationship or the circumstances mean that he/she can no longer be objective.

## professional competence and due care

Professional competence requires the accountant to be aware of and have an understanding of technical, professional and business developments. Examples of achieving this include continuing professional development (CPD) and ensuring that professional staff receive appropriate training and supervision.

Due care requires the accountant to act in accordance with the requirements of the current work assignment, carefully, thoroughly and on a timely basis.

## confidentiality

The accountant must maintain the confidentiality of information, unless the information is a matter of public knowledge. The requirement to maintain confidentiality includes:

- information disclosed by a client or prospective client
- information within the organisation where the accountant works
- when the accountant is in a social environment

Confidentiality extends to those with whom the accountant may have to consult, eg specialists, senior and junior professional staff. Also confidential information can only be used for the purpose for which it was legitimately acquired.

The principle of confidentiality continues after the end of the accountant's relationship with a client or an employer.

There are certain circumstances where confidential information can be disclosed. These are when:

- it is permitted by law and authorised by the client or employer
- it is required by law, eg in the course of legal proceedings, providing information to public authorities such as HM Revenue & Customs, of infringements of the law
- there is actual or suspected money laundering or terrorist financing which, by law, must be reported to the firm's Money Laundering Reporting Officer or to the National Crime Agency
- there is a professional duty or right to disclose, which is in the public interest and is not prohibited by law

## professional behaviour

To prevent ethical conflict, the accountant must be honest and truthful in all dealings so as not to bring the profession into disrepute. In particular accountants must not make:

- exaggerated claims for the services they offer, the qualifications they have, or the experience they have gained
- disparaging references or unsubstantiated comparisons to the work of others

# How Ethics Impacts on Accounting

We have already seen on page 196 how the principles of ethical behaviour affect the accountant in business and in public practice, together with the safeguards that can be put into place to eliminate threats or to reduce them to acceptable levels.

In this section we see how ethical behaviour impacts on organisations within accounting:

- the role and composition of the board of directors
- the role of auditors and the audit report
- the role and composition of the remuneration committee
- corporate governance
- corporate social responsibility

## the board of directors

Most companies are managed by a board of directors who are appointed or elected by the shareholders to run the company on their behalf. Directors are subject to re-election at regular intervals – usually at the company's annual general meeting (AGM) – by the shareholders.

The *role of the board of directors* is to ensure the long-term success of the company by setting the company's strategy, financial objectives, and level of risk to be taken. The board provides leadership of the company, to include ethics, corporate governance and corporate social responsibility.

The *composition of the board of directors* of a large public limited company will comprise a chairman, executive directors and non-executive directors. (Executive directors are employees who work for the company full-time, while non-executive directors are part-time.)

The principles of ethical behaviour impact on the board of directors in the following way:

- **integrity** – the directors act in good faith and are not put in a position where their duties and personal interests conflict
- **objectivity** – the directors exercise their powers in the best interests of the company without benefit to themselves
- **professional competence and due care** – the statutory duties for directors, as set out in the Companies Act 2006 (see page 114), are followed
- **confidentiality** – information learned as a director is not disclosed outside the business
- **professional behaviour** – the directors do not take actions to the detriment of the company

## auditors and the audit report

External auditors are independent of the company being audited and are appointed by the shareholders at a company's AGM.

Note that a large company will also have internal auditors who are employees of the company which they audit. They are concerned with the internal checking and control procedures of the company – for example, procedures for the control of cash, authorisation of purchases and disposal of property, plant and equipment. The nature of this work requires that they should have a degree of independence within the company and they will usually report directly to the company's finance director.

The *role of external auditors* is to examine the company's accounts to ensure that they have been prepared properly and that the financial statements give a true and fair view of the company's affairs in accordance with the legal and regulatory frameworks which relate to the accounting sector. (See page 127 for more on the audit report, and note that most small private companies are exempt from audit requirements.)

The principles of ethical behaviour impact on external auditors in the following way:

- **integrity** – auditors are independent from the company being audited; they must be honest in assessing whether the financial statements present a true and fair view of the company's affairs
- **objectivity** – auditors must avoid the situation where one large audit client dominates their business
- **professional competence and due care** – auditors should be up-to-date with developments in accountancy – including continuous professional development (CPD) – and must ensure that only appropriately qualified staff carry out audits
- **confidentiality** – information learned as auditors is not disclosed to outsiders unless the audit client has given proper and specific authority, or there is a legal or professional right to disclose
- **professional behaviour** – auditors must not bring the accountancy profession into disrepute and must follow the Ethical Standard for reporting accountants (set by the Financial Reporting Council)

## the remuneration committee

A large company or organisation will have a remuneration committee whose role is to recommend and review aspects of payments (both salary and benefits) for the senior management, including the executive directors and the chairman. The remuneration committee will usually comprise at least three non-executive directors – the committee will probably meet two or three times a year.

The *role of the remuneration committee* is to ensure that the company's remuneration policies for senior management fit with the plans of the company both in the short-term and the medium-term, and to recommend and monitor the level and structure of remuneration.

The principles of ethical behaviour impact on the remuneration committee in the following way:

- **integrity** – the remuneration committee must act independently from the board of directors and must be honest in their dealings

- **objectivity** – the committee should be properly constituted and act within its role and authority; no director is to be involved in deciding their own remuneration

- **professional competence and due care** – the committee must be up-to-date on the accounting rules of payments and reporting, including the requirements of corporate governance

- **confidentiality** – only recommendations to the board of directors are to be disclosed; all other information should not be discussed outside of the committee

- **professional behaviour** – the committee must not take actions that bring the company or the accountancy profession into disrepute

## corporate governance

Corporate governance sets out the systems by which companies are directed and controlled. It involves balancing the interests and requirements of a company's stakeholders – shareholders, employees, management, customers, suppliers, government, lenders, local community – and ensuring that management can deliver long-term success for the company.

The UK's Corporate Governance Code – issued by the Financial Reporting Council – sets out the standards of good practice for areas such as composition of the board of directors, remuneration, shareholder relations, accountability and audit.

The principles of ethical behaviour impact on corporate governance in the following way:

- **integrity** – a company's board of directors must act within the best interests of the company and in accordance with the law

- **objectivity** – the board of directors sets out the company's strategic aims in order to ensure that its obligations to stakeholders are met

- **professional competence and due care** – the board of directors and its various committees must have the skills, experience and knowledge to discharge their duties and responsibilities effectively

- **confidentiality** – where appropriate, confidentiality is maintained and the company adheres to all ethical principles

- **professional behaviour** – the directors should be up-to-date with their skills and knowledge and must not bring the company into disrepute

## corporate social responsibility

Most large companies acknowledge obligations to their staff and to the environment in which they work. They do this through their policies on corporate social responsibility (CSR) which often cover issues such as:

- a respect for the environment (eg running fuel efficient lorries)
- sourcing products with integrity (eg buying coffee beans from ethical suppliers)
- creating a good workplace for employees (eg allowing flexible hours for employees with childcare responsibilities)
- providing support to the community in which they operate (eg supporting employees to carry out voluntary activities)

The principles of ethical behaviour impact on corporate social responsibility in the following way:

- **integrity** – the company has a policy of buying its goods and services from local and/or ethical suppliers; it acts with integrity in all its business dealings
- **objectivity** – the company has a policy of doing things for the community within which it operates, eg donations to local charities, allowing staff to take part in charitable or community work, and continues to do this even if profits are reduced
- **professional competence and due care** – ensuring that the company has a positive impact on the community in which it operates and has respect for the environment
- **confidentiality** – where appropriate, confidentiality is maintained and the company adheres to all ethical principles
- **professional behaviour** – the company complies with laws; treats suppliers, staff and customers properly and with respect; contributes to a healthy, safe and secure workplace

# ACTING ETHICALLY WHEN WORKING WITH OTHERS

Members of accounting bodies must always act ethically when working with others, whether it is clients, suppliers, colleagues or stakeholders. Acting ethically includes understanding and applying:

- the principles of ethical behaviour (see pages 193-194)
- the codes of practice of the CCAB and CIMA (see pages 192-193)
- the regulatory framework of the accounting sector, eg the Companies Act 2006, the Financial Reporting Council, etc (see pages 188-192)

The Institute of Business Ethics (IBE) has produced a 'Simple ethical test for a business decision'. This test has three elements or questions to ask when faced with a business decision. These are:

- transparency – do I mind others knowing what I have decided?
- effect – who does my decision affect or hurt?
- fairness – would my decision be considered fair by those affected?

By considering these three questions an individual within an organisation will consider the ethical implications of the decision made.

# Dealing With Unethical Behaviour or Illegal Acts

Accountants must be vigilant in their work to prevent and to detect instances of unethical behaviour or illegal acts that have been, or may be, committed by an employer, colleague or client. It is the implementation of a strong code of conduct in the organisation and a positive corporate culture that encourages ethical behaviour from employees in order to minimise the risks of unethical behaviour or illegal acts.

The appropriate course of action for resolving ethical conflict such as unethical behaviour or illegal acts is to take the following steps:

- obtain and check all the facts
- is the behaviour unethical or the act illegal?
- identify the fundamental ethical principle(s) affected:
    - integrity
    - objectivity
    - professional competence and due care
    - confidentiality
    - professional behaviour
- evaluate the significance of threats to the fundamental principles:
    - self-interest
    - self-review
    - familiarity
    - intimidation
    - advocacy
- identify possible courses of action to resolve
- seek external help when necessary, eg auditor, professional body, legal advice

An accountant may be put under pressure by an employer, colleague or client, not to comply with the fundamental ethical principles. He or she may face pressure to:

- break the law
- breach the rules and standards of their profession
- be part of a plan for unethical or illegal earnings
- lie or mislead (including by keeping silent) auditors or regulators, or
- put his/her name to or otherwise be associated with a statement which materially misrepresents the facts

All of the above are very serious situations. Each one clearly conflicts with the ethical standards expected of a professional accountant.

Breaking the law is obviously not something anyone, never mind a professional accountant, should do. The rules and standards of the accounting professional are clearly there for a purpose and should not be broken by members of the profession. Note that breaching ethical standards includes not only active deception, but also an accountant misleading auditors by just keeping quiet when he/she knows the auditors have got something wrong.

So what happens if an employed accountant is put in a position where pressure is put on him/her to do one (or more) of the above? Possible action that the accountant could take can be summarised as follows:

- if the law has been broken, the accountant should try hard to persuade the employer not to continue with the unlawful activity and to rectify the situation as soon as possible

- if there is a difference of opinion between the accountant and the employer regarding an accounting or ethical matter, wherever possible this should be resolved with the involvement of more senior staff within the organisation. If necessary, the issue should be dealt with using the employer's formal dispute resolution process

- where the issue between the employer and the accountant cannot be resolved and the accountant considers that he/she has exhausted all other possible alternatives then he/she may have no option but to offer to resign. In this case the employed accountant should explain to the employer the reasons for his/her resignation, and should at the same time maintain the duty of confidentiality to the employer

It is worth noting here that the accounting profession and the code of ethics strongly recommends that the employed accountant should obtain advice from his/her professional body or legal advice before taking the step of offering to resign. One important reason for this is that the law now protects an employee from dismissal for 'whistleblowing', ie breaking confidentiality. In other words, the employee should not have to be put in the position of having to lose his/her job when the matter is serious enough to be made public. Only the accountant's professional body or a lawyer (or both) can advise in this situation.

The process of dealing with ethical conflict is summarised in the diagram below.

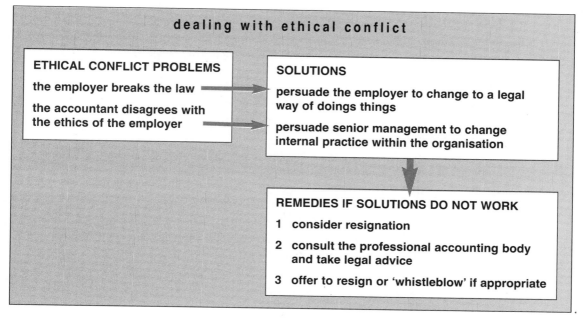

**dealing with ethical conflict**

**ETHICAL CONFLICT PROBLEMS**

the employer breaks the law

the accountant disagrees with the ethics of the employer

**SOLUTIONS**

persuade the employer to change to a legal way of doings things

persuade senior management to change internal practice within the organisation

**REMEDIES IF SOLUTIONS DO NOT WORK**

1  consider resignation

2  consult the professional accounting body and take legal advice

3  offer to resign or 'whistleblow' if appropriate

## WORKED EXAMPLE: RESOLVING ETHICAL CONFLICT

### situation

Jayne Simms is an accountant working for Durning & Co. She provides financial advice to two clients, Aye Limited and Bee Limited, who are both in the same line of business. Recently another company, Cee Limited, has been offered for sale and both Aye Limited and Bee Limited have expressed an interest to Jayne in buying Cee Limited. Each has asked Jayne to act for them in financial matters in order to progress this potential acquisition.

### solution

The steps that Jayne must take to resolve this ethical conflict are:

1.  **The relevant facts**

    Both Aye Limited and Bee Limited have asked Jayne to act for them in financial matters to progress the potential acquisition of Cee Limited.

2.  **The ethical issues involved**

    Jayne will be acting for two clients, each of whom is considering the acquisition of the same third company.

3.  **The fundamental principles**

    Two fundamental principles of ethical behaviour are at risk here:

    *   objectivity – it will be difficult for Jayne to act for both her existing clients and to remain independent
    *   confidentiality – Jayne will find it difficult to keep information about each client confidential

    These two clients may learn that Jayne is acting for them both and may perceive that she will favour one rather than the other, or may use confidential information for the benefit of one client.

4.  **The established internal procedures**

    The first consideration is whether Durning & Co has established procedures for dealing with conflicts of interest between clients. For example, another accountant within the firm could be asked to take over the work of one client.

5.  **Alternative courses of action**

    Jayne should discuss the issue with her line manager and/or the senior management of Durning & Co. Both the issue and the discussion should be documented.

    It may be that Jayne will only be able to act for one of her clients. However, this may not eliminate the threat to her fundamental ethical principles or reduce them to an acceptable level. If this is the case, then Jayne will not be able to act for either of her clients.

# CHAPTER SUMMARY

- The legal and regulatory framework of the accounting sector comprises:
  - accounting standards
  - company law
  - Conceptual Framework for Financial Reporting

- Organisations involved in the legal and regulatory framework include:
  - The Financial Reporting Council (FRC)
  - The Government Department for Business, Energy and Industrial Strategy (BEIS)
  - The European Union

- The professional accounting bodies have a role to play in establishing and enforcing codes of ethical conduct on their members.

- The fundamental principles of ethical behaviour are:
  - integrity
  - objectivity
  - professional competence and due care
  - confidentiality
  - professional behaviour

- Potential threats to the fundamental ethical principles are:
  - self-interest threats
  - self-review threats
  - familiarity threats
  - intimidation threats
  - advocacy threats

- Safeguards are put in place to eliminate threats or to reduce them to an acceptable level. Two categories of safeguards are:
  - safeguards created by the accountancy profession
  - safeguards in the work environment

- The principles of ethical behaviour impact on:
  - the role of the accountant in business
  - the role of the accountant in public practice

- the role and composition of the board of directors
- the role of auditors and the audit report
- the role and composition of the remuneration committee
- corporate governance
- corporate social responsibility

- Acting ethically when working with others includes understanding and applying:
  - the principles of ethical behaviour
  - the codes of practice of the CCAB and CIMA
  - the regulatory framework of the accounting sector

- Accountants must be vigilant in their work to prevent and to detect instances of unethical behaviour or illegal acts that have been, or may be, committed by an employer, colleague or client.

- Resolving ethical conflict takes a step-by-step approach; check facts; identify the ethical principles affected; evaluate the threats; identify courses of action, seek external help when necessary.

This chapter concludes the financial accounting part of the A-level Accounting course. The next section moves on with a study of management accounting, picking up from topics covered in A-level Accounting year 1.

# QUESTIONS

visit
www.osbornebooks.co.uk
to take an online test

An asterisk (*) after the question number means that the answer is given at the end of this book.

**9.1**   Which of the following comprises the regulatory framework of the accounting sector?

| | | |
|---|---|---|
| **A** | Accounting standards, the European Union, the Department for Business, Energy and Industrial Strategy | |
| **B** | Company law, Conceptual Framework for Financial Reporting, professional accounting bodies | |
| **C** | Accounting standards, the Financial Reporting Council, the Department for Business, Energy and Industrial Strategy | |
| **D** | Accounting standards, company law, Conceptual Framework for Financial Reporting | |

**9.2\***   Outline the purposes of using accounting standards.

**9.3\***   Professional accounting bodies in the UK have established ethical codes of conduct which apply to their members.

**(a)**   Explain what is contained in these codes of conduct.

**(b)**   How do accountancy bodies deal with members who are guilty of misconduct?

**9.4\***   You are the accountant preparing the financial statements of Faye Ltd for the financial year just ended. The directors wish to show the lowest possible profit for the year in order to pay less tax. To achieve this they are pressuring you to report a reduced and incorrect figure for revenue.

Which fundamental principle of ethical behaviour is threatened by this situation?

| | | |
|---|---|---|
| **A** | Professional competence and due care | |
| **B** | Confidentiality | |
| **C** | Objectivity | |
| **D** | Integrity | |

**9.5\*** You are the accountant preparing the financial statements of Rayner Ltd for the financial year just ended. A friend of yours works for Rayner Ltd and you know that she receives an annual bonus based on the profits of the company. At a social event your friend asks, "How are the profits looking for the year? I am hoping for a good bonus this year".

Which fundamental principle of ethical behaviour is threatened by this situation?

| A | Professional behaviour | |
|---|---|---|
| B | Confidentiality | |
| C | Objectivity | |
| D | Integrity | |

**9.6\*** A friend of yours is currently studying for her professional accounting examinations. A few days ago you saw an advertisement in the local newspaper where your friend offers a full range of professional accountancy services, stating that she has many years of experience, and has a large number of satisfied clients.

Which fundamental principle of ethical behaviour is threatened by this situation?

| A | Professional behaviour | |
|---|---|---|
| B | Professional competence and due care | |
| C | Confidentiality | |
| D | Objectivity | |

**9.7** For each of the following statements identify the fundamental principle of ethical behaviour.

| Statement | Fundamental principle of ethical behaviour |
|---|---|
| The manager of an accountancy firm arranges appropriate training and supervision for staff | |
| An accountant suggests to a prospective client that the client's current accountants are providing a poor service | |
| An accounting report contains a misleading statement | |
| An accountant must avoid situations that unduly influence professional judgement | |
| An accountant discusses the financial results of a client's business with friends | |

**9.8\***

You are a trainee accountant for Omega Accountants. You have been asked to help in the preparation of the financial statements of Foss Ltd, a manufacturer of children's toys, for the year ended 31 December 20-1.

At a business event in your city a bank manager looking for new business asks you to let her have a copy of Foss Ltd's most recent financial statements. You know that Foss Ltd banks with a different bank.

Identify and explain the relevant fundamental principle of ethical behaviour that is threatened by this situation.

**9.9**

You are a trainee accountant working for Blenheim Accountants. A client of Blenheim Accountants is Towan Ltd, a boat builder.

As a result of cash flow problems Towan Ltd has been very slow in paying its trade payables. Having recently helped in the preparation of the financial statements of Towan Ltd you are aware that the cash flow problem remains. The directors ask you to provide a letter which assures the suppliers of Towan Ltd that all future payments will be made on time in accordance with normal trade terms.

Identify and explain the relevant fundamental principle of ethical behaviour that is threatened by this situation.

**9.10\***

You are a trainee accountant working for King Accountants. You have been asked to help in the preparation of the financial statements of Porth Ltd, a manufacturer of surfboards, for the year ended 31 December 20-1.

The directors of Porth Ltd approach you saying that they wish to reduce the company's tax charge to the minimum possible. They ask you to implement ways to achieve this, one suggestion from them being to reduce the valuation of closing inventory.

Identify and explain the relevant fundamental principle of ethical behaviour that is threatened by this situation.

**9.11\***

Brenda is a professional accountant who works as a sole-practitioner. One of her larger clients, Avon Holidays Ltd, has recently taken over one of its rivals, Severn Leisure Ltd. Avon Holidays Ltd intends to continue to operate Severn Leisure Ltd as a separate entity. They have asked Brenda to take on Severn Leisure Ltd as a client. If she accepts this offer it will mean that the combined fee income from these two companies will be 30% of her total fee income.

**(a)**     Explain which of Brenda's fundamental principles is most threatened by this situation and the type of threat that she is facing.

**(b)**     Should Brenda accept the additional work?

**9.12\***

Lesley is a professional accountant who works for the accountancy partnership of Gunn and Rood. She has recently returned from a week's holiday to find a thank you card on her desk from Matt, the finance director of one of her clients. The card includes the following note together with a £100 gift voucher.

> Hi Lesley,
>
> Thank you for all your hard work on our financial statements this year. We are delighted that you decided not to raise the significant reduction in our allowance for doubtful debts with the partners at Gunn and Rood. This has meant that our profit for the year is in line with the forecast we gave our shareholders, rather than much lower as it would have been without your help.
>
> Please find enclosed a gift voucher as a small thank you.
>
> Best wishes
>
> Matt
>
> PS I would appreciate it if we could keep this arrangement between us as it may not look good for you if the partners at Gunn and Rood knew about this.

**(a)** If Lesley knowingly reduced the allowance for doubtful debts, explain which **two** of Lesley's fundamental ethical principles are most threatened by this situation.

**(b)** What type of threat does Lesley face to her fundamental ethical principles?

**(c)** If Lesley genuinely believed that the allowance for doubtful debts was correct, are there any reasons that she cannot accept the gift voucher from Matt?

**9.13**

Paul Bowral is a professional accountant who works for Sebel Ltd, a manufacturing company. The managing director of Sebel Ltd, Tom Hardy, has recently leased a hospitality box at the local premiership rugby club for the whole season. Tom has said that Paul, a keen rugby supporter, can use the box for the cup final if he works late for the next week to ensure that the financial statements are completed on time.

**(a)** Explain what type of threat Paul faces to his fundamental ethical principles.

**(b)** Explain which **two** of Paul's fundamental principles are threatened in this situation.

**(c)** What safeguards can he put in place to eliminate this threat or reduce it to an acceptable level?

**9.14** Tom is a professional accountant who works for Star Software Ltd. His partner, Johanna, is an accountant who works for Berrima Ltd, a company that makes computer games. The managing director of Berrima Ltd has recently announced that she wishes to retire and is looking for a buyer for the company.

The managing director at Star Software Ltd has asked Tom to find out from Johanna what sort of price she thinks her managing director will accept for the business. He adds that Tom and Johanna will be most welcome to use his holiday cottage in Cornwall if his bid for Berrima Ltd is successful.

(a) Identify which of Tom and Johanna's fundamental ethical principles are threatened by this situation.

(b) What action could Tom take in these circumstances?

**9.15\*** Sam is a recently qualified professional accountant in business working for Goulburn Ltd. She has been asked by her manager to prepare some complex depreciation calculations on properties owned by the business which have recently been revalued. She has not carried out work like this before.

State **two** safeguards that Sam should consider to reduce the threats to her fundamental ethical principle of professional competence and due care.

**9.16** Edward is a newly qualified accountant who has recently started work with Thirl & Mere, a medium-sized firm of accountants. On his curriculum vitae (CV) Edward stated that he has experience in completing VAT returns when in fact he has only ever completed a VAT return in his professional accounting examinations. Edward has been asked to take responsibility for completing the quarterly VAT return for one of Thirl & Mere's larger clients.

What should Edward do in these circumstances?

**9.17** Will, an accountant in practice, has been asked by Rachel, one of his clients, to provide her with some financial information about another of his clients, who is one of Rachel's customers. Rachel is currently in a legal dispute with her customer.

Explain whether Will can provide Rachel with any information about his other client.

**9.18\*** Michael is a professional accountant who works for Botany Ltd, an audit firm. His manager has recently overhead Michael in the pub telling a friend all about a confidential matter at work. The manager has told Michael that he will now face disciplinary procedures because he has behaved unethically.

Decide whether or not each of the following organisations can or cannot bring disciplinary procedures against Michael for his unethical behaviour.

|   |   | Can | Cannot |
|---|---|---|---|
| **A** | The Department for Business, Energy and Industrial Strategy | | |
| **B** | Botany Ltd | | |
| **C** | Michael's professional body | | |

Select **one** option for each organisation.

**9.19\*** Julia Steyne is a professional accountant who works as a sole practitioner. One of her larger clients is Corso Ltd, which runs a chain of fast-food outlets. Julia provides accountancy services to Corso Ltd, including payroll services.

Today Tom, an accounts assistant at Julia's practice, asks to speak to Julia. He has been processing the payroll for Corso Ltd and has noticed that it is paying a number of its employees at rates below the national minimum wage. He is concerned that Corso Ltd is acting illegally.

What steps should Julia take to deal with this matter?

**9.20** John Kerr is a professional accountant who works for the accountancy partnership of Maxwell and Payne. John is responsible for preparing the financial statements of New Glaze Ltd, a double-glazing business. From the financial statements of New Glaze Ltd that have just been prepared, John has become aware that the company has liquidity problems.

A national double-glazing company, Clear Glass Ltd, has expressed an interest in buying New Glaze Ltd. However, Clear Glass Ltd requires assurances about the liquidity of New Glaze Ltd. The directors of New Glaze Ltd have asked John to confirm to the potential buyers that it has no liquidity problems as, without such confirmation, the sale to Clear Glass Ltd will not go through.

What steps should John take to deal with this matter?

**9.21*** What is the role of a company's remuneration committee?

| | | |
|---|---|---|
| **A** | To negotiate with the executive directors in order to agree their remuneration | |
| **B** | To review the salary and benefits payments for senior management of the company | |
| **C** | To circulate the minutes of its meetings to the company's directors | |
| **D** | To review the salary and benefits payments for all staff of the company, except for the executive directors | |

**9.22** For a limited company, explain what is meant by:

- Corporate governance

- Corporate social responsibility

**9.23** Explain the steps that an employed accountant should take to deal with unethical behaviour or illegal acts committed by an employer?

# Management Accounting

This section of the book develops further the management accounting techniques you have acquired in year 1 studies. The areas it covers include:

- features of management accounting – how it differs from financial accounting

- the preparation and use of budgets – their role in the planning and control of a business

- marginal, absorption and activity based costing – selecting and applying the cost concepts to be used in decision-making

- standard costing and variance analysis – the purpose of standard costing, including the calculation and interpretation of variances

- capital investment appraisal techniques – payback and net present value

# 10 MANAGEMENT ACCOUNTING: THE USE OF BUDGETS

Management accounting differs from financial accounting in that it produces different reports and statements – although both types of accounting obtain their data from the same sources of accounting information carried out by the business over a period of time. In this chapter we recap on the features of management accounting, which have been discussed in Chapter 1 (page 16).

The chapter also looks at a number of budgets that can be used by businesses to help with planning and control. In particular we focus on budgets for:

- sales
- production
- purchases
- labour
- cash

## FEATURES OF MANAGEMENT ACCOUNTING

The diagram on the next page illustrates the main features of management accounting, contrasted with financial accounting:

Management accounting is very much about providing information to help with:

- decision-making – short-term and the use of marginal costing, long-term and the use of capital investment appraisal
- planning – the preparation of budgets
- control – including the use of standard costing

Information is also provided in management accounting reports that help with setting prices for products being sold.

See also Chapter 1 (page 16) where the differences between these two types of accounting were considered.

| MANAGEMENT ACCOUNTING | FINANCIAL ACCOUNTING |
|---|---|
| Focus is on the preparation of reports to help the management of a business with decision-making, planning, and control. | Focus is on accounting records and the preparation of financial statements. |
| Reports are based on the recent past and projections for the future. | Financial statements are based on business transactions carried out over a period of time. |
| Reports are set out in a format that meets the needs of the business, with no legal requirement to produce them. Apart from checking the reports, there is no requirement for auditing. | Reports are in a set format – often required by law – to comply with the Companies Act, accounting standards, HM Revenue and Customs, etc. The financial statements of limited companies may be required to be audited by external auditors. |
| Reports are prepared primarily for internal stakeholders such as management, employees, owners; some external stakeholders – such as lenders – may see the reports. | Reports are prepared for internal and external stakeholders such as shareholders, suppliers, lenders, government and, for companies, are filed at Companies House where they are in the public domain. |
| Information is prepared as frequently as circumstances demand; speed is often vital as information may go out-of-date quickly. | Generally timing is not critical for preparing financial statements, although once a year is customary. |

# USING BUDGETS IN A BUSINESS

**A budget is a financial plan for a business, prepared in advance and generally covering a period of up to 12 months.**

Budgets are part of the planning aspect of a business and are prepared for specific sections of the business: these budgets can then be controlled by a budget holder, who may be the manager or supervisor of the specific section. Such budgets include:

- sales budget
- production budget
- purchases budget
- labour budget
- cash budget

The end result of the budgeting process is often the production of a master budget, which takes the form of budgeted financial statements – budgeted income statement and statement of financial position (a budgeted statement of cash flows is often also included in the master budget). The master budget is the 'master plan' which shows how all the other budgets 'work together'. The diagram on the next page shows how all the budgets are linked to each other.

The starting point for the budgeting process is generally the sales budget, because it is usually sales that determine the other activities of the business. Consequently the order in which the budgets will be prepared is usually:

- **sales budget** – what can the business expect to sell in the coming months, and how much money will be received?
- **production budget** – how can the business make/supply all the items which it plans to sell?
- **purchases budget** – what does the business need to buy to make/supply the goods it plans to sell, and at what cost?
- **labour budget** – what will be the cost of labour to make/supply the goods?
- **cash budget** – what money will be flowing in and out of the bank account? – will an overdraft be needed?
- **master budget** – a summary of all the budgets to provide a budgeted income statement and statement of financial position

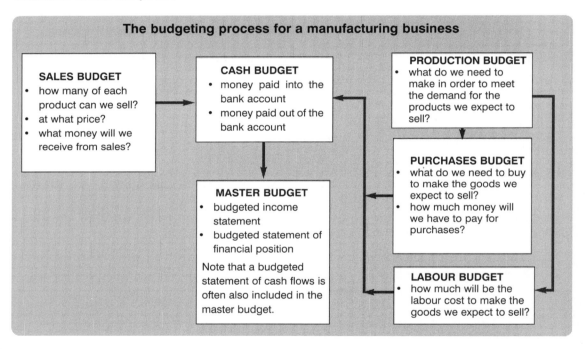

### The budgeting process for a manufacturing business

## Sales Budget

**A sales budget is used to estimate sales in units and revenue. It is linked to the production budget and the master budget.**

The sales budget is often the starting point for the budgeting process in any type of business. It is the plan which will project the sales of:

- products made by a **manufacturing** business, eg cars, DVDs, breakfast cereals
- services provided by a **service** business, eg holidays, educational courses, bus and train journeys

It is from the sales budget that a business is able to estimate what it needs to produce, thus giving a link between the sales and production budgets. Sales budget also links to the master budget – when the sales figure is used in the budgeted income statement.

## planning the sales budget

The accuracy of the sales budget is critical for the success of the business. If a business overestimates sales, it will be left with unsold goods or under-utilised services; if sales are underestimated, then customers will be lost to competitors. Both overestimating and underestimating sales can lose money. While budgeting is not an exact science, and is unlikely to be 100% accurate, it is essential that as much accurate information as possible is gathered; this can include:

- details of past sales performance, including seasonal variations – available within the business
- present sales figures – up-to-date figures from sales representatives
- what the competition is doing – estimates of market share
- assessment of whether the market is expanding or declining
- forecasts made – by sales representatives and market researchers
- trading conditions – the economic climate and the business cycle

A sales budget will start off by estimating the number of units to be sold over the next year and then applying a selling price to produce an estimate of the income figure in money terms.

An example of a sales budget follows:

### sales budget

| | January | February | March | April | May | June |
|---|---|---|---|---|---|---|
| Sales units | 500 | 500 | 550 | 550 | 600 | 600 |
| Sales value | £5,000 | £5,000 | £5,500 | £5,500 | £6,000 | £6,000 |

Note how the budget uses:

**budget periods** – the subdivision of the budget into monthly, four-weekly (which divides a 52-week year into 13 four-weekly periods), or weekly

**budget headings** – the subdivision of the budget into sales units and sales value

## PRODUCTION BUDGET

**A production budget shows the level of production in units needed to meet the demand for expected sales and identifies any production problems that may need to be resolved. It is linked to the purchases and labour budgets.**

When a business has established its sales budget it is then in a position to work out its production budget (for a manufacturing business), or its operating budget (for a service). Note that production/operating budgets are normally prepared using units of output (rather than money amounts).

A production budget links to purchases budget – which records the materials that need to be bought – and the labour budget – which shows the labour hours and the cost needed to produce the goods.

## planning the production budget

When planning a production/operating budget, management must gather together information about the business' resources and consider a range of external factors in order to assess what can and cannot be achieved. These include:

- **timing**     When during the year are the products required? Are there any seasonal fluctuations (Christmas cards, fireworks) which will produce uneven demands on production facilities? Will the business need to hold quantities of products in advance?

- **capacity**     Can the existing production facilities cope with the expected demand? Will new non-current assets be needed? Should some work be subcontracted to other businesses?

- **labour cost**   Does the business have the right number of staff with the necessary skills? Will more staff be needed? Will there need to be training? Will overtime need to be worked, or is an additional shift required?

- **materials**     Can the right quality and quantity of materials be obtained at the right price?

When all of this information has been gathered and analysed, the business should then be in a position to prepare the production budget, taking into account:

- the projected monthly sales (in units)
- the number of units of goods at the beginning and end of each month

The production budget is usually prepared in terms of units of production. Some of the factors listed above will need to be considered, for example:

- there may be a maximum level of inventory that can be held in the warehouse/stores
- management may require that each month's closing inventory is a set percentage of next month's sales

## WORKED EXAMPLE: PRODUCTION BUDGET

This production budget (in units) has been prepared where there are the following constraints:
- each month's closing inventory is to be 20% of the following month's sales units
- the maximum capacity of the warehouse is 100 units

## production budget

| | January | February | March | April | May | June |
|---|---|---|---|---|---|---|
| | units | units | units | units | units | units |
| Sales | 250 | 300 | 280 | 600 | 325 | 300 |
| Opening inventory | (50) | (60) | (56) | (100) | (65) | (60) |
| Closing inventory | 60 | 56 | *100 | 65 | 60 | **65 |
| Production | 260 | 296 | 324 | 565 | 320 | 305 |

 *   maximum capacity of the warehouse

 **   sales in July are estimated to be 325 units, so closing inventory at the end of June is budgeted to be 65 units

**Tutorial note:**
- To calculate the production units for each month, deduct the opening inventory from sales and add the closing inventory. For example, in January:

| | | Units |
|---|---|---|
| | sales | 250 |
| *less* | opening inventory | 50 |
| *add* | closing inventory | 60 |
| *equals* | production | 260 |

Opening inventory is deducted because it is used for sales for the month – for example in January, if there were to be no closing inventory, production would need to be 250 units – 50 units opening inventory = 200 units; however, closing inventory is 60 units, so production needs to be 260 units.

## benefits of a production budget

The use of a production budget enables a business to:

- identify the production capacity available
- schedule resources – eg cash, materials, labour – effectively
- meet sales demand
- make best use of spare capacity

# PURCHASES BUDGET

**A purchases budget shows the number and value of the goods that need to be bought in order to meet the demands of the production department. It is linked to the master budget.**

Purchases budget is a development of the sales and production budgets. It is used to work out the level of purchases that will have to be made:

- either, to meet the requirements for materials in the production process of a manufacturing business
- or, to provide the goods to be sold in a shop

Purchases budget is expressed in terms of units of goods to be bought, together with the purchases cost.

Purchases budget links to the master budget – where the purchases figure is used in the budgeted income statement.

## planning the purchases budget

The layout for this budget is very similar to that for production, using sales, opening inventory and closing inventory to calculate purchases in units. A bottom row shows the money amounts of purchases.

As with the production budget, there may be factors to consider when preparing the purchases budget, for example:

- there may be a maximum level of inventory that can be held in the warehouse/stores
- management may require that each month's closing inventory is a set percentage of next month's sales
- there must be a link to the production budget so that sufficient goods are bought to meet the requirements of the production department

## WORKED EXAMPLE: PURCHASES BUDGET

This purchases budget has been prepared where there are the following constraints:
- each month's closing inventory is to be 50% of the following month's sales units
- the maximum capacity of the warehouse is 350 units
- the purchase cost of each unit is £10

Sales units are shown in the budget; sales in July are estimated to be 640 units.

### purchases budget

|  | January | February | March | April | May | June |
|---|---|---|---|---|---|---|
|  | units | units | units | units | units | units |
| Sales | 500 | 550 | 600 | 780 | 570 | 620 |
| Opening inventory | (250) | (275) | (300) | (350) | (285) | (310) |
| Closing inventory | 275 | 300 | *350 | 285 | 310 | **320 |
| Purchases | 525 | 575 | 650 | 715 | 595 | 630 |
| Purchases cost | £5,250 | £5,750 | £6,500 | £7,150 | £5,950 | £6,300 |

\*   maximum capacity of the warehouse

\*\*  sales in July are estimated to be 640 units, so closing inventory at the end of June is budgeted to be 320 units

**Tutorial notes:**
- To calculate the number of units to be purchased each month, deduct the opening inventory from sales and add the closing inventory.
- The row for purchases cost is included in the purchases budget and is the number of units to be bought multiplied by the purchase cost of each unit.

# Labour Budget

**A labour budget is used to plan and control the labour hours and labour costs of production-line employees.**

A labour budget links with the production budget to ensure that a business will have the right number of labour hours available for the planned level of production. It is not only the right number of hours available, but other factors to consider include:

- are staff of the correct grade available?
- do we need to train any staff to bring them up to the grade needed?
- do we need to recruit more staff?
- do we have too many staff and, if so, do we need to consider redundancies?

The use of a labour budget allows any shortfalls in labour hours to be identified so that corrective action can be taken. Shortfalls in the right number and grade of staff available may mean that labour costs increase because, in order to keep production going, it is necessary to:

- hire in temporary staff
- pay overtime
- work extra shifts
- use more skilled and more expensive staff than is necessary

## planning the labour budget

Working from the production budget the number of labour hours to make each unit of output needs to be determined. At the same time the grade of staff needed to carry out the work and their pay rate needs to be known. If there are any pay rises expected to be paid within the budget period, these should be allowed for when preparing the budget.

A labour budget consists of the number of labour hours expected for each budget period – eg weekly, four-weekly or monthly. The rate paid to staff is then used to calculate an estimate of the labour cost.

An example of a labour budget follows on the next page:

**labour budget**

|  | January | February | March | April | May | June |
|---|---|---|---|---|---|---|
| Labour hours | 400 | 450 | 450 | 500 | 500 | 450 |
| Labour cost | £6,000 | £6,750 | £6,750 | £7,500 | £7,500 | £6,750 |

An adaptation of labour budget can be used to show the:

- labour hours required to meet planned production
- labour hours available
- any surplus or shortfall of labour hours

The surplus or shortfall indicates that action needs to be taken:

- a surplus of hours available in some months could be used to manufacture inventory in advance of months when the budget shows a shortfall, subject to the costs of manufacturing and storing the extra inventory
- a surplus of hours available could indicate that the business is employing too many staff for its production needs, and should consider reducing overtime, cutting back on the number of shifts, laying off temporary staff, or making some staff redundant
- a shortfall of hours available could indicate that the business needs to consider increasing overtime, working additional shifts, taking on temporary staff, recruiting permanent staff, or training other staff to work on this production

An example of a labour budget showing surpluses and shortfalls of labour hours follows:

**labour budget**

|  | January | February | March | April | May | June |
|---|---|---|---|---|---|---|
| Production in units | 200 | 225 | 225 | 250 | 250 | 225 |
| Labour hours at 2 hours per unit | 400 | 450 | 450 | 500 | 500 | 450 |
| Labour hours available | 450 | 450 | 450 | 450 | 500 | 500 |
| Surplus/(shortfall) of labour hours | 50 | – | – | (50) | – | 50 |

- the surplus hours in January could be used to make extra units to be held in inventory until April
- the surplus hours in June could be used to build up inventory before employees begin their summer holidays

## benefits of a labour budget

The use of a labour budget enables a business to:

• plan and control the cost of labour

• identify any surplus or shortfall in the number of labour hours available for planned production, allowing corrective action to be taken and changes made to overtime and shift working

• plan labour requirements for future production, identifying when more or fewer labour hours will be needed, and linking to recruitment or redundancy issues for the Human Resources Department

# CASH BUDGET

**A cash budget details the forecast cash/bank receipts and payments, usually on a month-by-month basis, for the next three, six or twelve months, in order to show the forecast bank balance at the end of each month throughout the budget period.**

Note that, although we call it a cash budget, it includes both cash and bank receipts and payments.

From the cash budget, the managers of a business can decide what action to take when a surplus of cash is shown to be available or, as is more likely, when a bank overdraft needs to be arranged.

## layout of a cash budget

A format for a cash budget, with example figures, follows.

| MIKE ANDERSON, TRADING AS 'ART SUPPLIES' CASH BUDGET FOR THE SIX MONTHS ENDING 30 JUNE 20-8 | | | | | | |
|---|---|---|---|---|---|---|
| | Jan £ | Feb £ | Mar £ | Apr £ | May £ | Jun £ |
| **Receipts** | | | | | | |
| Capital introduced | 20,000 | | | | | |
| Trade receivables | – | – | 3,000 | 6,000 | 6,000 | 10,500 |
| Total receipts for month | 20,000 | – | 3,000 | 6,000 | 6,000 | 10,500 |
| **Payments** | | | | | | |
| Non-current assets | 8,000 | | | | | |
| Inventory | 5,000 | | | | | |
| Trade payables | – | 2,000 | 4,000 | 4,000 | 7,000 | 7,000 |
| Operating expenses | 1,600 | 1,600 | 1,600 | 1,600 | 1,600 | 1,600 |
| Drawings | 1,000 | 1,000 | 1,000 | 1,000 | 1,000 | 1,000 |
| Total payments for month | 15,600 | 4,600 | 6,600 | 6,600 | 9,600 | 9,600 |
| Net cash flow | 4,400 | (4,600) | (3,600) | (600) | (3,600) | 900 |
| Opening bank balance (overdraft) | – | 4,400 | (200) | (3,800) | (4,400) | (8,000) |
| Closing bank balance (overdraft) | 4,400 | (200) | (3,800) | (4,400) | (8,000) | (7,100) |

## sections of a cash budget

A cash budget consists of three main sections:

- receipts for the month
- payments for the month
- summary of bank account

**Receipts** are analysed to show the amount of money that is expected to be received from cash sales, trade receivables, sale of non-current assets, capital introduced/issue of shares, loans received etc.

**Payments** show how much money is expected to be paid in respect of cash purchases, trade payables, expenses (often described in cash budgets as operating expenses), purchases of non-current assets, repayment of capital/shares and loans. Note that non-cash expenses (such as depreciation and doubtful debts) are not shown in the cash budget.

The **summary of the bank account** at the bottom of the cash budget shows **net cash flow** (total receipts less total payments) added to the bank balance at the beginning of the month, and resulting in the estimated closing bank balance or overdraft at the end of the month. An overdraft is shown in brackets.

## benefits of a cash budget

The use of a cash budget enables a business to:

- monitor its cash resources
- plan future expenditure, eg the financing of new non-current assets
- control costs and revenues to ensure that either:
  - a bank overdraft is avoided (so saving interest and charges payable), or
  - a bank overdraft or loan can be arranged in advance
- reschedule payments where necessary to avoid bank borrowing, eg delay the purchase of non-current assets
- co-ordinate the activities of the various sections of the business, eg the production department buys in materials not only to meet the expected sales of the sales department but also at a time when there is cash available
- communicate the overall aims of the business to the various sections and to check that the cash will be available to meet their needs
- identify any possible cash surpluses in advance and take steps to invest the surplus on a short-term basis (so earning interest)

# CASH FLOWS FROM TRADE RECEIVABLES AND TO TRADE PAYABLES

Within a cash budget it is necessary to take note of the timing of receipts from trade receivables and payments to trade payables. This is because many businesses buy their materials and sell their products on credit terms – the payments and receipts may well not be in the same months as indicated by the purchases and sales budgets. The Worked Examples on the next pages show how payments and receipts can be calculated.

## trade receivables

The period of credit allowed to customers – the time between making a sale and receiving payment – affects the cash flow of the business as this period is being financed by the seller. It is important that, as well as having good products and being able to sell them, cash flows in from customers are received without delay and by the due date. It is a shortage of cash that causes most business failures.

Receipts from customers link to the cash budget, which records receipts from trade receivables – and the master budget – where the amount of trade receivables is shown as an asset on the forecast statement of financial position.

For example, a business has agreed trade terms of 30 days with its customers. This means that sales made in January should be paid for in February, the sales made in February should be paid for in March, etc. The cash budget needs to record these receipts from credit sales for the month when it is expected they will be received.

Note that, for trade receivables, it may be necessary to allow for cash discount allowed and irrecoverable debts – these will affect the expected cash receipts shown in the cash budget.

## WORKED EXAMPLE: RECEIPTS FROM TRADE RECEIVABLES

### situation

You are to calculate receipts from trade receivables for January to June using the following information:
- the amount of trade receivables at 1 January is £14,000
- credit sales are budgeted to be £30,000 per month from January to March, and £40,000 per month from April to June
- half of the trade receivables pay in the month of sale and take advantage of 2% cash discount allowed
- the remainder of trade receivables pay in the month after sale, without cash discount – however, 3% of these will not pay and should be regarded as irrecoverable debts

### solution

### receipts from trade receivables

|  | January £ | February £ | March £ | April £ | May £ | June £ |
|---|---|---|---|---|---|---|
| Month of sale | 15,000 | 15,000 | 15,000 | 20,000 | 20,000 | 20,000 |
| Cash discount | (300) | (300) | (300) | (400) | (400) | (400) |
| Following month | 14,000 | 15,000 | 15,000 | 15,000 | 20,000 | 20,000 |
| Irrecoverable debts | (420) | (450) | (450) | (450) | (600) | (600) |
| Receipts for month | 28,280 | 29,250 | 29,250 | 34,150 | 39,000 | 39,000 |

Note that the trade receivables figure for the budgeted statement of financial position at 30 June will be £19,400 (ie £20,000 – £600 irrecoverable debt).

## trade payables

An important aspect of running a business is to ensure that trade receivables are paid on time. Delaying payment beyond the due date may well mean that suppliers refuse to deliver any further goods, which will lead to production problems and have an effect on the whole business. Suppliers usually offer a period of credit, and so the period between taking delivery of the goods and making payment for them gives the buyer a period when its purchases are being financed by the seller. Nevertheless, the buyer needs to ensure that cash is available in the bank account to meet payments to trade receivables as they fall due.

Payments to suppliers link to the cash budget, which records payments to trade payables – and the master budget – where the amount of trade payables is shown as a liability on the forecast statement of financial position.

For example, a business has agreed trade terms of 60 days with its suppliers. This means that purchases made in January should be paid for in March, the purchases made in February should be paid for in April, etc. The cash budget needs to record these payments for credit purchases for the month when it is expected to be made.

Note that for trade payables, it may be necessary to allow for cash discount received, which will affect the expected cash payments shown in the cash budget.

### WORKED EXAMPLE: PAYMENTS TO TRADE PAYABLES

**situation**

You are to calculate payments to trade payables for July to December using the following information:
- the amount of trade payables at 1 July is £12,000
- credit purchases are budgeted to be £25,000 per month in July and August, £30,000 per month in September and October, and £34,000 per month in November and December
- half of the trade payables allow cash discount of 3% and are paid in the month of purchase
- the remainder of trade payables are paid in the month after sale, without cash discount

**solution**

#### payments to trade payables

|  | July | August | September | October | November | December |
|---|---|---|---|---|---|---|
|  | £ | £ | £ | £ | £ | £ |
| Month of purchase | 12,500 | 12,500 | 15,000 | 15,000 | 17,000 | 17,000 |
| Cash discount | (375) | (375) | (450) | (450) | (510) | (510) |
| Following month | 12,000 | 12,500 | 12,500 | 15,000 | 15,000 | 17,000 |
| Payments for month | 24,125 | 24,625 | 27,050 | 29,550 | 31,490 | 33,490 |

Note that the trade payables figure for the budgeted statement of financial position at 31 December will be £17,000.

# MASTER BUDGET

A master budget takes the form of budgeted financial statements – budgeted income statement and statement of financial position. (A budgeted statement of cash flows is also often included in the master budget.)

A cash budget does not indicate the profits (or losses) being made by a business. It does not follow that a cash budget which reveals an increasing bank balance necessarily indicates a profitable business. A **master budget** is the next logical step once all other budgets, including the cash budget, have been prepared.

## WORKED EXAMPLE: MASTER BUDGET

### situation

A friend of yours, Mike Anderson, has recently been made redundant from his job as a sales representative for an arts and crafts company. Mike has decided to set up in business on his own selling art supplies to shops and art societies. He plans to invest £20,000 of his savings into the new business. He has a number of good business contacts, and is confident that his firm will do well. He thinks that some additional finance will be required in the short term and plans to approach his bank for this.

Mike has prepared a cash budget for his new business (see page 225) and asks for your assistance in producing a budgeted income statement for the next six months, together with a budgeted statement of financial position at 30 June 20-8.

He provides the following information:

- The business, which is to be called 'Art Supplies' will commence in January 20-8.

- Non-current assets costing £8,000 will be bought in early January. These will be paid for immediately and are expected to have a five-year life, at the end of which they will be worthless.

- An initial purchase of goods costing £5,000 will be bought and paid for at the beginning of January, and will be maintained at this level.

- Monthly purchases of inventory will then be made at a level sufficient to replace forecast sales for that month, ie the goods he expects to sell in January will be replaced by purchases made in January, and so on.

- Forecast monthly sales are:

| January | February | March | April | May | June |
|---------|----------|-------|-------|-----|------|
| £3,000 | £6,000 | £6,000 | £10,500 | £10,500 | £10,500 |

- The selling price of goods is fixed at the cost price plus 50 per cent; for example, the goods he expects to sell in January for £3,000 will have cost him £2,000 (two-thirds of the selling price), ie his mark-up is 50%.

- To encourage sales, he will allow two months' credit to customers; however, only one month's credit will be received from suppliers (but the initial purchase will be paid for immediately).

- Operating expenses of the business, including rent of premises, but excluding depreciation of non-current assets, are estimated at £1,600 per month and are paid for in the month in which they are incurred.

- Mike intends to take drawings of £1,000 each month in cash from the business.

## solution

| MIKE ANDERSON, TRADING AS 'ART SUPPLIES' BUDGETED INCOME STATEMENT FOR THE SIX MONTHS ENDING 30 JUNE 20-8 | | |
|---|---|---|
| | £ | £ |
| **Revenue** | | 46,500 |
| Opening inventory | 5,000 | |
| Purchases £46,500 x 2/3 | 31,000 | |
| | 36,000 | |
| Less Closing inventory | 5,000 | |
| Cost of sales | | 31,000 |
| **Gross profit** | | 15,500 |
| Less expenses: | | |
| Operating expenses | 9,600 | |
| Depreciation of non-current assets | | |
| (£8,000 ÷ 5 years) ÷ 2, ie six months | 800 | |
| | | 10,400 |
| **Profit for the period** | | 5,100 |

**MIKE ANDERSON, TRADING AS 'ART SUPPLIES'**
**BUDGETED STATEMENT OF FINANCIAL POSITION AS AT 30 JUNE 20-8**

| | £ | £ | £ |
|---|---|---|---|
| **Non-current Assets** | | | |
| At cost | | | 8,000 |
| Less Depreciation | | | 800 |
| Carrying amount | | | 7,200 |
| | | | |
| **Current Assets** | | | |
| Inventory | | 5,000 | |
| Trade receivables  £10,500 x 2 months | | 21,000 | |
| | | 26,000 | |
| **Less Current Liabilities** | | | |
| Trade payables | 7,000 | | |
| Bank overdraft | 7,100 | | |
| | | 14,100 | |
| **Net Current Assets** | | | 11,900 |
| **NET ASSETS** | | | 19,100 |
| | | | |
| **FINANCED BY** | | | |
| **Capital** | | | |
| Opening capital | | | 20,000 |
| Add Profit for the period | | | 5,100 |
| | | | 25,100 |
| Less Drawings | | | 6,000 |
| | | | 19,100 |

Notes:
* purchases are two-thirds of the sales values (because selling price is cost price plus 50 per cent)
* customers pay two months after sale, ie trade receivables from January settle in March
* suppliers are paid one month after purchase, ie trade payables from January are paid in February

**Points to note when preparing budgeted financial statements:**

* The revenue figure used is the total amount of goods sold, whether paid for or not (sales made, but not yet paid for, are recorded as trade receivables in the statement of financial position).

* Likewise, the figure for purchases is the total of goods bought, with amounts not yet paid for recorded as trade payables in the statement of financial position.

* Depreciation, which *never* appears in the cash budget, is shown amongst the expenses in the income statement, and deducted from the cost of the non-current asset in the statement of financial position. (Note that, in the example above, depreciation is for a period of six months.)

## benefits of the master budget

The master budget involves preparation of budgeted financial statements – budgeted income statement and statement of financial position. These benefit a business in a number of ways:

- the budgeted profit can be calculated and compared with the actual profit of the previous year
- the budgeted profit shows the effect of changes in the selling price of products, the volume of units sold, the buying price, and in expenses
- management of a business can take action by reviewing their selling prices, volume of sales, buying prices, and overhead expenses
- the actual gross and profit for the period can be compared with the budgeted profit, and any differences can be investigated

## differences between cash and profit

While a cash budget shows the budgeted bank balance during the budget period, the master budget shows the budgeted profit for the budget period. Sometimes people in business get confused between 'cash' and 'profit' and may say: "I am making a profit, but why is my bank overdraft increasing?"

The difference between cash and profit is:

- cash is money in the bank or held as physical cash (eg in a cash till)
- profit is a calculated figure which shows the surplus of income over expenditure for the period; it takes note of adjustments for accruals and prepayments and non-cash items such as depreciation and provision for doubtful debts; it does not include capital expenditure (ie the purchase of non-current assets, or owner's drawings/dividends).

The reasons why a business can be making a profit but its bank balance is reducing (or its bank overdraft is increasing) include:

- capital expenditure – the purchase of non-current assets reduces cash but profit is affected only by the amount of depreciation on the asset
- increase in trade receivables – if more goods are being sold, this should lead to an increase in profit but, until trade receivables pay, there is no benefit to the bank balance
- decrease in trade payables – if trade payables are paid earlier than usual there will be no effect on profit but the bank balance will reduce (or a bank overdraft will increase)
- increase in inventory – if more inventory is purchased there will be an increase in profit as it is sold, but paying for inventory will reduce the money at bank (or increase an overdraft)
- prepayment of expenses at the year end – as the prepayment is an expense for next year, early payment will have no effect on the current year's profit, but the bank balance will be affected by the payment
- repayment of a loan – this has no effect on profits (although loan interest may be reduced), but the bank balance will be affected by the repayment
- drawings/dividends paid to owners – will have no effect on profit, but the bank balance will be affected by the payment

Clearly the above will work in reverse for a business that is making reduced profits (or losses) but whose bank balance is increasing (or its bank overdraft is reducing).

Note that a statement of cash flows (see Chapter 7) demonstrates the link between profit and changes in cash. The master budget often also includes a budgeted statement of financial position.

# CHAPTER SUMMARY

- Management accounting focuses on the preparation of reports to help the management of a business with decision-making, planning, and control.

- Management reports are set out in a format that meets the needs of the business and are prepared primarily for internal stakeholders – management, employees, owners.

- A budget is a financial plan for a business, prepared in advance and generally covering a period of up to 12 months.

- Budgets are prepared for each section of the business, eg sales, production, purchases, labour, cash.

- Responsibility for budgets is given to managers and supervisors – the budget holders.

- The master budget is compiled from the separate budgets of a business.

- The master budget comprises:
  - budgeted income statement
  - budgeted statement of financial position
  - a budgeted statement of cash flows is also often included in the master budget

In the next chapter we look at absorption costing and activity based costing, and compare them with marginal costing. We also see how selling prices of products are calculated when using these two methods of costing.

# QUESTIONS

visit
www.osbornebooks.co.uk
to take an online test

An asterisk (*) after the question number means that the answer is given at the end of this book.

**10.1*** Which of the following statements describe features of financial accounting and which describe features of management accounting?

| Statement | Financial accounting | Management accounting |
|---|---|---|
| Reports relate to what has happened in the past | | |
| May be required by law | | |
| Gives estimates of costs and income for the future | | |
| May be available in the public domain | | |
| Gives up-to-date reports which can be used for controlling the business | | |
| Is used by people outside the business | | |
| Is designed to meet the requirements of people inside the business | | |
| Shows details of the expected costs of materials, labour and expenses | | |
| Records accurate amounts, not estimates | | |

**10.2*** The following budgeted information is available for Product E for the month of August:

- finished goods inventory at 1 August      2,500 units
- direct labour hours per unit      2 hours
- budgeted sales of Product E      5,000 units
- decrease in finished goods inventory      300 units

How many direct labour hours will be required for Product E during August?

| | | |
|---|---|---|
| **A** | 10,000 hours | |
| **B** | 9,400 hours | |
| **C** | 10,600 hours | |
| **D** | 5,000 hours | |

**10.3**

The following budgeted information is available for Product D for the month of July:

- quantity of material per unit of Product D          4 kg
- budgeted sales of Product D                                 2,000 units
- decrease in inventory of material                        1,500 kg
- increase in finished goods inventory of Product D    200 units

How many kilos of material will be purchased during July?

| A | 8,000 kg | |
|---|----------|---|
| B | 10,300 kg | |
| C | 7,300 kg | |
| D | 8,800 kg | |

**10.4**

Fence Right Ltd makes metal fence panels with built-in posts. The production manager gives you the following information in order to produce a production budget for the six months of January to June:

- Demand is expected to be 1,000 panels in January. In February this should increase by 20% and then, for March, April and May should increase by 5% each month based on the demand for the previous month. In June and July demand is expected to be 1,200 panels each month.

- The inventory to be held at the end of each month is to be maintained at a level of 25% of the following month's sales, but the maximum capacity of the warehouse is 325 panels.

- The inventory at the start of January is 250 panels.

**REQUIRED:**

Prepare a production budget for the months of January to June (where necessary, round up to the nearest whole fence panel).

| | January units | February units | March units | April units | May units | June units |
|---|---|---|---|---|---|---|
| Sales | | | | | | |
| Opening inventory | | | | | | |
| Closing inventory | | | | | | |
| Production | | | | | | |

**10.5\*** **(a)** **You are to** calculate receipts from trade receivables for April to September using the following information:

- the amount of trade receivables at 1 April is £10,000

- credit sales are budgeted to be £25,000 per month from April to July, and £30,000 per month in August and September

- half of the trade receivables pay in the month of sale and take advantage of 3% cash discount allowed

- the remainder of trade receivables pay in the month after sale, without cash discount – however, 2% of these will not pay and should be regarded as irrecoverable debts

**RECEIPTS FROM TRADE RECEIVABLES**

|  | April | May | June | July | August | September |
|---|---|---|---|---|---|---|
|  | £ | £ | £ | £ | £ | £ |
|  |  |  |  |  |  |  |
|  |  |  |  |  |  |  |
|  |  |  |  |  |  |  |
|  |  |  |  |  |  |  |
| Receipts for month |  |  |  |  |  |  |

**(b)** State the amount of trade receivables for the budgeted statement of financial position at 30 September.

**10.6** **(a)** **You are to** calculate payments to trade payables for October to March using the following information:

- the amount of trade payables at 1 October is £12,500

- credit purchases are budgeted to be £30,000 per month in October and November, £40,000 per month in December and January, and £35,000 per month in February and March

- half of the trade payables allow cash discount of 2% and are paid in the month of purchase

- the remainder of trade payables are paid in the month after sale, without cash discount

## PAYMENTS TO TRADE PAYABLES

|  | October £ | November £ | December £ | January £ | February £ | March £ |
|---|---|---|---|---|---|---|
|  |  |  |  |  |  |  |
|  |  |  |  |  |  |  |
|  |  |  |  |  |  |  |
| Payments for month |  |  |  |  |  |  |

**(b)** State the amount of trade payables for the budgeted statement of financial position at 31 March.

**10.7\*** You are preparing the cash budget of Wilkinson Limited for the first six months of 20-8. The following budgeted figures are available:

|  | Sales £ | Purchases £ | Wages and salaries £ | Other expenses £ |
|---|---|---|---|---|
| January | 65,000 | 26,500 | 17,500 | 15,500 |
| February | 70,000 | 45,000 | 18,000 | 20,500 |
| March | 72,500 | 50,000 | 18,250 | 19,000 |
| April | 85,000 | 34,500 | 18,500 | 18,500 |
| May | 65,000 | 35,500 | 16,500 | 20,500 |
| June | 107,500 | 40,500 | 20,000 | 22,000 |

The following additional information is available:

- Sales income is received in the month after sale, and sales for December 20-7 amounted to £57,500

- 'Other expenses' each month includes an allocation of £1,000 for depreciation; all other expenses are paid for in the month in which they are incurred

- Purchases, and wages and salaries are paid for in the month in which they are incurred

- The bank balance at 1 January 20-8 is £2,250

**REQUIRED:**

**(a)** Prepare a month-by-month cash budget for the first six months of 20-8, using the layout on the next page.

**(b)** Calculate the total net cash outflow for the six months.

**WILKINSON LIMITED**
**CASH BUDGET FOR THE SIX MONTHS ENDING 30 JUNE 20-8**

| | Jan £ | Feb £ | Mar £ | Apr £ | May £ | Jun £ |
|---|---|---|---|---|---|---|
| **Receipts** | | | | | | |
| | | | | | | |
| | | | | | | |
| Total receipts for month | | | | | | |
| **Payments** | | | | | | |
| | | | | | | |
| | | | | | | |
| | | | | | | |
| | | | | | | |
| Total payments for month | | | | | | |
| Net cash flow | | | | | | |
| Add Opening bank balance (overdraft) | | | | | | |
| Closing bank balance (overdraft) | | | | | | |

10.8

Jim Smith has recently been made redundant; he has received a redundancy payment and this, together with his accumulated savings, amounts to £10,000. He has decided to set up his own business selling stationery and this will commence trading with an initial capital of £10,000 on 1 January. On this date he will buy a van for business use at a cost of £6,000. He has estimated his purchases, sales, and expenses for the next six months as follows:

| | Purchases £ | Sales £ | Expenses £ |
|---|---|---|---|
| January | 4,500 | 1,250 | 750 |
| February | 4,500 | 3,000 | 600 |
| March | 3,500 | 4,000 | 600 |
| April | 3,500 | 4,000 | 650 |
| May | 3,500 | 4,500 | 650 |
| June | 4,000 | 6,000 | 700 |

He will pay for purchases in the month after purchase; likewise, he expects his customers to pay for sales in the month after sale. All expenses will be paid for in the month they are incurred.

**REQUIRED:**

**(a)** Jim realises that he may need a bank overdraft before his business becomes established. Prepare a month-by-month cash budget for the first six months of Jim Smith's business, using the layout below.

**(b)** What is the maximum bank overdraft shown by the cash budget? Suggest two ways in which Jim Smith could amend his business plan in order to avoid the need for a bank overdraft.

**JIM SMITH**
**CASH BUDGET FOR THE SIX MONTHS ENDING 30 JUNE**

|  | Jan £ | Feb £ | Mar £ | Apr £ | May £ | Jun £ |
|---|---|---|---|---|---|---|
| **Receipts** |  |  |  |  |  |  |
|  |  |  |  |  |  |  |
|  |  |  |  |  |  |  |
| Total receipts for month |  |  |  |  |  |  |
| **Payments** |  |  |  |  |  |  |
|  |  |  |  |  |  |  |
|  |  |  |  |  |  |  |
|  |  |  |  |  |  |  |
|  |  |  |  |  |  |  |
| Total payments for month |  |  |  |  |  |  |
| Net cash flow |  |  |  |  |  |  |
| Opening bank balance (overdraft) |  |  |  |  |  |  |
| Closing bank balance (overdraft) |  |  |  |  |  |  |

**10.9\***

Mayday Limited was recently formed and plans to commence trading on 1 June 20-1. During May the company will issue 200,000 ordinary shares of £1 each at par (ie nominal value) and the cash will be subscribed at once. During the same month £130,000 will be spent on plant and £50,000 will be invested in inventory, resulting in a cash balance on 1 June of £20,000.

Plans for the twelve months commencing 1 June 20-1 are as follows:

- Inventory costing £40,000 will be sold each month at a mark-up of 25%. Customers are expected to pay in the second month following sale.

- Month-end inventory levels will be maintained at £50,000 and purchases will be paid for in the month following delivery.

- Wages and other expenses will amount to £6,000 per month, payable in the month during which the costs are incurred.

- Plant will have a ten-year life and no scrap value. Depreciation is to be charged on the straight-line basis.

**REQUIRED:**

**(a)** A month-by-month cash budget for Mayday Limited for the year to 31 May 20-2.

**(b)** The company's budgeted income statement for the year ending 31 May 20-2, together with a budgeted statement of financial position at that date.

**10.10**

The statement of financial position of Antonio's Speciality Food Shop at 31 August 20-1 was:

|  | £ Cost | £ Depreciation | £ Carrying amount |
|---|---|---|---|
| **Non-current Assets** | 15,000 | 3,000 | 12,000 |
| **Current Assets** |  |  |  |
| Inventory |  | 5,000 |  |
| Trade receivables |  | 800 |  |
|  |  | 5,800 |  |
| **Less Current Liabilities** |  |  |  |
| Trade payables | 3,000 |  |  |
| Bank overdraft | 1,050 |  |  |
|  |  | 4,050 |  |
| **Net Current Assets** |  |  | 1,750 |
| **NET ASSETS** |  |  | 13,750 |
|  |  |  |  |
| **FINANCED BY** |  |  |  |
| **Capital** |  |  | 13,750 |

On the basis of past performance, Antonio expects that his sales during the coming six months will be:

| September | October | November | December | January | February |
|-----------|---------|----------|----------|---------|----------|
| £8,000    | £8,000  | £10,000  | £20,000  | £6,000  | £6,000   |

Antonio allows credit to some of his regular customers, and the proportions of cash and credit sales are expected to be:

|                   | Cash sales | Credit sales |
|-------------------|------------|--------------|
| November          | 80%        | 20%          |
| December          | 60%        | 40%          |
| All other months  | 90%        | 10%          |

Customers who buy on credit normally pay in the following month. Antonio's gross profit margin is consistently 25% of his selling price. He normally maintains his inventory at a constant level by purchasing goods in the month in which they are sold: the only exception to this is that in November he purchases in advance 50 per cent of the goods he expects to sell in December.

Half of the purchases each month are made from suppliers who give a 2 per cent cash discount for immediate payment and he takes advantage of the discount. He pays for the remainder (without discount) in the month after purchase.

Expenditure on wages, rent and other expenses of the shop are consistently £2,000 per month paid in the month in which they are incurred.

Non-current assets are depreciated at 10 per cent per annum on cost price.

**REQUIRED:**

(a)  A cash budget showing Antonio's bank balance or overdraft for each month in the six months ending 28 February 20-2.

(b)  Antonio's budgeted statement of financial position at 28 February 20-2.

(c)  If Antonio's bank manager considered it necessary to fix the overdraft limit at £3,500, explain what Antonio should do in order to observe the limit.

10.11

Raj, Sam and Tam are partners in RST & Co, a firm of accountants. Their capital account figures are currently: Raj £40,000, Sam £30,000 and Tam £25,000. Profits and losses are shared 50%, 30% and 20% respectively.

The partners ask you, as their accounts assistant, to prepare a cash budget for April, May and June based on the following information:

- The bank balance at 31 March is expected to be £2,180.

- The partnership charges fee income to their clients; the actual and forecast fee income for each partner is:

|  | Actual | | Forecast | |
|---|---|---|---|---|
|  | March | April | May | June |
|  | £ | £ | £ | £ |
| Raj | 15,000 | 18,000 | 10,000 | 16,000 |
| Sam | 12,000 | 10,000 | 15,000 | 8,000 |
| Tam | 8,000 | 9,000 | 6,000 | 7,500 |

Clients are invoiced as soon as the work is completed and 50% will pay immediately. The remaining clients will pay within 30 days – however, 3% of these will not pay and should be regarded as irrecoverable debts.

- The forecast operating expenses of the partnership are £18,225 per month, payable in the month they occur. Included in operating expenses is £2,000 per month for depreciation of office equipment.

- A car is to be bought for Tam in May at a cost of £30,000.

- Partners' drawings are based on their individual fee income each month:

  - Raj intends to withdraw 30% of his fee income in April, May and June

  - Sam intends to withdraw 25% of his fee income in April and May, but none in June

  - Tam intends to withdraw 20% of her fee income in April, none in May and 30% in June

- The partnership bank account has an overdraft facility of £15,000. The interest rate on borrowing is currently 12% per year. In preparing the cash budget the partners instruct you to calculate any interest to be charged in a month based on the closing bank balance of the previous month.

**You are to:**

**(a)** Prepare the cash budget for the partnership for the months of April, May and June.

### CASH BUDGET OF RAJ, SAM AND TAM FOR APRIL, MAY AND JUNE

| | April £ | May £ | June £ |
|---|---|---|---|
| | | | |
| | | | |
| | | | |
| | | | |
| | | | |
| | | | |
| | | | |
| | | | |
| | | | |
| | | | |
| | | | |
| | | | |
| | | | |
| | | | |
| | | | |
| | | | |
| | | | |

**(b)** The partners are considering a bank loan as an alternative to using the bank overdraft to purchase the car for Tam. The bank offers 80% of the cost on a four-year loan, with monthly repayments at a variable rate of interest which, initially, would be 5%.

Write a note for the partners which sets out whether the car should be purchased using the bank overdraft or a bank loan.

**10.12\*** A friend of yours runs a manufacturing business. You are helping your friend to prepare a business cash budget for the next six months. Your friend comments: 'This is all a bit of an effort and I can't see how it will benefit my business.'

**REQUIRED:**

Explain three benefits of preparing a cash budget for a business.

# 11 ABSORPTION AND ACTIVITY BASED COSTING

This chapter studies the costing methods of absorption costing and activity based costing. The technique of marginal costing has already been covered in year 1 studies – see Accounting for AQA: AS and A-level year 1, Chapter 20.

This chapter develops the use of management accounting and covers:

● an explanation of cost units and cost centres

● an overview of the main costing methods and their purposes

● the use of absorption costing, comparing it with marginal costing

● the use of activity based costing, including an explanation of cost drivers and cost pools

● the benefits and limitations of absorption costing, activity based costing, and marginal costing

● the use of absorption costing and activity based costing to calculate the selling price of a product

## COST UNITS AND COST CENTRES

Costing methods make use of cost centres and cost units. Before we look in detail at costing methods we need to explain cost units and cost centres.

**Cost units are units of output to which costs can be charged.**

A cost unit can be:

• a unit of production from a factory such as a car, a television, an item of furniture

• a unit of service, such as a passenger-mile on a bus, a transaction on a bank statement, an attendance at a swimming pool, a gigabyte of usage on the internet

Within an individual business – particularly in the service industry – there may well be several cost units that can be used. For example, in a hotel the cost units in the restaurant will be meals, and for the rooms, the cost units will be guest nights.

Costs also need to be charged to a specific part of a business – a **cost centre.**

**Cost centres are sections of a business to which costs can be charged.**

A cost centre in a manufacturing business, for example, is a department of a factory, a particular stage in the production process, or even a whole factory. In a college, examples of cost centres are the teaching departments, or particular sections of departments such as the college's administration office. In a hospital, examples of cost centres are the hospital wards, operating theatres, specialist sections such as the X-ray department and the pathology department.

Collecting costs together in cost centres assists with control of the business. The manager of a cost centre can be held responsible for its costs.

# COSTING METHODS – AN OVERVIEW

The main costing methods used in management accounting are:

- absorption costing – the total costs of the whole business are absorbed amongst all of the cost units
- marginal costing – the cost of producing one extra unit of output
- activity based costing – the overheads of the business are attributed to output on the basis of activities
- standard costing – a pre-determined cost for materials, labour and overheads is set in advance of production

The diagram on the next page shows the purpose of each of these costing methods. The use of each costing method is dependent on the information needs of the business:

- do we require a figure for profit? (use absorption costing)
- why are the overheads so high for the production line making 'Product Exe'? (use activity based costing)
- can we afford to sell 1,000 units each month to Megastores Limited at a discount of 20 per cent? (use marginal costing)
- how much will it cost us to make 'Product Wye' next month? (use standard costing)

Note that absorption costing, marginal costing, and activity based costing are all methods that can be used in conjunction with standard costing, if required.

In this chapter we study absorption costing – making comparisons with marginal costing – and activity based costing. Standard costing, together with the use of variance analysis, is covered in detail in Chapter 13.

Note that each of these costing methods focuses on how the overheads – the indirect costs – are applied to the output of the business. The direct costs – direct materials and direct labour – are always allocated directly to the output at the cost incurred.

## COSTING METHODS AND THEIR PURPOSES

**purposes of methods**

**costing methods**

| purposes of methods | costing methods |
|---|---|
| to calculate profit and to calculate inventory valuation for the financial statements | absorption costing |
| to help with decision-making | marginal costing |
| to identify reasons why overheads are incurred for a particular activity | activity based costing |
| to calculate costs in advance of production – particularly where businesses operate a production line, eg a car factory | standard costing |

# ABSORPTION COSTING

**Absorption costing absorbs the total costs of the whole business amongst all of the cost units.**

Absorption costing answers the question, "What does it cost to make one unit of output?"

The absorption cost of a unit of output is made up of the following costs:

|  |  | £ |
|---|---|---|
|  | direct materials | x |
| *add* | direct labour | x |
| *add* | direct expenses | x |
| *add* | overheads (fixed and variable) | x |
| *equals* | ABSORPTION COST | x |

Note that:

- the overheads of a business comprise the indirect factory and the office costs, ie those costs that cannot be identified directly with units of output – the non-production overheads
- under some circumstances, absorption costing includes only production costs, ie it excludes all costs beyond production, such as distribution expenses, selling and marketing expenses, administration expenses, and finance costs.

## WORKED EXAMPLE: ABSORPTION COSTING

### situation

The Wyvern Bike Company makes 100 bikes each week and its costs are as follows:

| WEEKLY COSTS FOR PRODUCING 100 BIKES | |
|---|---:|
| | £ |
| direct materials (£30 per bike) | 3,000 |
| direct labour (£25 per bike) | 2,500 |
| PRIME COST* | 5,500 |
| overheads (fixed) | 3,500 |
| TOTAL COST | 9,000 |

*prime cost = direct materials + direct labour + direct expenses (if any)

- there are no direct expenses incurred by the company
- the selling price of each bike is £100

What is the absorption cost of producing one bike, and how much profit does the company make each week?

### solution

The absorption cost of producing one bike is:

$$\frac{\text{total cost (direct and indirect costs)}}{\text{units of output}} = \frac{£9,000}{100 \text{ bikes}} = £90 \text{ per bike}$$

With a selling price of £100 per bike, the income statement is:

| INCOME STATEMENT FOR 100 BIKES | | |
|---|---|---:|
| | | £ |
| | selling price  (100 bikes x £100) | 10,000 |
| *less* | total cost | 9,000 |
| *equals* | PROFIT | 1,000 |

As the Worked Example shows, each cost unit bears an equal proportion of the costs of the overheads of the business. Because of its simplicity, absorption costing is a widely used system which tells us how much it costs to make one unit of output. It works well where the cost units are identical, eg 100 identical bikes, but is less appropriate where some of the cost units differ in quality, eg 100 bikes, of which 75 are standard models and 25 are handbuilt to the customers' specifications. It also ignores the effect of changes in the level of output on the cost structure. For example, if the bike manufacturer reduces output to 50 bikes a week:

• will direct materials remain at £30 per bike? (buying materials in smaller quantities might mean higher prices)

• will direct labour still be £25 per bike? (with lower production, the workforce may not be able to specialise in certain jobs, and may be less efficient)

• will the overheads remain fixed at £3,500? (perhaps smaller premises can be used and the factory rent reduced)

In Chapter 12 we will see how, under absorption costing, overheads are attributed to output using direct labour and machine hour methods. Such overhead absorption rates allow different products to be charged with the amount of overheads that reflect the direct labour or machine hours used in their production.

# MARGINAL COSTING AND ABSORPTION COSTING COMPARED

Marginal costing tells the management of a business the cost of producing one extra unit of output, while the distinction between fixed and variable costs forms the basis of break-even analysis (seen in AQA year 1 studies). Nevertheless, costing methods should ensure that all the costs of a business are recovered by being charged to production. This is achieved by means of absorption costing. A comparison between these two methods of costing is as follows:

• *marginal costing*

Marginal costing recognises that fixed costs vary with time rather than activity, and identifies the cost of producing one extra unit. For example, the rent of a factory relates to a certain time period, eg one month, and remains unchanged whether 100 units of output are made or whether 500 units are made; by contrast, the production of one extra unit will incur an increase in prime costs, ie direct materials, direct labour and direct expenses – this increase is the marginal cost.

• *absorption costing*

As we have seen in this chapter, absorption costing absorbs all production costs into each unit of output. Thus each unit of output in a factory making 100 units will bear a greater proportion of the factory rent than will each unit when 500 units are made in the same time period.

The diagram on the next page demonstrates how the terms in marginal costing relate to the same production costs as those categorised under absorption costing terms. When using marginal costing it is the behaviour of the cost – fixed or variable – that is important, not the origin of the cost.

| ABSORPTION COSTING | MARGINAL COSTING |
|---|---|
| **prime costs**<br>direct materials<br>direct labour<br>direct expenses | **variable costs**<br>variable direct materials<br>variable direct labour<br>variable direct expenses<br>variable overheads |
| **indirect costs**<br>variable overheads<br>fixed overheads | **fixed costs**<br>fixed direct costs<br>fixed overheads |

## marginal costing and absorption costing: profit comparisons

Because of the different ways in which marginal costing and absorption costing treat fixed costs, the two methods produce different levels of profit when there is a closing inventory figure. This is because, under marginal costing, the closing inventory is valued at variable production cost; by contrast, absorption cost includes a share of fixed production costs in the closing inventory valuation. This is illustrated in the Worked Example which follows, looking at the effect of using marginal costing and absorption costing on the income statement of a manufacturing business.

Note that the marginal cost approach helps with management decision-making – eg break-even. However, for financial accounting, absorption costing must be used for inventory valuation purposes in order to comply with international accounting standard number 2, *Inventories*. Under IAS 2, closing inventory valuation must be based on the costs of direct materials, direct labour, direct expenses (if any), and production overheads. Note that non-production overheads are not included, as they are charged in full to the income statement in the year to which they relate.

## WORKED EXAMPLE: MARGINAL AND ABSORPTION COSTING

### situation

Chairs Limited commenced business on 1 January 20-7. It manufactures a special type of chair designed to alleviate back pain. Information on the first year's trading is as follows:

| | |
|---|---|
| number of chairs manufactured | 5,000 |
| number of chairs sold | 4,500 |
| selling price | £110 per chair |
| direct materials | £30 per chair |
| direct labour | £40 per chair |
| fixed production overheads | £100,000 |

The directors ask for your help in producing income statements using the marginal costing and absorption costing methods. They say that they will use 'the one that gives the higher profit' to show to the company's bank manager.

**solution**

**CHAIRS LIMITED**

**INCOME STATEMENT FOR THE YEAR ENDED 31 DECEMBER 20-7**

| | MARGINAL COSTING | | ABSORPTION COSTING | |
|---|---|---|---|---|
| | £ | £ | £ | £ |
| **Revenue** 4,500 chairs at £110 each | | 495,000 | | 495,000 |
| **Variable costs** | | | | |
| Direct materials at £30 each | 150,000 | | 150,000 | |
| Direct labour at £40 each | 200,000 | | 200,000 | |
| | 350,000 | | | |
| Less Closing inventory (marginal cost) | | | | |
| 500 chairs at £70 (£30 + £40) each | 35,000 | | | |
| | | 315,000 | | |
| **CONTRIBUTION** | | 180,000 | | |
| **Fixed production overheads** | | 100,000 | 100,000 | |
| | | | 450,000 | |
| Less Closing inventory (absorption cost) | | | | |
| 500 chairs at £90 (£450,000 / 5,000) each | | | 45,000 | |
| Less Cost of sales | | | | 405,000 |
| **Gross profit** | | 80,000 | | 90,000 |
| Less Non-production overheads | | 50,000 | | 50,000 |
| **Profit for the year** | | 30,000 | | 40,000 |

Notes:

•    Closing inventory is always calculated on the basis of this year's costs.

•    The difference in the profit figures is caused by the closing inventory figures: £35,000 under marginal costing and £45,000 under absorption costing – the same costs have been used, but fixed production overheads have been treated differently.

•    Only fixed production overheads are dealt with differently using the techniques of marginal and absorption costing – both methods charge non-production overheads *in full* to the income statement in the year to which they relate.

With marginal costing, the full amount of the fixed production overheads has been charged in this year's income statement; by contrast, with absorption costing, part of the fixed production overheads (here, £10,000) has been carried forward to next year in the inventory valuation. Because of this, profit will always be higher under absorption costing in accounting periods of increasing inventory levels.

With regard to the directors' statement that they will use 'the one that gives the higher profit', two points should be borne in mind:

- A higher profit does *not* mean more money in the bank.
- The two costing methods simply treat fixed production overheads differently and, in a year when there is no closing inventory, total profits *to date* are exactly the same – but they occur differently over the years.

Note that, for financial accounting purposes, Chairs Limited will have to use the absorption cost closing inventory valuation of £45,000 in order to comply with IAS 2, *Inventories*.

# ACTIVITY BASED COSTING

**Activity based costing (ABC) attributes overheads to output on the basis of activities.**

Activity based costing is a costing method which has developed from absorption costing, but adopts a different approach to charging – attributing – overheads to output. ABC identifies what causes overheads to be incurred, rather than simply charging total overheads for a particular period.

Traditional costing systems usually charge overheads to output on the basis of direct labour hours (or labour cost), or machine hours. For example, for each labour hour – or machine hour – required by the output, £x of overheads is charged through an *overhead absorption rate* (see Chapter 12). While this method may be suitable for industries which are labour intensive, or where production requires the use of heavy machinery, it is not always appropriate for today's capital intensive, low-labour industries, as the example which follows shows.

**example**

ExeWye Limited manufactures two products, Exe and Wye. Product Exe is produced on a labour-intensive production line, using basic machinery; product Wye is produced using the latest 'state of the art' computer-controlled machinery, which requires few employees. ExeWye's costs are:

| | | |
|---|---|---|
| **direct materials, total** | £500,000 | |
| – product Exe | £250,000 | |
| – product Wye | £250,000 | |
| **direct labour, total** | £250,000 | (25,000 hours) |
| – product Exe | £200,000 | (20,000 hours) |
| – product Wye | £50,000 | (5,000 hours) |
| **overheads (fixed), total** | £250,000 | |

- a major proportion of these relate to maintenance and depreciation of the computer controlled machinery used to make product Wye

ExeWye Limited uses labour hours as the basis by which to charge overheads to production. Therefore, the overhead will be split between the two products as:

overhead for product Exe = four-fifths (ie 20,000 out of 25,000 hours) of total overheads of £250,000 = £200,000

overhead for product Wye = one-fifth (ie 5,000 out of 25,000 hours) of total overheads of £250,000 = £50,000

Thus, the majority of the overhead is charged to the labour-intensive production line (product Exe), and relatively little to the capital intensive line (product Wye). As a major proportion of the costs relates to product Wye, this has the effect of undercosting this product (and overcosting product Exe). Instead, a more appropriate costing system is needed, and activity based costing can be used to attribute overheads to output on the basis of activities.

## the use of cost drivers

### Cost drivers are activities which cause costs to be incurred.

In the example looked at above, the cost driver used to attribute overheads to output was – inappropriately – labour costs. Instead of using a cost driver linked to the volume of business (as above), activity based costing uses cost drivers linked to the *way in which business is conducted*: this concept is illustrated in the example which follows:

### example

AyeBee Limited manufactures two products, Aye and Bee. Product Aye is produced in batches of 500 units of output; product Bee is produced in batches of 100 units of output. Each unit of production – whether Aye or Bee – requires one direct labour hour.

Production of each batch of Aye and Bee requires the following overheads:

- the machinery to be set up at a cost of £400 per batch (to cover the engineer's time, test running of the machinery, etc)
- quality inspection at a cost of £200 per batch (to cover the inspector's time, cost of rejects, etc)

In a typical week the company produces 500 units of product Aye, ie one batch of 500 units, and 500 units of product Bee, ie five batches of 100 units. Thus the set-up and quality inspection costs for the week will be:

| | | |
|---|---|---|
| 6 set-ups at £400 each | = | £2,400 |
| 6 quality inspections at £200 each | = | £1,200 |
| TOTAL | | £3,600 |

Note: each 'box' represents one set-up and one quality inspection

As each unit of output requires one direct labour hour, ie product Aye 500 hours, product Bee 500 hours, the overhead costs of set-ups and quality inspection, using traditional costing systems, will be charged to output as follows:

| product Aye | = | £1,800 |
|---|---|---|
| product Bee | = | £1,800 |
| TOTAL | | £3,600 |

We can see that this is an incorrect basis on which to charge overheads to output, because product Aye required just one set-up and one quality inspection, while product Bee took five set-ups and five quality inspections. By using the system of activity based costing, with set-up and inspection as cost drivers, we can attribute overheads as follows:

**product Aye**

| 1 set-up at £400 | = | £400 |
|---|---|---|
| 1 quality inspection at £200 | = | £200 |
| TOTAL | | £600 |

**product Bee**

| 5 set-ups at £400 | = | £2,000 |
|---|---|---|
| 5 quality inspections at £200 | = | £1,000 |
| TOTAL | | £3,000 |

By using the activity based costing system, there is a more accurate reflection of the cost of demand on the support functions of set-up and quality inspection: it reduces the cost of 500 units of product Aye by £1,200 (ie £1,800 – £600) and increases the cost of 500 units of product Bee by £1,200 (ie from £1,800 to £3,000). This may have implications for the viability of product Bee, and for the selling price of both products.

## other cost drivers

Cost drivers must have a close relationship with an activity, which can then be related to output. Examples of activities and their cost drivers include:

| Activity | Cost driver |
|---|---|
| • set-ups of machinery | • number of set-ups of machinery |
| • quality control | • number of quality inspections |
| • processing orders to suppliers | • number of orders |
| • processing invoices received | • number of invoices |
| • processing orders to customers | • number of orders |
| • processing invoices to customers | • number of invoices |
| • marketing | • number of advertisements |
| • telephone sales | • number of telephone calls made |

As has been seen in the example above, by using activity based costing, the emphasis is placed on which activities cause costs. It answers the question why costs are incurred, instead of simply stating the amount of the cost for a given period. By using ABC, the responsibility for the cost is established and so steps can be taken to minimise the cost for the future.

## the use of cost pools

**Cost pools are groups of overhead costs that are incurred by the same activity.**

When using activity based costing it is advisable to group together those overhead costs which are attributed to the same activity in a cost pool. For example, the purchasing costs for goods to be used in production will include the wages of the firm's purchasing staff, the cost – or proportionate cost – of the purchasing office, the cost of telephone/post/email relating to purchasing.

The use of a cost pool makes the attribution of costs through cost drivers that much easier – there is no need to seek a separate cost driver for each overhead cost, when similar activities can be grouped together.

## using activity based costing

The steps to applying activity based costing are illustrated in the following diagram:

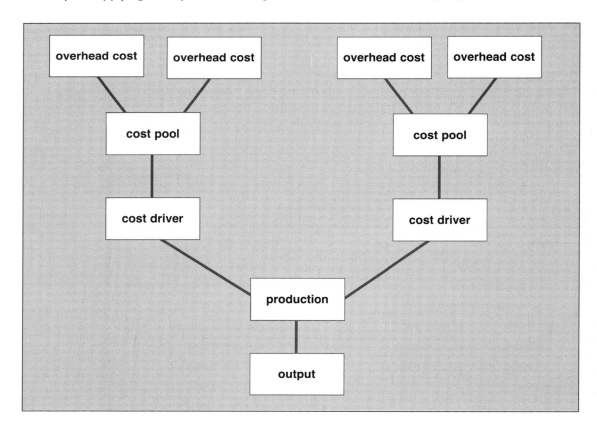

- The first step is to group together in a cost pool the overhead costs which are incurred by the same activity, for example, the purchasing costs for goods to be used in production.
- The second step is to identify the factor which influences the costs – the cost driver. Once identified, the rate for each cost can be calculated. For example, the cost driver could be the cost of placing an order for the purchase of goods to be used in production.
- The third step is to charge the rate for each cost to production based on the use of the activity. For example, if a product requires two purchase orders to be placed, it will be charged with the cost of two activities.

## advantages of using activity based costing

The main advantages of using ABC:

- cost information is more accurate because cost drivers are used to identify the activity which causes costs to be incurred
- it is more objective because it is able to identify the overhead costs relating to different products, rather than the overheads of the whole business
- with its focus on overhead costs ABC gives the management of a business a good understanding of why costs are incurred and how they will be altered by changes in production
- it leads to the more accurate calculation of selling prices because overhead costs are attributed to the products which use the activities
- it may identify areas of waste and inefficiency
- management decision-making is improved, eg in pricing policy
- ABC is appropriate for capital-intensive industries where overheads are high and complex in nature

# COMPARISON OF COSTING METHODS

The table, on the next page, gives a comparison between marginal costing, absorption costing, and activity based costing, including a note on the benefits and the limitations of each. The Worked Example on pages 257-259 compares these three costing methods in a practical situation.

A further costing method, standard costing, is discussed in Chapter 13.

## Comparison of marginal, absorption and activity based costing

|  | Marginal costing | Absorption costing | Activity based costing |
|---|---|---|---|
| Main use | • to help with short-term decision-making such as make or buy decisions, acceptance of additional work, price setting, target profit, etc | • to calculate selling prices using cost plus profit<br>• to calculate inventory valuation for financial statements | • to identify what causes overheads to be incurred for a particular activity |
| How does it work? | • focuses on product costs<br>• costs are classified as either fixed or variable<br>• contribution to fixed costs is calculated as selling price less variable costs | • focuses on product and period costs<br>• production overheads are charged to production through an overhead absorption rate, often on the basis of direct labour hours or machine hours | • focuses on product costs<br>• cost drivers are identified<br>• production overheads are attributed to production on the basis of activities |
| Main focus | • marginal cost<br>• contribution | • production overheads charged to production<br>• calculating selling prices and profit<br>• calculating inventory values | • identifying cost drivers as a way of attributing production overheads to production |
| Benefits | • concept of contribution is easy to understand<br>• useful for short-term decision-making, but no consideration of overheads | • acceptable under IAS 2, *Inventories*<br>• appropriate for traditional industries where production overheads are charged to production on the basis of direct labour hours or machine hours | • acceptable under IAS 2, *Inventories*<br>• more accurate calculation of selling prices because production overheads are analysed to the products which use the activities<br>• appropriate for capital-intensive industries where overheads are high and complex in nature |
| Limitations | • costs have to be identified as either fixed or variable<br>• all overheads have to be recovered, otherwise a loss will be made<br>• not acceptable under IAS 2, *Inventories*<br>• calculation of selling prices may be less accurate than other costing methods | • not as useful in short-term decision-making as marginal costing<br>• may provide less accurate basis for calculation of selling prices where overheads are high and complex in nature | • time-consuming to set up and record costs (because of the detail required)<br>• the selection of cost drivers can be difficult<br>• the cost drivers and cost pools need to be kept up-to-date<br>• period costs – such as rent and rates – still need to be recovered |

# WORKED EXAMPLE: WHICH COSTING METHOD TO USE?

### situation

EssTee Limited manufactures two products, Ess and Tee.

Weekly production is 500 units of each product. Each unit of production – whether Ess or Tee – requires one direct labour hour.

Products are made in batches – before a batch can be made the production machinery must be set up, checked for accuracy and test run. Each batch produced has to be inspected to ensure that it is of the required standard, with any rejects being identified.

Currently the company uses absorption costing.

Details of each product are:

*Product Ess*

–       made in batches of 500 units

–       selling price per unit, £100

–       direct materials per unit, £30

–       direct labour per unit, £10

*Product Tee*

–       made in batches of 100 units

–       selling price per unit, £80

–       direct materials per unit, £20

–       direct labour per unit, £10

*Fixed production costs each week are:*

–       set-up costs of machinery, £12,000

–       inspection costs of production, £6,000

These costs are currently attributed to output on the basis of direct labour hours.

The management accountant of EssTee Limited asks for your help to show how marginal costing, absorption costing and activity based costing will deal differently with the costs.

**solution**

**Marginal costing**

|  |  | Product Ess | | Product Tee | | Total |
|---|---|---|---|---|---|---|
|  |  | £ | £ | £ | £ | £ |
|  | revenue |  | 50,000 |  | 40,000 |  |
| *less* | variable costs: |  |  |  |  |  |
|  | direct materials | 15,000 |  | 10,000 |  |  |
|  | direct labour | 5,000 |  | 5,000 |  |  |
|  |  |  | 20,000 |  | 15,000 |  |
| *equals* | contribution |  | 30,000 |  | 25,000 | 55,000 |
| *less* | fixed production costs |  |  |  |  | 18,000 |
| *equals* | profit for the week |  |  |  |  | 37,000 |

- With marginal costing, the focus is on the contribution – both by product and in total.
- Fixed production costs are treated as a period cost – ie a cost of time (such as a week, as here) rather than being product related.

**Absorption costing**

|  |  | Product Ess | | Product Tee | | Total |
|---|---|---|---|---|---|---|
|  |  | £ | £ | £ | £ | £ |
|  | revenue |  | 50,000 |  | 40,000 |  |
| *less* | direct materials | 15,000 |  | 10,000 |  |  |
|  | direct labour | 5,000 |  | 5,000 |  |  |
|  | PRIME COST | 20,000 |  | 15,000 |  |  |
|  | fixed production costs | *9,000 |  | *9,000 |  |  |
|  | TOTAL COST |  | 29,000 |  | 24,000 |  |
| *equals* | profit for the week |  | 21,000 |  | 16,000 | 37,000 |

* 500 direct labour hours for each product per week, so fixed production costs are £18,000 ÷ 2 = £9,000 per product.

- With absorption costing, the focus is on profit – both by product and in total.
- Overhead costs are absorbed by production before profit is calculated.

## Activity based costing

|  | Fixed production costs: | set-ups | | inspections | |
|---|---|---|---|---|---|
|  |  | number | £ | number | £ |
|  | product Ess | 1 | 2,000 | 1 | 1,000 |
|  | product Tee | 5 | 10,000 | 5 | 5,000 |
|  |  |  | 12,000 |  | 6,000 |

- set-ups: £12,000 ÷ 6 = £2,000 per set-up
- inspections: £6,000 ÷ 6 = £1,000 per inspection

|  |  | Product Ess | | Product Tee | | Total |
|---|---|---|---|---|---|---|
|  |  | £ | £ | £ | £ | £ |
|  | revenue |  | 50,000 |  | 40,000 |  |
| *less* | direct materials | 15,000 |  | 10,000 |  |  |
|  | direct labour | 5,000 |  | 5,000 |  |  |
|  | PRIME COST | 20,000 |  | 15,000 |  |  |
|  | fixed production costs |  |  |  |  |  |
|  | set-ups | 2,000 |  | 10,000 |  |  |
|  | inspections | 1,000 |  | 5,000 |  |  |
|  | TOTAL COST |  | 23,000 |  | 30,000 |  |
| *equals* | profit for the week |  | 27,000 |  | 10,000 | 37,000 |

- With activity based costing, which is a development of absorption costing, the focus is on identifying the overhead costs for a particular activity.
- It gives more accurate costing information and shows that smaller batches (as here with product Tee) cost more to produce.

# CALCULATING THE SELLING PRICE

**Selling price is the amount of money that is agreed between a buyer and a seller which enables the exchange of a product – goods or a service – to take place.**

The direct costs (materials and labour) and the indirect costs (overheads), together with the profit, make up the selling price of a product. How do we work out the selling price? One way is to calculate the direct and indirect costs of a product and then to apply cost-plus pricing. This uses the cost price of making a product or providing a service and adds on a percentage of the cost to give the selling price, ie

*cost price + profit = selling price*

Cost is usually calculated on the basis of the full cost of either absorption costing or activity based costing which add together all the costs of each unit. Profit is calculated as a percentage mark-up on cost price (ie the profit, being a percentage of cost price, is added to cost price to give selling price).

The disadvantage of using cost-plus pricing is that the selling price may be uncompetitive with other, similar products or services. This could lead to an insufficient number of units of output being sold to recover costs.

## WORKED EXAMPLE: USING COST-PLUS PRICING

**situation**

Leathercraft Limited makes seats for aircraft. Its costs per seat are:

|  | £ |
|---|---|
| Direct materials | 140 |
| Direct labour | 60 |
| PRIME COST | 200 |
| Fixed overheads | 50 |
| TOTAL COST | 250 |

The company is currently reviewing its selling prices and is considering cost-plus pricing based on a 20 per cent mark-up on absorption cost (ie profit is 20 per cent of cost price, which is added to cost price to give selling price).

**solution**

*percentage mark-up on absorption cost*

selling price is calculated as:

|  | £ |
|---|---|
| total cost per seat | 250 |
| 20 per cent mark-up (20% x £125) | 50 |
| selling price per seat | 300 |

**important note**

Using cost-plus pricing does not mean that Leathercraft Limited will be able to sell its seats at the price of £300 each. It might be that customers will find a supplier who is able to produce seats of the same quality but at a cheaper price. This could lead Leathercraft Limited into selling an insufficient number of seats to recover its costs. In these circumstances decisions about the selling price may have to be reconsidered.

A business can use cost-plus pricing in conjunction with either absorption costing or activity based costing. To compare the use of these in setting selling prices:

*absorption costing*

- calculates a total cost – variable costs and fixed costs – to recover all overheads in the selling price
- bases overhead absorption rates often on either machine hours or labour hours – whilst they may not be entirely accurate, they provide a reasonable estimate of overhead costs
- uses cost-plus pricing to ensure that, provided the business sets its selling price above total cost, a profit will be made

*activity based costing*

- produces more accurate cost information than absorption costing because cost drivers are used to identify the activity which causes costs to be incurred
- is more objective than absorption costing because it is able to identify, and differentiate between, the overhead costs relating to different products
- leads to the more accurate calculation of selling prices because overhead costs are analysed to the products which use the activities

As well as cost-plus pricing, a business may also have to consider

- market-led pricing, with the selling price of goods set in line with other suppliers of the same or similar products and services
- marginal cost/contribution pricing, which determines the minimum selling price to be charged for products and services, although overhead costs need to be covered by the contribution from all sales before a profit can be made

**Tutorial note:** price setting is covered in more detail in Accounting for AQA: AS and A-level year 1, Chapter 21.

# CHAPTER SUMMARY

● The costing methods of absorption costing, activity based costing and standard costing make use of cost centres and cost units.

● Cost units are units of output to which costs can be charged.

● Cost centres are sections of a business to which costs can be charged.

● The main costing methods are:

  –   absorption costing

  –   marginal costing

  –   activity based costing

  –   standard costing (covered in Chapter 13)

● Absorption costing absorbs the total costs of the whole business amongst all of the cost units.

● Activity based costing (ABC) attributes overheads to production on the basis of activities.

● ABC makes use of cost drivers and cost pools.

● Cost drivers are activities which cause costs to be incurred.

● Cost pools are groups of overhead costs that are incurred by the same activity.

● Cost-plus pricing is where a mark-up is added to the cost price – calculated using either absorption or activity based costing – in order to determine the selling price.

In the next chapter we look at the allocation and apportionment of overhead costs, together with the use of overhead absorption rates to charge overhead costs to production.

# QUESTIONS

An asterisk (*) after the question number means that the answer is given at the end of this book.

**11.1**  Which **one** of the following is an example of a cost unit?

| A | The salary paid to the office supervisor | |
|---|---|---|
| B | The production department of a business | |
| C | A passenger mile on a bus | |
| D | The pathology department of a hospital | |

**11.2***  Which **one** of the following is an example of a cost centre?

| A | A gigabyte of usage on the internet | |
|---|---|---|
| B | A quality inspection in a factory | |
| C | A car made in a factory | |
| D | A teaching department of a college | |

**11.3**  Which **one** of the following is an example of a cost driver?

| A | The cost of a set-up of machinery in a factory | |
|---|---|---|
| B | The cost of an operation in a hospital | |
| C | The costs of a business's marketing department | |
| D | The cost of indirect labour in a factory | |

**11.4**  **(a)**  Distinguish between cost units and cost centres.

**(b)**  Suggest one cost unit and two cost centres for:
- a firm of accountants
- a parcel delivery company
- a college of further education
- a mixed farm, growing crops and raising cattle

**11.5** Suggest likely cost centres for each of the following:

- A theatre in a provincial town, where touring productions are staged. The theatre has a bar and a confectionery counter. Ticket sales are dealt with by the theatre's box office, and the plays are advertised locally.

- A garage, which sells new and used cars of two different makes. Cars are also repaired, serviced and valeted.

**11.6\*** Coffeeworks Limited manufactures coffee machines for domestic use. The management of the company is considering next year's production and has asked you to help with certain financial decisions.

The following information is available:

| | |
|---|---|
| Selling price (per machine) | £80 |
| Direct materials (per machine) | £25 |
| Direct labour (per machine) | £20 |
| Overheads (fixed) | £270,000 per year |

The company is planning to manufacture 15,000 coffee machines next year.

**(a)** Calculate the marginal cost per coffee machine.

**(b)** Calculate the absorption cost per coffee machine.

**(c)** Prepare an income statement to show the profit or loss if 15,000 coffee machines are sold.

**11.7** Cook-It Limited makes garden barbecues. The management of the company is considering the production for next year and has asked for help with certain financial decisions.

The following information is available:

| | |
|---|---|
| Wholesale selling price (per barbecue) | £90 |
| Direct materials (per barbecue) | £30 |
| Direct labour (per barbecue) | £25 |
| Fixed overheads | £150,000 per year |

The company is planning to manufacture 10,000 barbecues next year.

**REQUIRED:**

You are to calculate:

- The marginal cost per barbecue
- The absorption cost per barbecue
- The profit or loss if 10,000 barbecues are sold

**11.8\***  Maxxa Limited manufactures one product, the Maxx. For the month of January 20-7 the following information is available:

| | |
|---|---|
| Number of units manufactured | 4,000 |
| Number of units sold | 3,000 |
| Selling price | £8 per unit |
| Direct materials for month | £5,000 |
| Direct labour for month | £9,000 |
| Fixed production overheads | £6,000 |
| Non-production overheads | £3,000 |

There was no inventory of finished goods at the start of the month. Both direct materials and direct labour are variable costs.

**REQUIRED:**

You are to produce income statements using marginal costing and absorption costing methods.

**11.9**  Activtoys Limited commenced business on 1 January 20-1. It manufactures the 'Activ', an outdoor climbing frame. Information on the first year's trading is as follows:

| | |
|---|---|
| Number of climbing frames manufactured | 1,500 |
| Number of climbing frames sold | 1,300 |
| Selling price | £125 per frame |
| Direct materials | £25 per frame |
| Direct labour | £30 per frame |
| Fixed production overheads | £82,500 |
| Non-production overheads | £4,000 |

**REQUIRED:**

**(a)**  The directors ask for your help in producing income statements using the marginal costing and absorption costing methods. They say that they will use "the one that gives the higher profit" to show to the company's bank manager.

**(b)**  Write a note to the directors explaining the reason for the different profit figures and commenting on their statement.

**11.10** Durning Limited manufactures one product, the Durn. For the month of April 20-4 the following information is available:

| | |
|---|---|
| Number of units manufactured | 10,000 |
| Number of units sold | 8,000 |
| Selling price | £4 per unit |
| Direct materials for month | £8,000 |
| Direct labour for month | £16,000 |
| Fixed production overheads for month | £10,000 |
| Non-production overheads | £2,000 |

There was no finished goods inventory at the start of the month. Both direct materials and direct labour are variable costs.

**REQUIRED:**

**(a)** Produce income statements for April 20-4, using:

- marginal costing

- absorption costing

**(b)** Explain briefly the reason for the difference between recorded profits under the alternative costing methods.

**11.11\*** **(a)** Explain the term 'activity based costing'.

**(b)** Explain the terms 'cost driver' and 'cost pool'.

**11.12** 'Activity based costing is a costing method which has developed from absorption costing.'

**REQUIRED:**

**(a)** How is activity based costing used in the calculation of the cost of a product?

**(b)** Give two benefits of using activity based costing rather than absorption costing.

**11.13** Mereford Manufacturing Limited makes two products, Aye and Bee. Product Aye is made in batches of 10,000 units, and Product Bee is made in batches of 1,000 units. Each batch has the following set-up and quality inspection costs:

- set-up £250
- quality inspection £150

Each week, the company produces 50,000 units of Aye and 50,000 units of Bee. At present the company charges overheads to output on the basis of labour hours, which are 500 hours per week for Aye and 500 hours for Bee.

**(a)** Calculate the overheads attributed to Aye and Bee each week, on the basis of labour hours.

**(b)** Calculate the overheads attributed to Aye and Bee each week, using activity based costing with the cost drivers of set-up and quality inspection.

**(c)** Advise the management of Mereford Manufacturing Limited which is the more appropriate method of charging overheads to output.

**11.14** ExeWye Limited manufactures two products, Exe and Wye.

Weekly production is 1,000 units of each product. Each unit of production – whether Exe or Wye – requires two direct labour hours.

Products are made in batches – before a batch can be made the production machinery must be set-up, checked for accuracy and test run. Each batch produced has to be inspected to ensure that it is of the required standard, with any rejects being identified.

Currently the company uses absorption costing.

Details of each product are:

**Product Exe**
- made in batches of 500 units
- selling price per unit, £200
- direct materials per unit, £60
- direct labour per unit, £20

**Product Wye**
- made in batches of 100 units
- selling price per unit, £160
- direct materials per unit, £40
- direct labour per unit, £20

**Fixed production costs each week:**
- set-up costs of machinery, £24,000
- inspection costs of production, £12,000

These costs are currently attributed to output on the basis of direct labour hours.

**REQUIRED:**

Show how marginal costing, absorption costing, and activity based costing will deal differently with the costs.

**11.15\*** Ando-Zalso Ltd manufactures two products: Ando and Zalso.

The direct costs of each product are:

|  | Ando | Zalso |
|---|---|---|
|  | £ | £ |
| Direct materials per unit | 5.00 | 8.00 |
| Direct labour per unit | 6.00 | 4.00 |

The company's total factory overheads are £22,150 per month.

Monthly production is:

- Ando  2,000 units

- Zalso  3,500 units

Ando is sold for £18.00 per unit and Zalso for £15.00 per unit.

The company uses activity based costing with the following cost pools and cost drivers:

| Cost pool | Cost driver | Overhead cost per month | Each product |
|---|---|---|---|
| Machinery adjustments | Number of times production machinery is adjusted during production | £10,150 | Ando: 2 adjustments per unit Zalso: 3 adjustments per unit |
| Quality inspections | Number of times products are inspected during production | £12,000 | Ando: 3 inspections per unit Zalso: 4 inspections per unit |

**REQUIRED:**

**(a)** Calculate the cost of making each unit of Ando and each unit of Zalso.

**(b)** Calculate the profit or loss per unit for each product.

**11.16\*** Duchy Private Hospital Limited carries out a large number of minor operations for day patients. For next year it plans 2,500 operations based on the following costs:

**annual costs for 2,500 minor operations**

|  | £ |
|---|---|
| Direct materials (£100 per operation) | 250,000 |
| Direct labour (£200 per operation) | 500,000 |
| PRIME COST | 750,000 |
| Fixed overheads | 250,000 |
| TOTAL COST | 1,000,000 |

The hospital is reviewing its pricing policy for minor operations and is considering cost-plus pricing based on a 20 per cent mark-up on absorption cost.

**REQUIRED:**

Calculate the price per minor operation using cost-plus pricing.

**11.17** Compare the advantages of using absorption costing with the advantages of activity based costing to calculate the selling price of a product.

# 12 OVERHEADS AND OVERHEAD ABSORPTION

In this chapter, we examine how overheads – the cost of indirect materials, indirect labour and indirect expenses – are calculated for a product or service and are added to the direct costs. We will be studying:

● the need to recover the cost of overheads through units of output

● the collection of overhead costs together in cost centres

● the process of allocating and apportioning the cost of overheads into the units of output

● the different bases of apportionment of overheads

● apportionment of service department costs

● two commonly-used overhead absorption rates and their relative merits

● the application of overhead absorption rates to actual work done

## OVERHEADS

In year 1 studies we saw the difference between direct costs and indirect costs (Accounting for AQA: AS and A-level year 1, Chapter 20). Direct and indirect costs can be set out as follows:

| DIRECT MATERIALS | INDIRECT MATERIALS |
|---|---|
| + DIRECT LABOUR | + INDIRECT LABOUR |
| + DIRECT EXPENSES | + INDIRECT EXPENSES |
| = TOTAL DIRECT COST OR PRIME COST | = TOTAL INDIRECT COST OR OVERHEAD |

As we have seen in Chapter 11, direct costs can be identified directly with each unit of output and are allocated directly to output.

Indirect costs or overheads cannot be identified directly with each unit of output. Overheads do not relate to particular units of output but must, instead, be shared amongst all of the cost units (units of output to which costs can be charged) to which they relate. For example, the cost of the factory rent must be included in the cost of the firm's output.

The important point to remember is that all the overheads of a business, together with the direct costs (materials, labour and expenses), must be covered by money flowing in from the firm's output – the sales of products or services. This point is demonstrated in the Worked Example which follows.

## WORKED EXAMPLE: OVERHEAD ABSORPTION

### situation

CoolHeads is a new hairdressing business, being set up by Nathan and Morgan in a rented shop.

Nathan and Morgan are preparing their price list. They must set the prices sufficiently high to cover all their costs and to give them a profit.

They have details of the costs of all the materials they need (shampoos, colourings and so on) from a specialist supplier. Nathan and Morgan have decided the rate to charge to the business for their own work and they do not intend to employ anyone else for the time being.

But there are other costs which they will also incur – their overheads – and they are not so sure how they will work these into their pricing structure. Nathan asks:

*'What about the shop rent and the business rates we have to pay? What about the electricity, the insurance, the telephone bill and all the advertising we have to do? How are we going to cover these costs?'*

*'How much will it cost us in total to deal with each customer?'*

*'How do we make sure that we are going to make a profit?'*

### solution

For pricing purposes, Nathan and Morgan need to include overheads in the cost of each item on their price list.

In a small business like this, the whole business could be a single cost centre. All the overheads could be allowed for in a single rate to charge for a haircut.

Suppose Nathan and Morgan estimate that their total overheads for the first year of trading will be £27,000. They expect to be working on hairstyling for 1,500 hours each during the year, ie a total of 3,000 hours between them.

Therefore, they could decide in advance that each hour of their work should be charged £27,000 ÷ 3,000 = £9 for overheads. A job that takes two hours to complete would then be charged 2 x £9 = £18 for overheads.

Notice that in a service business such as hairdressing, direct materials costs are likely to be relatively small in comparison with the cost of direct labour and overheads. It is essential for Nathan and Morgan to consider the cost of overheads when they are setting their prices and the labour hourly rate is one way of doing this. This is called an 'overhead absorption rate' and we will look in more detail at this idea later in this chapter.

In larger businesses, overheads are usually classified by function under headings such as:

- factory or production expenses, eg factory rent and rates, indirect factory labour, indirect factory materials, heating and lighting of factory
- selling and marketing expenses, eg salaries of sales staff, costs of advertising
- distribution expenses, eg delivery costs, vehicle costs
- administration expenses, eg office rent and rates, office salaries, heating and lighting of office, indirect office materials
- finance costs, eg bank interest, bank charges

Each of these functions or sections of the business is likely to be a separate cost centre (a section of a business to which costs can be charged).

In order to deal with the overheads we need to know how the whole business is split into cost centres. This will depend on the size of the business and the way in which the work is organised.

## COLLECTING OVERHEADS IN COST CENTRES

### allocation of overheads

Some overheads belong entirely to one particular cost centre, for example:

- the salary of a supervisor who works in only one cost centre
- the rent of a separate building in which there is only one cost centre
- the cost of indirect materials that have been issued to one particular cost centre

Overheads like these can therefore be allocated to the cost centre to which they belong.

**Allocation of overheads is the charging – attributing – to a particular cost centre of overheads that are incurred entirely by that cost centre.**

### apportionment of overheads

Overheads that cannot be allocated to a particular cost centre have to be shared or **apportioned** between two or more cost centres.

**Apportionment of overheads is the sharing of overheads over a number of cost centres to which they relate. Each cost centre is charged with a proportion of the overhead cost.**

For example, a department which is a cost centre within a factory will be charged a proportion of the factory rent and rates. Another example is where a supervisor works within two departments, both of which are separate cost centres: the indirect labour cost of employing the supervisor is shared between the two cost centres.

With apportionment, a suitable **basis** – or method – must be found to apportion overheads between cost centres; the basis selected should be related to the type of cost. Different methods might be used for each overhead – the example on the next page indicates some methods that can be used.

| OVERHEAD | BASIS OF APPORTIONMENT |
|---|---|
| rent, business rates | floor area (or volume of space) of cost centres |
| heating, lighting | floor area (or volume of space) of cost centres |
| buildings insurance | floor area (or volume of space) of cost centres |
| buildings depreciation | floor area (or volume of space) of cost centres |
| machinery insurance | cost or carrying amount of machinery and equipment |
| machinery depreciation | value of machinery, or machine usage (hours) |
| canteen | number of employees in each cost centre |
| supervisory costs | number of employees in each cost centre, or labour hours worked by supervisors in each cost centre |

It must be stressed that apportionment is used for those overheads that cannot be allocated to a particular cost centre. For example, if a college's Business Studies Department occupies a building in another part of town from the main college building, the rates for the building can clearly be allocated to the Business Studies cost centre. By contrast, the rates for the main college building must be apportioned amongst the cost centres on the main campus.

## review of allocation and apportionment

It is important that the allocation and apportionment of overheads are reviewed at regular intervals to ensure that the methods being used are still valid. For example:

- *allocation*

  The role of a supervisor may have changed – whereas previously the supervisor worked in one department only, he or she might now be working in two departments.

- *apportionment*

  Building work may have expanded the floor area of a department, so that the apportionment basis needs to be reworked for costs such as rent and rates.

Any proposed changes to allocation and apportionment must be discussed with senior staff and their agreement obtained before any changes to methods are implemented. Accounting staff will often have to consult with staff (such as managers and supervisors) working in operational departments, to discuss how overheads are charged to their departments, and to resolve any queries.

## apportionment and ratios

It is important to understand the method of apportionment of overheads using ratios. For example, overheads relating to buildings are often shared in the ratio of the floor area used by the cost centres.

Now read through the example below which shows the use of ratios in apportionment, and then the Worked Example on the next page.

**example of apportionment using ratios**

AyeBee Limited has four cost centres: two production departments, Aye and Bee, and two non-production cost centres, stores and maintenance. The total rent per year for the business premises is £12,000. This is to be apportioned on the basis of floor area, given as:

|  | Production dept Aye | Production dept Bee | Stores | Maintenance |
|---|---|---|---|---|
| Floor area (square metres) | 400 | 550 | 350 | 200 |

**Step 1**

Calculate the total floor area: 400 + 550 + 350 + 200 = 1,500 square metres

This shows the ratio in which costs are apportioned to each department as 400:550:350:200.

**Step 2**

Divide the total rent by the total floor area: £12,000 ÷ 1,500 = £8

This gives a rate of £8 per square metre.

**Step 3**

Multiply the floor area in each cost centre by the rate per square metre. This gives the share of rent for each cost centre. For example, in production department Aye, the share of rent is 400 x £8 = £3,200. The results are shown in the table:

|  | Production dept Aye | Production dept Bee | Stores | Maintenance |
|---|---|---|---|---|
| Floor area (square metres) | 400 | 550 | 350 | 200 |
| Rent apportioned | £3,200 | £4,400 | £2,800 | £1,600 |

**Step 4**

Check that the apportioned amounts agree with the total rent:

£3,200 + £4,400 + £ 2,800 + £1,600 = £12,000.

## WORKED EXAMPLE: OVERHEAD ALLOCATION AND APPORTIONMENT

### situation

Pilot Engineering Limited, which makes car engine components, uses some of the latest laser equipment in one department, while another section of the business continues to use traditional machinery. Details of the factory are as follows:

Department Exe is a 'hi-tech' machine shop equipped with laser-controlled machinery which cost £80,000. This department has 400 square metres of floor area. There are three machine operators: the supervisor spends one-third of the time in this department.

Department Wye is a 'low-tech' part of the factory equipped with machinery which cost £20,000. The floor area is 600 square metres. There are two workers who spend all their time in this department: the supervisor spends two-thirds of the time in this department.

The overheads to be allocated or apportioned are as follows:

| | | |
|---|---|---|
| 1 | Factory business rates | £12,000 |
| 2 | Wages of the supervisor | £21,000 |
| 3 | Factory heating and lighting | £2,500 |
| 4 | Depreciation of machinery | £20,000 |
| 5 | Buildings insurance | £2,000 |
| 6 | Insurance of machinery | £1,500 |
| 7 | Specialist materials for the laser equipment | £2,500 |

How should each of these be allocated or apportioned to each department?

### solution

The recommendations are:

1   Factory business rates – apportioned on the basis of floor area.

2   Supervisor's wages – apportioned on the basis of time spent, ie one-third to Department Exe, and two-thirds to Department Wye. If the time spent was not known, an alternative basis could be established, based on the number of employees.

3   Factory heating and lighting – apportioned on the basis of floor area.

4   Depreciation of machinery – apportioned on the basis of machine value.

5   Buildings insurance – apportioned on the basis of floor area.

6   Insurance of machinery – apportioned on the basis of machine value.

7   Specialist materials for the laser equipment – allocated to Department Exe because this cost belongs entirely to Department Exe.

It is important to note that there are no fixed rules for the apportionment of overheads – the only proviso is that a fair proportion of the overhead is charged to each department which has some responsibility for the cost being incurred. Methods of apportionment will need to be reviewed at regular intervals to ensure that they are still valid; changes can only be implemented with the agreement of senior staff.

The apportionment of overheads for Pilot Engineering Limited is as follows (sample workings are shown below the table):

| Overhead | Basis of apportionment | Total | Dept Exe | Dept Wye |
|---|---|---|---|---|
| | | £ | £ | £ |
| Factory rates | Floor area | 12,000 | 4,800 | 7,200 |
| Wages of supervisor | Time spent | 21,000 | 7,000 | 14,000 |
| Heating and lighting | Floor area | 2,500 | 1,000 | 1,500 |
| Dep'n of machinery | Machine value | 20,000 | 16,000 | 4,000 |
| Buildings insurance | Floor area | 2,000 | 800 | 1,200 |
| Machinery insurance | Machine value | 1,500 | 1,200 | 300 |
| Specialist materials | Allocation | 2,500 | 2,500 | – |
| | | 61,500 | 33,300 | 28,200 |

For example, the floor areas of the two departments are:

| | | |
|---|---|---|
| Dept Exe | 400 | square metres |
| Dept Wye | 600 | square metres |
| Total | 1,000 | square metres |

Factory business rates are apportioned as follows:

$$\frac{£12,000}{1,000} = £12 \text{ per square metre}$$

| | | | |
|---|---|---|---|
| Dept Exe rates | £12 x 400 | = | £4,800 |
| Dept Wye rates | £12 x 600 | = | £7,200 |
| Total | | | £12,000 |

Note that overhead apportionment is often, in practice, calculated using a spreadsheet.

# SERVICE DEPARTMENTS

Many businesses have departments which provide services within the business; for example, maintenance, transport, stores or stationery. Each service department is likely to be a cost centre, to which a proportion of overheads is charged. As service departments do not themselves have any cost units to which their overheads may be charged, the costs of each service department must be re-apportioned to the production departments (which do have cost units to which overheads can be charged). A suitable basis of re-apportionment must be used, for example:

* the overheads of a maintenance department might be re-apportioned to production departments on the basis of value of machinery or equipment, or on the basis of time spent in each production department
* the overheads of a stores or stationery department could be re-apportioned on the basis of value of goods issued to production departments
* the overheads of a subsidised canteen could be re-apportioned on the basis of the number of employees

Re-apportionment of service department overheads is considered in the next section.

# RE-APPORTIONMENT OF SERVICE DEPARTMENT OVERHEADS

The overheads of service departments are charged to production cost centres using the **elimination method** with either:

* direct apportionment, where service departments provide services to production departments only, or
* step-down, where service departments provide services to production departments and to some other service departments

To illustrate re-apportionment, we will apply the elimination method to a business with two production departments, Cee and Dee, and two service departments, stores and maintenance. After allocation and apportionment of production overheads, the totals are:

|  | Total | Production dept Cee | Production dept Dee | Stores | Maintenance |
|---|---|---|---|---|---|
|  | £ | £ | £ | £ | £ |
| Overheads | 20,400 | 10,000 | 5,000 | 2,400 | 3,000 |

## elimination method, with direct apportionment

Here the service departments do not provide services to one another. Their costs are directly apportioned to production departments using a suitable basis. In the example on the previous page:

- stores overheads are re-apportioned on the basis of the number of stores requisitions – department Cee has made 150 requisitions; department Dee has made 50
- maintenance overheads are re-apportioned on the value of machinery – department Cee has machinery with a carrying amount value of £20,000, department Dee's machinery has a carrying amount of £10,000

Using direct apportionment, the overheads of the service departments are re-apportioned as shown in the table below. The method of calculation using ratios is the same as used for apportionment.

Notice that the total is taken out of the service cost centre column when it is shared between the production cost centres.

| | Total | Production dept Cee | Production dept Dee | Stores | Maintenance |
|---|---|---|---|---|---|
| | £ | £ | £ | £ | £ |
| Overheads | 20,400 | 10,000 | 5,000 | 2,400 | 3,000 |
| Stores | – | 1,800 | 600 | (2,400) | – |
| Maintenance | – | 2,000 | 1,000 | – | (3,000) |
| | 20,400 | 13,800 | 6,600 | – | – |

Thus all the overheads have now been charged to the production departments where they can be 'absorbed' into the cost units which form the output of each department. We will see how the absorption is carried out later in this chapter.

## elimination method, with step-down

This is used where one service department provides services to another.

Using the figures from the example, the stores department deals with requisitions from the maintenance department, but no maintenance work is carried out in the stores department. Under the elimination method with step-down, working from the information which follows (next page), we re-apportion firstly the overheads of the stores department (because it does not receive any services from the maintenance department), and secondly the overheads of the maintenance department.

- number of stores requisitions
  - department Cee        150
  - department Dee        50
  - maintenance            50

- value of machinery
  - department Cee        £20,000
  - department Dee        £10,000

The re-apportionment of the production overheads of the service departments, using step-down, is as follows:

|  | Total | Production dept Cee | Production dept Dee | Stores | Maintenance |
|---|---|---|---|---|---|
|  | £ | £ | £ | £ | £ |
| Overheads | 20,400 | 10,000 | 5,000 | 2,400 | 3,000 |
| Stores | – | 1,440 | 480 | (2,400) | 480 |
|  |  |  | – |  | *3,480 |
| Maintenance | – | 2,320 | 1,160 | – | (3,480) |
|  | 20,400 | 13,760 | 6,640 | – | – |

* Note that a new total is calculated for the maintenance department before it is re-apportioned. £480 from stores is added to the original £3,000 overheads in the maintenance department.

All the overheads have now been charged to the production departments.

# ALLOCATION AND APPORTIONMENT – A SUMMARY

The diagram on the next page summarises the allocation and apportionment of overheads that we have seen in this chapter. It shows:

- allocation of overheads directly to cost centres
- apportionment of overheads on an equitable basis to cost centres
- re-apportionment of service department costs to production cost centres

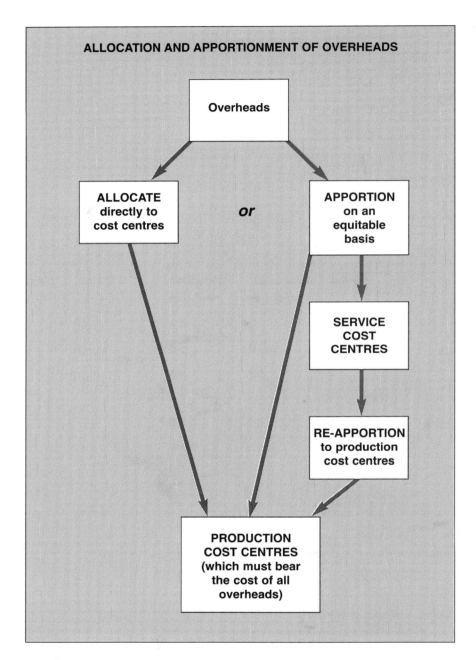

**ALLOCATION AND APPORTIONMENT OF OVERHEADS**

Overheads

ALLOCATE
directly to
cost centres

*or*

APPORTION
on an
equitable
basis

SERVICE
COST
CENTRES

RE-APPORTION
to production
cost centres

PRODUCTION
COST CENTRES
(which must bear
the cost of all
overheads)

## OVERHEAD ABSORPTION

Once overheads have been allocated or apportioned to production cost centres, the final step is to ensure that the overheads are charged to cost units. In the language of cost accounting this is known as 'absorption', ie the cost of overheads is charged to the cost units which pass through that particular production department.

We saw in the Worked Example on page 271 (CoolHeads hairdressing) how overheads could be allowed for when deciding on selling prices.

Similarly, if you take a car to be repaired at a garage, the bill may be presented as follows:

|  | £ |
|---|---|
| Parts | 70.00 |
| Labour: 3 hours at £40 per hour | 120.00 |
| Total | 190.00 |

Within this bill are the three main elements of cost: materials (parts), labour and overheads. The last two are combined as labour – the garage mechanic is not paid £40 per hour; instead the labour rate might be £15 per hour, with the rest, ie £25 per hour, being absorption of the overhead and the profit of the garage. Other examples are accountants and solicitors, who charge a 'rate per hour', part of which is used to contribute to the cost of overheads and profit.

To be profitable, a business must ensure that its selling prices more than cover all its costs:

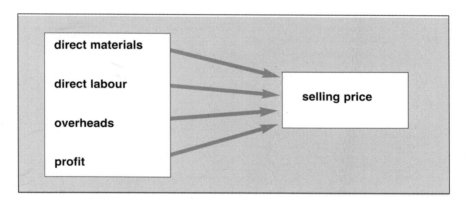

## calculating overhead absorption rates

In order to absorb the overheads of a department, there are two steps to be followed:

1  calculation of the overhead absorption rate (OAR)

2  application of this rate to actual work done

The overhead absorption rate is calculated using budgeted figures as follows, for a given time period:

$$OAR = \frac{budgeted\ overheads}{budgeted\ activity}$$

The amount of budgeted activity must be measured in a suitable way, usually:

- labour hours, or
- machine hours

These methods are illustrated below.

## labour hour method

With this method, production overhead is absorbed on the basis of the number of direct labour hours worked.

1  Calculation of the overhead absorption rate, using budgeted figures:

$$\frac{budgeted\ overheads}{budgeted\ direct\ labour\ hours} = cost\ per\ labour\ hour$$

2  Application of the rate:

*direct labour hours worked x overhead absorption rate*

*= overhead absorbed and charged to production*

---

**example**

Department Jay    budgeted overheads for year                £40,000
                  budgeted direct labour hours for year        5,000
                  actual direct labour hours in March            450

1    Overhead absorption rate:
$$\frac{£40,000}{5,000\ hours} = £8\ per\ direct\ labour\ hour$$

2    Application of the rate:
          450 hours  x  £8    = £3,600 of overhead absorbed in March

---

## machine hour method

Here the production overhead is absorbed on the basis of machine hours.

1  Calculation of the overhead absorption rate, using budgeted figures:

$$\frac{budgeted\ overheads}{budgeted\ machine\ hours} = cost\ per\ machine\ hour$$

2  Application of the rate:

*machine hours worked  x  overhead absorption rate*

*= overhead absorbed and charged to production*

**example**

Department Kay     budgeted overheads for year           £216,000
                         budgeted machine hours for year        36,000
                         actual machine hours in March           3,500

1     Overhead absorption rate:

$$\frac{£216,000}{36,000 \text{ hours}} = £6 \text{ per machine hour}$$

2     Application of the rate:

       3,500 hours x £6   =   £21,000 of overhead absorbed in March

## which method to use?

Only one overhead absorption rate will be used in a particular department (cost centre), and the method selected must relate to the reason why the costs are incurred. For example, a cost centre which is machine based, where most of the overheads incurred relate to machinery, will use a machine hour basis.

The labour hour method is popular where the cost centre is labour intensive (eg the garage mentioned earlier). Overheads are absorbed on a time basis – a cost unit that requires twice the labour of another cost unit will be charged twice the overhead. However, this method will be inappropriate where some units are worked on by hand while others quickly pass through a machinery process and require little labour time.

A machine hour rate is particularly appropriate where expensive machinery is used in the department. However, it would be unsuitable where not all products pass through the machine but some are worked on by hand: in the latter case, no overheads would be charged to the cost units.

It is important to select the best method of overhead absorption for the particular business, otherwise wrong decisions will be made on the basis of the costing information. The particular absorption method selected for a department will need to be reviewed at regular intervals to ensure that it is still valid. For example, the labour hour method is unlikely to continue to be appropriate where a machine has been brought in to automate processes that were previously carried out by hand. As noted earlier, any proposed changes must be discussed with senior staff and their agreement obtained before any changes to methods are implemented. The changes will need to be discussed with staff (such as managers and supervisors) working in operational departments to explain how overheads will be charged to their departments in the future, and any queries will need to be resolved.

## using a pre-determined rate

Most businesses calculate a pre-determined overhead absorption rate (OAR) for each department. This is then applied to all production passing through that department.

The OAR is calculated in advance using budgeted amounts – this avoids having to calculate the rate regularly, which may result in changes over quite short time periods. Instead the rate is smoothed out over fluctuations in cost and activity over a longer accounting period.

# Over- or Under-Absorption of Overheads

Most businesses will find that the amount of overheads absorbed into the cost of their actual work during the year is not the same as the amount that has been spent. If the amount absorbed is the greater, the difference is called 'over-absorption' of overheads. If the amount absorbed is less than the amount spent, the difference is called 'under-absorption'.

**Over-absorption or under-absorption is the difference between the total amount of overheads absorbed in a given period and the total amount spent on overheads.**

## over-absorption of overheads

The following example shows a calculation for over-absorption – with the overhead absorption rate based on direct labour hours.

---

Department Exe

| | |
|---|---|
| overhead absorption rate (based on direct labour hours) | £6.00 per labour hour |
| actual labour hours in year | 6,300 hours |
| actual overheads for year | £36,000 |

- actual overheads for the department are £36,000
- actual overhead absorbed: 6,300 hours x £6.00 per hour = £37,800
- over-absorption of overhead: £37,800 – £36,000 = £1,800

At the end of the financial year the income statement is credited with the amount of over-absorbed overhead.

---

On first impressions, over-absorption of overheads seems to be a 'bonus' for a business – profits will be higher; however, it should be remembered that the overhead rate may have been set too high. As a consequence, sales might have been lost because the selling price has been too high. The overhead absorption rate (OAR) will need to be reviewed with the manager and supervisors of the operational department if over-absorption continues on a regular basis – they may be able to explain the reason for the difference.

## under-absorption of overheads

With under-absorption, the actual overhead absorbed is less than the actual overheads for the department. For example, if in Department Exe (above) actual labour hours in the year were 5,500, the calculations would be:

---

- actual overheads for the department are £36,000
- actual overhead absorbed: 5,500 hours x £6.00 per hour = £33,000
- under-absorption of overhead: £36,000 – £33,000 = £3,000

At the end of the financial year the income statement is debited with the amount of under-absorbed overhead.

---

Under absorption of overheads is a cost to a business, so reducing profitability. It may be that the selling price of output has been set too low, or output is less than expected, or actual overhead is more than expected. The OAR will need to be revised if under-absorption continues on a regular basis.

## CHAPTER SUMMARY

- Direct costs can be identified directly with each unit of output and are allocated to the output at the cost incurred.

- Indirect costs (overheads) do not relate to particular units of output, but must be shared amongst all the cost units to which they relate.

- Overheads are:
  - allocated to a specific cost centre, if they belong entirely to that cost centre
  - apportioned between cost centres, if they are shared

- Apportionment is done on a suitable basis, using ratios of floor area, numbers of employees, etc.

- The total overheads allocated and apportioned to the service cost centres are then re-apportioned to the production cost centres using the elimination method.

- After re-apportionment of the service cost centre overheads, the total overheads in each production cost centre can be calculated.

- Overhead absorption rates (OAR) are calculated using the total budgeted overheads in each cost centre.

- An OAR is calculated as follows:

  *overhead absorption rate* $= \dfrac{\textit{budgeted overheads}}{\textit{budgeted activity}}$

  where the budgeted activity be measured, often in terms of direct labour hours or machine hours.

- Two commonly-used OARs are labour hour and machine hour.

- Overhead absorption rates are applied to the actual work carried out. A direct labour hour absorption rate is applied as follows, for example:

  *direct labour hours worked x overhead absorption rate $=$ overhead absorbed*

- At the end of a given period, the amount of overhead absorbed may differ from the amount actually spent on the overheads. The difference is:
  - either, over-absorption (when the amount absorbed is more than the amount spent)
  - or, under-absorption (when the amount absorbed is less than the amount spent)

In the next chapter we focus on standard costing, one of the four main methods of costing, and look at its purpose, advantages, and its role in variance analysis.

# QUESTIONS

visit
**www.osbornebooks.co.uk**
to take an online test

An asterisk (*) after the question number means that the answer is given at the end of this book.

**12.1*** Which formula is used to calculate the overhead absorption rate in a cost centre?

| A | Budgeted overheads/budgeted activity | |
|---|---|---|
| B | Actual overheads/budgeted activity | |
| C | Budgeted overheads/actual activity | |
| D | Budgeted activity/budgeted overheads | |

**12.2** Beacon Ltd operates a system of absorption costing. It apportions factory administration overheads to the four departments of cutting, moulding, finishing and stores on the basis of the floor area in each department.

| Department | Cutting | Moulding | Finishing | Stores |
|---|---|---|---|---|
| Floor area (square metres) | 100 | 40 | 50 | 20 |

The factory administration overheads for the next year are budgeted to be £176,400.

How much of the factory administration overheads will be apportioned to the moulding department?

| A | £16,800 | |
|---|---|---|
| B | £33,600 | |
| C | £42,000 | |
| D | £84,000 | |

**12.3*** The following information is available for Product Bee:

- budgeted overhead absorption rate      £8.00 per direct labour hour
- direct labour hours per unit      3 hours
- finished goods inventory at 1 January 20-4      60 units
- finished goods inventory at 31 January 20-4      80 units

Indicate the difference between:
- – the profit for the month using absorption costing
- – the profit for the month using marginal costing

| A | Absorption costing profit would be £480 higher | |
|---|---|---|
| B | Absorption costing profit would be £480 lower | |
| C | Marginal costing profit would be £960 higher | |
| D | Marginal costing profit would be £960 lower | |

**12.4\*** Distinguish between:

- allocation of overheads

- apportionment of overheads

**12.5\*** Wyvern Fabrication Company has two production departments – moulding and finishing.

The company absorbs overheads on the basis of machine hours and the following overhead analysis information is available to you (note that service department overheads have already been apportioned to production departments):

| OVERHEAD ANALYSIS SHEET | | |
|---|---|---|
| | **Moulding** | **Finishing** |
| Budgeted total overheads (£) | 9,338 | 3,298 |
| Budgeted machine hours | 1,450 | 680 |
| Budgeted overhead absorption rate (£) | | |

Details of a particular job of work are as follows:

| JOB NUMBER 1234: OVERHEAD ANALYSIS SHEET | | |
|---|---|---|
| | **Moulding** | **Finishing** |
| Machine hours | 412 | 154 |
| Budgeted overhead absorption rate (£) | | |
| Overhead absorbed (£) | | |

**You are to:**

**(a)** Calculate the overhead absorption rate for each of the two departments and complete the overhead analysis sheet.

**(b)** Calculate the production overhead absorbed by job number 1234 and complete the job overhead analysis sheet.

**(c)** Suggest an alternative overhead absorption rate that the company might use and comment on the circumstances that would make it appropriate.

**12.6**

Mereford Management College is a private college that has two teaching departments – accountancy and management.

The college charges overheads on the basis of lecturer hours. The following overhead analysis information is available to you (note that support services overheads – such as the administration office, reprographics department and learning resources – have already been apportioned to the teaching departments):

| OVERHEAD ANALYSIS SHEET FOR JANUARY 20-8 | | |
|---|---|---|
| | Accountancy department | Management department |
| Budgeted total overheads (£) | 22,143 | 17,251 |
| Budgeted lecturer hours | 1,525 | 1,300 |
| Budgeted overhead absorption rate (£) | | |

Details of a particular course – 'Finance for Managers' – that is taught in both the accountancy and management departments are as follows:

| OVERHEAD ANALYSIS SHEET COURSE: FINANCE FOR MANAGERS | | |
|---|---|---|
| | Accountancy department | Management department |
| Lecturer hours | 45 | 20 |
| Budgeted overhead absorption rate (£) | | |
| Overhead absorbed by course (£) | | |

**You are to:**

**(a)** Calculate the overhead absorption rate for each of the two departments and complete the overhead analysis sheet.

**(b)** Calculate the overhead absorbed by the 'Finance for Managers' course and complete the course overhead analysis sheet.

**12.7\*** ABC Limited is a manufacturing business with three cost centres: Departments A, B and C. The following are the budgeted factory overheads for the forthcoming year:

| | |
|---|---|
| Rent and rates | £7,210 |
| Depreciation of machinery | £10,800 |
| Supervisor's salary | £12,750 |
| Insurance of machinery | £750 |

Departmental information is:

| | Dept A | Dept B | Dept C |
|---|---|---|---|
| Floor area (sq m) | 300 | 150 | 250 |
| Value of machinery | £25,000 | £15,000 | £10,000 |
| Number of production-line employees | 8 | 4 | 3 |

**You are to:**

**(a)** Apportion the overheads to the cost centres, stating the basis of apportionment. (Use a layout based on the the one shown on page 276.)

**(b)** Calculate the overhead absorption rate (to two decimal places) of each department, based on labour hours. Note that the factory works a 37 hour week for 48 weeks in a year.

**12.8** Wye Engineering Limited offers specialist engineering services to the car industry. It has two production departments – machining and finishing – and a service department which maintains the machinery of both departments. Budgeted production overheads for the forthcoming year are:

| | £ |
|---|---|
| Rent and rates | 5,520 |
| Buildings insurance | 1,320 |
| Insurance of machinery | 1,650 |
| Lighting and heating | 3,720 |
| Depreciation of machinery | 11,000 |
| Supervisory salaries | 30,000 |
| Maintenance department salary | 16,000 |
| Factory cleaning | 4,800 |

The following information is available:

| | Machining | Finishing | Maintenance |
|---|---|---|---|
| Floor area (square metres) | 300 | 200 | 100 |
| Number of employees | 6 | 3 | 1 |
| Value of machinery | £40,000 | £15,000 | – |

The factory works a 35 hour week for 47 weeks each year.

**You are to:**

**(a)** Prepare an analysis of production overheads showing the basis of allocation and apportionment to the three departments of the business (use the layout below).

**(b)** Re-apportion the service department overheads to production departments on the basis of value of machinery (use the layout below).

**(c)** Calculate an overhead absorption rate based on labour hours for each of the two production departments.

**(d)** Discuss an alternative overhead absorption rate that the company could use.

| Overhead | Basis of apportionment | Total | Machining | Finishing | Maintenance |
|---|---|---|---|---|---|
| | | £ | £ | £ | £ |
| Rent and rates | | | | | |
| Buildings insurance | | | | | |
| Machinery insurance | | | | | |
| Lighting and heating | | | | | |
| Dep'n of machinery | | | | | |
| Supervisory salaries | | | | | |
| Maintenance dept salary | | | | | |
| Factory cleaning | | | | | |
| | | | | | |
| Re-apportionment of maintenance dept | | | | | |
| | | | | | |

**12.9\*** Mercia Tutorial College has two teaching departments – business studies and general studies – and two service departments – administration and technical support. The overheads of each department are as follows:

|  |  | £ |
|---|---|---|
| • | business studies | 40,000 |
| • | general studies | 20,000 |
| • | administration | 9,600 |
| • | technical support | 12,000 |

The basis for re-apportioning the overheads of the service departments is:

* technical support, on the value of equipment in each department – business studies, £50,000; general studies, £25,000; administration, £25,000

* administration, on the number of students in the teaching departments – business studies 500; general studies, 250

**You are to** use the elimination method with step-down to re-apportion the two service department overheads to the two teaching departments.

**12.10\*** Rossiter and Rossiter is a firm of chartered accountants, with two partners. Overhead costs for next year are budgeted to be:

|  | £ |
|---|---|
| Office rent | 20,000 |
| Office salaries | 60,000 |
| Rates | 9,600 |
| Heating and lighting | 4,800 |
| Stationery | 4,000 |
| Postage and telephone | 10,200 |
| Car expenses | 11,200 |

The two partners plan to work for 47 weeks next year. They will each be in the office for 40 hours per week, but will be working on behalf of their clients for 35 hours per week.

**(a)** What is the overhead absorption rate per partner hour?

**(b)** If each partner wishes to earn a salary of £60,000 per year, what is the combined hourly rate per partner, which includes overheads and their salaries?

**(c)** If both partners actually work on their clients' behalf for 37 hours per week, what will be the total over-absorption of overheads for the year?

**12.11**

A friend of yours is about to start in business making garden seats. She plans to make two different qualities – 'Standard' and 'De Luxe'. Costs per unit for direct materials and labour are budgeted to be:

|  | Standard | De Luxe |
|---|---|---|
|  | £ | £ |
| Direct materials | 12.50 | 20.00 |
| Direct labour: |  |  |
| 3 hours at £8.00 per hour | 24.00 | – |
| 3.5 hours at £10.00 per hour | – | 35.00 |
|  | 36.50 | 55.00 |
| Machine hours | 1 | 2.5 |

Production overheads are expected to be £1,000 per month.

Production is expected to be 80 'Standard' seats and 40 'De Luxe' seats per month.

**(a)** Suggest two different methods by which overheads can be absorbed and calculate the overhead absorption rate.

**(b)** Calculate the production cost of each of the two qualities of garden seats using the two different methods of overhead absorption (to two decimal places).

**(c)** Compare the results of your calculations and suggest to your friend the most appropriate method of overhead absorption for this business.

**12.12\***

Durning Limited manufactures and sells household furniture. The company's operations are organised by departments, as follows:

- Warehouse
- Manufacturing
- Sales
- Administration

The fixed overheads of the company for November 20-7 were as follows:

|  | £ | £ |
|---|---|---|
| Depreciation of non-current assets |  | 9,150 |
| Rent |  | 11,000 |
| Other property overheads |  | 6,200 |
| Administration overheads |  | 13,450 |
| Staff costs: |  |  |
| – warehouse | 3,600 |  |
| – indirect manufacturing | 9,180 |  |
| – sales | 8,650 |  |
| – administration | 5,940 |  |
|  |  | 27,370 |
| **Total fixed overheads** |  | 67,170 |

The following information is also available:

| Department | % of floor space occupied | Carrying amount of non-current assets £000 |
|---|---|---|
| Warehouse | 15% | 120 |
| Manufacturing | 60% | 400 |
| Sales | 10% | 20 |
| Administration | 15% | 60 |
| | 100% | 600 |

Overheads are allocated and apportioned between departments using the most appropriate basis.

**REQUIRED:**

**(a)** Please refer to the text and table on the next page.

**(b)** Manufacturing fixed overheads are absorbed on the basis of budgeted machine hours. The budgeted number of machine hours for November 20-7 was 10,000 hours.

Calculate the budgeted fixed overhead absorption rate for the manufacturing department for November 20-7.

**For use with Question 12.12 (a) on previous page**

Complete the following table showing the allocation and apportionment of fixed overheads between the four departments.

| Fixed overheads for November 20-7 | Basis of apportmnt | Total £ | Warehouse £ | Manufacturing £ | Sales £ | Administration £ |
|---|---|---|---|---|---|---|
| Depreciation of non-current assets | | 9,150 | | | | |
| Rent | | 11,000 | | | | |
| Other property overheads | | 6,200 | | | | |
| Administration overheads | | 13,450 | | | | |
| Staff costs | | 27,370 | | | | |
| | | 67,170 | | | | |

**12.13** Wyvern Private Hospital plc has two patient wards – a day care ward for minor operations where the patients go home at the end of the day, and a surgical ward for patients who remain in the hospital for several days. There are two service departments – the operating theatre and administration.

The overheads of each department for last month were as follows:

|  |  | £ |
|---|---|---|
| • | day care ward | 28,750 |
| • | surgical ward | 42,110 |
| • | operating theatre | 32,260 |
| • | administration | 9,075 |

The basis for re-apportioning the overheads of the service departments is:

• operating theatre, on the number of operations carried out – day care ward, 160; surgical ward, 120

• administration, on the number of staff in each department – day care ward, 10; surgical ward, 25; operating theatre, 20

**You are to** use the elimination method with step-down to re-apportion the two service department overheads to the two patient wards.

**12.14** Fox Furniture Limited makes tables and chairs for school and college use. There are two production lines – tables and chairs – and two service departments – stores and maintenance.

The overheads of each department for last month were as follows:

|  |  | £ |
|---|---|---|
| • | tables | 12,000 |
| • | chairs | 8,000 |
| • | stores | 3,000 |
| • | maintenance | 2,000 |

The basis for re-apportioning the overheads of the service departments is:

• stores, on the number of requisitions – tables, 100; chairs, 80; maintenance, 20

• maintenance, on the value of equipment in each department – tables, £30,000; chairs, £20,000

**You are to** use the elimination method with step-down to re-apportion the two service department overheads to the two production departments.

**12.15**

Milestone Motors Limited sells and services cars. The company's operations are organised into four departments, as follows:

- New car sales
- Used car sales
- Servicing
- Administration

The fixed overheads of the company for the four weeks ended 28 April 20-4 were as follows:

|  | £ | £ |
|---|---|---|
| Depreciation of non-current assets | | 8,400 |
| Rent | | 10,000 |
| Other property overheads | | 4,500 |
| Staff costs: | | |
|   – new car sales | 11,080 | |
|   – used car sales | 7,390 | |
|   – servicing | 9,975 | |
|   – administration | 6,850 | |
| | | 35,295 |
| Administration overheads | | 3,860 |
| **Total fixed overheads** | | 62,055 |

The following information is also available:

| Department | % of floor space occupied | Carrying amount of non-current assets £000 |
|---|---|---|
| New car sales | 40% | 50 |
| Used car sales | 30% | 30 |
| Servicing | 20% | 100 |
| Administration | 10% | 20 |
| | 100% | 200 |

Overheads are allocated and apportioned using the most appropriate basis. The total administrative overheads are then re-apportioned to the three departments using the following percentages.

- New car sales    20%
- Used car sales   30%
- Servicing        50%

**REQUIRED**

**(a)** Please refer to the text and table on the next page.

**(b)** Servicing department fixed overheads are absorbed on the basis of budgeted direct labour hours. The budgeted number of direct labour hours for the servicing department during the four weeks ended 28 April 20-4 was 1,025 hours.

Calculate the budgeted fixed overhead absorption rate per direct labour hour for the servicing department during the period.

**For use with Question 12.15 (a) on previous page**

Complete the following table showing:

- the basis for allocation or apportionment of each overhead;

- the allocation and apportionment of fixed overheads between the four departments;

- the re-apportionment of the total administration overheads.

| Fixed overheads for four weeks ended 28 April 20-4 | Basis of apportmnt | Total £ | New car sales £ | Used car sales £ | Servicing £ | Administration £ |
|---|---|---|---|---|---|---|
| Depreciation of non-current assets | | 8,400 | | | | |
| Rent | | 10,000 | | | | |
| Other property overheads | | 4,500 | | | | |
| Staff costs | | 35,295 | | | | |
| Administration overheads | | 3,860 | | | | |
| | | 62,055 | | | | |
| Administration | | 62,055 | | | | |

**12.16\*** Wentworth Limited's budgeted overheads and activity levels for the next quarter are:

|  | Cutting | Assembly |
|---|---|---|
| Budgeted overheads (£) | 165,600 | 318,750 |
| Budgeted direct labour hours | 18,400 | 12,750 |
| Budgeted machine hours | 8,280 | 4,250 |

**(a)** What would be the budgeted overhead absorption rate for each department if this were set based on their both being heavily automated?

| A | Cutting £9 per hour; assembly £25 per hour |  |
|---|---|---|
| B | Cutting £9 per hour; assembly £75 per hour |  |
| C | Cutting £20 per hour; assembly £25 per hour |  |
| D | Cutting £20 per hour; assembly £75 per hour |  |

**(b)** What would be the budgeted overhead absorption rate for each department if this were set based on their both being labour intensive?

| A | Cutting £9 per hour; assembly £25 per hour |  |
|---|---|---|
| B | Cutting £9 per hour; assembly £75 per hour |  |
| C | Cutting £20 per hour; assembly £25 per hour |  |
| D | Cutting £20 per hour; assembly £75 per hour |  |

**Additional data:**

At the end of the quarter actual overheads incurred were found to be:

|  | Cutting | Assembly |
|---|---|---|
| Actual overheads (£) | 158,200 | 322,250 |

**(c)** Assuming that exactly the same amount of overheads was absorbed as budgeted, what were the budgeted under- or over-absorptions in the quarter?

| A | Cutting over-absorbed £7,400; assembly over-absorbed £3,500 |  |
|---|---|---|
| B | Cutting over-absorbed £7,400; assembly under-absorbed £3,500 |  |
| C | Cutting under-absorbed £7,400; assembly under-absorbed £3,500 |  |
| D | Cutting under-absorbed £7,400; assembly over-absorbed £3,500 |  |

**12.17** Crosskeys Ltd has the following information for its machining and finishing departments:

| Quarter 1 | Machining | Finishing |
|---|---|---|
| Budgeted direct labour hours | 1,385 | 1,320 |
| Budgeted machine hours | 2,650 | 750 |
| Actual direct labour hours | 1,430 | 1,450 |
| Actual machine hours | 2,750 | 810 |
| Budgeted overheads | £38,425 | £24,750 |
| Actual overheads | £41,250 | £26,550 |

**(a)** The budgeted overhead absorption rate for the machining department based upon machine hours, and for the finishing department based upon labour hours, is:

| | Machining £ | Finishing £ |
|---|---|---|
| Budgeted overhead absorption rate | per hour | per hour |

**(b)** Complete the following sentence by selecting the appropriate item and inserting the correct amount:

In Quarter 1 overheads for the machining department were

OVER-ABSORBED / UNDER-ABSORBED

by £ 

**(c)** In Quarter 2, if the overhead absorption rate for the finishing department is £19 per labour hour, the actual overheads incurred were £26,550 and the actual labour hours used were 1,450, complete the following table:

| | Overheads incurred £ | Overheads absorbed £ | Difference absorbed £ | Under/over absorption |
|---|---|---|---|---|
| Finishing department | | | | |

# 13 STANDARD COSTING AND VARIANCE ANALYSIS

This chapter focuses on standard costing, which can be used in conjunction with marginal costing, absorption costing and activity based costing.

Standard costing is used to calculate costs – materials, labour and overheads – in advance of production. It is a way of controlling costs: standard costs are compared with actual costs by calculating variances, and action is taken where appropriate to improve performance.

In this chapter we look at the:

●     purpose of standard costing

●     role of standard costing in variance analysis

●     main variances for materials, labour and sales

●     interrelationships of variances

●     reconciliation of budget and actual figures for cost, profit and sales

●     advantages and disadvantages of standard costing

## PURPOSE OF STANDARD COSTING

**Standard costing sets the planned cost for materials, labour and overheads in a period of time.**

All businesses need methods of controlling the costs of materials, labour and overheads that go to make up the finished product (we have seen, in Chapter 10, how budgets can be set and controlled). Imagine a factory where the cost and amount of materials to make the product is not known, where the hours of work and rates of pay have not been recorded and where there is no indication of the cost of overheads. Under such circumstances, the costs could not be controlled, and it would be impossible to quote a price for the product to a customer. Therefore many businesses establish a standard or budgeted cost for their output. Thus a standard cost can be calculated for things as diverse as a product manufactured in a factory, a hospital operation, servicing a car and a meal in a restaurant.

Standard costing is ideal for situations where components are identical and manufacturing operations are repetitive.

The standard cost for units of output is calculated or budgeted in advance of production and working on the assumption of either an *ideal standard* (ie no poor quality material, no labour idle time, no machine breakdowns), or an *attainable standard*, which allows for a pre-determined amount of loss or wastage and a given level of efficiency.

Standard costs are set for:

* **materials**

   The quantity and quality of each type of direct material to be used in production, and the price of such materials is pre-determined. Standard materials cost is the expected quantity and quality of materials multiplied by expected material price.

* **labour**

   The direct labour hours required to manufacture a quantity of goods, and the cost of the labour is pre-determined. Standard labour cost is the expected labour hours multiplied by expected wage rates.

* **overheads**

   The expected quantity of output within a time period divided into the expected overheads will determine the standard overhead cost.

Note that standard costing is used in conjunction with the other costing methods, ie the standard cost is set in advance of production using absorption costing, or marginal costing, or activity based costing methods.

## setting standards

In standard costing, it is important that care should be taken over the setting of standards. Poorly set standards will be of no help to the management of a business when the figures are used in further analysis.

The main departments within an organisation which can provide information to enable standards to be set are:

* **Purchasing**

   The buying department of a business will be able to determine prices, and the expected trends, of materials used.

* **HR (Human Resources)**

   This department will have current wage and salary rates, together with bonus and overtime details, of the various grades of employees; forecasts of changes can also be ascertained.

* **Management services**

   Often called work study, this department will determine the standard amount of time that each work-task in the production process should take.

* **Production**

   This department has overall responsibility for production and will know the quantities of materials required for each unit of production, and the value of production will be linked to the overhead costs.

## WORKED EXAMPLE: SETTING A STANDARD COST

### situation

AMC Engineering Limited manufactures car bumper mouldings. It has been asked by its major customer, Okassa Limited, to prepare a quotation for mouldings for a new car, which is code-named OK10. The elements of cost for 100 mouldings have been calculated by AMC Engineering Limited as:

| | |
|---|---|
| *materials:* | polycarbonate (of specified quality), 200 kilos at £1.10 per kilo |
| | finishing material, 10 litres at £5.40 per litre |
| *labour:* | 5 hours at £11.50 per hour |
| | 2 hours at £12.75 per hour |
| *overheads:* | 13 hours at £20 per hour |

What is the standard cost of producing 100 bumper mouldings?

### solution

| | £ | £ |
|---|---|---|
| *materials* | | |
| polycarbonate: 200 kilos at £1.10 per kilo | 220.00 | |
| finishing material: 10 litres at £5.40 per litre | 54.00 | |
| | | 274.00 |
| *labour* | | |
| 5 hours at £11.50 per hour | 57.50 | |
| 2 hours at £12.75 per hour | 25.50 | |
| | | 83.00 |
| | | 357.00 |
| *overheads* | | |
| 13 hours at £20 per hour | | 260.00 |
| STANDARD COST | | 617.00 |

This standard cost will then be used by AMC Engineering Limited to help establish the selling price to the customer, ie: standard cost + profit = selling price.

# THE ROLE OF STANDARD COSTING IN VARIANCE ANALYSIS

**A variance is the difference between the standard cost/expected revenue and the actual cost/revenue.**

A business using the standard costing system monitors the outcomes by comparing the standard costs set with the results that actually occurred and by calculating variances. An outline of the monitoring process is shown in the diagram which follows on the next page.

### THE MONITORING PROCESS FOR STANDARD COSTS

| | |
|---|---|
| *set* | standard costs |
| *compare* | standard costs with actual costs |
| *calculate* | total variance |
| *analyse* | total variance |
| *explain* | reasons for variance |
| | *take action* |

The full amount by which the actual cost of a product differs from the standard cost is known as the cost variance. It is calculated by deducting actual cost from standard cost, for example:

---

**Cost of making 1,200 garden walling blocks**

| | £ |
|---|---|
| standard cost | 1,000 |
| actual cost | 980 |
| COST VARIANCE | 20 \*FAV |

\* Variances are either favourable (FAV) or adverse (ADV):
- favourable is where actual cost is less than standard cost
- adverse is where actual cost is more than standard cost

The cost variance is made up of the variances for each of the main elements of cost – materials, labour and overheads. Note that we do not study overhead variances in AQA A-level Accounting. The variance for each element can be further analysed into a number of sub-variances which are used to identify the *reasons* for the variance.

A summary of the cost variances and sub-variances for materials and labour is shown in the diagram below.

**SUMMARY OF COST VARIANCES AND SUB-VARIANCES FOR MATERIALS AND LABOUR**

As the diagram shows, the cost variance can result from a combination of different factors:

- **materials variance**
- price variance, caused by a price rise or price fall in the cost of materials
- usage variance, caused by a change in the amount of materials used

The materials price variance and usage variance make up the materials variance.

- **labour variance**
- rate variance, caused by a rise in pay rates, or the need to use a different grade of employee (at a higher or lower wage rate)
- efficiency variance resulting in more or fewer hours worked

The labour rate variance and efficiency variance make up the labour variance.

**Tutorial note:** overheads variances are not studied in AQA A-level Accounting.

As well as cost variances, there are also variances for sales, as follows:

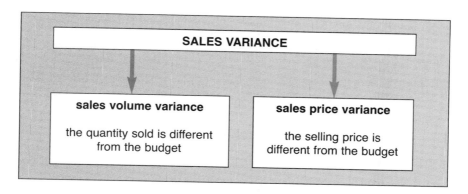

In the next section we will see how the variances – or sub-variances – for materials, labour and sales are identified and calculated. The principle of variance analysis is that variances and sub-variances are identified and calculated until they can be seen to be the responsibility of an individual employee, or small section within the business. For example, a materials price variance, where the cost of materials is different from the standard cost, is the responsibility of the purchasing department; it is this department that will have to explain to management the reason(s) for any variance. Note that a variance can only identify that a problem exists; it is for the appropriate section of the business to investigate the cause of the variance.

# MATERIALS VARIANCES

**Materials variance is the difference between the standard cost of material and the actual cost of material for the actual production.**

The materials variance =

<table>
<tr><td>the standard cost of material for the actual output</td><td>minus</td><td>the actual cost of material</td></tr>
</table>

This can be expressed as:

*(standard quantity x standard price)  –  (actual quantity x actual price)*

The materials variance is analysed into the **materials price variance** and the **materials usage variance.** As their names suggest, the first sub-variance measures the amount of the cost difference due to the price of material, and the second, the cost difference due to the amount of material used.

## material price variance

The material price variance =

| the standard cost of the actual quantity of material used | minus | the actual cost of the actual quantity of material used |
|---|---|---|

This can be expressed as:

*actual quantity  x  (standard price – actual price)*

## material usage variance

The material usage variance =

| the standard quantity of material for the actual production at standard price | minus | the actual quantity of material used at standard price |
|---|---|---|

This can be expressed as:

*standard price x  (standard quantity – actual quantity)*

**Tutorial note:**

The above formulas have been presented so that positive answers will give rise to favourable variances, and a negative answer will mean the variance will be adverse. However it is best to determine favourable or adverse from logic since formulas can be remembered incorrectly. Simply, if it costs more than standard, or the usage is more than standard, the variance must be adverse.

## linking of materials variances

Materials variances are often linked in the following way:

• the use of cheaper material of lower quality may result in a favourable price variance, but may lead to an adverse usage variance as the material may be more difficult to work with and have higher wastage (eg the use of cheap paper in a computer printer may jam the printer)

• the use of more expensive material of higher quality may result in an adverse price variance, but may lead to a favourable usage variance because the material is easier to work with and there is less wastage

## WORKED EXAMPLE: CALCULATING MATERIALS VARIANCES

### situation

Wyvern Walling is a manufacturer of garden wall blocks. The management accountant has prepared the following costs for a batch of 1,200 wall blocks:

- the standard price of concrete is 25p per kilogramme (kg)
- the standard usage is 1,200 kgs

The results achieved for the latest batch are:

- the actual price of concrete used was 30p per g
- the actual usage was 900 kgs

In short, the concrete has cost more, but less has been used for each wall block.

What are the variances for materials costs?

### solution

Here both the price and usage have differed from the standard to give the following *materials variance*:

*(standard quantity x standard price) – (actual quantity x actual price)*

(1,200 kgs x 25p per kg) – (900 kgs x 30p per kg) =

£300 – £270 = £30 FAVOURABLE

While the total materials variance is favourable by £30, as both price *and* usage differ from standard, the sub-variances must be calculated:

### material price sub-variance

*actual quantity* x *(standard price – actual price)*

900 kgs x (25p – 30p) = £45 ADVERSE

### material usage sub-variance

*standard price* x *(standard quantity – actual quantity)*

25p x (1,200 kgs – 900 kgs) = £75 FAVOURABLE

MATERIALS VARIANCE £30 FAVOURABLE

For a batch of 1,200 wall blocks, the materials variance is £30 FAV. Although materials have cost more, this extra cost has been more than offset by the reduced usage. It might be that the higher price paid has meant that better quality materials have been purchased resulting in less wastage.

# LABOUR VARIANCES

**Labour variance is the difference between the standard cost of labour and the actual cost of labour for the actual production.**

The labour variance  =

| the standard cost of labour for the actual output | minus | the actual cost of labour |
|---|---|---|

This can be expressed as:

*(standard hours x standard rate)  –  (actual hours x actual rate)*

Labour variance is analysed into two sub-variances in a similar way to materials variances. The **labour rate variance** measures the labour cost difference due to the rate paid, and the **labour efficiency variance** measures the cost difference due to the amount of labour time used. The concept of labour 'rate' is similar to materials 'price', and labour 'efficiency' is similar to materials 'usage'. This makes remembering the calculation method and interpreting the variances much easier.

## labour rate variance

The labour rate variance  =

| the standard cost of the actual labour hours worked | minus | the actual cost of the actual labour hours worked |
|---|---|---|

This can be expressed as:

*actual labour hours  x  (standard rate – actual rate)*

Note how similar this is to the materials price variance.

## labour efficiency variance

The labour efficiency variance  =

| standard labour hours for actual production at standard rate | minus | actual labour hours worked at standard rate |
|---|---|---|

This can be expressed as:

*standard rate x  (standard hours – actual hours)*

This also has a strong resemblance to the materials usage variance; we are simply considering the efficiency of the workforce instead of the quantity of material.

## linking of labour variances

Labour variances are often linked in the following way:

* the use of a lower grade of staff may result in a favourable labour rate variance, but may lead to an adverse labour efficiency variance as they will be less skilled at carrying out the work

* the use of a higher grade of staff may result in an adverse labour rate variance, but may lead to a favourable labour efficiency variance as they will be more skilled and so will get the work done more quickly and to a higher standard

## WORKED EXAMPLE: CALCULATING LABOUR VARIANCES

### situation

The management accountant of Wyvern Walling has prepared the following labour costs for a batch of 1,200 wall blocks.

* the standard cost of direct labour is £12.00 per hour
* the standard time is 25 hours per batch

The results achieved for the latest batch are:

* the actual cost of direct labour was £10.00 per hour
* the actual production took 32 hours

In short, the wage rates are lower, but the employees have not worked as efficiently as expected.

What are the variances for labour costs?

### solution

Here both the rate and efficiency have differed from the standard to give the following *labour variance*:

*(standard hours x standard rate) – (actual hours x actual rate)*

(25 hours x £12.00 per hour) – (32 hours x £10.00 per hour) =

£300 – £320 = £20 ADVERSE

Note: The calculation gives a negative figure of £20; this means that the actual cost is more than the standard cost, ie it is adverse, and profits will reduce. By contrast, a favourable cost variance is a positive figure, ie the actual cost is less than the standard cost, and profits will increase.

While the labour variance is adverse by £20, as both rate and efficiency differ from standard, the sub-variances must be calculated:

**labour rate sub-variance**

| *actual hours* | x | *(standard rate – actual rate)* | |
|---|---|---|---|
| 32 hours | x | (£12.00 – £10.00) | = £64 FAVOURABLE |

**labour efficiency sub-variance**

| *standard rate* | x | *(standard hours – actual hours)* | |
|---|---|---|---|
| £12.00 | x | (25 hours – 32 hours) | = £84 ADVERSE |
| LABOUR VARIANCE | | | = £20 ADVERSE |

For a production run of 1,200 wall blocks, the labour variance is £20 ADV. Although the workforce has been paid less (or lower grade employees have been used), this cost saving has been more than offset by lower efficiency.

# SALES VARIANCES

**Sales variance is the difference between the standard sales revenue and the actual sales revenue for the product or service.**

The sales variance =

| the actual sales revenue for the product or service | minus | the standard sales revenue for the product or service |
|---|---|---|

This can be expressed as:

*(actual quantity x actual price) – (standard quantity x standard price)*

The sales variance is analysed into two sub-variances. The **sales volume variance** measures the sales income difference due to the quantity sold, and the **sales price variance** measures the sales income difference due to the price received.

## sales volume variance

The sales volume variance =

| the actual quantity of sales at the standard selling price | minus | the standard quantity of sales at the standard selling price |
|---|---|---|

This can be expressed as:

*(actual quantity – standard quantity) x standard price*

## sales price variance

The sales price variance =

| the actual quantity of sales at the actual selling price | minus | the actual quantity of sales at the standard price |
| --- | --- | --- |

This can be expressed as:

*(actual price − standard price) x actual quantity*

**Tutorial note:**

Take care when determining whether sales variances are favourable or adverse – it is better to use logic. Simply, if more have been sold than standard, or the selling price is higher than standard, the variance must be favourable.

## linking of sales variances

Sales variances are often linked in the following way:

• a lower selling price may result in an adverse sales price variance, but may lead to a favourable ' sales volume variance as more of the product is sold

• a higher selling price may result in a favourable sales price variance, but may lead to an adverse sales volume variance as customers switch to cheaper products

# WORKED EXAMPLE: CALCULATING SALES VARIANCE

## situation

The management accountant of Wyvern Walling has prepared the following estimates for sales:

• expected sales next week are 5,000 wall blocks

• expected selling price is £1.00 per wall block

At the end of the week the results are:

• actual sales for the week were 4,500 wall blocks

• actual selling price was £1.10 per wall block

In short, the sales volume is lower than estimated, but the selling price is higher.

What are the variances for sales?

**solution**

Here both sales volume and price have differed from what was estimated to give the following *sales variance*:

*(actual quantity x actual selling price) – (standard quantity x standard price)*

| (4,500 wall blocks x £1.10 each) | – | (5,000 wall blocks x £1.00 each) | | = |
| --- | --- | --- | --- | --- |
| £4,950 | – | £5,000 | = £50 ADVERSE | |

This adverse variance will reduce profits by £50. As both sales volume *and* price differ from what was estimated, the sub-variances must be calculated:

**sales volume sub-variance**

*(actual quantity – standard quantity) x standard price*

(4,500 – 5,000) x £1.00            = £500     ADVERSE

**sales price sub-variance**

*(actual price – standard price) x actual quantity*

(£1.10 – £1.00) x 4,500            = £450     FAVOURABLE

SALES VARIANCE                    = £50      ADVERSE

The sales variance for the week is £50 ADV – the selling price is higher, but fewer wall blocks have been sold. The reduction in the volume of sales has not been offset by the higher selling price.

## THE INTERRELATIONSHIPS OF VARIANCES

Once you are familiar with the figures used for calculating variances, and with what each variance means, it is necessary then to consider the possible causes of variances. It should be possible to think your way logically through each situation in order to assess its impact on variances. In the AQA examination you may calculate, or be given, a number of variances and asked to suggest the possible causes. When doing this, think about the *interrelationships of variances* where a situation causes more than one variance. Examples include:

- buying cheaper material of lower quality may result in a favourable price variance but, if there is higher wastage, may lead to an adverse usage variance
- using a higher grade of labour may result in an adverse labour rate variance but, because of the greater skill of the workforce, may lead to a favourable labour efficiency variance
- using better quality material, which is more expensive, may affect not just material variances but labour variances too – a lower grade of labour might be used and, because of the good quality material, labour efficiency might be improved, resulting in both labour sub-variances being favourable

- reducing the selling price of a product is likely to give an adverse sales price variance but, if more is sold, a favourable sales volume variance
- the quality of materials and/or the grade of labour used is likely to affect the sales variances – customers are less likely to buy products made cheaply, but may be prepared to pay a price premium for a well-made quality product

The following table gives examples of possible causes of variances. Please read it carefully, and ensure that you can appreciate the logic of including each item, and its effect. There may be situations where you can envisage the cause creating further variances, since the table is not intended to be exhaustive.

'A' or 'F' refers to whether adverse or favourable variances may result.

| | Material price | Material usage | Labour rate | Labour efficiency | Sales volume | Sales price |
|---|---|---|---|---|---|---|
| **Possible Cause:** | | | | | | |
| Poorly set standard | A or F | A or F | A or F | A or F | | |
| Different material supplier | A or F | | | | | |
| Different material quality | A or F | A or F | | A or F | | |
| Unexpected discounts | F | | | | | |
| Higher grade staff | | F | A | F | | |
| Lower grade staff | | A | F | A | | |
| Unexpected pay rise | | | A | | | |
| High inflation | A | | A | | | |
| Low inflation | F | | F | | | |
| Improved production machinery | | F | | F | | |
| Exchange rate fluctuations | A or F | | | | | A or F |
| Reduction in selling price | | | | | F | A |
| Increase in selling price | | | | | A | F |

# RECONCILIATION STATEMENTS

Variances can be brought together in a reconciliation statement which may take the form of:

- a cost reconciliation statement, or
- a profit reconciliation statement, or
- a sales reconciliation statement

Reconciliation statements set out the variances and demonstrate to the management of a business how the budgeted cost, profit or revenue has been affected by variances to give the actual profit or cost or revenue for the period. It is then for management to decide which variances require further investigation and, where appropriate, they can be passed to the responsible department with a request for investigation.

## cost reconciliation statement

This statement reconciles the budgeted cost with the actual cost in the following way:

| | £ ADV | £ FAV | £ |
|---|---|---|---|
| **WYVERN WALLING** | | | |
| **COST RECONCILIATION STATEMENT FOR THE WEEK ENDED ..........** | | | |
| Budgeted total cost | | | 500 |
| Material price variance | 45 | | |
| Material usage variance | | 75 | |
| Labour rate variance | | 64 | |
| Labour efficiency variance | 84 | | |
| | 129 | 139 | (10) |
| Actual total cost | | | 490 |

Note that, for a cost reconciliation statement, favourable cost variances are deducted because they reduce costs, while adverse cost variances are added because they increase costs.

## profit reconciliation statement

This statement reconciles the budgeted profit – here, for example, £1,000 – with the actual profit in the following way:

**WYVERN WALLING**

**PROFIT RECONCILIATION STATEMENT FOR THE WEEK ENDED ..........**

| | £ | £ | £ |
|---|---|---|---|
| | ADV | FAV | |
| Budgeted profit | | | 1,000 |
| Material price variance | 45 | | |
| Material usage variance | | 75 | |
| Labour rate variance | | 64 | |
| Labour efficiency variance | 84 | | |
| | 129 | 139 | 10 |
| Actual profit | | | 1,010 |

Note that, for a profit reconciliation statement, favourable cost variances are added to increase profit, while adverse cost variances are deducted to reduce profit.

A further version of the reconciliation statement is to prepare a statement reconciling the budgeted revenue and costs with the actual revenue and costs. Here it is necessary to calculate figures on the basis of actual output rather than budgeted output. This technique is known as *flexing the budget*.

Flexing the budget to actual output is illustrated in the following Worked Example which also requires the calculation of sales and cost sub-variances. A sales reconciliation statement is shown after the Worked Example.

## WORKED EXAMPLE: RECONCILING THE VARIANCES

### situation

Sally Johnson Ltd manufactures one product, the SJ 003. The company operates a standard costing system.

The managing director asks you, the management accountant, to explain why the actual profit in May of £46,500 differs from the budgeted profit of £35,000.

| | Budget for May | Actual for May |
|---|---|---|
| Sales and production | 5,000 units at £75 each | 6,000 units at £70 each |
| Materials | 5 metres per unit at £4.00 per metre | 5.5 metres per unit at £3.50 per metre |
| Labour | 2 hours 30 minutes per unit at £12 per hour | 2 hours per unit at £14 per hour |
| Overheads | £90,000 | £90,000 |
| Profit for the month | £35,000 | £46,500 |

To provide the managing director with an explanation, you decide to:

**(a)** calculate the:

– sales volume and price variances

– material price and usage variances

– labour rate and efficiency variances

**(b)** prepare a reconciliation statement which shows how the variances have caused profit to alter.

**solution**

**(a)** Sales volume variance:

(6,000 units – 5,000 units) x £75       =     £75,000 FAVOURABLE

Sales price variance:

(£70 – £75) x 6,000 units       =     £30,000 ADVERSE

Material price variance:

33,000 metres x (£4.00 – £3.50)       =     £16,500 FAVOURABLE

Material usage variance:

£4.00 x (30,000 metres – 33,000 metres)       =     £12,000 ADVERSE

Labour rate variance:

12,000 hours x (£12.00 – £14.00)       =     £24,000 ADVERSE

Labour efficiency variance:

£12.00 x (15,000 – 12,000 hours)       =     £36,000 FAVOURABLE

**(b)**

> **Tutorial note:** the original budget is flexed, which is then compared with actual production revenue and costs

### SALLY JOHNSON LTD
### RECONCILIATION STATEMENT OF SALES AND COSTS FOR THE MONTH

| | Original budget 5,000 units £ | Flexed budget 6,000 units £ | Actual 6,000 £ | Variances £ |
|---|---|---|---|---|
| Sales | 375,000 | *450,000 | 420,000 | 30,000  ADV |
| | | volume 75,000  FAV | | price 30,000  ADV |
| Less costs | | | | |
| Materials | 100,000 | 120,000 | 115,500 | 4,500  FAV |
| | | | | price 16,500  FAV |
| | | | | usage 12,000  ADV |
| Labour | 150,000 | 180,000 | 168,000 | 12,000  FAV |
| | | | | rate 24,000  ADV |
| | | | | efficiency 36,000  FAV |
| CONTRIBUTION | 125,000 | 150,000 | 136,500 | 13,500  ADV |
| Overheads | 90,000 | 90,000 | 90,000 | – |
| Profit for the month | 35,000 | 60,000 | 46,500 | 13,500  ADV |

*6,000 units at £75 each

**Notes:**

- the flexed budget is calculated on the basis of the original budget's revenue and costs
- sales volume variance is indicated by the flexed budget figure, ie £450,000 – £375,000 = £75,000 FAV
- the 'flexed budget' and 'actual' figures are compared to give the variances in the right-hand column
- the management of Sally Johnson Ltd will wish to study the interrelationships between the labour and materials variances, for example:
  - favourable material price variance could indicate that the material is of poorer quality which has led to an adverse material usage variance because there is more wastage
  - adverse labour rate variance may have been caused because a higher grade of labour has had to be used with the skills to work with poorer quality material while the more skilled workforce has been more efficient in production

## sales reconciliation statement

This statement reconciles the budgeted sales revenue with the actual total revenue in the following way (using figures from Worked Example just seen):

---

**SALLY JOHNSON LTD**

**SALES RECONCILIATION STATEMENT FOR THE MONTH ..........**

| | £ |
|---|---|
| BUDGETED sales (5,000 UNITS AT £75 each) | 375,000 |
| Sales volume variance (FAV) | 75,000 |
| Sales price variance (ADV) | (30,000) |
| Actual sales (6,000 UNITS AT £70 each) | 420,000 |

Note that, for a sales reconciliation statement, favourable sales variances are added to increase revenue, while adverse sales variances are deducted to reduce revenue.

---

Note: some AQA examination questions may combine a sales reconciliation statement with a cost reconciliation statement to show why the actual profit differs from the budgeted profit.

# ADVANTAGES AND DISADVANTAGES OF STANDARD COSTING

The main *advantages of standard costing* are that it can be used:

- to help with *decision-making* – for example, with the selling price of a product
- to assist in *planning* – for example, to plan the quantity and cost of resources needed for production
- as a means of *controlling* costs – standard costs are compared with actual costs and variances calculated so that action can be taken by the responsible manager or department when appropriate

In addition to these, there may be other benefits:

- the detailed study of current production techniques that is needed to set up a standard costing system may reveal hidden inefficiencies and unnecessary expenditure
- the close monitoring of costs should increase the awareness of cost consciousness of both employees and management, and encourage them to achieve the standard costs which have been set
- standard costing lends itself to exception reporting – results are reported only when they are outside a pre-set range and so, in this way, major variations from standard are spotted and dealt with quickly, eg with a standard cost of £10,000 a difference of £10 would not be investigated, whereas a £1,000 difference would be investigated, this being the exception

The main *disadvantages of standard costing* are:

- the standard cost of making a product or providing a service may be set incorrectly, leading either to reduced sales because the product is priced too high, or to increased sales which are being sold at too low a price to make a profit

- prices of materials, labour and overheads may fluctuate frequently (eg the price of raw materials) so that the standard cost quickly goes out-of-date

- while a standard cost represents one way of making the product or providing a service there may be others – eg switching production from a labour-intensive process to a machine-intensive production line

- the use of variance analysis may be more complex than a variance from the standard cost, eg the use of better quality materials might lead to increased output and lower labour costs

# CHAPTER SUMMARY

- Standard costing sets the planned cost for materials, labour and overheads in a period of time.

- A variance is the difference between the standard cost revenue and the actual cost/revenue.

- With standard costing, variances and sub-variances can be calculated for materials, labour and overheads. Note that overheads variances are not studied in AQA A-level Accounting.

- Materials variance = (standard quantity x standard price) – (actual quantity x actual price).

- Materials price variance = actual quantity x (standard price – actual price).

- Materials usage variance = standard price x (standard quantity – actual quantity).

- Labour variance = (standard hours x standard rate) – (actual hours x actual rate).

- Labour rate variance = actual labour hours x (standard rate – actual rate).

- Labour efficiency variance = standard rate x (standard hours – actual hours).

- As well as materials and labour variances, there are also variances for sales.

- Sales variance = (actual quantity x actual price) – (standard quantity x standard price).

- Sales volume variance = (actual quantity – standard quantity) x standard price.

- Sales price variance = (actual price – standard price) x actual quantity.

- The *interrelationships of variances* is where one variance has an effect on another variance.

● Variances can be brought together in a *reconciliation statement* which may take the form of:

  – a cost reconciliation statement, or

  – a profit reconciliation statement, or

  – a sales reconciliation statement

  Such statements demonstrate to the management of a business how the budgeted cost/profit/revenue has been affected by variances to give the actual cost/profit/revenue.

● A reconciliation of forecast costs with actual costs requires all costs to be based on actual output (rather than budgeted output) – this is known as flexing the budget.

● Standard costing can be used:

  – to help with *decision-making*

  – to assist in *planning*

  – as a means of *controlling* costs

In the next chapter we look at how business decision-making can be helped by the use of capital investment appraisal techniques.

# QUESTIONS

visit
**www.osbornebooks.co.uk**
to take an online test

An asterisk (*) after the question number means that the answer is given at the end of this book.

**13.1\***   Standard costing is used to set:

| | | |
|---|---|---|
| **A** | The planned cost for materials, labour and overheads in a period of time | |
| **B** | The actual cost per unit of output in a period of time | |
| **C** | The actual cost for materials, labour and overheads in a period of time | |
| **D** | The break-even cost per unit of output in a period of time | |

**13.2**   A variance is:

| | | |
|---|---|---|
| **A** | The difference between the actual revenue and the standard cost of a unit of output | |
| **B** | The difference between the standard cost/revenue and the actual cost/revenue | |
| **C** | The difference between sales revenue and variable costs | |
| **D** | The difference between fixed costs and variable costs | |

**13.3\***   The following information is available for the materials used in making Product E for April:

- standard cost 100 kilos at £8 per kilo

- actual cost 110 kilos at £7 per kilo

Which **one** of the following statements is correct?

| | | |
|---|---|---|
| **A** | Material price variance £110 adverse; material usage variance £80 favourable | |
| **B** | Material price variance £80 adverse; material usage variance £110 favourable | |
| **C** | Material price variance £30 favourable; material usage variance £0 | |
| **D** | Material price variance £110 favourable; material usage variance £80 adverse | |

**13.4** The following information is available for the labour required to make Product F in May:
- standard cost 40 hours at £15 per hour
- actual cost 38 hours at £16 per hour

Which **one** of the following statements is correct?

| | | |
|---|---|---|
| **A** | Labour rate variance £38 adverse; labour efficiency variance £30 favourable | |
| **B** | Labour rate variance £30 adverse; labour efficiency variance £38 favourable | |
| **C** | Labour rate variance £38 favourable; labour efficiency variance £30 adverse | |
| **D** | Labour rate variance £8 adverse; labour efficiency variance £0 | |

**13.5\*** The following information is available for sales of Product G in June:
- expected sales 1,000 units at £17 each
- actual sales 1,200 units at £15 each

Which **one** of the following statements is correct?

| | | |
|---|---|---|
| **A** | Sales volume variance £2,400 favourable; sales price variance £3,400 adverse | |
| **B** | Sales volume variance £3,400 favourable; sales price variance £2,400 adverse | |
| **C** | Sales volume variance £3,400 adverse; sales price variance £2,400 favourable | |
| **D** | Sales volume variance £0; sales price variance £1,000 favourable | |

**13.6** The following information is available for sales of Product H in July:
- standard selling price          £15 per unit
- budgeted sales          4,250 units
- actual sales          4,500 units
- actual sales revenue          £65,250

What is the sales price variance for July?

| | | |
|---|---|---|
| **A** | £3,750 adverse | |
| **B** | £2,250 adverse | |
| **C** | £3,750 favourable | |
| **D** | £2,250 favourable | |

**13.7**   **(a)**   What is meant by standard costing?

**(b)**   What are the main advantages to a business in using such a costing method?

**13.8\***   Calculate the materials variance for each of the following, and analyse the variance between a price variance and a usage variance. (Indicate whether each variance is *adverse* or *favourable*.)

*Material: sheet steel*

| | |
|---|---|
| Standard quantity | 0.5 sq metres |
| Standard price | £5 per sq metre |
| Actual quantity | 0.5 sq metres |
| Actual price | £6 per sq metre |

*Material: alloy*

| | |
|---|---|
| Standard quantity | 2 kgs |
| Standard price | £1.50 per kg |
| Actual quantity | 2.5 kgs |
| Actual price | £1.50 per kg |

*Material: flour*

| | |
|---|---|
| Standard quantity | 0.5 kgs |
| Standard price | 50p per kg |
| Actual quantity | 0.6 kgs |
| Actual price | 40p per kg |

*Material: gelling fluid*

| | |
|---|---|
| Standard quantity | 3 litres |
| Standard price | £1.50 per litre |
| Actual quantity | 2.5 litres |
| Actual price | £2 per litre |

**13.9\*** Calculate the labour variance for each of the following, and analyse the variance between a rate variance and an efficiency variance. (Indicate whether each variance is *adverse* or *favourable*.)

*Casting*

| | |
|---|---|
| Standard hours | 5 hours |
| Standard rate | £10 per hour |
| Actual hours | 6 hours |
| Actual rate | £10 per hour |

*Machining*

| | |
|---|---|
| Standard hours | 2 hours |
| Standard rate | £13 per hour |
| Actual hours | 2 hours |
| Actual rate | £15 per hour |

*Finishing*

| | |
|---|---|
| Standard hours | 1 hour |
| Standard rate | £12 per hour |
| Actual hours | 1.25 hours |
| Actual rate | £12.80 per hour |

*Packing*

| | |
|---|---|
| Standard hours | 1 hour |
| Standard rate | £16 per hour |
| Actual hours | 0.75 hours |
| Actual rate | £14.40 per hour |

**13.10** From the following data you are to calculate:

**(a)** material price variance

**(b)** material usage variance

**(c)** materials variance

(Indicate whether each variance is *adverse* or *favourable*.)

| | Standard price | Standard quantity | Actual price | Actual quantity |
|---|---|---|---|---|
| **Material A** | £5 per kg | 100 kgs | £4 per kg | 120 kgs |
| **Material B** | £20 per unit | 120 units | £22 per unit | 100 units |
| **Material C** | £10 per litre | 600 litres | £9 per litre | 500 litres |
| **Material D** | £2 per metre | 300 metres | £3 per metre | 250 metres |

**13.11**  From the following data you are to calculate:

**(a)**   labour rate variance

**(b)**   labour efficiency variance

**(c)**   labour variance

(Indicate whether each variance is *adverse* or *favourable*.)

| | Standard hours | Standard rate | Actual hours | Actual rate |
|---|---|---|---|---|
| Product 1 | 8 | £10.00 | 7 | £11.00 |
| Product 2 | 3 | £15.00 | 4 | £16.00 |
| Product 3 | 24 | £12.00 | 30 | £11.50 |
| Product 4 | 12 | £16.00 | 15 | £17.00 |

**13.12**  The following information is available for the manufacture of 600 ornamental clay garden pots, showing variances for materials and labour:

| | Standard cost | | Actual cost | | Variances | | |
|---|---|---|---|---|---|---|---|
| | | £ | | £ | | £ | |
| materials | 900 kgs | | 800 kgs | | price | 40 | ADV |
| | at 75p per kg | 675 | at 80p per kg | 640 | usage | 75 | FAV |
| | | | | | materials | 35 | FAV |
| labour | 150 hours | | 140 hours | | rate | 140 | ADV |
| | at £10.00 per hour | 1,500 | at £11.00 per hour | 1,540 | efficiency | 100 | FAV |
| | | | | | labour | 40 | ADV |

**REQUIRED:**

**(a)**   Show how the variances for materials and labour have been calculated.

**(b)**   Explain why the variances may have occurred and how they will be used to monitor costs.

**13.13**   Zelah Ltd sells a single product, the Zel, at £5 per unit. The company's budgeted sales for the year ended 31 December 20-9 were 20,000 units.

At the year end, the company had actually sold 18,000 units for £108,000.

**REQUIRED:**

**(a)**   Calculate the sales price variance and state the formula used.

**(b)**   Calculate the sales volume variance and state the formula used.

**(c)**   Prepare a reconciliation statement of sales for the year.

**(d)**   Explain why the sales variances may have occurred.

**13.14***   The budget for direct labour is £10,800; the actual cost is £12,200. The budget for direct materials is £4,600; the actual cost is £4,350.

Which **one** of the following statements is correct?

| | |
|---|---|
| **A** | Direct labour variance £1,400 adverse; direct materials variance £250 adverse |
| **B** | Direct labour variance £1,400 favourable; direct materials variance £250 favourable |
| **C** | Direct labour variance £1,400 adverse; direct materials variance £250 favourable |
| **D** | Direct labour variance £1,400 favourable; direct materials variance £250 adverse |

**13.15**   The budget for direct labour is £15,900; the actual cost is £14,800. The budget for direct materials is £8,200; the actual cost is £8,650.

Which **one** of the following statements is correct?

| | |
|---|---|
| **A** | Direct labour variance £1,100 adverse; direct materials variance £450 adverse |
| **B** | Direct labour variance £1,100 favourable; direct materials variance £450 favourable |
| **C** | Direct labour variance £1,100 adverse; direct materials variance £450 favourable |
| **D** | Direct labour variance £1,100 favourable; direct materials variance £450 adverse |

**13.16\*** A budget for 8,000 units of output shows a direct materials cost of £17,400 and a direct labour cost of £12,600. Actual output is 9,000 units.

Which **one** of the following gives the correct figures for the flexed budget?

| A | Direct materials £19,575; direct labour £14,175 | |
| B | Direct materials £19,575; direct labour £12,600 | |
| C | Direct materials £17,400; direct labour £14,175 | |
| D | Direct materials £17,400; direct labour £12,600 | |

**13.17\*** Identify the correct variance from the causes of variances given by putting a tick in the relevant column of the table below.

| Cause of variance | Adverse | Favourable |
|---|---|---|
| Increase in material prices | | |
| Fewer materials are wasted | | |
| Cheaper materials are used | | |
| Theft of materials | | |
| An increase in direct labour pay | | |
| More efficient usage of direct labour | | |
| Overtime is paid to direct labour | | |
| Selling prices are increased | | |
| An increase in the number of units sold | | |

**13.18***

**Tutorial note:** this question requires a flexed bludget in order to show how the variances have caused a change in profit

FunPlay Ltd manufactures wooden garden slides. The company operates a standard costing system.

The managing director is concerned that the actual profit last month of £4,400 is significantly less than the budgeted profit of £60,600. She asks for an explanation.

The management accountant provides the following information:

|  | **Budget for last month** | **Actual for last month** |
|---|---|---|
| Sales and production | 1,200 slides at £260 each | 1,300 slides at £220 each |
| Materials | 12 metres per slide at £6.00 per metre | 14 metres per slide at £5.50 per metre |
| Labour | 5 hours per slide at £20 per hour | 7 hours per slide at £15 per hour |
| Overheads | £45,000 | £45,000 |
| Profit for the month | £60,000 | £4,400 |

The management accountant has calculated the relevant variances as follows:

| **Variance** | **£** |
|---|---|
| Sales – price | 52,000 ADV |
| Sales – volume | 26,000 FAV |
| Materials – price | 9,100 FAV |
| Materials – usage | 15,600 ADV |
| Labour – rate | 45,500 FAV |
| Labour – efficiency | 52,000 ADV |

**REQUIRED:**

**(a)** Prepare a reconciliation statement which shows how the variances have caused the reduction in the profit.

**(b)** Suggest possible causes for the variances.

# 14 CAPITAL INVESTMENT APPRAISAL

In this chapter we see how accounting information is used to help a business to make decisions involving capital investment projects. For example, if we need a new printer for the office, shall we buy a Toshiba or a Canon model?

The main methods of capital investment appraisal are:

● payback period

● net present value, also known as discounted cash flow

In this chapter we will explain what capital investment appraisal involves, and then study these two methods by means of a Worked Example, and make comparisons between them.

## WHAT IS CAPITAL INVESTMENT APPRAISAL?

**Capital investment appraisal enables a business to make decisions as to whether or not to invest in a particular capital investment project and, where there are alternatives, to assist in deciding in which to invest.**

You will readily appreciate that, whether at home or at work, resources are limited and, as a result, there is a need to use them in such a way as to obtain the maximum benefits from them. To do this it is necessary to choose between various financial alternatives available; for example, on a personal level, we have to make decisions such as:

*Should I save my spare cash in a bank's instant access account, or should I deposit it for a fixed term?*

*Should I save up for a car, or should I buy on hire purchase?*

*Which make of car, within my price range, should I buy?*

*Should I rent a house or should I buy, taking out a mortgage?*

While these decisions are personal choices, the management of businesses of all sizes are faced with making choices, as are other organisations such as local authorities and central government.

The management of any business is constantly having to make decisions on what goods or services to produce, where to produce, how to produce, and how much to produce. For each major choice to be made, some method of appraisal has to be applied to ensure that, whatever decisions are taken, they are consistent with the objectives of the business. This means that it is necessary to look at all the alternatives available and to choose the one that is going to give the most benefit. For example, a business may have to decide whether to replace its existing machinery with new, more up-to-date machinery. If it decides on new machinery, it then has to choose between different makes of machine and different models, each having a different cost and each capable of affecting output in a different way. The decision will affect the performance of the business – its profit or loss and its cash flow.

# WHAT IS A CAPITAL INVESTMENT PROJECT?

A capital investment project is the spending of money now in order to receive benefits (or reduce costs) in future years; it is illustrated in the diagram below.

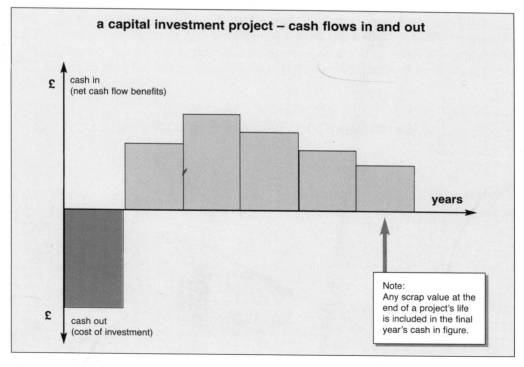

Here, the cost of the investment, or capital expenditure, is being spent at the start – either at the very beginning of the project (often stated as 'year 0'), or during the first year. The difference between these two is illustrated by the following:

* buying a new printer is a cash outflow at the beginning of the project
* the installation of a new production line may well incur cash outflows during the first year

The cost of the investment brings benefits (or reduced costs) in future years for as long as the project lasts. Any expected scrap value at the end of the project's life is included in the final year's net cash inflow.

## CAPITAL APPRAISAL MEASURES IN EVALUATING PROJECTS

Businesses need to apply capital appraisal methods when evaluating projects to ensure that the decisions they make are the correct choices. As well as the cash flows in and out for a capital investment project, a number of other factors need to be considered before a decision is made. In particular, a business cannot make decisions in isolation – it is part of a wider community, with responsibilities to its employees, the local economy and the environment.

Even small businesses have responsibilities to others, while large businesses must take great care to consider the effect of their decisions – the public and the media (in the form of television, radio, newspapers, the internet) will certainly scrutinise their every move.

The diagram below shows some of the factors which affect business decision-making. This shows that, while internal factors such as the effect on profit and cash is important, external factors need to be considered also. External factors are often referred to as 'social accounting' and will impact on decision-making at a variety of levels. More decisions are made at lower levels than at higher levels – although it is the latter that get most attention in the media. For example (next page):

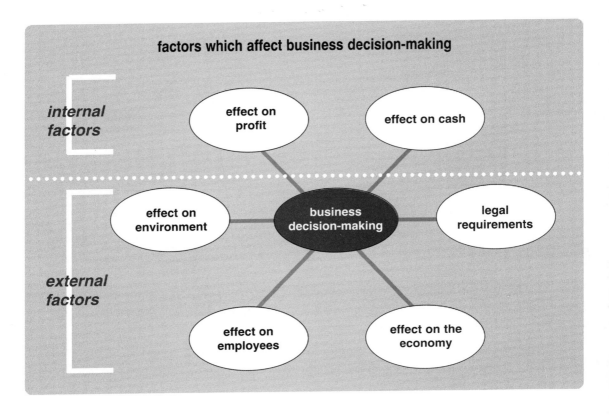

- higher level decisions:
    - we are going to close our factory in Scotland
    - our call centre will be transferred to India
    - we will only buy furniture which uses timber from managed forests
- lower level decisions:
    - we have a first-aid training programme
    - all our photocopying is done on recycled paper
    - the tea used in our canteen comes from 'fairtrade' suppliers

The conclusion to draw is that we all make decisions – both in business and in our personal lives. We need to consider not only the internal factors, but also the external factors.

The following is a summary of the main financial factors and the non-financial factors that should be considered when evaluating projects:

## Financial factors

- *Source of finance.* Where is the money coming from to finance the project? Is it from a cash surplus, an existing or new bank overdraft and loans? A large project may warrant a share or loan issue to raise specific finance. Assets such as machinery, equipment and vehicles are often financed using hire purchase and leasing.

- *Cost of capital.* All finance has a cost – often the return on its capital employed that the business expects, plus the rate of interest it has to pay when borrowing. Interest rates will be different for each source of finance – from the interest foregone on cash surpluses, to that which must be paid on bank overdrafts and loans. With ordinary shares, the cost of capital is the dividend that shareholders expect to receive. Hire purchase and leasing payments include the interest cost. Note that, with variable interest rates, cost of capital may well change during the life of a project.

- *Total estimated cost of project.* It is important to forecast accurately the total capital expenditure cost of projects. Historically, the cost of large-scale projects has often been under-estimated and the final actual cost has been much higher than anticipated, leading to financial difficulties.

- *Taxation implications.* A project will usually include both tax allowances and payments. The allowances occur when new assets – such as machinery, equipment and vehicles – are purchased. Called writing down allowances, these reduce the amount of tax to be paid. However, the cost savings or increasing profits of the investment project will increase overall profitability of the business and will lead to more tax being paid.

- *Working capital requirements.* Most projects will also require an investment in working capital – inventory, trade receivables and trade payables. Thus an amount of working capital is needed at the start, and throughout the project's life. It will only be recovered at the end of the project.

- *Audit of project.* It is important to keep a regular check on costs and revenues to ensure that they are in line with the estimates. There are three separate phases that should be audited:
    - costs of bringing the project into commission
    - operational costs and revenues
    - decommissioning costs

**Non-financial factors**

- Economic climate – recession or period of growth.
- Political implications – a possible change of government may affect investment decisions.
- Commissioning – the length of time that it will take for the project to be up and running.
- Training – the costs and implications of staff training.
- Location – where the project is to be located, and subsequent effects on the culture of the business.
- Capacity – effect on overall output of the business.
- Product life cycle – the implications on the project of the stage of the output within the product life cycle.

## WORKED EXAMPLE: MAKING THE DECISION

### situation

A business is investing in a new project and has to make the choice between Project Aye and Project Bee. The initial cost and the net cash flow (income, less expenses but not depreciation) to the business have been calculated over five years for each project as follows:

|  | PROJECT AYE | PROJECT BEE |
|---|---|---|
| Initial cost at the beginning of the project | £20,000 | £28,000 |
| Net cash inflow: |  |  |
| Year 1 | £8,000 | £10,000 |
| Year 2 | £12,000 | £10,000 |
| Year 3 | £5,000 | £8,000 |
| Year 4 | £4,000 | £9,000 |
| Year 5 | £2,000 | £9,000 |

- At the end of year 5, both projects will have a scrap value of £1,000; this amount is already included in the year 5 cash inflows.
- Only one project can be undertaken.
- The business requires an annual rate of return of 10 per cent on new projects.

Which project should be chosen?

### solution

The two methods commonly used to appraise a capital investment project such as this are:

- payback period
- net present value, also known as discounted cash flow

These methods will be considered in this chapter in order to help the business to make its decision.

# PAYBACK PERIOD

**Payback is the period of time it takes for the initial cost of capital investment to be repaid from net cash flow inflows.**

From the Worked Example of Projects Aye and Bee, seen earlier, the cash flows and the cumulative cash flows (ie net cash flows to date) are shown in the table below. From this information it can be seen that project Aye costs £20,000 (paid out at the beginning of the project) and it is expected that the net cash flow over the first two years will equal the cost. The payback period for Project Aye is, therefore, two years, while that for Project Bee is three years. So, using payback, Project Aye is preferable because it has the shorter payback period.

## WORKED EXAMPLE: PAYBACK CALCULATIONS

| Year | PROJECT AYE | | PROJECT BEE | |
|---|---|---|---|---|
| | Cash flow | Cumulative cash flow | Cash flow | Cumulative cash flow |
| | £ | £ | £ | £ |
| 0 | (20,000) | (20,000) | (28,000) | (28,000) |
| 1 | 8,000 | (12,000) | 10,000 | (18,000) |
| 2 | 12,000 | – | 10,000 | (8,000) |
| 3 | 5,000 | 5,000 | 8,000 | – |
| 4 | 4,000 | 9,000 | 9,000 | 9,000 |
| 5 | 2,000 | 11,000 | 9,000 | 18,000 |

The payback period is indicated by the shading

Although these payback periods work out to exact years, they rarely do so in practice. Be prepared to calculate part years in the examination. For example, if Project Aye had an initial cost of £22,000, the payback would require £2,000 of the £5,000 cash flow in year 3. The payback period would then be:

- 2 years + (£2,000/£5,000 x 12 months)
  = 2 years and 4.8 months, or

- 2 years + (£2,000/£5,000 x 52 weeks)
  = 2 years and 20.8 weeks, or

- 2 years + (£2,000/£5,000 x 365 days)
  = 2 years and 146 days

Note that, in calculating part years, we are making the assumption that cash flows occur at an even rate throughout the year – this may not be the case for all projects – sales (and costs) may be higher at certain times: for example, retailers are likely to have high sales in the pre-Christmas shopping period.

The shorter the payback period the better, particularly where high technology or fashion projects are concerned – they may be out-of-date before they reach the end of their useful lives.

Earlier cash flows are likely to prove more accurate estimates than later cash flows. Thus, if two projects have the same payback, the one with the greater cash flow in the early years is preferred.

For example, consider two projects with a payback period of two years from the following cash flows:

|  | Wye | Zed |
|---|---|---|
| Year 1 | £8,000 | £12,000 |
| Year 2 | £12,000 | £8,000 |

While both projects have the same payback period of two years, Zed is the preferred project under the payback method because of earlier cash flows.

## benefits of payback

- it is easy to calculate
- it is easy to understand
- it places emphasis on the earlier cash flows, which are more likely to be accurate than later cash flows
- an ideal capital investment appraisal method for high technology projects

## limitations of payback

- all cash flows after the payback period are ignored
- within the payback period it fails to consider the timing of net cash flows, eg Project Aye would still have had a payback of two years even if the cash flows for years one and two had been reversed (as noted above, greater cash flows in earlier years are to be preferred)
- the effects of inflation are ignored
- the time value of money is ignored, unlike the discounted cash flow method
- the life of the asset is not considered
- the estimates of cash flows may be inaccurate

# NET PRESENT VALUE

**Net present value (discounted cash flow) is a method of capital investment appraisal which recognises that money has a time value – it compares net cash flows, at their present values, with the initial cost of the capital investment to give a net present value), or discounted return, on the investment.**

A quick example of a net present value decision is where a friend asks you to lend her £1 and offers to repay you either tomorrow, or in one year's time. Which will you choose? The answer is clear: you would want the money back sooner rather than later because, if you don't intend to spend it, you can always save it in a bank, where it may earn some interest. Thus the rate of interest represents the time value of money.

Using £1 as an example, if it is saved with a bank at an interest rate of 10 per cent* per year, it will increase as follows:

\* an interest rate of 10 per cent per year on a savings rate is too good to be true but is used here for illustrative purposes!

| | |
|---|---|
| original investment | £1.00 |
| interest at 10% on £1 | £0.10 |
| value at end of first year | £1.10 |
| interest at 10% on £1,10 | £0.11 |
| value at end of second year | £1.21 |

This uses the technique of compound interest. So, with interest rates of 10 per cent per year, we can say that the future value of £1 will be £1.10 at the end of year one, £1.21 at the end of year two, and so on; thus £1 set aside now will gain in value so that, at some time in the future, we will have access to a larger sum of money. However, supposing that we were to receive £1 at the end of year one, what is it worth to us now? To find the answer to this, we need to carry out the following calculation:

$$\text{£1} \quad \times \quad \frac{100}{110^*} \quad = \quad \text{£0.91}$$

\* 100 per cent, plus the rate of interest (in this example, 10 per cent).

Therefore, if we had £0.91 now and invested it at 10 per cent per year, we would have £1 at the end of year one. We can say that the *present value* of £1 receivable in one year's time is £0.91. In the same way, £1 receivable in two years' time is £0.83, calculated as follows:

$$\text{£1} \quad \times \quad \frac{100}{110} \quad \times \quad \frac{100}{110} \quad = \quad \text{£0.83}$$

We can build up a *table of discount factors* (for 10 per cent interest rate) as shown below:

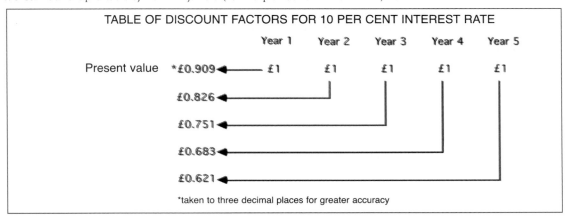

| TABLE OF DISCOUNT FACTORS FOR 10 PER CENT INTEREST RATE | | | | | |
|---|---|---|---|---|---|
| | Year 1 | Year 2 | Year 3 | Year 4 | Year 5 |
| Present value   *£0.909 ◄——— £1 | £1 | £1 | £1 | £1 | |
| £0.826 ◄ | | | | | |
| £0.751 ◄ | | | | | |
| £0.683 ◄ | | | | | |
| £0.621 ◄ | | | | | |

\*taken to three decimal places for greater accuracy

Note that there is no need to learn how to calculate discount factors – the correct factors will always be given to you in the examination.

The table of factors reminds us of the basic principle that *money has a time value* and, from this, the further into the future that we expect to receive money, then the lower is its *present value*. Thus the discount factors relate to interest rates which represent the cost of capital (ie either the rate of return that the business expects on its money, or the rate of interest it has to pay when borrowing).

Let us now return to the Worked Example where a business has to choose between Projects Aye and Bee. We will look at this assuming a cost of capital – or rate of return – of 10 per cent. For each project, the expected net cash flows are multiplied by the relevant discount factor to give the *discounted cash flow*; the difference between total discounted cash flow and the initial cost is the *net present value* of the project.

## WORKED EXAMPLE: DISCOUNTED CASH FLOW CALCULATIONS

### Project Aye

|  | Cash flow £ |  | Discount factor |  | Discounted cash flow £ |
|---|---|---|---|---|---|
| Year 0* | (20,000) | x | 1.000 | = | (20,000) |
| Year 1 | 8,000 | x | 0.909 | = | 7,272 |
| Year 2 | 12,000 | x | 0.826 | = | 9,912 |
| Year 3 | 5,000 | x | 0.751 | = | 3,755 |
| Year 4 | 4,000 | x | 0.683 | = | 2,732 |
| Year 5 | 2,000 | x | 0.621 | = | 1,242 |
|  |  |  | Net Present Value | = | 4,913 |

\* Year 0 is the beginning of the project when the initial cost is paid. Some projects such as the installation of a new production line – may well incur cash outflows during the first year.

Notes:

- The initial cost is shown in brackets because it is a cost, whereas the net cash inflows are positive amounts. Net Present Value is the net sum of all the discounted cash inflows and outflows.

- When using discount factors, the assumption is made that cash flows occur at the end of each year – apart, that is, from the Year 0 initial cash flow.

**Project Bee**

|  | Cash flow £ | | Discount factor | | Discounted cash flow £ |
|---|---|---|---|---|---|
| Year 0 | (28,000) | x | 1.000 | = | (28,000) |
| Year 1 | 10,000 | x | 0.909 | = | 9,090 |
| Year 2 | 10,000 | x | 0.826 | = | 8,260 |
| Year 3 | 8,000 | x | 0.751 | = | 6,008 |
| Year 4 | 9,000 | x | 0.683 | = | 6,147 |
| Year 5 | 9,000 | x | 0.621 | = | 5,589 |
| | | | Net Present Value | = | 7,094 |

Here, with a cost of capital – or rate of return – of 10 per cent, Project Bee is better, producing a considerably higher net present value than Aye. Note that both projects give a positive net present value at 10 per cent: this means that either project will be of benefit to the business but Bee is preferable; a negative net present value would indicate that a project should not go ahead.

Thus, using a discounted cash flow method, future cash flows are brought to their present value; this means that, the further on in time that cash flows are receivable, the lower is the net present value.

## benefits of discounted cash flow

- all cash flows are considered
- the time value of money is used
- the timing of cash flows is taken into account
- although more complex to calculate than payback, when using a table of factors the calculations are easy to make

## limitations of discounted cash flow

- the cost of capital rate – or rate of return – is, in practice, difficult to ascertain and may also vary over the life of the project
- the meaning of net present value is not always clear to users of the information
- when comparing two projects, the one with the higher net present value does not always represent the better project for the business – other factors need to be considered, eg quality of output, compatibility with existing equipment and systems
- the estimates of cash flows may be inaccurate

Tutorial note: in the AQA Examination, do not abbreviate the terms 'net present value' and 'discounted cash flow'.

# CAPITAL INVESTMENT APPRAISAL: COMPARISON

It is unlikely that a business will rely on one investment appraisal method only; instead both methods might need to be satisfied before a capital project is given the go-ahead. Supposing, for example, that the business in the Worked Example which has to choose between Projects Aye and Bee, applied the following criteria: "projects must have a payback period not exceeding two-and-a-half years, and must have a positive net present value at a 10 per cent rate of return." How do the two projects compare?

|  | Project Aye | Project Bee |
|---|---|---|
| Payback period | 2 years | 3 years |
| Net present value at 10 per cent | £4,913 | £7,094 |

Under the criteria that the business has laid down, Aye would be chosen. However, Bee seems a better project on the net present value basis and is only rejected because it does not meet the payback period requirement. However, the capital expenditure required for Bee is £8,000 greater than Aye, being £28,000 compared with £20,000; so it seems that Project Aye is, on balance, the better of the two.

# OTHER CONSIDERATIONS

As we have seen earlier in this chapter (page 332), in addition to the numerical techniques that can be used for capital investment appraisal, a business must consider a number of other financial and non-financial factors before making the final decision. These include:

- **Total implications.** The effect of the project on the business as a whole will include implications for:
  - sales, with possible increases in output
  - output, with changes in techniques, eg a switch from labour-intensive to machine-intensive output
  - employees, with possible redundancies, training needs, pay structure
  - working capital required for the project
  - needs, such as premises, transport, materials, skilled employees
- **Cost of finance.** Possible changes in the cost of capital will have a direct effect on the viability of the project. For example, an increase in the general level of interest rates will reduce the project's overall profitability. Projects are often financed through fixed interest rate loans, or through hire purchase and leasing, thus establishing some part of the finance at fixed rates; however, invariably working capital is financed by a bank overdraft at variable interest rates.
- **Taxation considerations.** The project will include the implications of both tax allowances and charges. However, a change in the general level of taxation could affect the viability of the project.
- **Forecasting techniques.** These can be used to answer 'what if?' questions: for example, "what if sales increase by 25 per cent?" or "what if materials costs fall by 5 per cent?" In this way, a business can use the technique of sensitivity analysis to see how the project is affected by changes to any of the data used in the appraisal.

- **Size of the investment.** A major project can be destabilising for a small business if cash inflows prove to be lower than expected.

# REPORTING DECISIONS

Capital investment appraisal decisions often have to be reported to managers, or other appropriate people, in a clear and concise way. The information should include recommendations which are supported by well-presented reasoning.

To conclude, we include a written report addressed to the General Manager of the business on Projects Aye and Bee, which we have looked at in this chapter. The company has the following criteria: "projects must have a payback period not exceeding two-and-a-half years, and must have a positive net present value at a 10 per cent cost of capital."

---

**REPORT**

| | |
|---|---|
| **To:** | General Manager |
| **From:** | AQA Accounting Student |
| **Date:** | Today |

Projects Aye and Bee

Introduction
- This report applies capital investment appraisal methods to these two projects.
- In this appraisal, the cash inflows and outflows used are those that have been given.

Report
- Please refer to the calculation sheet (tutorial note: on pages 335 and 338-339).
- Both projects are acceptable from a financial viewpoint because they each return a positive net present value at a discount rate of 10%, as follows: Project Aye £4,913; Project Bee £7,094. These calculations assume that net cash inflows occur at the end of each year.
- The payback periods are: Project Aye, 2 years; Project Bee, 3 years.

Conclusion
- Project Aye meets both the company requirements of payback within two-and-a-half years, and a positive net present value at a 10 per cent rate of return.
- Project Bee does not meet the payback requirement, but does have a positive net present value at a 10 per cent rate of return.
- Project Aye has a lower net present value than Project Bee.
- On balance, Project Aye is recommended:
  - lower initial cost
  - high cash inflows in the first two years
  - quick payback
  - positive net present value

---

# THE USE OF DISCOUNT FACTORS TO MINIMISE COSTS

In this chapter we have used discounted cash flow to appraise capital investment projects, ie capital expenditure at the start of the project with cash inflows over the life of the project. A further use of discounted cash flow is to minimise costs – eg making a choice between alternative electricity or telephone suppliers. The same principles are applied as with capital investment projects but, because we are looking at costs, the preferred choice will be the one with the lower net present cost. This is shown by the following:

* Estimated annual electricity costs from two suppliers, based on a three-year contract:

|  | POWER UK | MERCIAN ENERGY |
|---|---|---|
| Year 1 | £2,000 | £1,500 |
| Year 2 | £2,000 | £2,000 |
| Year 3 | £2,000 | £2,500 |

* At a cost of capital of 10 per cent, with discount factors of 0.909, 0.826 and 0.751 for years 1, 2 and 3 respectively, the net present costs of the two suppliers are:

|  | POWER UK | | | MERCIAN ENERGY | | |
|---|---|---|---|---|---|---|
|  | £ | | £ | £ | | £ |
| Year 1 | (2,000) x 0.909 | = | (1,818) | (1,500) x 0.909 | = | (1,364) |
| Year 2 | (2,000) x 0.826 | = | (1,652) | (2,000) x 0.826 | = | (1,652) |
| Year 3 | (2,000) x 0.751 | = | (1,502) | (2,500) x 0.751 | = | (1,878) |
| Net Present Cost | | | (4,972) | | | (4,894) |

The preferred supplier – based solely on the calculations – is Mercian Energy, because it has the lower net present cost.

Net present cost can be used in a number of circumstances – both in business and personally – such as:

– choosing a utility supplier

– making finance cost comparisons when buying a car, etc

– comparing loan/mortgage deals from banks

# CHAPTER SUMMARY

● Capital investment appraisal uses two main methods to help in decision-making:
  - payback period
  - net present value, also known as discounted cash flow

● Capital investment appraisal enables a business to make decisions as to whether or not to invest in a particular capital investment project and, where there are alternatives, to assist in deciding in which to invest.

● Businesses often use a combination of appraisal methods before making decisions about capital projects.

● Payback is the length of time it takes for the initial cost of a capital investment to be repaid from net cash inflows.

● Using discount factors is a method of capital investment appraisal which recognises that money has a time value – it compares net cash flows, at their present values, with the initial cost of the capital investment to give a net present value of the capital project.

● Cost of capital is the percentage cost of financing an investment – often the return on its capital employed that the business expects, plus the rate of interest it has to pay when borrowing.

● Before deciding on a capital project, other factors include:
  - total implications for the business
  - cost of finance, and effect of changes
  - taxation
  - sensitivity analysis to answer 'what if?' questions
  - size of the investment relative to the size of the business

● Discount factors can also be used to minimise costs.

# QUESTIONS

| | visit |
| | **www.osbornebooks.co.uk** |
| An asterisk (*) after the question number means that the answer is given at the end of this book. | **to take an online test** |

**14.1\***  Which best describes the payback method of investment appraisal?

| A | The period of time it takes for the initial cost of the investment to be repaid from gross cash inflows | |
|---|---|---|
| B | The period of time it takes for the investment to begin generating net cash inflows | |
| C | The period of time for which the investment is expected to last | |
| D | The period of time it takes for the initial cost of the investment to be repaid from net cash inflows | ✓ |

**14.2\*** Which best describes the net present value method of investment appraisal?

| | |
|---|---|
| A | Net present value is gross cash inflows minus the initial cost of the investment |
| B | Net present value is the return on capital employed for the investment |
| C | Net present value is the amount of the discounted return on the investment |
| D | Net present value is the rate at which the cost of the investment equals the discounted value of net inflows from the investment |

**14.3** ABC Ltd is investing in new machinery for its factory. The machinery is to cost £650,000. The expected cash flows are shown below and are assumed to accrue evenly during the year.

| Year | Cash inflow £ | Cash outflow £ |
|---|---|---|
| 1 | 400,000 | 200,000 |
| 2 | 550,000 | 300,000 |
| 3 | 750,000 | 350,000 |

*(handwritten annotations: 200 000 (450 ; 250,000 (200, ; 400,000 200,)*

What is the payback period for the machinery to the nearest day?

| | |
|---|---|
| A | 1 year 166 days |
| B | 2 years 0 days |
| C | 2 years 183 days |
| D | 2 years 272 days |

*(handwritten tick next to C)*

**14.4** DEF Ltd is investing in new machinery for its factory. The machinery is to cost £500,000 and will last for four years.
The management accountant has calculated the following at a discount rate of 10%:

| Year | Net cash inflow £ | Discount factor 10% | Discounted cash flow £ |
|---|---|---|---|
| 1 | 200,000 | 0.909 | 181,800 |
| 2 | 200,000 | 0.826 | 165,200 |
| 3 | 160,000 | 0.751 | 120,160 |
| 4 | 180,000 | 0.683 | 122,940 |

What is the net present value for the machinery?

| | |
|---|---|
| A | £60,000 |
| B | £90,100 |
| C | £500,000 |
| D | £590,100 |

**14.5\***  Sesame Shoes Limited is appraising the financial effects of a project to develop a new range of shoes. The company requires an annual rate of return of 10% on any new project.

The following information relates to this project.

|  | Year 0 | Year 1 | Year 2 | Year 3 | Year 4 | Year 5 |
|---|---|---|---|---|---|---|
|  | £ | £ | £ | £ | £ | £ |
| Design costs | 95,000 | – | – | – | – | – |
| Sales revenue | – | 60,000 | 80,000 | 100,000 | 100,000 | 50,000 |
| Variable costs | – | 30,000 | 40,000 | 50,000 | 50,000 | 25,000 |
| 10% discount factor | 1.000 | 0.909 | 0.826 | 0.751 | 0.683 | 0.621 |

**REQUIRED**

Calculate for the new project:

**(a)**   The payback period.

**(b)**   The net present value.

**14.6\***  Robert Smith is considering two major capital investment projects for his business. Only one project can be chosen and the following information is available:

|  |  | Project Exe | Project Wye |
|---|---|---|---|
|  |  | £ | £ |
| Initial cost at the beginning of the project |  | 80,000 | 100,000 |
| Net cash inflows, year: | 1 | 40,000 | 20,000 |
|  | 2 | 40,000 | 30,000 |
|  | 3 | 20,000 | 50,000 |
|  | 4 | 10,000 | 50,000 |
|  | 5 | 10,000 | 40,000 |

The initial cost occurs at the beginning of the project and you may assume that the net cash inflows will arise at the end of each year. Robert Smith requires an annual rate of return of 12 per cent. Neither project will have any residual value at the end of five years.

The discount factors at 12 per cent are:

|        |       |
|--------|-------|
| Year 1 | 0.893 |
| Year 2 | 0.797 |
| Year 3 | 0.712 |
| Year 4 | 0.636 |
| Year 5 | 0.567 |

**REQUIRED:**

**(a)** Produce numerical assessments of the two projects based on the following capital investment appraisal methods:

- the payback period

- the net present value

**(b)** Write a report to Robert Smith on the relative merits of the capital investment appraisal methods, advising which capital investment, if either, should be undertaken.

14.7* The Wyvern Bike Company is planning to introduce a new range of bikes in addition to its existing range. The company requires an annual rate of return of 12 per cent on any new project. The managing director has asked you to appraise the financial effects of introducing the new range. The following information relates to this project.

|                    | Year 0 | Year 1 | Year 2 | Year 3 | Year 4 | Year 5 |
|--------------------|--------|--------|--------|--------|--------|--------|
|                    | £      | £      | £      | £      | £      | £      |
| Development costs  | 40,000 | 60,000 | –      | –      | –      | –      |
| Sales revenue      | –      | –      | 75,000 | 90,000 | 150,000 | 100,000 |
| Variable costs     | –      | –      | 30,000 | 35,000 | 60,000 | 40,000 |
| 12% discount factor | 1.000 | 0.893 | 0.797 | 0.712 | 0.636 | 0.567 |

**REQUIRED:**

**(a)** Calculate for the new project:

- the payback period
- the net present value

**(b)** Use the data from part (a) to prepare a report to the managing director on the new bike project. Your report should:

- identify **two** additional items of information relevant to appraising this project
- make a recommendation to accept or reject the project based on its net present value

**14.8**

The following information relates to two major capital investment projects being considered by Newell Limited. For financial reasons, only one project can be accepted.

|  | | **Project Ess** | **Project Tee** |
|---|---|---|---|
|  | | £ | £ |
| Initial cost at the beginning of the project | | 100,000 | 115,000 |
| Net cash inflows, year: | 1 | 40,000 | 50,000 |
| | 2 | 60,000 | 35,000 |
| | 3 | 20,000 | 30,000 |
| | 4 | 20,000 | 30,000 |
| | 5 | 10,000 | 30,000 |
| Expected scrap value* at end of year 5 | | 5,000 | 7,000 |

*Note: remember to add the expected scrap value to the year 5 net cash inflow.*

The initial cost occurs at the beginning of the project and you may assume that the net cash inflows will arise at the end of each year. Newell Limited requires an annual rate of return of 10 per cent.

The discount factors at 10 per cent are:

| | |
|---|---|
| Year 1 | 0.909 |
| Year 2 | 0.826 |
| Year 3 | 0.751 |
| Year 4 | 0.683 |
| Year 5 | 0.621 |

**REQUIRED:**

**(a)** Produce numerical assessments of the two projects based on the following capital investment appraisal methods:

- the payback period
- the net present value

**(b)** Write a report to the managing director on the relative merits of the project appraisal methods, and advising which capital investment, if either, should be undertaken.

**14.9**   The Chester Carpet Company is considering a capital investment project to purchase a new machine for the production department.

The machine will cost £65,000 and will have a useful life of four years. The cash inflows are expected to be:

|  | £ |
|---|---|
| Year 1 | 17,000 |
| Year 2 | 25,000 |
| Year 3 | 31,000 |
| Year 4 | 24,000 |

At the end of the project, the machine will be sold as scrap for an expected amount of £4,000. The expected scrap value should be added to the year 4 cash inflow.

The Chester Carpet Company requires an annual rate of return of 10 per cent for net present value, and a maximum payback period of three years.

**REQUIRED:**

**(a)** Use the working paper on the next page to calculate the net present value and the payback period of the proposed project. Calculate all money amounts to the nearest £.

**(b)** Write a report to the General Manager evaluating the proposal from a financial viewpoint. State any assumptions you have made in your analysis.

**THE CHESTER CARPET COMPANY**

**Working paper for the financial appraisal of a new machine**

**for the production department**

DISCOUNTED CASH FLOW

| Year | Cash flow | Discount factor at 10% | Discounted cash flow |
|------|-----------|------------------------|----------------------|
|      | £         |                        | £                    |
| 0    | _____ | 1.000                 | _____           |
| 1    | _____ | 0.909                 | _____           |
| 2    | _____ | 0.826                 | _____           |
| 3    | _____ | 0.751                 | _____           |
| 4    | _____ | 0.683                 | _____           |
| Net Present Value | | | _____ |

PAYBACK PERIOD

| Year | Cash flow | Cumulative cash flow |
|------|-----------|----------------------|
|      | £         | £                    |
| 0    | _____ | _____          |
| 1    | _____ | _____          |
| 2    | _____ | _____          |
| 3    | _____ | _____          |
| 4    | _____ | _____          |

Payback period =  _____

**14.10** The research department of Zelah Chemical Company has discovered a wonder drug which cures the symptoms of the common cold within a matter of hours. The company has decided to develop the new drug – to be called 'Zelahcold' – and the managing director has asked you to appraise the financial effects of this project.

For all new projects the company requires an annual rate of return of 10 per cent for net present value, and a maximum payback period of three years.

The following information relates to this project.

|  | Year 0 | Year 1 | Year 2 | Year 3 | Year 4 | Year 5 |
|---|---|---|---|---|---|---|
|  | £ | £ | £ | £ | £ | £ |
| Development costs | 110,000 | – | – | – | – | – |
| Sales revenue | – | 55,000 | 90,000 | 120,000 | 120,000 | 120,000 |
| Variable costs | – | 35,000 | 30,000 | 40,000 | 40,000 | 35,000 |
| 10% discount factor | 1.000 | 0.909 | 0.826 | 0.751 | 0.683 | 0.621 |

**REQUIRED:**

**(a)** Calculate for the new project:
- the payback period
- the net present value

**(b)** Use the data from part (a) to prepare a report to the managing director on the new product. Your report should:
- identify **two** additional items of information relevant to appraising this project
- make a recommendation to accept or reject the project

**14.11\***

Tara Kassim is the managing director of Boxit Ltd, which makes cardboard boxes from recycled paper. The current production machinery is old and needs to be replaced.

Tara has prepared two alternative investment projects – whichever project is chosen, the company will have to borrow the initial investment from the bank at a variable interest rate of 7% per annum.

**Project A**

This project involves replacing the old production line with new automated machinery designed to use recycled paper to make the boxes. As the machinery is automated 50% of the production staff – which is 20 people – will no longer be needed and will have to be made redundant or take early retirement. The remaining production staff will need to be retrained to use the new machinery.

**Project B**

This project involves replacing the old production line with new machinery that is simple to operate and relatively cheap to buy. This machinery can only make cardboard boxes from ordinary paper that has not been recycled. No production staff will have to be made redundant and retraining costs will be minimal. Tara is unsure how the customers of Boxit Ltd will react to boxes which are not made from recycled paper. However, she believes that this is the better option as it will impact less on the cash resources of the business.

The management accountant of Boxit Ltd has carried out investment appraisals on both projects, which is summarised as follows:

|  | Project A | Project B |
|---|---|---|
| Initial investment | £800,000 | £250,000 |
| Net present value | £650,000 | £175,000 |
| Payback period | 5 years | 3 years |
| Estimated life of project | 12 years | 9 years |

Net present value has been calculated using a discount rate of 12% for both projects. This is based on the current return on capital employed of 5% plus the bank interest rate of 7%.

**REQUIRED:**

Assess the two projects and recommend to the directors of Boxit Ltd which one they should select.

---

**Tutorial note**

With this question it is appropriate to structure your answer around headings such as:

- comparison of the financial data for the two projects

- consideration of non-financial factors, eg impact on the environment

- an analysis of the financial data, eg sensitivity analysis of higher interest rates

- recommendation to the directors

**14.12** Durning Traders Ltd is considering two capital investment projects, Project Exe and Project Wye.

The management accountant has summarised company policy and her calculations of the two projects as follows:

| Appraisal method | Notes | Company policy | Project Exe | Project Wye |
|---|---|---|---|---|
| Payback method | – | 2.5 years maximum | 2 years | 3 years |
| Net present value | Discounted at 12% cost of capital | Accept if positive | +£12,450 | +£18,930 |

Show which project(s) meet the company's criteria?

| | | |
|---|---|---|
| **A** | Project Exe | |
| **B** | Project Wye | |
| **C** | Project Exe and Project Wye | |
| **D** | Neither Project Exe nor Project Wye | |

# Answers to Selected Questions

Answers to questions marked with an asterisk (*) are provided in this section. These are set out in the fully worked layout that should be used, which is very important in accounting.

Answers to all other questions are available to tutors who adopt this textbook for their students. For further information, visit the Tutor Resources section at www.osbornebooks.co.uk

## 1.1

### NICK JOHNSON

#### INCOME STATEMENT FOR THE YEAR ENDED 31 DECEMBER 20-3

| | £ | £ |
|---|---:|---:|
| Revenue (Sales) | | 310,000 |
| Opening inventory | 25,000 | |
| Purchases | 210,000 | |
| | 235,000 | |
| Less Closing inventory | 21,000 | |
| Cost of sales | | 214,000 |
| **Gross profit** | | 96,000 |
| Less expenses: | | |
| Administration expenses | 12,000 | |
| Wages | 41,000 | |
| Interest paid | 9,000 | |
| Depreciation | | |
| Property | 4,000 | |
| Machinery | 6,000 | |
| | | 72,000 |
| **Profit for the year** | | 24,000 |

---

### STATEMENT OF FINANCIAL POSITION AS AT 31 DECEMBER 20-3

| | £ Cost | £ Depreciation | £ Carrying amt |
|---|---:|---:|---:|
| **Non-current Assets** | | | |
| Property | 200,000 | 44,000 | 156,000 |
| Machinery | 40,000 | 30,000 | 10,000 |
| | 240,000 | 74,000 | 166,000 |
| **Current Assets** | | | |
| Inventory (closing) | | 21,000 | |
| Trade receivables | | 31,000 | |
| Bank | | 900 | |
| Cash | | 100 | |
| | | 53,000 | |
| **Less Current Liabilities** | | | |
| Trade payables | | 25,000 | |
| **Net Current Assets** | | | 28,000 |
| | | | 194,000 |
| **Less Non-current Liabilities** | | | |
| Loan from bank | | | 80,000 |
| **NET ASSETS** | | | 114,000 |
| **FINANCED BY:** | | | |
| **Capital** | | | |
| Opening capital | | | 100,000 |
| Add Profit for the year | | | 24,000 |
| | | | 124,000 |
| Less Drawings | | | 10,000 |
| | | | 114,000 |

1.3

A

E

## 1.5

**Financial accounting:**
- focus is on accounting records and the preparation of financial statements (income statement, statement of financial position, company's annual report)
- based on transactions carried out over a period of time
- reports are in a set format
- prepared for stakeholders such as shareholders, suppliers, lenders, government

**Management accounting:**
- focus is on reports to help the management of a business with decision-making, planning and control
- reports are based on the recent past and projections for the future
- reports are in a format that meets the needs of the business
- prepared for internal stakeholders such as management, employees, owners

## CHAPTER 2   Incomplete records

| | |
|---|---|
| 2.1 | C |
| 2.2 | D |
| 2.4 | D |
| 2.6 | C |
| 2.8 | £260,000 ie £200,000 + £60,000 (30% of revenue) |
| 2.10 | £20,000 ie £320,000 ÷ 16 |

**2.12**

**JAYNE HARVEY**
**CALCULATION OF GOODS FOR OWN USE**
**FOR THE YEAR ENDED 30 JUNE 20-8**

| | £ | £ |
|---|---:|---:|
| Opening inventory | | 21,500 |
| Purchases | | 132,000 |
| **Cost of inventory available for sale** | | 153,500 |
| Sales | 180,000 | |
| Less Normal gross profit margin (30%) | 54,000 | |
| **Cost of sales** | | 126,000 |
| Estimated closing inventory | | 27,500 |
| Less Actual closing inventory | | 26,000 |
| **Value of goods for own use** | | 1,500 |

**2.14**

**(a)**

**Sales Ledger Control Account**

| Dr | | £ | | | Cr | £ |
|---|---|---:|---|---|---|---:|
| 20-4 | | | | 20-4 | | |
| 31 Dec | Sales (to income statement) | 156,000 | | 31 Dec | Receipts from trade receivables | 153,500 |
| | | | | | Balance c/d | 2,500 |
| | | 156,000 | | | | 156,000 |
| 20-5 | | | | 20-5 | | |
| 1 Jan | Balance b/d | 2,500 | | | | |

**(b)**

**Purchases Ledger Control Account**

| Dr | | £ | | | Cr | £ |
|---|---|---:|---|---|---|---:|
| 20-4 | | | | 20-4 | | |
| 31 Dec | Payments to trade payables | 95,000 | | 31 Dec | Purchases (to income statement) | 160,000 |
| 31 Dec | Balance c/d | 65,000 | | | | |
| | | 160,000 | | | | 160,000 |
| | | | | 20-5 | | |
| | | | | 1 Jan | Balance b/d | 65,000 |

**(c)**

**Shop Rent Control Account**

| Dr | | £ | | | Cr | £ |
|---|---|---:|---|---|---|---:|
| 20-4 | | | | 20-4 | | |
| 31 Dec | Payments for rent | 8,750 | | 31 Dec | Rent (to income statement) | 8,500 |
| | | | | 31 Dec | Balance c/d | 250 |
| | | 8,750 | | | | 8,750 |
| 20-5 | | | | 20-5 | | |
| 1 Jan | Balance b/d | 250 | | | | |

**Shop Wages Control Account**

| Dr | | £ | | | Cr | £ |
|---|---|---:|---|---|---|---:|
| 20-4 | | | | 20-4 | | |
| 31 Dec | Payments for wages | 15,000 | | 31 Dec | Wages (to income statement) | 15,550 |
| 31 Dec | Balance c/d | 550 | | | | |
| | | 15,550 | | | | 15,550 |
| | | | | 20-5 | | |
| | | | | 1 Jan | Balance b/d | 550 |

(d)

## JANE PRICE
### INCOME STATEMENT FOR THE YEAR ENDED 31 DECEMBER 20-4

| | £ | £ |
|---|---|---|
| Revenue | | 156,000 |
| Purchases | 160,000 | |
| Less Closing inventory | 73,900 | |
| Cost of sales | | 86,100 |
| **Gross profit** | | **69,900** |
| Less expenses: | | |
| Advertising | 4,830 | |
| Shop rent | 8,500 | |
| Shop wages | 15,550 | |
| General expenses | 5,000 | |
| Depreciation: shop fittings | 10,000 | |
| | | 43,880 |
| **Profit for the year** | | **26,020** |

(e)

## JANE PRICE
### STATEMENT OF FINANCIAL POSITION AS AT 31 DECEMBER 20-4

| | Cost £ | Depreciation £ | Carrying amount £ |
|---|---|---|---|
| **Non-current Assets** | | | |
| Shop fittings | 50,000 | 10,000 | 40,000 |
| **Current Assets** | | | |
| Inventory | | 73,900 | |
| Trade receivables | | 2,500 | |
| Prepayment of shop rent | | 250 | |
| Bank* | | 19,900 | |
| | | 96,550 | |
| **Less Current Liabilities** | | | |
| Trade payables | 65,000 | | |
| Accrual of shop wages | 550 | | |
| | | 65,550 | |
| **Net Current Assets** | | | 31,000 |
| **NET ASSETS** | | | 71,000 |
| **FINANCED BY** | | | |
| **Capital** | | | |
| Opening capital (introduced at start of year) | | | 60,000 |
| Add Profit for the year | | | 26,020 |
| | | | 86,020 |
| Less Drawings | | | 15,020 |
| | | | 71,000 |

* Bank account summary:

| | £ |
|---|---|
| • total receipts for year | 213,500 |
| • less total payments for year | 193,600 |
| • **balance at year end** | **19,900** |

# Partners' Current Accounts

| Dr | Lysa £ | Mark £ | | Lysa £ | Mark £ |
|---|---|---|---|---|---|
| **20-4** | | | **20-4** | | |
| 31 Dec Drawings | 13,000 | 12,250 | 1 Jan Balances b/d | 420 | 1,780 |
| 31 Dec Balance c/d | – | 830 | 31 Dec Interest on capital | 2,500 | 2,000 |
| | | | 31 Dec Share of profits | 9,300 | 9,300 |
| | | | 31 Dec Balance c/d | 780 | – |
| | 13,000 | 13,080 | | 13,000 | 13,080 |
| **20-5** | | | **20-5** | | |
| 1 Jan Balance b/d | 780 | – | 1 Jan Balance b/d | – | 830 |

(a)

4.9

### SIGRID AND TOMASCZ IN PARTNERSHIP, TRADING AS 'S & T PLUMBERS'
### PARTNERSHIP APPROPRIATION ACCOUNT FOR THE YEAR ENDED 30 JUNE 20-2

| | £ | £ | £ |
|---|---|---|---|
| **Profit for the year** | | | 50,500 |
| Add interest charged on partners' drawings: | | | |
| Sigrid | | 1,280 | |
| Tomascz | | 920 | 2,200 |
| | | | 52,700 |
| **Less appropriation of profit:** | | | |
| Salary: Tomascz | | | 12,000 |
| Interest allowed on partners' capitals: | | | |
| Sigrid £40,000 x 10% | | 4,000 | |
| Tomascz £30,000 x 10% | | 3,000 | 7,000 |
| | | | 33,700 |
| **Share of remaining profit:** | | | |
| Sigrid (60%) | | 20,220 | |
| Tomascz (40%) | | 13,480 | |
| | | | 33,700 |

---

# CHAPTER 3   Computer accounting

**3.1** Explanation of two advantages out of the list on page 62. The most obvious advantages are speed of input, accuracy of transaction recording, accessibility of up-to-date information and document printing (eg invoices, credit notes and statements).

**3.2** The main two advantages are that a spreadsheet saves time in calculation and secondly that if any of the figures should alter, the remaining dependent figures will automatically be recalculated.

**3.3** Three from:
- ledger accounting, eg sales ledger, purchases ledger, cash book
- management reports, eg aged trade receivables' analysis
- trial balance
- financial statements, eg income statement, statement of financial position
- VAT return

**3.4** Two from: hacking from outside (or inside), theft from outside (or inside), computer breakdown when periodic back-ups have not been made, viruses, inefficient back-up policy.

# CHAPTER 4   Partnership financial statements

**4.1** B

**4.2** C

**4.3** A

**4.7**

### Partners' Capital Accounts

| Dr | Lysa £ | Mark £ | | Lysa £ | Mark £ |
|---|---|---|---|---|---|
| **20-4** | | | **20-4** | | |
| 31 Dec Balances c/d | 50,000 | 40,000 | 1 Jan Balances b/d | 50,000 | 40,000 |
| **20-5** | | | **20-5** | | |
| | | | 1 Jan Balances b/d | 50,000 | 40,000 |

## (b)

**Partners' Capital Accounts**

| Dr | | Sigrid £ | Tomascz £ | | | Cr Sigrid £ | Tomascz £ |
|---|---|---|---|---|---|---|---|
| 20-2 | | | | 20-1 | | | |
| 30 Jun | Balances c/d | 40,000 | 30,000 | 1 Jul | Balances b/d | 40,000 | 30,000 |
| | | | | 20-2 | | | |
| | | 40,000 | 30,000 | 1 Jul | Balances b/d | 40,000 | 30,000 |

**Partners' Current Accounts**

| Dr | | Sigrid £ | Tomascz £ | | | Cr Sigrid £ | Tomascz £ |
|---|---|---|---|---|---|---|---|
| 20-1 | | | | 20-1 | | | |
| 1 Jul | Balance b/d | – | 2,500 | 1 Jul | Balance b/d | 1,200 | – |
| 20-2 | | | | 20-2 | | | |
| 30 Jun | Interest on drawings | 1,280 | 920 | 30 Jun | Salary | – | 12,000 |
| 30 Jun | Drawings | 26,000 | 21,500 | 30 Jun | Interest on capital | 4,000 | 3,000 |
| 30 Jun | Balance c/d | – | 3,560 | 30 Jun | Share of profits | 20,220 | 13,480 |
| | | | | 30 Jun | Balance c/d | 1,860 | – |
| | | 27,280 | 28,480 | | | 27,280 | 28,480 |
| 20-2 | | | | 20-2 | | | |
| 1 Jul | Balance b/d | 1,860 | – | 1 Jul | Balance b/d | – | 3,560 |

## 4.10 (a)

**Partners' Capital Accounts**

| Dr | | James £ | Hill £ | | | Cr James £ | Hill £ |
|---|---|---|---|---|---|---|---|
| 20-4 | | | | 20-4 | | | |
| 31 Dec | Balances c/d | 38,000 | 32,000 | 1 Jan | Balances b/d | 38,000 | 32,000 |
| | | | | 20-5 | | | |
| | | 38,000 | 32,000 | 1 Jan | Balances b/d | 38,000 | 32,000 |

**Partners' Current Accounts**

| Dr | | James £ | Hill £ | | | Cr James £ | Hill £ |
|---|---|---|---|---|---|---|---|
| 20-4 | | | | 20-4 | | | |
| 1 Jan | Balance b/d | 3,000 | – | 1 Jan | Balance b/d | – | 1,000 |
| 31 Dec | Drawings | 10,000 | 22,000 | 31 Dec | Salary | – | 15,000 |
| 31 Dec | Balances c/d | 800 | 7,200 | 31 Dec | Interest on capital | 3,800 | 3,200 |
| | | | | 31 Dec | Share of profits | 10,000 | 10,000 |
| | | 13,800 | 29,200 | | | 13,800 | 29,200 |
| | | | | 20-5 | | | |
| | | | | 1 Jan | Balances b/d | 800 | 7,200 |

## (b)

### JOHN JAMES AND STEVEN HILL IN PARTNERSHIP, TRADING AS 'GRAPES'
### INCOME STATEMENT FOR THE YEAR ENDED 31 DECEMBER 20-4

| | £ | £ |
|---|---|---|
| **Gross profit** | | 89,000 |
| Less expenses: | | |
| Rent and rates | 7,500 | |
| Advertising | 12,000 | |
| Heat and light | 3,500 | |
| Wages and salaries | 18,000 | |
| Sundry expenses | 4,000 | |
| Depreciation: shop fittings | 2,000 | |
| | | 47,000 |
| **Profit for the year** | | 42,000 |
| | | |
| **Less appropriation of profit:** | | |
| Salary: Hill | | 15,000 |
| Interest allowed on partners' capitals | | |
| James £38,000 x 10% | 3,800 | |
| Hill £32,000 x 10% | 3,200 | |
| | | 7,000 |
| | | 20,000 |
| **Share of remaining profit:** | | |
| James | | 10,000 |
| Hill | | 10,000 |
| | | 20,000 |

### STATEMENT OF FINANCIAL POSITION AS AT 31 DECEMBER 20-4

| | Cost £ | Depreciation £ | Carrying amt £ |
|---|---|---|---|
| **Non-current Assets** | | | |
| Shop fittings | 20,000 | 2,000 | 18,000 |
| **Current Assets** | | | |
| Inventory | | 35,000 | |
| Trade receivables | | 6,000 | |
| Bank | | 29,000 | |
| | | 70,000 | |
| **Less Current Liabilities** | | | |
| Trade payables | | 10,000 | |
| **Net Current Assets** | | | 60,000 |
| **NET ASSETS** | | | 78,000 |
| | | | |
| **FINANCED BY** | | | |
| **Capital Accounts** | | | |
| James | | 38,000 | |
| Hill | | 32,000 | |
| | | | 70,000 |
| **Current Accounts** | | | |
| James | | 800 | |
| Hill | | 7,200 | |
| | | | 8,000 |
| | | | 78,000 |

(c)
- The balance on the partners' current accounts represents the balance owed or owing between the business and the individual partners after transactions such as salaries, interest on capital, share of profits, and drawings have been taken into account.
- A debit balance on a partner's current account means that the partner has drawn out more than his/her entitlement of salary, interest on capital and share of profits.
- A credit balance on a partner's current account means that the partner has drawn out less than his/her entitlement of salary, interest on capital and share of profits.

## 4.11 (a)

### Partners' Capital Accounts

| Dr | Clark | Pearce | | Cr | Clark | Pearce |
|---|---|---|---|---|---|---|
| | £ | £ | 20-3 | | £ | £ |
| 20-4 | | | 1 Jul Balances b/d | | 60,000 | 30,000 |
| 30 Jun Balances c/d | 60,000 | 30,000 | | | | |
| | 60,000 | 30,000 | | | 60,000 | 30,000 |
| 20-4 | | | | | | |
| | | | 1 Jul Balances b/d | | 60,000 | 30,000 |

### Partners' Current Accounts

| Dr | Clark | Pearce | | Cr | Clark | Pearce |
|---|---|---|---|---|---|---|
| | £ | £ | 20-3 | | £ | £ |
| 20-4 | | | 1 Jul Balances b/d | | 430 | 300 |
| 30 Jun Drawings | 20,600 | 15,700 | 20-4 | | | |
| 30 Jun Balance c/d | – | 4,840 | 30 Jun Salary | | – | 12,000 |
| | | | 30 Jun Share of profits | | 16,480 | 8,240 |
| | | | 30 Jun Balance c/d | | 3,690 | – |
| | 20,600 | 20,540 | | | 20,600 | 20,540 |
| 20-4 | | | 20-4 | | | |
| 1 Jul Balance b/d | 3,690 | – | 1 Jul Balance b/d | | – | 4,840 |

(b)

### CLARK AND PEARCE, IN PARTNERSHIP
### INCOME STATEMENT FOR THE YEAR ENDED 30 JUNE 20-4

| | £ | £ |
|---|---|---|
| Gross profit | | 105,000 |
| Less expenses: | | |
| Salaries | 30,400 | |
| Electricity | 2,420 | |
| Telephone | 3,110 | |
| Rent and rates | 10,000 | |
| Discount allowed | 140 | |
| Office expenses | 10,610 | |
| Irrecoverable debts written off | 1,200 | |
| Depreciation: office equipment | 10,400 | |
| | | 68,280 |
| **Profit for the year** | | 36,720 |
| | | |
| **Less appropriation of profit:** | | |
| Salary: Pearce | | 12,000 |
| | | 24,720 |
| **Share of remaining profit:** | | |
| Clark (two-thirds) | | 16,480 |
| Pearce (one-third) | | 8,240 |
| | | 24,720 |

### STATEMENT OF FINANCIAL POSITION AS AT 30 JUNE 20-4

| | Cost £ | Depreciation £ | Carrying amt £ |
|---|---|---|---|
| **Non-current Assets** | | | |
| Office equipment | 52,000 | 31,200 | 20,800 |
| **Current Assets** | | | |
| Inventory | | | 41,570 |
| Trade receivables | | 20,000 | |
| Less provision for doubtful debts | | 780 | 19,220 |
| Bank | | | 21,750 |
| | | | 82,540 |
| **Less Current Liabilities** | | | |
| Trade payables | | | 12,190 |
| **Net Current Assets** | | | 70,350 |
| **NET ASSETS** | | | 91,150 |
| | | | |
| **FINANCED BY** | | | |
| **Capital Accounts** | | | |
| Clark | | 60,000 | |
| Pearce | | 30,000 | |
| | | | 90,000 |
| **Current Accounts** | | | |
| Clark | | (3,690) | |
| Pearce | | 4,840 | |
| | | | 1,150 |
| | | | 91,150 |

**5.2   A**

**5.3   B**

**5.5**

### Partners' Capital Accounts

| Dr | | Jim £ | Maisie £ | Matt £ | | Cr | | Jim £ | Maisie £ | Matt £ |
|---|---|---|---|---|---|---|---|---|---|---|
| 20-4 | | | | | | 20-4 | | | | |
| 1 Jan | Goodwill written off | 24,000 | 16,000 | 8,000 | | 31 Dec | Balances b/d | 60,000 | 40,000 | – |
| 31 Dec | Drawings | 12,000 | 12,000 | 8,000 | | 20-5 | | | | |
| 31 Dec | Balances c/d | 82,800 | 51,200 | 22,000 | | 1 Jan | Goodwill created | 28,800 | 19,200 | – |
| | | | | | | 1 Jan | Bank | | | 28,000 |
| | | | | | | 31 Dec | Share of profit | 30,000 | 20,000 | 10,000 |
| | | 118,800 | 79,200 | 38,000 | | | | 118,800 | 79,200 | 38,000 |
| | | | | | | 20-6 | | | | |
| | | | | | | 1 Jan | Balances b/d | 82,800 | 51,200 | 22,000 |

**5.6**

### Partners' Capital Accounts

| Dr | | Andy £ | Beth £ | Cath £ | | Cr | | Andy £ | Beth £ | Cath £ |
|---|---|---|---|---|---|---|---|---|---|---|
| | Bank | 57,000 | | | | | Balances b/d | 30,000 | 15,000 | 10,000 |
| | Goodwill written off | – | 15,000 | 15,000 | | | Revaluation | 12,000 | 8,000 | 4,000 |
| | Bank | – | 500 | | | | Goodwill created | 15,000 | 10,000 | 5,000 |
| | Balances c/d | – | 17,500 | 17,500 | | | Bank | – | – | 13,500 |
| | | 57,000 | 33,000 | 32,500 | | | | 57,000 | 33,000 | 32,500 |
| | | | | | | | Balances b/d | – | 17,500 | 17,500 |

**5.8**

### Revaluation Account

| Dr | | £ | | Cr | | £ |
|---|---|---|---|---|---|---|
| 20-9 | | | | 20-9 | | |
| 1 Jan | Inventory write-off | 3,000 | | 1 Jan | Property | 30,000 |
| 1 Jan | Irrecoverable debts written off | 2,000 | | | | |
| 1 Jan | Capital accounts: | | | | | |
| | Henry (3/5) | 15,000 | | | | |
| | Jenny (2/5) | 10,000 | | | | |
| | | 30,000 | | | | 30,000 |

### Goodwill Account

| Dr | | £ | | Cr | | £ |
|---|---|---|---|---|---|---|
| 20-9 | | | | 20-9 | | |
| 1 Jan | Capital accounts: | | | 1 Jan | Capital accounts: | |
| | Henry (3/5) | 24,000 | | | Henry (2/5) | 16,000 |
| | Jenny (2/5) | 16,000 | | | Jenny (2/5) | 16,000 |
| | | | | | Kylie (1/5) | 8,000 |
| | | 40,000 | | | | 40,000 |

### Partners' Capital Accounts

| Dr | | Henry £ | Jenny £ | Kylie £ | | Cr | | Henry £ | Jenny £ | Kylie £ |
|---|---|---|---|---|---|---|---|---|---|---|
| 20-9 | | | | | | 20-9 | | | | |
| 1 Jan | Goodwill written off | 16,000 | 16,000 | 8,000 | | 1 Jan | Balances b/d | 100,000 | 90,000 | – |
| 1 Jan | Balances c/d | 123,000 | 100,000 | 42,000 | | 1 Jan | Revaluation | 15,000 | 10,000 | – |
| | | | | | | 1 Jan | Goodwill created | 24,000 | 16,000 | – |
| | | | | | | 1 Jan | Bank | – | – | 50,000 |
| | | 139,000 | 116,000 | 50,000 | | | | 139,000 | 116,000 | 50,000 |
| | | | | | | 1 Jan | Balances b/d | 123,000 | 100,000 | 42,000 |

**6.2** The benefits to a company's shareholders of the statement of changes in equity are that it highlights the changes that have taken place to their stake in the company. It includes not only the *realised* profit or loss from the income statement, but also *unrealised* profits (such as the gain on the upwards revaluation of property) which are taken directly to reserves. It also highlights the dividends that have been paid to shareholders.

**6.4** Items to be included in a directors' report (four items required for the answer):

- the principal activities of the company
- a review of the activities of the company over the past year
- likely developments that will affect the company in the future, including research and development activity
- directors' names and their shareholdings in the company
- proposed dividends
- any significant differences between the book value and market value of property
- political and charitable contributions
- the company's policies on:
  - employment of disabled people
  - health and safety at work of employees
  - actions taken on employee involvement and consultation
  - payment of suppliers

**6.6** **(a)** **(1)** *Current assets*, eg trade receivables, inventory, cash or cash equivalents

Assets which are:

- cash or cash equivalent
- those to be realised, sold or used within the normal operating cycle
- assets held for trading and expected to be realised within twelve months

**(2)** *Current liabilities*, eg trade payables, tax liabilities, bank overdraft

Liabilities which are:

- those expected to be settled within the normal operating cycle
- liabilities held for trading and expected to be settled within twelve months
- where the company does not have the right to defer payment beyond twelve months

**(b)** **(1)** Dividends; activities; review of business; list of directors and their shareholdings; employees; charity/political contributions; health and safety; payment of suppliers, etc.

**(2)** The directors are responsible for preparing the financial statements in accordance with company law and (international) accounting standards.

Auditors are responsible for forming an opinion on the financial statements – that they give a true and fair view in accordance with company law and (international) accounting standards.

---

### HENRY, JENNY AND KYLIE

**STATEMENT OF FINANCIAL POSITION AS AT 1 JANUARY 20-9**

| | £ | £ |
|---|---:|---:|
| **Non-current Assets** | | |
| Property (revaluation) | | 180,000 |
| Vehicles (carrying amount) | | 30,000 |
| | | 210,000 |
| **Current Assets** | | |
| Inventory 20,000 – 3,000 | 17,000 | |
| Trade receivables 25,000 – 2,000 | 23,000 | |
| Bank 3,000 + 50,000 | 53,000 | |
| | 93,000 | |
| **Less Current Liabilities** | | |
| Trade payables | 28,000 | |
| **Net Current Assets** | | 65,000 |
| **NET ASSETS** | | 275,000 |
| **FINANCED BY** | | |
| **Capital Accounts** | | |
| Henry | | 123,000 |
| Jenny | | 100,000 |
| Kylie | | 42,000 |
| | | 265,000 |
| **Current Accounts** | | |
| Henry | 8,500 | |
| Jenny | 1,500 | |
| | | 10,000 |
| | | 275,000 |

**6.8** This answer may be set out either vertically or horizontally.

| Non-current Assets | |
|---|---|
| *Property, plant and equipment* | £000 |
| Carrying amount at start of year | 3,832 |
| Additions at cost | 722 |
| Less Disposals during year £1,076 – £695 | 381 |
| Less Depreciation for year (*missing figure*) | 589 |
| Carrying amount at end of year | 3,584 |

**Non-current Assets**

| | Carrying amt at start £000 | Additions at cost £000 | Disposals £000 | Depreciation £000 | Carrying amt at end £000 |
|---|---|---|---|---|---|
| Property, plant and equipment | 3,832 | 722 | (381) | (589) | 3,584 |

**6.10**

### NELSON PLC
### INCOME STATEMENT FOR THE YEAR ENDED 31 MARCH 20-2

| | £000 | £000 |
|---|---|---|
| Revenue | | 1,935 |
| Opening inventory | 140 | |
| Purchases | 960 | |
| | 1,100 | |
| Less Closing inventory | 180 | |
| Cost of sales | | 920 |
| **Gross profit** | | 1,015 |
| Less expenses: | | |
| Distribution expenses (note 1) | 486 | |
| Administration expenses (note 2) | 329 | |
| | | 815 |
| **Profit/(loss) for the year from operations** | | 200 |
| Less Finance costs | | – |
| **Profit/(loss) for the year before tax** | | 200 |
| Less Tax | | 15 |
| **Profit/(loss) for the year after tax** | | 185 |

### STATEMENT OF CHANGES IN EQUITY FOR THE YEAR ENDED 31 MARCH 20-2

| | Share capital | Share premium | Revaluation reserve | Retained earnings | Total |
|---|---|---|---|---|---|
| | £000 | £000 | £000 | £000 | £000 |
| Balances at 1 April 20-1 | 500 | 140 | – | 245 | 885 |
| Profit for the year | – | – | – | 185 | 185 |
| Revaluation surplus | – | – | 100 | – | 100 |
| Dividends paid | – | – | – | (40) | (40) |
| Issued share capital | – | – | – | – | – |
| Balances at 31 March 20-2 | 500 | 140 | 100 | 390 | 1,130 |

### NELSON PLC
### STATEMENT OF FINANCIAL POSITION AS AT 31 MARCH 20-2

| Non-current Assets | Valuation | Cost | Depreciation | Carrying amount |
|---|---|---|---|---|
| | £000 | £000 | £000 | £000 |
| *Property, plant and equipment* | | | | |
| Property | 500 | – | – | 500 |
| Plant and equipment | – | 550 | 430 | 120 |
| | 500 | 550 | 430 | 620 |
| | | | | (note 3) |

| Current Assets | £000 | £000 |
|---|---|---|
| Inventory | 180 | |
| Trade and other receivables | 570 | |
| Cash and cash equivalents | 35 | |
| | 785 | |
| Less Current Liabilities | | |
| Trade and other payables | 260 | |
| Tax liabilities | 15 | |
| | 275 | |
| Net Current Assets | | 510 |
| NET ASSETS | | 1,130 |

| EQUITY | £000 |
|---|---|
| **Issued Share Capital** | |
| Ordinary shares of £1 each, fully paid | 500 |
| **Capital Reserves** | |
| Share premium | 140 |
| Revaluation reserve | 100 |
| **Revenue Reserve** | |
| Retained earnings | 390 |
| **TOTAL EQUITY** | 1,130 |

**7.1** B

**7.3** B

**7.5**

| Transaction | Inflow of cash | Outflow of cash | No effect on cash |
|---|---|---|---|
| A Cash purchases | | ✓ | |
| B Sold goods on credit | | | ✓ |
| C Bought goods on credit | | | ✓ |
| D Bought a non-current asset paying by cheque | | ✓ | |
| E A trade receivable pays by bank transfer | ✓ | | |
| F Paid expenses in cash | | ✓ | |
| G Paid a trade payable by bank transfer | | ✓ | |

---

**Working note 1 (£000)**

| | |
|---|---|
| Distribution expenses | 420 |
| Depreciation | *66 |
| | 486 |

* depreciation: plant and equipment £550 x 20% = £110 x 60%

**Working note 2 (£000)**

| | |
|---|---|
| Administration expenses | 285 |
| Depreciation | *44 |
| | 329 |

* depreciation as per distribution expenses, but at 40%

**Working note 3 (£000)**

Accumulated depreciation at 31 March 20-2:

£320 + £110 = £430

**6.12  C**

**6.14**

DURNING PLC

STATEMENT OF CHANGES IN EQUITY FOR THE YEAR ENDED 30 JUNE 20-5

| | Share capital £ | Share premium £ | Retained earnings £ | Total £ |
|---|---|---|---|---|
| At 1 July 20-4 | 600,000 | 90,000 | 330,000 | 1,020,000 |
| Issue of shares | 150,000 | 90,000 | | 240,000 |
| Profit for the year | | | 365,000 | 365,000 |
| Dividends paid | | | (220,000) | (220,000) |
| At 30 June 20-5 | 750,000 | 180,000 | 475,000 | 1,405,000 |

## 7.7 HALL LIMITED
### STATEMENT OF CASH FLOWS FOR THE YEAR ENDED 30 SEPTEMBER 20-5

| | £ | £ |
|---|---|---|
| Profit from operations | 24,000 | |
| Adjustments for: | | |
| Depreciation | 318,000 | |
| Increase in inventory | (251,000) | |
| Increase in trade receivables | (152,000) | |
| Increase in trade payables | 165,000 | |
| **Cash from operating activities** | 104,000 | |
| Interest paid | (218,000) | |
| Tax paid | (75,000) | |
| *Net cash used in operating activities* | | (189,000) |
| **Investing activities** | | |
| Purchase of non-current assets | (358,000) | |
| Proceeds from sale of non-current assets | 132,000 | |
| *Net cash used in investing activities* | | (226,000) |
| **Financing activities** | | |
| Issue of share capital | 150,000 | |
| Non-current loan | 200,000 | |
| Dividends paid | (280,000) | |
| *Net cash from financing activities* | | 70,000 |
| **Net decrease in cash and cash equivalents** | | (345,000) |
| **Cash and cash equivalents at beginning of year** | | 395,000 |
| **Cash and cash equivalents at end of year** | | 50,000 |

## 7.8 J SMITH LIMITED
### STATEMENT OF CASH FLOWS FOR THE YEAR ENDED 31 DECEMBER 20-2

| | £ | £ | £ |
|---|---|---|---|
| Profit from operations (Working 1) | 13,000 | | |
| Depreciation | 1,000 | | |
| Increase in inventory | (3,500) | | |
| Increase in trade receivables | (550) | | |
| Increase in trade payables | 250 | | |
| **Cash from operating activities** | 10,200 | | |
| Interest paid | (250) | | |
| Tax paid | (1,000) | | |
| *Net cash from operating activities* | | 8,950 | |
| **Investing activities** | | | |
| Purchase of non-current assets (Working 2) | (2,000) | | |
| *Net cash used in investing activities* | | (2,000) | |
| **Financing activities** | | | |
| Dividends paid | (9,000) | | |
| *Net cash used in financing activities* | | (9,000) | |
| **Net decrease in cash and cash equivalents** | | (2,050) | |
| **Cash and cash equivalents at beginning of year** | | 850 | |
| **Cash and cash equivalents at end of year** | | (1,200) | |

# 1. Working for profit from operations

| | £ | £ |
|---|---|---|
| Increase in retained earnings: | | |
| Retained earnings at 31 December 20-2 | 4,000 | |
| Less Retained earnings at 31 December 20-1 | 2,000 | |
| | | 2,000 |
| Add back: | | |
| Dividends paid | | 9,000 |
| Tax provision | | 1,750 |
| Finance costs | | 250 |
| Profit from operations | | 13,000 |

# 2. Working for purchase of PPE

| | £ |
|---|---|
| PPE at cost on 31 December 20-2 | 5,000 |
| Less PPE at cost on 31 December 20-1 | 3,000 |
| Purchase of non-current assets | 2,000 |

## SHEEHAN LIMITED

### STATEMENT OF CASH FLOWS FOR THE YEAR ENDED 31 OCTOBER 20-3

| | £000 | £000 |
|---|---|---|
| Profit from operations (Working 1) | 2,520 | |
| Depreciation | 318 | |
| Loss on asset disposal (Working 3) | 3 | |
| Increase in inventory | (15) | |
| Decrease in trade receivables | 15 | |
| Increase in trade payables | 27 | |
| **Cash from operating activities** | 2,868 | |
| Interest paid | (168) | |
| Tax paid | (744) | |
| *Net cash from operating activities* | | 1,956 |
| **Investing activities** | | |
| Purchase of non-current assets | (629) | |
| Proceeds from sale of non-current assets | 8 | |
| *Net cash used in investing activities* | | (621) |
| **Financing activities** | | |
| Receipts from issue of share capital (Working 4) | 627 | |
| Repayment of non-current loans (£2,400 - £600) | (1,800) | |
| Dividends paid | (144) | |
| *Net cash used in financing activities* | | (1,317) |
| **Net increase in cash and cash equivalents** | | 18 |
| **Cash and cash equivalents at start of the year** | | 30 |
| **Cash and cash equivalents at end of the year** | | 48 |

**8.1**   A

**8.2**   B

**8.3**   C

**8.8**   (a)   cash is the actual amount of money held in the bank or as cash

profit is a calculated figure which shows the surplus of income over expenditure for a period

(b)   Examples of how a business can make good profits during a year when the bank balance reduces or the bank overdraft increases (the question asks for two examples):

- purchase of non-current assets – cash decreases; no effect on profit (but there is likely to be an amount for depreciation in the income statement)
- repayment of a loan – cash decreases; no effect on profit
- payment of dividends/drawings – cash decreases; no effect on profit
- an increase in inventory – cash decreases, profit increases
- an increase in trade receivables – cash decreases; no effect on profit
- a decrease in trade payables – cash decreases; no effect on profit

## 1. Working for profit from operations

|  | £000 | £000 |
|---|---|---|
| Increase in retained earnings: |  |  |
| Retained earnings at 31 October 20-3 | 3,411 |  |
| Less Retained earnings at 31 October 20-2 | 1,953 |  |
|  |  | 1,458 |
| Add back: |  |  |
| Dividends paid |  | 144 |
| Tax provision |  | 750 |
| Finance costs |  | 168 |
| Profit from operations |  | 2,520 |

## 2. Working for cost of asset sold during the year

|  | £000 | £000 |
|---|---|---|
| Non-current assets at cost at 31 October 20-3 |  | 9,000 |
| Less Additions |  | 629 |
|  |  | 8,371 |
| Less Non-current assets at cost at 31 October 20-2 |  | 8,400 |
| Cost of asset sold during the year |  | 29 |

## 3. Working for profit or loss on disposal of a non-current asset

|  | £000 |
|---|---|
| Cost of asset sold during year (Working 2) | 29 |
| Less Depreciation on asset sold | 18 |
|  | 11 |
| Proceeds of sale | 8 |
| Loss on disposal | 3 |

## 4. Working for receipts from issue of share capital

|  | £000 | £000 |
|---|---|---|
| Increase in share capital: |  |  |
| Share capital at 31 October 20-3 | 3,000 |  |
| Less Share capital at 31 October 20-2 | 2,550 |  |
|  |  | 450 |
| Increase in share premium |  | 177 |
| Issue of share capital |  | 627 |

---

**REPORT**

To:     Steve Horan

From:   AQA Accounting student

Subject: Shareholding in Blenheim plc

Date:   Today

As requested I have looked into the financial situation of Blenheim plc.

(1) The **gross profit margin** has deteriorated.

Less gross profit is being generated by sales/gross profit margin on sales.

Deterioration may be due to decreasing its sales price or increasing the cost of sales or both.

Could have been a change in the product mix.

(2) The **profit in relation to revenue** has improved.

More profit is being generated from sales – possibly an increase in sales volume.

Either an increase in the sales margins or a decrease in expenses, or both.

As the gross margins have deteriorated, must be the result of a decrease in expenses.

(3) The **rate of inventory turnover (days)** has deteriorated.

It now takes eighteen days more to sell the inventory, on average, than it took the year before. This results in increased holding costs and possible inventory deterioration.

The increase might be due to slow moving inventory that might indicate possible obsolescence problems.

(4) **Trade receivable days** have deteriorated.

It now takes fifteen days more to collect the debts, on average, than it took the year before.

It might be due to old debts which might become irrecoverable debts in the future.

(5) **Trade payable days** have deteriorated.

It now takes eight days more to pay credit suppliers, on average, than it took the year before. This may be as a result of the longer time being taken to collect debts from customers.

If trade payables are not paid on time they could refuse to supply further goods to the company.

---

**(b)**

Steve should be advised to consider selling his shares since only the profit in relation to revenue percentage has improved. The use of resources needs to be urgently reviewed by management as the periods for inventory, trade receivables and trade payables have all deteriorated.

Before making a final decision Steve should seek further financial information from the company.

**8.13 a&b**

• *shareholders*

– dividends

– profits

Dividends enable shareholders to see how much cash they are receiving from their investment and to enable comparison with previous years/other investments.

Profits enable shareholders to see how much was retained in the company for investment and to assess the future prospects of the company.

• *lenders*

– total loans

– profits

There may be other lenders which need to be repaid, so reducing the ability of the company to repay its lending.

Profits enable the loan providers to assess the likelihood of receiving their finance charges and loan repayments.

• *suppliers*

– current assets, net current assets

– profits

The current assets/net current assets will enable trade payables to look at the liquidity of the company (ie the stability of the company on a short-term basis) and to assess its ability to pay suppliers.

A company that is generating profits is likely to be able to pay its suppliers. Also, the company may be expanding, so creating an increased level of purchases from its suppliers; comparison of profits with previous years.

• *employees*

– profits

– net assets

A profitable company may be able to afford pay rises; comparison of profits with previous years.

The net assets show the financial strength of the company and indicate its ability to continue in business, so assuring future employment prospects.

**Report**

To: Birgitta

From: AQA Accounting student

Subject: Evaluation of Avon plc and Severn plc

Date: Today

1 The number of shares that you could purchase and the expected income:

- Avon plc

£50,000 investment ÷ £1.20 current market price = 41,666 shares

At current dividends your income is 41,666 shares x 10.5p per share = £4,375 (approx) per year

- Severn plc

£50,000 ÷ £3.50 = 14,285 shares

Income 14,285 x 7.0p = £1,000 (approx) per year

2 A comparison of the investor ratios for the two companies shows:

- Avon is better than Severn
  - dividend per share
  - dividend yield
- Severn is better than Avon
  - dividend cover
  - earnings per share
  - price earnings ratio

Other data shows that:

- Severn appears to be a larger company than Avon (based on PPE amounts)
- Avon has a higher return on capital employed than Severn
- Severn is lower geared than Avon, whose gearing may be too risky for investors
- Severn's share price appears to be more stable – fluctuating within a narrower range than that of Avon

3 An analysis will help you with the investment decision.

- You wish, initially, to maximise income – Avon will give you a much higher income.
- However, Avon's share price is less stable than that of Severn (note that the difference in the share prices is not an indicator of a better or worse company). This could offer larger capital gains if it rises, but with the possibility of losses if it falls.

- Avon's higher return on capital employed could be as a result of the company making more efficient use of its capital employed.
- Avon's higher capital gearing represents a riskier investment – 70% means that non-current liabilities are greater than equity.
- Other factors to consider include:
  - what is your attitude to investment risk?
  - Is the line of business in which both companies operate acceptable to you?
  - Is other data, both historical and future, available?

4 The conclusion is that, if you wish to maximise income, you should make your investment in Avon. However, this is a more volatile company – share price, gearing – and your investment will be more at risk. If you wish to invest for the longer-term, both for income and capital gain (share price increase), you should consider making your investment in Severn.

## CHAPTER 9 Accounting regulations and ethics

9.2 The purposes of using accounting standards:

- to provide a framework for preparing and presenting financial statements
- to standardise financial statements
- to reduce the variations of accounting treatments used in financial statements
- to help to ensure high quality financial accounting for users
- to enable compliance with the Companies Act and audit requirements
- to allow users of financial statements to make comparisons between firms

9.3 (a) The ethical codes of conduct established by the professional accounting bodies in the UK set out:

- the required standards of professional behaviour that accountants should maintain
- gives guidance on how to achieve these standards

(b) Failure by an accountant to comply with applicable regulations and codes of practice of an accounting body may result in the member being disciplined.

Misconduct is either:

- bringing the accounting profession into disrepute
- acting in breach of the rules and regulations of the accounting body

Professional accounting bodies have disciplinary processes and sanctions for misconduct. These are a disciplinary investigation, a decision and, if found guilty, a penalty (ranging from a fine, suspension of membership, or expulsion from membership).

**9.4** C

**9.5** B

**9.6** A

**9.8** The relevant fundamental principle of ethical behaviour is confidentiality. An accountant must maintain the confidentiality of information, unless the information is a matter of public knowledge, or the accountant has the client's authority to disclose information. The requirement to maintain confidentiality includes when the accountant is in a social environment.

**9.10** The relevant fundamental principle is objectivity. An accountant must not allow bias, conflict of interest or the undue influence of others to override professional or business judgements.

**9.11**

**(a)** If Brenda accepts the new company as a client the fee income from the two companies will represent a substantial proportion of her total fee income. This could represent a self-interest threat to Brenda's objectivity as she could be reliant on the fees from Avon Holidays Ltd and its acquisition, Severn Leisure Ltd.

**(b)** Brenda should not accept the additional work for Avon Holidays as she cannot reduce the self-interest threat she would face to an acceptable level.

**9.12**

**(a)** The two fundamental ethical principles that are most threatened by this situation are:

Integrity: if Lesley knows that the provision for doubtful debts was too low she has deliberately produced incorrect financial information which is both misleading to the users and dishonest.

Professional behaviour: knowingly allowing inaccurate and misleading information to be included in a client's financial statements breaches accounting regulations and consequently brings the accounting profession into disrepute.

**(b)** Lesley faces an intimidation threat from Matt's statement that 'it may not look good for you if the partners at Gunn and Rood knew about this'.

**(c)** Professional accountants should use their professional judgement to decide whether it is appropriate to accept gifts or hospitality from clients. Even if Lesley believes that she has not done anything wrong, the comments that Matt has made in the thank you card, together with its significant value, mean that Lesley cannot accept the gift voucher from Matt.

**9.15** Two of the following:

- obtain additional advice or training
- ensure that she has adequate time to carry out the work
- obtain assistance from someone with the necessary expertise
- consult with a more senior member of staff at Goulburn Ltd, independent experts or her professional accounting body

**9.18** A cannot; B can; C can

**9.19** There is an ethical issue here and Julia must take steps to resolve it:

1. **The relevant facts**

   Julia must check the payroll calculations for Corso Ltd to see whether any of its employees are being paid at rates below the national minimum wage.

2. **The ethical issues involved**

   If the practice continues to process the payroll for the client, it is doing so in the knowledge that a number of the client's employees are being paid less than they should legally receive.

3. **The fundamental principles**

   If Corso Ltd is paying employees below the national minimum wage, Julia's professional behaviour is being threatened as her practice is processing payroll that does not comply with relevant laws and regulations.

   There is also a threat to Julia's integrity as she is knowingly allowing the client to act dishonestly and, therefore, is acting dishonestly herself.

4. **The established internal procedures**

   Julia must first establish whether this is a genuine mistake on the part of her client. If it is, then she must advise Corso Ltd to increase the rate of pay to minimum wage. If it is not a mistake, and the client refuses to change the pay rate, then the first consideration is whether Julia's practice has established procedures for dealing with a client who is not complying with legal requirements. Certainly, Julia must gather the facts and present them to the directors of Corso Ltd. She must ensure that she fully advises them of the implications of what they are doing.

5. **Alternative courses of action**

   Julia should consult with her professional body and/or take legal advice. She may need to report Corso Ltd's actions to the relevant authorities, but should not do so before taking advice.

   Ultimately, Julia may have to cease providing accounting services for this client.

**9.21** B

## 10.1

| Statement | Financial accounting | Management accounting |
|---|---|---|
| Reports relate to what has happened in the past | ✓ | |
| May be required by law | ✓ | |
| Gives estimates of costs and income for the future | | ✓ |
| May be available in the public domain | ✓ | |
| Gives up-to-date reports which can be used for controlling the business | | ✓ |
| Is used by people outside the business | ✓ | |
| Is designed to meet the requirements of people inside the business | | ✓ |
| Shows details of the expected costs of materials, labour and expenses | | ✓ |
| Records accurate amounts, not estimates | ✓ | |

## 10.2　B

## 10.5　(a)

### RECEIPTS FROM TRADE RECEIVABLES

| | April £ | May £ | June £ | July £ | August £ | September £ |
|---|---|---|---|---|---|---|
| Month of sale | 12,500 | 12,500 | 12,500 | 12,500 | 15,000 | 15,000 |
| Cash discount | (375) | (375) | (375) | (375) | (450) | (450) |
| Following month | 10,000 | 12,500 | 12,500 | 12,500 | 12,500 | 15,000 |
| Irrecoverable debts | (200) | (250) | (250) | (250) | (250) | (300) |
| Receipts for month | 21,925 | 24,375 | 24,375 | 24,375 | 26,800 | 29,250 |

(b)　£14,700, ie £15,000 – £300

## 10.7　(a)

### WILKINSON LIMITED
### CASH BUDGET FOR THE SIX MONTHS ENDING 30 JUNE 20-8

| | Jan £ | Feb £ | Mar £ | Apr £ | May £ | Jun £ |
|---|---|---|---|---|---|---|
| **Receipts** | | | | | | |
| Trade receivables | 57,500 | 65,000 | 70,000 | 72,500 | 85,000 | 65,000 |
| Total receipts for month | 57,500 | 65,000 | 70,000 | 72,500 | 85,000 | 65,000 |
| **Payments** | | | | | | |
| Trade payables | 26,500 | 45,000 | 50,000 | 34,500 | 35,500 | 40,500 |
| Wages and salaries | 17,500 | 18,000 | 18,250 | 18,500 | 16,500 | 20,000 |
| Other expenses | 14,500 | 19,500 | 18,000 | 17,500 | 19,500 | 21,000 |
| Total payments for month | 58,500 | 82,500 | 86,250 | 70,500 | 71,500 | 81,500 |
| Net cash flow | (1,000) | (17,500) | (16,250) | 2,000 | 13,500 | (16,500) |
| Opening bank balance (overdraft) | 2,250 | 1,250 | (16,250) | (32,500) | (30,500) | (17,000) |
| Closing bank balance (overdraft) | 1,250 | (16,250) | (32,500) | (30,500) | (17,000) | (33,500) |

(b)　Total net net cash flow may be calculated in two ways:

- £2,250 (opening balance 1 January) + £33,500 overdraft (closing balance 30 June) = (£35,750) total net cash outflow
- (£1,000) + (£17,500) + (£16,250) + £2,000 + £13,500 + (£16,500) = (£35,750) net cash outflow

# MAYDAY LIMITED
## CASH BUDGET FOR THE YEAR ENDING 31 MAY 20-2

|  | Jun £ | Jul £ | Aug £ | Sep £ | Oct £ | Nov £ | Dec £ | Jan £ | Feb £ | Mar £ | Apr £ | May £ |
|---|---|---|---|---|---|---|---|---|---|---|---|---|
| **Receipts** | | | | | | | | | | | | |
| Trade receivables | – | – | 50,000 | 50,000 | 50,000 | 50,000 | 50,000 | 50,000 | 50,000 | 50,000 | 50,000 | 50,000 |
| Total receipts for month | – | – | 50,000 | 50,000 | 50,000 | 50,000 | 50,000 | 50,000 | 50,000 | 50,000 | 50,000 | 50,000 |
| **Payments** | | | | | | | | | | | | |
| Trade payables | – | 40,000 | 40,000 | 40,000 | 40,000 | 40,000 | 40,000 | 40,000 | 40,000 | 40,000 | 40,000 | 40,000 |
| Wages and expenses | 6,000 | 6,000 | 6,000 | 6,000 | 6,000 | 6,000 | 6,000 | 6,000 | 6,000 | 6,000 | 6,000 | 6,000 |
| Total payments for month | 6,000 | 46,000 | 46,000 | 46,000 | 46,000 | 46,000 | 46,000 | 46,000 | 46,000 | 46,000 | 46,000 | 46,000 |
| Net cash flow | (6,000) | (46,000) | 4,000 | 4,000 | 4,000 | 4,000 | 4,000 | 4,000 | 4,000 | 4,000 | 4,000 | 4,000 |
| Opening bank balance (overdraft) | 20,000 | 14,000 | (32,000) | (28,000) | (24,000) | (20,000) | (16,000) | (12,000) | (8,000) | (4,000) | – | 4,000 |
| Closing bank balance (overdraft) | 14,000 | (32,000) | (28,000) | (24,000) | (20,000) | (16,000) | (12,000) | (8,000) | (4,000) | – | 4,000 | 8,000 |

(b)

## MAYDAY LIMITED

### BUDGETED INCOME STATEMENT FOR THE YEAR ENDING 31 MAY 20-9

| | £ | £ |
|---|---|---|
| **Revenue** | | 600,000 |
| Opening inventory | 50,000 | |
| Purchases | 480,000 | |
| | 530,000 | |
| Less Closing inventory | 50,000 | |
| Cost of sales | | 480,000 |
| **Gross profit** | | 120,000 |
| Less expenses: | | |
| Wages and other expenses | 72,000 | |
| Depreciation of non-current assets | 13,000 | |
| | | 85,000 |
| **Profit for the year** | | 35,000 |

### BUDGETED STATEMENT OF FINANCIAL POSITION AS AT 31 MAY 20-9

| | £ | £ |
|---|---|---|
| **Non-current assets** | | |
| At cost | | 130,000 |
| Less depreciation to date | | 13,000 |
| Carrying amount | | 117,000 |
| **Current assets** | | |
| Inventory | 50,000 | |
| Trade receivables | 100,000 | |
| Bank | 8,000 | |
| | 158,000 | |
| **Less Current liabilities** | | |
| Trade payables | 40,000 | |
| **Net Current Assets** | | 118,000 |
| **NET ASSETS** | | 235,000 |
| **FINANCED BY** | | |
| **Capital** | | |
| Share capital | | 200,000 |
| Add Profit for the year | | 35,000 |
| | | 235,000 |

**10.12** **Benefits of a cash budget (three required)**

The use of a cash budget enables a business to:

* monitor its cash resources

* plan future expenditure, eg the financing of new non-current assets

* control costs and revenues to ensure that either:

  – a bank overdraft is avoided (so saving interest and charges payable), or

  – a bank overdraft or loan can be arranged in advance

* reschedule payments where necessary to avoid bank borrowing, eg delay the purchase of non-current assets

* co-ordinate the activities of the various sections of the business, eg the production department buys in materials not only to meet the expected sales of the sales department but also at a time when there is cash available

* communicate the overall aims of the business to the various sections and to check that the cash will be available to meet their needs

* identify any possible cash surpluses in advance and take steps to invest the surplus on a short-term basis (so earning interest)

**11.2**  D

**11.6**

(a) *Marginal cost per coffee machine*

| | £ |
|---|---|
| Direct materials (per machine) | 25.00 |
| Direct labour (per machine) | 20.00 |
| MARGINAL COST (per machine) | 45.00 |

(b) *Absorption cost per coffee machine*

| | £ |
|---|---|
| Direct materials (per machine) | 25.00 |
| Direct labour (per machine) | 20.00 |
| PRIME COST (per machine) | 45.00 |
| Overheads (fixed) £270,000 ÷ 15,000 machines | 18.00 |
| TOTAL COST (per machine) | 63.00 |

(c)

**COFFEEWORKS LIMITED**

**INCOME STATEMENT: 15,000 COFFEE MACHINES**

| | £ | £ |
|---|---|---|
| Revenue (15,000 x £80) | | 1,200,000 |
| Direct materials (15,000 x £25) | 375,000 | |
| Direct labour (15,000 x £20) | 300,000 | |
| PRIME COST | 675,000 | |
| Overheads (fixed) | 270,000 | |
| TOTAL COST | | 945,000 |
| PROFIT FOR THE YEAR | | 255,000 |

---

**11.8**

**MAXXA LIMITED**

**INCOME STATEMENT FOR THE MONTH ENDED 31 JANUARY 20-7**

| | MARGINAL COSTING | | ABSORPTION COSTING | |
|---|---|---|---|---|
| | £ | £ | £ | £ |
| Revenue 3,000 units at £8 each | | 24,000 | | 24,000 |
| **Variable costs** | | | | |
| Direct materials at £1.25 each | 5,000 | | 5,000 | |
| Direct labour at £2.25 each | 9,000 | | 9,000 | |
| | 14,000 | | | |
| Fixed production overheads | | | 6,000 | |
| | | | | 20,000 |
| Less Closing inventory (marginal cost) | | | | |
| 1,000 units at £3.50 each | 3,500 | | | |
| | 10,500 | | | |
| Less Closing inventory (absorption cost) | | | | |
| 1,000 units at £5 each | | | 5,000 | |
| **CONTRIBUTION** | | 13,500 | | |
| Less Cost of sales | | | | 15,000 |
| Fixed production overheads | | 6,000 | | |
| **Gross profit** | | 7,500 | | 9,000 |
| Less Non-production overheads | | 3,000 | | 3,000 |
| **Profit for the month** | | 4,500 | | 6,000 |

Closing inventory is calculated on the basis of this month's costs:

*marginal costing*, variable costs only, ie £1.25 + £2.25 = £3.50 per unit

*absorption costing*, variable and fixed costs, ie £20,000 ÷ 4,000 units = £5 per unit

The difference in the profit is caused only by the closing inventory figures: £3,500 under marginal costing, and £5,000 under absorption costing. With marginal costing, the full amount of the fixed production overheads has been charged in this month's income statement; by contrast, with absorption costing, part of the fixed production overheads (here £6,000 x 25% = £1,500) has been carried forward in the inventory valuation.

**11.11**

(a) Activity based costing is a costing method which attributes overheads to output on the basis of activities. The cost per unit of a product can be calculated based on its use of activities.

(b)
• A cost driver is an activity which causes costs to be incurred.
• A cost pool is a group of overhead costs that are incurred by the same activity.

**11.15**

(a)

|  | Ando £ | Zalso £ |
|---|---|---|
| Direct materials | 10,000 | 28,000 |
| Direct labour | 12,000 | 14,000 |
| Total direct cost | 22,000 | 42,000 |
| Overheads: |  |  |
| Machinery adjustments (W1) | 2,800 | 7,350 |
| Quality inspections (W2) | 3,600 | 8,400 |
| Total cost | 28,400 | 57,750 |
| Total cost per unit (W3) | 14.20 | 16.50 |

W1
Ando: 2,000 units x 2 adjustments = 4,000 adjustments
Zalso: 3,500 units x 3 adjustments = 10,500 adjustments
Cost per adjustment: £10,150 ÷ 14,500 adjustments = 70p per adjustment

W2
Ando: 2,000 units x 3 inspections = 6,000 inspections
Zalso: 3,500 units x 4 inspections = 14,000 inspections
Cost per inspection: £12,000 ÷ 20,000 inspections = 60p per inspection

W3
Ando: total cost £28,400 ÷ 2,000 units = £14.20 per unit
Zalso: total cost £57,750÷ 3,500 units = £16.50 per unit

(b)

|  | Ando £ | Zalso £ |
|---|---|---|
| Cost per unit | 14.20 | 16.50 |
| Selling price per unit | 18.00 | 15.00 |
| Profit/(loss) per unit | 3.80 | (1.50) |

**11.16** Tutorial note: the calculations can be made either in total or per operation

*percentage mark-up on absorption cost*

| | £ |
|---|---|
| Selling price is calculated as: | |
| total cost (£400 per operation) | 1,000,000 |
| 20 per cent mark-up (£80 per operation) | 200,000 |
| selling price | 1,200,000 |

The price per minor operation will be:
£1,200,000 ÷ 2,500 operations = £480 per operation

## CHAPTER 12 Overheads and overhead absorption

**12.1** A

**12.3** A

Tutorial note: with absorption costing, the overheads are included in the closing inventory – this gives a higher amount for closing inventory than marginal costing (higher closing inventory = higher profit).

**12.4**

• allocation of overheads – the charging to a cost centre of those overheads that have been directly incurred by that cost centre
• apportionment of overheads – the charging to a cost centre of a proportion of overheads

**12.5** (a)

| OVERHEAD ANALYSIS SHEET | MOULDING | FINISHING |
|---|---|---|
| Budgeted total overheads (£) | 9,338 | 3,298 |
| Budgeted machine hours | 1,450 | 680 |
| Budgeted overhead absorption rate (£) | 6.44* | 4.85** |

\* £9,338 ÷ 1,450 hours
\*\* £3,298 ÷ 680 hours

**(b)**

### JOB 1234: OVERHEAD ANALYSIS SHEET

|  | MOULDING | FINISHING |
|---|---|---|
| Job machine hours | 412 | 154 |
| Budgeted overhead absorption rate (£) | 6.44 | 4.85 |
| Overhead absorbed by job (£) | 2,653.28* | 746.90** |

\* 412 hours x £6.44 per hour
\*\* 154 hours x £4.85 per hour

**(c) Labour hour**

- With this method, production overhead is absorbed on the basis of the number of direct labour hours worked.

- While this is a commonly-used method, it is inappropriate where some output is worked on by hand while other output passes quickly through a machinery process and requires little direct labour time.

- This method may be appropriate for Wyvern Fabrication; however, much depends on the balance between direct labour hours and machine hours in the two production departments.

**12.7 (a)**

| Overhead | Basis of apportionment | Total | Dept A | Dept B | Dept C |
|---|---|---|---|---|---|
|  |  | £ | £ | £ | £ |
| Rent and rates | Floor area | 7,210 | 3,090 | 1,545 | 2,575 |
| Dep'n of machinery | Value of machinery | 10,800 | 5,400 | 3,240 | 2,160 |
| Supervisor's salary | Production-line employees | 12,750 | 6,800 | 3,400 | 2,550 |
| Machinery insurance | Value of machinery | 750 | 375 | 225 | 150 |
|  |  | 31,510 | 15,665 | 8,410 | 7,435 |

**(b)**

37 hours x 48 weeks = 1,776 labour hours per employee

Dept A: 8 employees = 14,208 hours = £1.10 per labour hour
Dept B: 4 employees = 7,104 hours = £1.18 per labour hour
Dept C: 3 employees = 5,328 hours = £1.40 per labour hour

**12.9**

|  | Total | Business studies | General studies | Administration | Technical support |
|---|---|---|---|---|---|
|  |  | £ | £ | £ | £ |
| Overheads | 81,600 | 40,000 | 20,000 | 9,600 | 12,000 |
| Technical support | – | 6,000 | 3,000 | 3,000 | (12,000) |
|  |  |  |  | 12,600 | – |
| Administration | – | 8,400 | 4,200 | (12,600) | – |
|  | 81,600 | 54,400 | 27,200 | – | – |

**12.10 (a)**

$\dfrac{\text{total overheads}}{\text{total hours}}$ = $\dfrac{£119,800}{3,290}$ = £36.41 per partner hour

**(b)**

$\dfrac{£119,800 + £120,000}{3,290}$ = £72.89 per partner hour

**(c)**

2 hours x 47 weeks x £36.41 = £3,422.54 per partner
(ie £6,845.08 in total)

12.16 (a) D
    (b) A
    (c) B

## CHAPTER 13 Standard costing and variance analysis

13.1   A

13.3   D

13.5   B

13.8

|  | Sheet steel £ p | Alloy £ p | Flour £ p | Gelling fluid £ p |
|---|---|---|---|---|
| Material price variance | 0.50 ADV | – | 0.06 FAV | 1.25 ADV |
| Material usage variance | – | 0.75 ADV | 0.05 ADV | 0.75 FAV |
| Material variance | 0.50 ADV | 0.75 ADV | 0.01 FAV | 0.50 ADV |

13.9

|  | Casting £ p | Machining £ p | Finishing £ p | Packing £ p |
|---|---|---|---|---|
| Labour rate variance | – | 4.00 ADV | 1.00 ADV | 1.20 FAV |
| Labour efficiency variance | 10.00 ADV | – | 3.00 ADV | 4.00 FAV |
| Labour variance | 10.00 ADV | 4.00 ADV | 4.00 ADV | 5.20 FAV |

13.14   C

13.16   A

**12.12**   **(a)**

| Fixed overheads for November 20-7 | Basis of apportmnt | Total £ | Warehouse £ | Manufacturing £ | Sales £ | Administration £ |
|---|---|---|---|---|---|---|
| Depreciation of non-current assets | Carrying amount | 9,150 | 1,830 | 6,100 | 305 | 915 |
| Rent | Floor space | 11,000 | 1,650 | 6,600 | 1,100 | 1,650 |
| Other property overheads | Floor space | 6,200 | 930 | 3,720 | 620 | 930 |
| Administration overheads | Allocated | 13,450 |  |  |  | 13,450 |
| Staff costs | Allocated | 27,370 | 3,600 | 9,180 | 8,650 | 5,940 |
|  |  | 67,170 | 8,010 | 25,600 | 10,675 | 22,885 |

**(b)**     Budgeted fixed overhead absorption rate for the manufacturing department:

£25,600 ÷ 10,000 hours = £2.56 per machine hour

**13.17**

| Cause of variance | Adverse | Favourable |
|---|---|---|
| Increase in material prices | ✔ | |
| Fewer materials are wasted | | ✔ |
| Cheaper materials are used | | ✔ |
| Theft of materials | ✔ | |
| An increase in direct labour pay | ✔ | |
| More efficient usage of direct labour | | ✔ |
| Overtime is paid to direct labour | ✔ | |
| Selling prices are increased | | ✔ |
| An increase in the number of units sold | | ✔ |

Notes:

- sales volume variance is indicated by the flexed budget figure, ie £338,000 – £312,000 = £26,000 FAV
- the 'flexed budget' and 'actual' figures are compared to give the variances in the right-hand column

(b) Sales price
  – lower prices because of competition in the market
  – discount given to regular customers
  – lower price charged in order to clear surplus inventory

Sales volume
  – increased sales as a result of lower prices
  – seasonal increase in sales
  – fewer competitors

Materials price
  – cheaper materials purchased
  – discount negotiated with suppliers
  – market price of materials has fallen

Materials usage
  – lower quality materials
  – more wastage

Labour rate
  – lower grade of labour used
  – reduction in level of wage rates

Labour efficiency
  – less skilled lower grade of labour
  – lower quality materials causing production problems

**13.18 (a)**

## FUNPLAY LTD
### RECONCILIATION STATEMENT OF SALES AND COSTS FOR THE MONTH

| | Original budget 1,200 slides £ | Flexed budget 1,300 slides £ | Actual 1,300 £ | Variances £ |
|---|---|---|---|---|
| Sales | 312,000 | *338,000 volume 26,000 FAV | 286,000 | 52,000 ADV price 52,000 ADV |
| Less costs | | | | |
| Materials | 86,400 | 93,600 | 100,100 | 6,500 ADV price 9,100 FAV usage 15,600 ADV |
| Labour | 120,000 | 130,000 | 136,500 | 6,500 ADV rate 45,500 FAV efficiency 52,000 ADV |
| CONTRIBUTION | 105,600 | 114,400 | 49,400 | 65,000 ADV |
| Overheads | 45,000 | 45,000 | 45,000 | – |
| Profit for the month | 60,600 | 69,400 | 4,400 | 65,000 ADV |

*1,300 slides at £260 each

# CHAPTER 14 Capital investment appraisal

**14.1** D

**14.2** C

**14.5** The net cash flows are:

| | £ |
|---|---|
| year 0 | (95,000) |
| year 1 | 30,000 |
| year 2 | 40,000 |
| year 3 | 50,000 |
| year 4 | 50,000 |
| year 5 | 25,000 |

## (a) payback period

| Year | Cash flow £ | Cumulative cash flow £ | |
|---|---|---|---|
| 0 | (95,000) | (95,000) | |
| 1 | 30,000 | (65,000) | |
| 2 | 40,000 | (25,000) | |
| 3 | 50,000 | 25,000 | ∴ £25,000 required |
| 4 | 50,000 | 75,000 | |
| 5 | 25,000 | 100,000 | |

The design costs are recovered half-way through year 3: £30,000 + £40,000 + (£25,000/£50,000 x 12 months). Thus the payback period is 2 years and 6 months. Note that these assume even cash flows during the year.

## (b) net present value

| Year | Cash flow £ | Discount factor | Discounted cash flow £ |
|---|---|---|---|
| 0 | (95,000) | x 1.000 | (95,000) |
| 1 | 30,000 | x 0.909 | 27,270 |
| 2 | 40,000 | x 0.826 | 33,040 |
| 3 | 50,000 | x 0.751 | 37,550 |
| 4 | 50,000 | x 0.683 | 34,150 |
| 5 | 25,000 | x 0.621 | 15,525 |
| | | Net Present Value | 52,535 |

**14.6 (a) payback period**

| | PROJECT EXE | | | PROJECT WYE | |
|---|---|---|---|---|---|
| Year | Cash flow £ | Cumulative cash flow £ | | Cash flow £ | Cumulative cash flow £ |
| 0 | (80,000) | (80,000) | | (100,000) | (100,000) |
| 1 | 40,000 | (40,000) | | 20,000 | (80,000) |
| 2 | 40,000 | – | | 30,000 | (50,000) |
| 3 | 20,000 | 20,000 | | 50,000 | – |
| 4 | 10,000 | 30,000 | | 50,000 | 50,000 |
| 5 | 10,000 | 40,000 | | 40,000 | 90,000 |

**net present value**

| | | PROJECT EXE | | PROJECT WYE | |
|---|---|---|---|---|---|
| Year | Discount factor | Cash flow £ | Discounted cash flow £ | Cash flow £ | Discounted cash flow £ |
| 0 | 1.000 | (80,000) | (80,000) | (100,000) | (100,000) |
| 1 | 0.893 | 40,000 | 35,720 | 20,000 | 17,860 |
| 2 | 0.797 | 40,000 | 31,880 | 30,000 | 23,910 |
| 3 | 0.712 | 20,000 | 14,240 | 50,000 | 35,600 |
| 4 | 0.636 | 10,000 | 6,360 | 50,000 | 31,800 |
| 5 | 0.567 | 10,000 | 5,670 | 40,000 | 22,680 |
| Net Present Value | | | 13,870 | | 31,850 |

**14.7** **(a)** The net cash flows are:

|        | £        |
|--------|----------|
| year 0 | (40,000) |
| year 1 | (60,000) |
| year 2 | 45,000   |
| year 3 | 55,000   |
| year 4 | 90,000   |
| year 5 | 60,000   |

**payback period**

| Year | Cash flow<br>£ | Cumulative cash flow<br>£ |
|------|----------------|---------------------------|
| 0    | (40,000)       | (40,000)                  |
| 1    | (60,000)       | (100,000)                 |
| 2    | 45,000         | (55,000)                  |
| 3    | 55,000         | –                         |
| 4    | 90,000         | 89,000                    |
| 5    | 60,000         | 149,000                   |

The development costs are recovered at the end of year 3. Note that these assume even cash flows during the year.

**net present value**

| Year | Cash flow<br>£ |   | Discount factor | Discounted cash flow<br>£ |
|------|----------------|---|-----------------|---------------------------|
| 0    | (40,000)       | × | 1.000           | (40,000)                  |
| 1    | (60,000)       | × | 0.893           | (53,580)                  |
| 2    | 45,000         | × | 0.797           | 35,860                    |
| 3    | 55,000         | × | 0.712           | 39,160                    |
| 4    | 90,000         | × | 0.636           | 57,240                    |
| 5    | 60,000         | × | 0.567           | 34,020                    |
|      |                |   | Net Present Value | 72,700                  |

**(b)**

| REPORT |
|--------|
| To:     Robert Smith<br><br>From:   AQA Accounting Student<br><br>Date:   Today |

Capital investment projects: Exe and Wye

This report carries out an appraisal of these two projects, based on the information provided. Two techniques are used:

- payback
- net present value

The first of these, payback, sees how long it takes for the initial outlay of the project to be repaid by the net cash flow coming in. For Project Exe, the payback period is two years; for Project Wye, it is three years. Using this technique, Project Exe is more favourable.

Payback is an easy technique both to calculate and understand. However, it does have the disadvantage of ignoring all cash flows after the payback period. With these two projects, Wye has strong cash inflows in years 4 and 5, after the payback period (however, these could be a disadvantage if the project is likely to go out-of-date soon).

The net present value technique relies on discounting relevant cash flows at an appropriate rate of return, which is 12 per cent for these projects. Net present value is a more sophisticated technique than payback in that it uses all cash flows and takes the timing of cash flows into account. However, the meaning of Net Present Value is not always clear, and the rate of return required on the projects may vary over their life.

Project Wye has a higher net present value (but also a higher initial cost) at £31,850, when compared with Exe at £13,870. The fact that both figures are positive means that either project will be worthwhile. However, Project Exe is to be preferred because:

- it has the faster payback
- the initial capital outlay is smaller
- it has strong cash flows in the early years, which are likely to be more accurate than the amounts for later years.

(b)

**REPORT**

| | |
|---|---|
| **To:** | Managing Director |
| **From:** | AQA Accounting Student |
| **Date:** | Today |

Introduction of a new range of bikes

This report carries out an appraisal on the project, based on the information provided.

The net present value technique relies on discounting relevant cash flows at an appropriate rate of return. It would be helpful to know:

1. whether there are any additional cash flows beyond year 5

2. whether the introduction of a new range of bikes will affect sales of our existing bikes

On the basis of the information provided, the project has a payback period of three years and a positive net present value of £72,700. The project should be carried out.

14.11 Comparing the financial data

**Project A:**

- larger initial investment (£550,000 more)
- higher net present value (£475,000 more)
- longer payback period (by 2 years)
- longer life of project (by 3 years)

**Project B:**

- lower initial investment
- lower net present value
- shorter payback period
- shorter life of project

After the payback period, Project A has 7 years of life to produce cash flows while Project B has 6 years.

Non-financial factors

**Project A:**

- production staff redundancies/early retirement (impact on local economy and unemployment)
- cost of redundancy payments
- cost of retraining remaining staff
- continue to use recycled paper in the production process

**Project B:**

- no longer able to use recycled paper (customers may be lost if non-recyclable paper is used)
- no redundancies
- minimal staff retraining costs

Analysis of financial data

- discount rate based on current ROCE and interest rates (conduct sensitivity analysis at different ROCE and bank interest rates)
- will the company be able to borrow the funds required (initial investment, Project A redundancy payments, retraining costs)?
- how reliable are the cash flows in the future (Project A 12 years, Project B 9 years)?
- how reliable is the data used in the calculations?
- will demand for the company's products remain for 12 years (Project A) or 9 years (Project B)?

Recommendation

- In the short term, Project B is the safer option – lower initial investment, no impact on the local economy and unemployment.

- In the longer term, Project A is the more profitable option but requires a higher initial investment and will impact on the local economy and unemployment.

- Project B is unable to use recycled paper and this may cause customers to be lost and lead to adverse comment in the media.

- Much depends on future demand for the company's products over 9 or 12 years. If it is expected to continue, then Project A, although more risky, would seem to be the better choice in the long term. However, it does need considerably more finance than Project B and will have a much greater impact in the short term on the local economy and employment.

# Index